COCKCROFT AND THE ATOM

Professor J D Cockroft by Rodrigo Moynihan, RA, 1947
(Courtesy: Imperial War Museum).

COCKCROFT
and the
ATOM

Guy Hartcup MA
and
T E Allibone CBE, FRS
Visiting Professor of Physics,
The City University.

Emeritus Professor of Electrical Engineering,
Leeds University

ADAM HILGER, LTD, BRISTOL

British Library Catologuing in Publication Data

Hartcup, Guy
   Cockcroft and the atom.
   1. Cockcroft, *Sir* John
   2. Physicists – Biography
   3. Nuclear physics – Biography
   I. Title   II. Allibone, T. E.
   539.7′092′4   QC16.C/
ISBN 0-85274-759-4

Consultant Editor: **Professor A J Meadows**

Published by Adam Hilger Ltd
Techno House, Redcliffe Way, Bristol BS1 6NX

The Adam Hilger book-publishing imprint is owned by
The Institute of Physics.

Typeset by Mathematical Composition Setters Ltd, Salisbury, Wiltshire
Printed in Great Britain by J W Arrowsmith Ltd, Bristol

CONTENTS

ACKNOWLEDGMENTS

As joint authors we shared the task of preparing this biography in the following manner: TEA, because of his long-standing friendship with Sir John
Cockcroft stemming from the days when they were fellow students in the
Cavendish, was well qualified to assess the latter's contribution to fundamental physics, to engineering and to postwar applications of nuclear energy:
GH, as an historian with a special interest in science and technology, was
responsible for most of the biographical research, the structure of the book
and the writing of the first draft. We are glad to record that our different
approaches and backgrounds did not prevent us from reaching agreement on
the assessments and conclusions that have been reached. TEA had been
asked by Churchill College in 1968 to write the biography but was obliged,
reluctantly, to decline as he was in full employment; it has therefore been a
great privilege, as well as a pleasure, to share this task with his co-author.

We are grateful to the Cockcroft family for their readiness to cooperate and,
in particular, to Lady Cockcroft who generously made available to GH Sir
John's personal correspondence and papers for study and quotation, and to
other members of her family, especially Christopher and Catherine and her
son-in-law, Michael Blackburn. Sir John's brothers, (the late) Eric, Leo and
Keith Cockcroft also provided letters and gave reminiscences of their youth
at Birks House.

We have pleasure in recording our thanks to Sir William Hawthorne,
Master of Churchill College for his hospitality and encouragement. A number
of the Fellows provided information on the early days of the College and
GH is particularly indebted to the late Stephen Roskill who provided intro-
ductions and to Richard Hey whose kindness, advice and knowledge was invaluable. He is also grateful to Correlli Barnett, Keeper of the Archive and
Marion Stewart, the Archivist, who answered many questions and opened
doors to numerous sources relating to Cockcroft.

In the course of his research GH received help from the following: The
Leverhulme Trust which awarded him a Research Fellowship enabling him
to travel in the USA; Mr P J Searby, Secretary of the UK Atomic Energy
Authority for allowing him to make use of Sir John's personal files and those
of Sir James Chadwick; Mrs Lorna Arnold, the Authority Historian, who
never failed to answer questions and give advice; Mrs Margaret Graham until

recently in the Harwell Archive, Mrs Sylvia Penney and Miss Judy Robertson. Mr C A H James, Secretary of the Royal Commission for the Exhibition of 1851, kindly drew attention to files relating to industrial bursaries and other awards to Cavendish members in the 1920s and 30s. In Vienna, Dr Sigvard Eklund, Director General of the International Atomic Energy Agency allowed GH to see a number of records held by the Agency. In the USA he received generous assistance and hospitality from Professor Kenneth Bainbridge, Professor Joseph C Boyce, Professor Robert Brode, Dr John Gaunt, Dr John H Lawrence, Professor Edwin McMillan, Professor Isidor Rabi, Dr Bruce Wharton, Mr Carroll Wilson, and in Canada from Dr G C Butler, Dr Hugh Carmichael, Dr George Laurence, Professor W B Lewis, Dr D J Mackenzie and Dr Arthur Ward.

Our thanks are due to the following who read and commented on drafts, provided information, gave hospitality, and helped us in a variety of ways: Sir John Adams, Lord Adrian, Professor J F Allen, Dr C B Amphlett, Lord Beaumont of Whitley, Mr Peter Bicknell, Mrs Hanni Bretscher, Lord Bowden of Chesterfield, Lady Chadwick, Mrs Joan Charnock, Mrs Joy Clarke, Sir Robert Cockburn, Sir William Cook, Sir Alan Cottrell, Dr A Copisarow, Professor Glyn Daniel, the late Canon Duckworth, Dr J V Dunworth, Sir Monty Finniston, Lord Flowers, Lady Flowers, Dr D W Fry, Professor W Galbraith, Mr Carl Gilbert, Dr D W Ginns, Dr Bertrand Goldschmidt, Dr Jules Guèron, Mr John Hall, Major General J R C Hamilton, Lord Hinton of Bankside, Viscount Hood, Sir Friston How, Sir Leonard Huxley, Mr J F Jackson, Professor Peter Kapitza, Professor N Kemmer, Dr A E Kempton, Dr Alexander King, Mr F W Linsey, Dr A C Lynch, Professor R A Lyttleton, Dr W B Mann, the late Professor Sir Leslie Martin, Professor W V Mayneord, Mr George McKerrow, Dr Kenneth McQuillen, Sir Harrie Melville, Mr Michael Michaels, Professor C J Milner, Professor J S Mitchell, Professor Philip Moon, Professor Sir Charles Oatley, Professor Sir Mark Oliphant, Professor Sir Rudolf Peierls, Lord Penney, Sir Michael Perrin, Sir Donald Perrott, Mr Harold Pettitt, Dr T G Pickavance, Mr Chapman Pincher, Lord Plowden, Mrs Popović-Stansfield, Professor J A K Quartey, Colonel G W Raby, Dr J A Ratcliffe, Professor J Rotblat, Lord Sherfield, Professor David Shoenberg, Dr Henry Seligman, Miss Betty Short, Mrs Freida Stack, Professor George Steiner, Professor P C Thonemann, Lord Todd, Dr J Waldram, Professor E T S Walton, Sir Denys Wilkinson, Mr Denis Willson, Professor Herbet Vetter and Lord Zuckerman.

Help was willingly given us by the staffs of the following institutions: The Public Record Office, the Department of Documents of the Imperial War Museum, the Cambridge University Library Archive, the Cavendish Laboratory, The City University Library, St John's College Library, Cambridge, the Nuffield College Library, Oxford, the Royal Society Library, the Science Museum Library, the Institution of Mechanical Engineers Library, and the Bancroft Library, University of California, Berkeley, USA.

We thank the following for permission to use illustrations: the Atomic Energy Research Establishment, Harwell; the Cavendish Laboratory; Churchill College Archive, Cambridge; the Imperial War Museum; the

International Atomic Energy Agency; the Public Record Office for a photograph which is Crown copyright; the remainder belong to the Cockcroft family or to friends of Sir John and we wish to thank them also.

We wish to record the support we have received from our respective wives, in the case of TEA's for reading the whole of the text and introducing into it very many improvements and in the case of GH's for taking off his shoulders many household chores over the past five years. Last, but not least, we thank Mrs Patrica Inglis and Mrs Eileen Saunders for their competent typing of the final draft.

Guy Hartcup
T E Allibone

PROLOGUE

There have been a few scientific discoveries, or even theories, which have changed completely our way of life. Isaac Newton gave us the laws of motion essential for all calculations concerning mechanical transport, Einstein gave us the concept of the equivalence of mass and energy, a concept of little importance in our ordinary everyday life but of extreme importance when dealing with reactions between atomic nuclei with which the world is greatly concerned today. The discovery of penicillin and the development of similar pharmaceutical products has led to a situation where man can hardly die from bacteriological causes. The inventions of the steam and internal combustion engines gave us the first industrial revolution and the transistor is giving us the second.

Two great discoveries in the Cavendish Laboratory in Cambridge just 50 years ago, supplemented by another in the Kaiser Wilhelm Institute for Chemistry in Berlin in 1938, have led to the Nuclear Age, to the Bomb and to nuclear power stations which have supplemented man's older sources of energy, coal, oil and hydro, and may in a succeeding century be our main source of energy. The first discovery was made by James Chadwick, the second by John Cockcroft and Ernest Walton and the third by Otto Hahn and Fritz Strassmann; all appropriately received Nobel Prizes. Chadwick had been a research student under Rutherford in Manchester before World War I and in 1919 became his collaborator in Cambridge in the early experiments on the disintegration of atomic nuclei by alpha-particles from radium. In 1920 Rutherford had speculated upon the structure of atomic nuclei: in his Bakerian Lecture to the Royal Society he had suggested that an atomic nucleus was probably made up from some protons, the nuclei of hydrogen atoms, and from some particles of similar mass which had no electric charge, these were later called neutrons. He outlined the properties of these neutral particles—as they had no charge they might pass readily through matter without being deflected by the electric forces surrounding nuclei. In February 1932 Chadwick made the crucial experiment which proved that the neutron existed and that it had the properties which Rutherford had forecast.

Two months later the second discovery was made. Cockcroft and Walton had been accelerating hydrogen nuclei, protons, in a vacuum discharge tube to which over 300 000 volts were applied and had been bombarding the light element lithium with the fast beam of protons; suddenly they saw on a sensitive screen scintillations which could only be due to bombardment of the screen by fast alpha-particles; they proved that the compound nucleus of lithium plus one proton had split into two helium nuclei, alpha-particles, and in so doing had lost a small amount of their combined mass, which, according to the Einstein theory, had been converted into energy of motion of the helium nuclei. There had been a gain of energy in this simple experiment though far more energy had been used in generating the high voltage. It was, nevertheless, a beginning, a very important beginning, and was followed by experiments in laboratories in many countries, so that in the next six years many elements had been disintegrated, some by protons, some by neutrons, and some by heavier nuclei. Furthermore, in Rome the heaviest element, uranium, had been bombarded and had probably been converted into elements of even higher atomic weights.

Finally came the third great discovery; in Berlin it was shown conclusively by chemical methods that the uranium nucleus bombarded by a neutron had actually split into two roughly equal halves yielding, by a loss of mass, an enormous amount of energy; uranium fission had been discovered and soon the road ahead to man's conquest of the nucleus became clear.

John Cockcroft and Ernest Walton played the essential role in starting artificial disintegration of the elements and, in due course, Cockcroft played a prominent part in the development of nuclear energy. First, however, came World War II. Even in 1938 Britain was deeply involved in the development of radio-direction-finding (RDF), to enable the fighter plane to be in the right place at the right time and for Cockcroft this had to take priority. Later came the preparations for the nuclear weapon; in this he played an important though minor role, and then, as the war was drawing to a close, the consideration of power stations of the future based on uranium became his main task. Later in life he returned to his beloved Cambridge as Master of the new college subscribed for as a memento to Churchill.

Who was this man?—a student who began his professional life as a mathematician, served his Country in an artillery regiment, graduated as an electrical engineer and served an engineering apprenticeship; returned to his first love, mathematics, taking the Tripos in Cambridge, then working in the Cavendish Laboratory, Cambridge, where, in due course, he did the famous experiment with which his name will always be coupled.

CHAPTER ONE

BOYHOOD IN TODMORDEN

Cockcrofts have been living in and around the Calder valley in the West Pennines since the 16th century at least. Originally they were yeoman farmers, keeping cows, a few sheep and a horse or two. Their name, frequently found in local records, is thought to have originated as a by-name for one keeping cocks in a croft or small enclosure. Some of them became men of substance, being connected with wool and its processing. Weaving was at that time a cottage industry; the Cockcrofts, like their neighbours, grazing their stock on their small holdings in the summer months and spinning and weaving in the winter when the weather was too harsh for out-of-doors work.

By the end of the 18th century, the beginnings of the industrial revolution in the valleys tempted the hill farmers down from their heights. Tucked away into side valleys, or cloughs, as they are locally known, water-powered mills were built, enabling larger machines to be operated. Clusters of houses sprang up around them and these little centres of industry slowly supplanted the cottage looms. One of the enterprising farmers was John Cockcroft's great great grandfather who was known locally as 'Jack o' th' Heights'; he owned a farm under Stoodley Pike, kept sheep and was a 'putter-out'; he put out wool to be spun and woven by hand.

A fresh stimulus to local industry in Todmorden was the introduction of cotton, first from the Levant and later from America and by the 1780s it was being brought in quantity across the Atlantic. One of the first cotton mills was built by the strong-minded Quaker family of Fielden, the most gifted member of which was John Fielden, the factory-reforming MP of the 1840s. The mechanisation of spinning led to a rapid growth of industry and accompanying trades. Two significant signs of this growth were the building of a turnpike road from Todmorden to Halifax and, in 1789, the construction of a canal to transport cotton goods to the sea. In another twenty years steam had begun to replace water power in the mills and this more effective method of production led to further industrialisation. But the work was hard and unremitting; most people worked a six day week, putting in 14 to 17 hours a day for five days and working until twilight on the sixth.[1]

The Cockcrofts were characteristic of this independent breed, hard-working and thrifty. Some of the family were members of the Church of England, but usually they were Nonconformist, like most of the people in the

Calder valley. Two main branches of the family were at Mayroyd and at Heptonstall, a hill village a few miles to the east of Todmorden. Here in the parish register there are some 150 references to the family dating from 1550. The spelling varies from Cawcrofte to Cokecroft, but Cockcroft is the most common form. One Cockcroft went to North America to fight the French and decided to settle in New York, establishing a silk and cloth business on the banks of the Hudson and John Cockcroft made contact with this branch during his visits to the States, before, during and, more frequently, after World War II.

In the first years of the 19th century Jack o' th' Height's son, Henry Cockcroft, was a typical middleman of the district, distributing yarn to the weavers and collecting it when woven. He ran a draper's shop and his wife, Sally, supervised a number of dressmakers and by 1848 the business was flourishing enough for Henry to build a mill powered by steam at Lobmill on the Halifax Road. It produced striped tickings and fashionable check patterned ginghams. Henry, or 'Old Harry' as he was called, was a man of initiative and during the American Civil War, when cotton imports from across the Atlantic were stopped, his mill turned over to making linen articles.[2]

As soon as he was old enough, Henry's son John joined the business. In due course he married Sarah Ellen Gaukroger, who died prematurely from pneumonia. It was not long before he married again, adding four more children to the family. The eldest son was John Arthur who, in 1896, married a local girl, Maude Fielden, goodlooking, intelligent and with a strong personality, a distant relative of the John Fielden MP. She played important parts in amateur dramatics and as she had a good soprano voice she often took principal parts in leading musical events in the district including traditional oratorios such as the 'Messiah'. She had taught in Todmorden but had to abandon this when her mother was left a widow with three other children and together they ran a milliner's shop in Todmorden.

The young Cockcrofts started married life in Stanley Terrace, Todmorden where they lived in a stone-faced two-storey house with a tiny garden in front. Here their first child John Douglas was born on 27 May 1897, but as a result of financial difficulties arising from the mill, the business was transferred in 1899 to Birks Mill in Walsden, a mill powered both by steam and water, overlooking the canal in front and with the moors rising directly behind. The family took up residence in Birks House, a stone's throw from the mill.

By then, John already had a brother, Eric, and in the course of the next seven years three more sons were born, Phillip, Keith and Lionel (known to the family as Leo). While John was to become an international figure, his brothers played prominent parts in the life of the community. Eric was awarded the Order of the British Empire for organising the Savings Movement during the Second World War and Leo became Mayor of Todmorden in 1947, a year after John had been made a Freeman of the Borough. Eighteen years later, Keith was chosen to be Mayor.

Birks House, though of modest proportions, was surrounded by trees with a garden in front and a large meadow sloping down to the canal, where the children could play. Up a winding road behind the house lay the moors and here in summer they picked bilberries and in the winter tobogganed down the snow-covered slopes. Alongside the mill was a large dam which supplied water to turn the mill wheel, and here the boys learned to swim.

The mill itself, as Keith later recalled[3],

> provided endless fun. We were chased out of the boiler house by the boiler man who would turn on the steam valves below the water gauges to scare us. We could watch the slowly-turning beam engine as the engine man went round to fill the lubricators. This engine was a McNaught Beam Condensing Engine of a temperamental type; if the load was suddenly shed it would sometimes 'set off at Boggart' or increase its speed to an alarming extent.

Sometimes when all was quiet on a Sunday afternoon the boys, ignoring strict injunctions, used to play with the great water wheel, an enormous shadowy thing between two high walls of stone, cold and dripping with water, and rather frightening. They succeeded in getting the wheel to turn and, climbing on to it, were able to run along a kind of footway, keeping at the bottom of the wheel as it turned. What made it more exciting was that as each spoke of the wheel came round, an iron bar crossed the footway about 12 inches high and they had to jump this each time. One of the brothers, not so nimble as the others, once failed to clear one of these iron bars and his brothers were horrified to see him going right round the wheel clinging desperately to this iron bar.[4]

Barges continually passed up and down the canal and when it froze, a gang of men, carried by a barge, broke up the ice with a long rail. Sometimes huge horse-drawn drays brought loads of warps to the mill yard. When there was no work on, the boys played cricket in the yard with a weft box as a wicket; to hit a six was against the rules!

In the winter evenings, or when a wet mist settled in the valley, the boys entertained themselves with a 'mirrorscope', an early form of epidiascope in which the light was provided by an incandescent gas mantle, and comic picture postcards were projected on to a large screen in the kitchen. They had a chemistry set and sometimes John used to make violent explosions by mixing potash and sulphur in a steel nut, putting a loose bolt in the nut and dropping on to the bolt a large weight released by a string thrown over a tree. Nor were his brothers less inventive; during the Armistice celebrations in November 1918, Keith and Leo strung electric light bulbs on wires between the chimneys of Birks House and attached them to the mill dynamo across the road; when the band began to play the lights were switched on to the astonishment of the merrymakers in the field below.

The Cockcrofts were a happy family presided over by a firm but kind father who was, however, preoccupied with the running of the mill, so that Maude ran the house and brought up the children. She was an excellent cook and the Christmas dinners were feasts to remember; the puddings, usually twelve in number, were made well in advance and hung in cloth-covered basins from a beam on the kitchen ceiling to be ready for the dinners and parties planned for the Christmas and New Year season.

> Another well remembered annual event [wrote Keith] was our summer holiday, usually spent at St Anne's-on-Sea near Blackpool. We boys carried the

luggage to the station on a large handcart from the mill. Then when all the family were ready, the train was boarded and we proceeded via Manchester because my father had a railway contract which could be used by him for the Walsden to Manchester part of the journey. On arrival at St Anne's we were taken to our rooms in a horse-drawn landau which was a great thrill. We bought our own food which was prepared by our landlady and we had a private sitting room. The cost to my father of a ten day holiday for seven was about £20.

Thrift was not only necessary but cultivated; corduroy suits and trousers were handed down from older members of the family, the garments seemed unable to be worn out and could be washed indefinitely. The children were taught to be useful and capable members of society and their mother would tell them stories to point a moral, one was about a great-aunt brought up in the West Indies with servants at her beck and call, spoiling her and making her 'no good in this world'. The family all went to chapel and alcohol was discouraged.

Life, as for other children of that time, could be tough. When they suffered from toothache the family was taken to a 'rather ruthless doctor' who extracted teeth without any form of anaesthetic and he removed the tonsils of one of the boys after laying him out on the dining-room table; on recovering consciousness the boy, with remarkable *sang froid*, asked where the offending organs were as he thought the cat might like to have them!

When John was five, he was sent to the Church of England school in Walsden where 'half-time' system was still in operation; some of the children worked half-time in the mills and half-time in school, morning and afternoon on alternate weeks. At eleven he went to Roomfield Grammar School in Todmorden where the teaching was more specialised, and travelled to and from school by train. When the 'down' train was approaching Walsden Station a bell would ring and John and the other boys often had to make a desperate sprint to reach the station, cross the line by the bridge and board the train before it started. Lessons began with the singing of the hymn 'Awake, my soul, and with the sun thy daily stage of duty run'. Boys and girls were in separate classrooms, both under the beneficent care of one J W Crabtree, and here John learned the 'three Rs', was taught woodwork by 'Mannie' Pickles and, when he was old enough, moved upstairs to the old Higher Grade School.

There are few surviving memories of him at this time, though Annie Quinn remembered him when they were both about ten playing hide and seek at Meadow Bottom. More particularly, she recalled him as a serious boy in a dark Norfolk suit who said his favourite subject was arithmetic[5]. At the same time he enjoyed playing football and cricket, later distinguishing himself as a good batsman.

One of the girls attending the school was Eunice Elizabeth Crabtree whose parents lived at Stansfield Hall overlooking the town of Todmorden. The Crabtrees, like the Cockcrofts, and the Fieldens, had deep roots in the district; Elizabeth's father was a staunch Methodist, attending chapel regularly, a Justice of the Peace, a Liberal in politics and a teetotaller. John and Elizabeth soon became friends and in time this friendship ripened into a love which was to be lifelong. Elizabeth shared John's intellectual activities and his letters to her, written regularly throughout life, show clearly that he could unburden himself to her on matters which were currently besetting him.

His performance at school was outstanding, being top repeatedly and in the VIth form he got 100 per cent in several subjects. After matriculating, the headmaster, Mr E Farrar, encouraged him to try and win a scholarship to Manchester University. This he did in 1914, taking mathematics, physics, French and Latin; the geometry paper he found hard going, but felt happier with the physics paper followed by a practical in the University laboratory— his diary records 'Rotten apparatus but easy questions'.

On the day before the examination began the newspapers reported the assassination of the Archduke Franz Ferdinand at Sarajevo but at that moment the cataclysmic implications of this event were not appreciated, least of all by those with their heads bent over their desks in the examination hall.

On 17 July, the ordeal over, John set off with a party of friends to the Lake District to relax and enjoy themselves; four of the party were German students; one a West Indian; there were two Scots, one a 'red-hot socialist', the second being less opinionated. The weather was hot and as they tramped over the hills round Windermere, Grasmere and Coniston they stripped and bathed in the cool becks. At night they lay in their tents and sang songs, English, Scotch and German; and no doubt there were friendly arguments over religion and politics; the Germans assured their companions that their country would not go to war with France. Luckily, they saw no newspapers to alarm them about the course of events and on 25 July John returned to Birks House to find the country on the brink of war.

It is not difficult to imagine the anxiety felt by John's parents over the declaration of war on 4 August. No-one could have then foreseen that four years would elapse before peace returned and that many families in the neighbourhood would be bereaved, or that the fabric of society would be fundamentally altered, nor could they foresee how war would affect the family business. John's scholastic attainments had not deflected his interest in the business of the mill; during school holidays, because of his ability with figures, he had taken to helping his father with costings and the thought must have passed through the latter's mind that the boy might in due course succeed him as head of the firm of John Cockcroft & Sons. At the same time he could not ignore the testimonials from John's teachers and, like them, he was determined that John should go to university.

John was successful in the university examination, winning a West Riding County Major Scholarship, tenable for three years, and he entered for the BSc course in mathematics. Horace Lamb was the professor, a very distinguished mathematician, author of the famous text book on the calculus, a born teacher but rather awe-inspiring and looking back, John believed he had been too young to benefit from Lamb's erudition and he did not consider that he had outstanding ability in maths.

His real interest was in atomic physics and while at school he had read a book by J A Crowther, later Professor of Physics at Reading University, which gave a popular account of the pioneer work of J J Thomson and Ernest Rutherford. Rutherford had come to Manchester from Canada in 1907 and taken over the Physics Department, he was then at the height of his powers, a world authority on the science of radioactivity who had gathered together a team of exceptionally gifted scientists, many of whom were to become world renowned, H G J Moseley, Hans Geiger, Niels Bohr, Ernest Marsden, James Chadwick, Fritz Paneth, George von Hevesy, C G Darwin, and others. As A B Wood, one of Rutherford's students, later wrote:

> It would be difficult to find anywhere such a galaxy of scientific talent, either before or since, working together in the same physics laboratory all at the same time.

A number of these men later became friends and colleagues of Cockcroft, but arriving at Manchester after the outbreak of war, he found that they were already dispersing. Moseley, who was considered to be one of the best research physicists of the day, joined the army and in 1915 was killed by a Turkish bullet in the Dardanelles campaign. Geiger, inventor of the 'Geiger counter', von Hevesy and Paneth hurried back to Germany and Austria. Rutherford himself was out of the country when war broke out and returned from a visit to Australia and New Zealand (his home) in January 1915 to find a rapidly emptying laboratory.

Cockcroft attended the first-year lectures in physics. The lecturer was unable to keep order in the class and Rutherford, trying to catch up with the administrative paperwork on his desk after his prolonged absence abroad, was called upon to take over. The effect on the class was electric. Cockcroft retained

> the immediate impression that here was a great man who was not going to stand any nonsense; thereafter the lectures were delivered by Rutherford in perfect quiet except for the applause which greeted the beautiful demonstrations of Kay, the laboratory steward.[6]

CHAPTER TWO

THE CRUCIBLE OF WAR

By the end of June 1915 Cockcroft had completed his first year at Manchester University, passing the Intermediate Examination in Mathematics, Physics and French. Early optimism about a speedy end of the war had, by now, evaporated and the country was being mobilised for a long war. Conscription was not to be introduced for another year as there had been such an enthusiastic response to Kitchener's stern appeal for volunteers to form the new armies to reinforce the original British Expeditionary Force. But John and Eric would soon reach military age.

From its start John had followed the progress of the war with interest and the early, rapid advances of the German armies were charted in his diary. Although at first he did not join the Manchester University Officers Training Corps (OTC), because to do so would have completely eclipsed his studies, he later joined it, anticipating that, should he apply for a commission, the experience would be useful. He had no ambition to become an officer. 'I heard', he wrote at the time, 'an officer's life summed up as swank, women and general enjoyment, but there are big responsibilities'. Later, he wrote to his father in a similar vein. 'I'd far sooner go in the ranks first like many others better than myself. I've no desire to be the inefficient young sub who is neither capable nor respected'. This was a mature judgment from an eighteen year old and was probably based on what he had been told about officers holding safe appointments at home. All in good time he passed out of the OTC as being 'efficient'.

In the summer of 1915 he volunteered for service with the Young Men's Christian Association (YMCA) and spent some months at a large army camp at Kinmel Park near Rhyl in North Wales working in the canteen with little time for leisure. It provided a good introduction to the type of men with whom he would serve for most of the war; by September 1915 there were about 2000 men convalescing at Kinmel who had been through the retreat from Mons, the fighting at Neuve Chapelle and Loos, and the early battles of Ypres. In spare moments John studied Horace Lamb's *Infinitesmal Calculus*, feeling he should not neglect his mathematics.

On 24 November 1915 he enlisted at Halifax. Two months had elapsed since the Battle of Loos which brought about the replacement of the British Commander-in-Chief, Sir John French, by Sir Douglas Haig. The terrible battles of the Somme and Passchendaele, which made such savage inroads upon John's generation, were still to come.

He never changed his attitude towards war. As he wrote home, 'I'd sooner be saving life than destroying it, far sooner. I should think afterwards of some boys I'd robbed of friends'. But he was never a pacifist. In both World Wars he was a patriot in the best sense of the word and believed it was his duty to defend his country from its enemies, even if this meant using the Atomic Bomb. At first he wanted to join the chemical section of the Royal Engineers; failing that there was the Royal Artillery. Probably there were no vacancies in the Engineers and on 29 March 1916 John was drafted to Ripon to serve with the 59th Divisional Training Battery of the Royal Field Artillery.

For the next six months he was trained to be a signaller. Signallers were specialists whose job was to maintain contact between a forward observation post and a battery which might be a mile or more behind. Communication was by field telephone and signallers had to be proficient in morse using a buzzer. Messages were also passed by flash-lamp or flags. John qualified as a first class signaller achieving 100 per cent in each subject in which he was tested. As the field artillery was horse-drawn, every soldier had to be able to look after horses and unlike most country lads, he found this hard but he overcame his distaste for the work in the stables.

The battle of the Somme began in the first week of July 1916 and from the middle of that month John watched the drafts which had completed their training set off each night for France. He had a fortnight's leave at Birks House at the beginning of August and returned to Ripon to complete his riding course. On 28 September his draft left for Folkestone and crossed the Channel by troopship to Boulogne.

This was his first glimpse of a foreign country with its unfamiliar styles of architecture and different forms of dress. He was a keen observer and recorded his impressions in long letters written in a minute script either to his parents or to Elizabeth and his movements were briefly entered in a diary. Raw troops were sent to the 'Bull Ring' at Le Havre, with its hectoring non-commissioned officers, later described by Robert Graves and Siegfried Sassoon, where the troops were instructed in the latest techniques of trench warfare and were toughened up before going to the Front. Apart from being reprimanded for a dirty rifle barrel John survived the course and was posted to 'B' Battery, 92nd Field Artillery Brigade.

This unit was one of three artillery brigades supporting the three infantry brigades of the 20th (Light) Division, formed shortly after the outbreak of war[1]. It had arrived in France in July 1915 and since then had fought in the first two battles of Ypres and during the past summer had been heavily engaged on the Somme. Each artillery brigade consisted of three 18-pounder batteries and one howitzer battery. All three brigades had recently been concentrated uncomfortably close to one another on the edge of Delville Wood, where they had been shelled mercilessly by the enemy, losing 2 officers and 17 other ranks. The Brigade war diarist laconically recorded that they had been through a trying time but had acquitted themselves admirably[2].

Cockcroft's draft made the forward journey first by rail and then by lorry up the Amiens – Albert Road, their ears pricked for the first sound of gun fire.

Coming the opposite way was a column of infantry, officers and men, 'hardly dragging themselves along, wounded or exhausted'. As the roads and tracks were pitted with water-filled craters, fresh supplies of ammunition for the guns were no longer brought up by limber but by pack horses under cover of darkness. Cockcroft's first job was to accompany the Divisional Ammunition Column. He soon got over his 'fear of the 'orses', he wrote home, 'and it is not a bad job. It is certainly much better to be on the back of a horse ploughing through eight inches of mud than going through it yourself.' Back in the lines the horses had to be watered, groomed and fed and this had to be done before the men had their dinner. It was difficult to make a knot in a harness chain in the cold and wet, and by the end of the day, he wrote, 'I was just about plastered with mud for I had the job of stableman, making out feeds, cutting chaff, etc in that slimy compound'.

In the wagon lines there was a good deal of grumbling and grousing; the men, he observed, were inclined to be selfish and greedy and were disillusioned by the failure of the Somme offensive. Soon he experienced his first tour of duty in the observation post when his battery was supporting attacks against enemy positions west of Bapaume. He wrote to his parents:

> You take turns of six hours with another telephonist to be at the phone and the remainder of the time act as orderly, sleeping of course at night. There's a telephone dug-out with blankets to sleep on and just room for things. It's quite interesting on the phone—you run a little exchange and hear quite a lot of what is going on, in addition to receiving fire orders for the battery ... it would be quite possible to send a message off from here to England—if allowed.
>
> I've seen a little now of German activity; in some cases shells—one big one burst about 30 yards away from the dug-out I was in and all the mud rattled down after it. That was the only one which has affected me in any way as yet —you feel a little nervy for a minute or so after. The others have just been a matter of interest or speculation.
>
> There's a lot goes on up above us on clear days. There are German planes running over all the time and plenty of shrapnel. You see them wheeling and banking and the tut-tut-tut of the machine guns going till one of them turns about with sometimes a trail of smoke behind and makes for home.
>
> It has been freezing here these last two days and it was quite acceptable. You could keep dry and with fur jacket, muffler, etc you were warm for the most part.

On 13 December the Brigade marched back to rest in billets at the village of Moulancourt where they remained for the next four weeks. Cockcroft was able to have a bath, 'wonderful to relate, the first for two and a half months'. Christmas Day 1916 was spent exercising, grooming and feeding the horses. Then the men sat down to Christmas dinner, roast pork, beef, vegetables, Christmas pudding and wines from the local *estaminet*; afterwards they sang carols. Earlier in the day Cockcroft went into the village church but 'was afraid [his] ignorance of the ritual of the Mass could be construed as discourteous'.

Relaxation after the rigours of the front inevitably led to trouble with the villagers and he observed that 'some of our chaps have lost all sense of civility and dignity and their language and behaviour to the women are rotten'. Once he took the train to Amiens, about 20 miles away, for a day's leave, and visited the cathedral, its carvings protected by sandbags to prevent them from being damaged by shell fire like those at Rheims. Inside 'little choristers in white gowns fringed with red were singing the chants, other little boys holding long candles in silver holders and crucifixes. Old members of the ''Chapter'' wore black gowns on top of these white surplices fringed with fur or ermine or something'. Then he explored the town, looked at the bookshop, and turned into the Army Bath Unit. He paid 2½d for towel and soap and soaked himself for 'ten delicious minutes' after which he began to remove the ingrained dirt.

For the remainder of the winter and early spring of 1917 his battery supported a series of attacks against a German salient in the Combles area holding out after the offensive of the past year. The weather continued to be extremely cold until mid-February but when the thaw came, the ground was turned into a quagmire and every day at least two or three men slipped from the duck boards into deep mud and water. In mid-March 1917 the Germans withdrew to the Hindenburg Line—a series of strong points several miles back prepared over the winter months.

Cockcroft was responsible for laying a telephone wire up to the forward observation post.

> Two of you [he explained in a letter to his father] carry the big heavy reel of wire and walk on, dodging shell holes and ploughing through the mud as the wire runs out towards its destination. When crossing roads, of course, it has to be dug in and care has to be taken with it when crossing the multitudinous tracks. Then when you've got all fixed up in the telephone dug-outs you'll find you can't get through on it. Then you go back for a phone and begin tapping in and testing the wire especially at the joints. In time you will most likely find a faulty joint and after mending it everything is OK. Mending joints is none too nice on a snowy morning with a strong wind blowing. Your fingers almost refuse to move for you can't wear gloves on the job. Stray shrapnel shells add an extra touch of joy to the job.

With other Divisions of the British Fourth Army, the 20th (Light) followed up the German withdrawal to the Hindenburg Line. According to the Divisional history the ground crossed by the infantry was one of the wettest and muddiest places of the line. Looking out from his observation post John, writing to Elizabeth, saw 'just one expanse of shell-pitted clay. Once it was well-wooded land but now the trees are just splintered stumps barely more than a foot high for whose possession thousands of our chaps must have gone to rest'.

The spring weather made life a little easier. They gathered fresh vegetables from the untilled fields. 'Manure was still there; left in heaps ready for spreading; the reaping machines are lying in the fields and you can still see the root crops where they have been left to rot'. In April everyone was suffering from septic sores—toes, fingers, neck and body due to the water; and they had to boil their vests and pants regularly to discourage lice.

On the eve of his 20th birthday, 27 May 1917, John wrote to his mother from Havrincourt:

> On one side of us are green fields, on the other the old familiar black wastes.
> To me these last few years have gone only too quickly. If only I could have com-
> pleted finals at Manchester by this day, but we must just hope that the wasted
> time will not be much prolonged.

In the meantime, he asked for, and read Shakespeare's tragedies, Carlyle's
essays, George Eliot's *Romola*, Dickens' *David Copperfield*, Machiavelli's *The
Prince*, Tolstoy's *Anna Karenina* and Turgenev's *Virgin Soil*. Most of these
volumes were in the small Everyman's edition, convenient for a pocket or
haversack. Throughout his life he was to read not merely as a form of relaxation, he became an inveterate reader and was extremely well informed in
literature and in science.

The written reflections and observations available to the public of a man
like Cockcroft in the ranks in the First World War are rare. He wrote, for
example, about his religious beliefs showing that he had begun to form his
own views. Unlike some scientists, he believed that there is a need for religion
in society, but he had no time for hypocrisy. He thought the army chaplains
had little influence,

> They come and hold a service perhaps once in six weeks. We sing the hymns
> (though not always in the original wording) for the sake of the singing but the
> address we usually get leaves no influence at all. The chaplain is an officer and
> knows very little of what the true state of the men's mind is. If there were a
> minister who knew the ranks from within and tried to show what religion really
> is, it would be different. The only one I ever knew like that was a Welsh minister
> at Kinmel Park. I wish there were more like him.

He got on well with the other signallers or 'house mates' as he called them,
they formed a 'family on our own, apart from the gunners, often regarded
as being a fortunate lot, that is when they are not having a day off duty. When
we're out all night on a "bust" wire that's a different matter'. Similarly, he
approved of his officers and NCOs, the former were 'young, jolly good sports
on the whole; they're especially decent when you are on duty forward with
them and will show you anything you want'. He never complained of being
harassed by the NCOs.

Such comradeship was now to be a sustaining influence in the critical battle
of the summer of 1917, officially named the Third Battle of Ypres, but more
familiarly known as Passchendaele. Cockcroft's battey with the remainder of
the Divisional artillery moved up into the Ypres salient to form part of a great
concentration of guns early in July. It was, as one historian noted, the last
attempt to blast the enemy's front line with an overwhelming concentration
of fire power but without using surprise. The effect of the ten day's bombardment was to destroy all the surface drainage of the Flemish plain and
'create not merely the usual crater field but an irremedial slough'[3].

Before the battle they enjoyed 'the long grasses and brilliant patches of pop-
pies and yellow flowers everywhere'. A phenomenal period of wet weather
accompanied the fighting. While the gunners concentrated on laying the gun,
the telephone orderly awaited orders from headquarters but usually his work

Figure 1 Cockcroft on leave, October 1917

was finished; 'it [had] been done earlier in the day in laying wires and getting communication for the officers and perhaps doing preliminary work such as wire cutting'. 'Not an inch of ground [he continued] but which has been ploughed and reploughed by our long and machine-like preparations' and over which he had to lay wire. The rain had made his puttees 'one mud roll, my breeches ditto and boots like rags'. Machine guns contributed to the bombardment

> with their devilish mechanical chatter. In front a thick curtain of smoke hides most of what is going on but you can see the Very lights going up, all colours of the rainbow, as Fritz signals for help. Presently you see the prisoners return- ing, as often as not arm-in-arm with our wounded, often carrying stretchers. There are some amusing sights. You haven't much time for looking about though, for all your attention must be fixed on looking for the flickering light which may be sending tremendously important messages.

Gas was being used by both sides, it could be detected by the soft thud of the shell and when

> you sniff the stuff you make a dive for your helmet and it's on. You never forget to take it with you after one experience of it. Never shall I forget its sickly smell and the memories it brings back.

The enemy's artillery tactics changed during July. Instead of the usual counter-battery fire he withdrew his guns before daylight and brought them up again at night, inflicting heavy casualties on the British gunners. Cockcroft's battery suffered 24 killed and wounded on one night and it was probably on this occasion that he was the sole survivor at an observation post from which he maintained unbroken contact with the gun positions. For this he was mentioned in despatches. On 22 July the battery was withdrawn for a short rest, but most of August was spent in the salient supporting the main attack which began on the 16th. At the end of September the infantry brigades of 20th Division were relieved, but the artillery, as often happened, remained forward for another two weeks, 'although all ranks were well-nigh exhausted after two and a half months continuous fighting in the battle'. New positions were taken up on Pilckem Ridge east of the Yser Canal, infantry helping to move the guns throught the swamp. At last on 16 October the batteries were relieved after three months. 'It was the hardest time in the line that the Divi- sional artillery ever spent [recorded their historian] and the men were absolutely played out when on 13 October they were moved out of action to a train for Peronne'[4].

Cockcroft now went home on leave. Clearly he was wasting his talents in the ranks and his family, among others, persuaded him to apply for a commis- sion. Eric had already joined the Royal Flying Corps, after being advised by John to avoid the infantry, and later he qualified as a pilot of a Handley Page bomber.

On his return to the Front a fortnight later, he found the battery had gone back to Gouzeaucourt to prepare for the Cambrai offensive on 20 November, 1917 which, in contrast to Passchendaele, was intended to be a surprise attack. For the first time tanks were to be employed on a large-scale moving in front of the infantry, and instead of a massive preliminary barrage the guns were to fire at successive objectives in front of the tanks and infantry. But the inadequate performance of these lumbering land 'dreadnoughts' did not provide the deep penetration that was hoped for. On the 30th the Germans counter-attacked, infiltrating round the flanks of the British. Suddenly the gunners of the 20th Division saw their infantry streaming in disorder through the gun pits. They nevertheless continued to fire until the enemy was within 250 yards on both sides. The order was then given to remove sights and breech blocks, and withdraw. A desperate attempt was made to harness the horses to the limbers and move back the wounded and as much equipment as possible to a hastily organised rendezvous at the village of Metz-en-Couture[5]. In this withdrawal Cockcroft lost all his kit, including a small primus stove which he had acquired during leave.

A thorough reorganisation was necessary after this misfortune and the Brigade remained out of action for the rest of the month. Another severe winter had set in, reducing the amount of activity in the line. Cockcroft had one further spell of action in the latter part of January and in early February 1918 when the 20th Division went back to the Menin Road Sector south west of Ypres. Here he heard that his application for a commission had been approved and on 21 February he returned to England to be trained as a gunner officer.

He attended a preliminary course at Brighton where he was taught the theoretical aspects of gunnery and enjoyed returning to study: 'We work at and argue over gunnery formulae and angles. It's good to do a little swotting again after so long without'. He took the theoretical work in his stride, but found the majority of the cadets 'had a very hazy notion of maths'. What he found less acceptable was the prejudice against non-public school boys training for commissions, and this became more apparent when he went at the end of April to the Officer Cadet School at Weedon in Northamptonshire. The Commandant, he wrote to Elizabeth, has

> as good as said that BEF men who are not public school boys should not be here and that men who are not sufficiently educated will have to suffer... However, thanks to the opportunities I've had, I don't think he can trouble me at all. I think I can hold my own with any of the public school fellows quite easily.

Indeed, he found the other members of his class

> know nothing of simple fractions and decimals so now they're teaching us rudiments of algebra, trig and arithmetic. My officer appears to think I know nothing about it and when I take my turn at explaining things to the class he tries to pull me up every time.

As for practical work, the young veteran from the Western Front found much of it irksome, such as 'digging perfectly ridiculous gun pits and learning how to fill sandbags'. For the second time he had to endure the riding school to master equitation and jumping.

In his spare time he cycled round the Warwickshire countryside, visiting old houses like Compton Wynyates and exploring Stratford-on-Avon. He had begun to take a keen interest in architecture and, after visiting Coventry, wrote,

> Wouldn't it be nice if they had done [to the new industrial complex that had
> sprung up over the war years] as they do in Germany—according to a recent
> lecturer—leave the old town as it is and use it to live in and build all the factories
> two or three miles out, and all the workers returning from the city of mills to
> the garden city at night.

Early in November 1918 he was gazetted second lieutenant in the Royal
Field Artillery. At a farewell dinner held at the end of the course, 'we all *had*
to drink the King's health but my friend on my left kindly drank the rest of
my wine. I wonder how a TT† gets on in a mess.' He was posted to 4 Battery
Reserve Brigade at Boyton on Salisbury Plain, not far from Stonehenge, then
surrounded by hutted camps. His life in the mess confirmed what he had
always suspected about the officer class in general and he complained 'I'd
more responsibility as a signaller than ever I've had or am likely to have here'.

When the war ended on 11 November 1918 those who did not intend to
make the army their career were eager to be demobilised as soon as possible.
Until that day, Cockcroft observed, 'drinking seemed to be the only kind of
enjoyment; alternatively, playing cards and telling each other how bored they
are'. He found 'the necessity for constant shelling out' for mess bills and other
expenses were barely covered by a subaltern's pay. He was happier outside
the mess and playing football with the troops. He had his first and only
experience of fox hunting when a major, back from France, decided that the
subalterns should join the local hunt; on the first occasion the fox gave the
hounds the slip, John cleared the hedges successfully, noting with satisfaction
that several of the civilian riders, presumably more experienced, were
thrown. For the next meet he was allotted a 'really good charger. But the
snow was too thick and they called it off'.

Ten days after the Armistice he wrote to the Manchester Ministry of
Labour Office asking for details of a special course for ex-servicemen. He had
already decided that, instead of returning to the university to read science,
he should take a degree in electrical engineering at the Manchester College
of Technology.

> All I want [he wrote to Elizabeth, with whom his school friendship had now
> matured into love] is just work I can like and throw myself into so that 'our'
> day may come before we are very much older.

He had asked for text books to be sent him and in his spare time studied the
theory of electricity and 'made a start on calculus. I think I could get it all
back with a few weeks of good hard work.'

He had to spend Christmas and the New Year at Boyton. The local town
of Warminster was full of Australian troops celebrating; 'We had a rough
passage along the streets from the snowballers. No-one commanded respect,
not even their own colonel!' His eagerly-awaited release came through in mid-
January 1919 and he thankfully removed his uniform on which so much

---

†Although never a teetotaller, Cockcroft was abstemious throughout his life like the
rest of his family.

money had been spent. The war years had toughened him and taught him to endure and work in adverse conditions; they were to stand him in good stead no more than 18 years later in another war in which he was to play a leading part. Amazingly, he had escaped without a scratch. Looking back at the time, he summed up his part in the war:

> I would never have been satisfied with life at the base in France, nor would I have been happy at home. It feels different after you've had a spell in the line but until you've actually been, you always feel as if you're out of it when others are talking of their experiences.

CHAPTER THREE

UNDERGRADUATE AND APPRENTICE

Cockcroft returned to Manchester to the College of Technology after his demobilisation in January 1919 to take a BSc degree in electrical engineering. As he had passed his intermediate and Part I Mathematics examinations at the university he was allowed to proceed to the second year course of electrical engineering which began in June 1919. The head of the department was Professor Miles Walker, a brilliant engineer, 45 years old, who had occupied the chair since 1912[1]. After leaving Cambridge, he had joined the British Westinghouse Electrical and Manufacturing Company, formed in 1899 as an offshoot of the American firm[2], and was sent by them to the USA to study the latest techniques, returning to specialise in generators, induction motors and the design of measuring instruments.

During the summer vacation of 1919 Cockcroft worked in the testing department of British Thomson-Houston, another large electrical engineering works which, 20 years later, he was to visit frequently when in charge of army radar research and development. He stayed in a hostel full of young students of both sexes and, when this became too noisy, sought 'digs' in Bath Street, Rugby, which he shared with a friend. He used to stay in Todmorden for weekends and succumbed to the great postwar flu epidemic which laid low all his family with the exception of his mother.

He enjoyed working under Professor Walker. Looking back, he thought that he was an inspiring, rather than a lucid, lecturer, who made his students 'appreciate the interlinking of physics and engineering so that in industry they could stand on their own feet and attack new problems on a sure basis'. Walker was

> one of those professors round whom legends grow, the professors who really do leave their wives in the car† and go home by train, or after stopping to talk in the College entrance, enquire from the porter whether they were going in or coming out.[3]

---

†Cockcroft himself later acquired a reputation for absent-mindedness. He once left his wife in the car while visiting Allibone, went home without her and had to be recalled by phone.

His other lecturers included Gerdal Storey, who had worked with Parsons on turbines, and John Prescott who taught Cockcroft Bessel Functions. Outside the lecture room he continued to play cricket and football and used to go and watch J T Tyldesley and Spooner play in the Yorkshire versus Lancashire matches at Old Trafford, or the famous 1921 Test Match in which 'Warwick Armstrong, the Australian captain [used to sit] down on the pitch waiting for the barracking to subside'. He went for long walks in the Pennines and remembered 'climbing half a dozen peaks in a day'[4].

In June 1920 he graduated BSc Tech being placed in the First Division of the examination. Walker persuaded him to become a College Apprentice at Metropolitan – Vickers as British Westinghouse was now called† and for which Walker acted as a consultant. The Apprentice Scheme had begun in 1902 and was designed to capture talent from schools and universities for, in addition to university graduates, there were several other categories covering school leavers, students working in the vacations, technicians; hundreds of distinguished scientists and engineers owed their early training to the scheme. Walker must have suggested to Mr A P M Fleming, the Manager of the Research and Education Departments of the Metropolitan – Vickers Company that Cockcroft might, in his College Apprenticeship, pursue a subject on which he might be able to present an MSc Thesis: certainly we know that he registered for an MSc before he went to the Works and some arrangement was made whereby he was allowed, most probably encouraged, to visit Professor Walker frequently to report progress on his thesis work. He obtained an Industrial Bursary from the Royal Commission for the Exhibition of 1851 to supplement his apprentice salary of £75 a year[5]. These bursaries were financed from the profits of the Exhibition and were awarded annually to promising graduates to tide them over the critical period between leaving university and obtaining remunerative employment in industry. Cockcroft never forgot this financial support and in 1962 became a member of the Royal Commission and served on the Board of Management until his death.‡

He found digs at 60 Victoria Road, Stretford and, on 21 August 1921, entered the Research and Education Department of Metro – Vick, to meet Mr Fleming, a distinguished electrical engineer, and who, like Walker, was to take a close interest in Cockcroft's career. The College Apprenticeship introduced young graduates to many branches of the Company's activities, generally starting at the very bottom of the ladder, in the Foundry, in the Pattern Shop, in a Test Department, etc. John began in one of the many Test Departments and shortly wrote to Elizabeth,

> I have begun my initiation as labourer, spanner-holder, etc at the Works. I am in a department known as Condenser Test. We test everything in the vats which has liquid in it—water to be exact. All pumps and things come our way—really it's a hydraulic place. We live in a jerry-built erection of corrugated iron away from the main Works. We walk about on a floor which consists of planks and

†During the war, the British subsidiary of the American company had been absorbed by the Metropolitan Carriage, Wagon and Finance Company and Vickers.
‡As late as February 1967 he lobbied Anthony Crosland, the Minister for Education and Science, for an increase in the grant to the Commission.

many, many holes above a deep, deep pit or well. In winter I should imagine it gets rather breezy as the roof holds many holes too. I have spent most of my time so far erecting a series of pumps and motors for a test, hauling up large pipes and securing them in position... I went to see Professor Walker last night. He was quite affable after reading half my thesis *including* one of the appendices. I shall be at the Tech tomorrow and Friday doing a little work.

Usually he met Elizabeth at weekends and they used to go for long walks over the moors near Todmorden. After one excursion he wrote to her from Stretford:

I suppose we *ought* to have been at chapel† but the day was *too good* altogether. I wonder if ever they will hold open-air services again in the hills. I think one service I will never forget was one we had in the Dales in the open air—no instruments—just the finest of hymns, a short address from a man who had tramped over from a neighbouring place and really it had an appeal one rarely gets in formal services.

In his spare time he wired Birks House, then lit by gas, for electric light and, as the mains had not yet been laid, he connected the system to the mill dynamo. He and his brothers built a wireless set from copper wire and cardboard and fixed an aerial to the top of the mill chimney. Appropriately, their first reception came from the BBC Manchester transmitter (2ZY) located at Metro – Vick. He also took part in a production of Shaw's *You never can tell* by the old boys of Todmorden School and learned his lines from a copy on the handlebars as he cycled from his digs to the Works.

On 9 July 1921 he applied to the Royal Commission for a renewal of his bursary to cover a second year as College Apprentice. He summarised the work he had been doing such as testing magnetic materials, testing materials for large transformers, testing insulating materials, examining a large turbo-alternator, and preparing a design of an apparatus for the harmonic analysis of voltage and current waveforms at power-frequencies (which was the subject of his thesis for MSc)[6]. Attached was Fleming's report on his first year, noting that he had 'made excellent progress, given evidence of capacity and displayed a marked application to his work'.[7]

He had submitted his thesis to the College of Technology in June. It was divided into three sections under the following headings: (1) harmonic analysis for alternating currents; (2) the effect of annealing on iron-losses in iron used for electrical machines; (3) the possibility of free magnetic particles causing a breakdown of insulation between stator conductors and core. He concluded that while the method of harmonic analysis using resonance was very accurate, the apparatus was too complicated for general use[8]. The examiners were satisfied with the thesis which was a competent, well organised piece of work, showing Cockcroft's practical approach combined with his ability for painstaking analysis. Walker, *en route* to New York in the *Aquitania*, wrote: 'I am very pleased to hear of your success. I hope that you will have a good holiday. Would you

†His parents were then attending Bridge Street Chapel and the family was expected to be present.

care to get a renewal of your scholarship at Metro – Vickers in order to thoroughly complete the work?'[9].

Cockcroft agreed to continue for another year in the Works and spent it in Dynamo Test Department, dealing mainly with the testing of electrical machinery. At the end of this period Fleming reported that he had made 'highly satisfactory progress'[10]. On account of this Miles Walker strongly recommended that he should go to Cambridge to improve his mathematics, believing that it would be 'advantageous for future work in the industry'; in this he was supported by Mr Fleming, a man of very liberal views who, throughout life, was keen to help young men make progress in their profession. The problem was to find the money. His father could not help for his salary was under £600 a year and, apart from John, he had to support three sons, one at university and two at secondary schools. Although the mill had survived the war reasonably well, the post-war slump had forced a number of mills in the neighbourhood to close. He could only compete in the post-war world with modern machinery, though, by 1922, he had been able to convert the mill from steam to electric power and had installed beaming machines in the channel which had been occupied by the wheel, now dismantled. Walker suggested that Cockcroft should try and win a scholarship from Walker's old college, St John's. If he were successful Walker would be able to supplement this with a scholarship offered by the Institution of Electrical Engineers to assist promising engineering students. In addition Mr Fleming offered a small 'retaining fee' of £50 if Cockcroft were prepared to return to the Company after taking the maths degree.

This was an exciting prospect; as he explained in a letter to his parents, 'Properly taken advantage of, Cambridge could make all the difference between mediocrity and a first-class position'. He needed £316 for his first and £225 for his second year. Professor Walker, very kindly, was willing to finance him for two years provided that Cockcroft paid him back. This support was increased by £150 from one of his aunts. He needed another £60 to see him through the first year.

> I should spend [he continued to his parents] three months of the first summer vacation at the works again and getting, at any rate, a respectable income. The second year would have to be decided on later when I saw what scholarship I would get.
>   I have always to keep in mind that Elizabeth will not want to go on waiting for ever and it would take some time to make enough to set up after I left Cambridge. I am writing to her tonight to ask her what she thinks about it.
> [He was more pessimistic in another letter.] Assuming that the Works wouldn't help financially, it means that I should have to borrow something like £250. At the end of my period of starting then I should be found with a debt of that order and at the same time have to *begin* to save with a view to setting up. It is not a very inviting prospect is it? You will see that unless the Works do help I can hardly go.

If he won the St John's scholarship he would have enough money to cover his first year. Furthermore, Elizabeth was prepared to defer marriage until he got his degree. When Walker died in January 1941 Elizabeth wrote to

John, by then a scientist of international repute

> I wonder where you would have been today if Miles had never made you go to
> Cambridge? Perhaps we'd have been living in a semi-detached somewhere in
> Manchester and I'd have been a bad-tempered, over-worked female instead of
> the perfect wife I am now. Though more likely you'd have been the world's
> leading electrical engineer earning about £10 000 a year. But whatever it was,
> it couldn't have improved on things as they are now and so we must say a large
> thank you to the memory of Miles.

Early in June 1922 Cockcroft saw Cambridge for the first time when he
went to St John's College to be examined for election as a Proper Sizar on
Dr Dowman's Foundation worth £30 a year for three years. Not only was he
successful but he was simultaneously elected by the College to a Hoare
Exhibition worth £20, awarded to 'two undergraduates of limited means', on
the recommendation of Ebenezer Cunningham, a college lecturer in
mathematics, a man who was to be his future supervisor. The balance of £216
was paid by his aunt and Miles Walker. Cockcroft later acknowledged
Cunningham's help in his mathematical studies over the next two years and
he was always made welcome at the Cunninghams' home

When he passed through the splendid Tudor gateway of St John's he
entered a world that was to captivate him for the rest of his life. He might
have appointments of national importance outside the university and he was
to spend much of his time travelling around the world, but he put down his
roots in Cambridge and he was never happy to be away too long from this
academic haven.

> The college [he wrote] is a lovely old building with three courts and cloisters
> and then behind, alongside the river, rows of tennis courts, lawns and trees. The
> river was full of lazy punts carrying flannel-clad people slowly along. It's the last
> week of the May revels and all the colleges are giving balls. Sisters and cousins
> and others are here in myriads in wonderful frocks, etc.

Before going up as a freshman in October 1922, Cockcroft went climbing
in the French Alps and on the way to Dover he stayed with an uncle in
Woking, Surrey and took the opportunity to see the sights of London. He also
went to the National Physical Laboratory at Teddington where two friends,
J Hollingworth and R L Smith-Rose, who both later became distinguished
engineers, were assistants in the Electricity Department. They told him that
he could get a job there at a salary starting at £300 a year. 'If Metro–Vick
fail', (i.e. should they not offer him a job after leaving Cambridge) he wrote
to Elizabeth, 'I have something in prospect anyway'.

How would Cockcroft have appeared to his fellow freshmen? He was of
medium height with a slight, though athletic, figure. In the fashion of the day,
his medium brown hair was kept trim and he wore the customary tweed jacket
and grey flannels of the period. Towards the end of the 1930s he began to
wear glasses and, with his increasing commitments preventing him from
taking the regular exercise to which he was used, he began to put on weight
in later years. When he arrived in Cambridge he was a few years older than
most of the freshmen; he had experienced four years of war and had had

practical engineering experience in a large Works: these circumstances, combined with his rather detached manner, were not conducive to the making of many close friendships with fellow undergraduates.

As a graduate of another university he was excused the taking of Part I of the mathematical tripos so in his first year he concentrated exclusively on Part II, a two-year course. He declared in later years that having to cope with this subject at the age of 26 was the most difficult thing he had ever done. Cunningham, however, was not only a good lecturer, but a thorough supervisor who did not believe in merely coaching students to pass examinations. A student once asked him whether a certain question would be likely to come up in the Tripos, to which Cunningham replied, 'You're not interested in exams, you're interested in mathematics'. Cockcroft also attended the lectures of Sir Joseph Larmor, the celebrated physicist, a Fellow of St John's and one who stood between the old and the new physics. His lectures, Cockcroft remembered,

> were extraordinarily obscure and three or four of us used to take turns in attending until something we could understand turned up. In particular, I was very interested in his treatment of reflection of radio waves on the [Heaviside] layer†, which again was given by Larmor in his lectures and only published a great deal later[11].

The University had much to offer in addition to lectures and he took full advantage of the numerous societies and clubs that used to invite the celebrities of the day to speak and, afterwards, to discuss their subject with the audience. His letters to Elizabeth reveal the extent of his interests. He was a member of a group that met at the Dean of St John's rooms where 'they sat round the fire and discussed all manner of subjects from Einstein downwards'. On one of these occasions he took part in a 'philosophical discussion on the existence of God. The speaker put forward the ''intuitional point of view'', whether what you ''felt within you'' was any sort of thing to go by. No doubt, you will answer in the affirmative way.' He was then reading Bertrand Russell's *Mysticism and Logic* to see what he thought about it. Later he heard Russell give his reasons on 'Why I am a Socialist', though they appeared to be no more than 'some quite harmless generalisations to which no-one would take exception'. Lord Dawson of Penn, the famous physician, put the case for birth control, pleading for reason as against a 'blind trust in chance. The least desirable sections of the community provide three or four times the average number of children than the artisan class do, for example.' He was a member of the Heretics—a select society founded in 1909 by C K Ogden, President until 1924, a society described by Cockcroft as 'non-religious but highly respectable; of the Ten Commandments, it held that only six need be attempted'. Papers ranged from literary to scientific. J B S Haldane read a paper in defence of chemical warfare, Cockcroft agreed with his conclusions—but was doubtful about their application to the civilian population—an interesting attitude in view of the dilemma later to be faced by scientists of his generation in making up their minds whether to advocate

†An electrically-charged layer in the atmosphere.

the use of an atomic bomb. It was about this time that Einstein spoke to the Cavendish Physical Society which used to meet every other Wednesday during term and some 30 years later Cockcroft recalled the occasion when he wrote to congratulate Einstein on his 80th birthday:

> Your work [he declared] for me has always been one of the most important components in our knowledge and way of thinking about the physical world and time has brought maturity to those first contributions you have made.[12]

Sometimes he went to the Union debating society. One of the debates was on prohibition, the teetotallers only lost 'by seven votes in 300 which is remarkable for Cambridge'. Another time he cast his vote against the prospect of a Conservative administration, this time there being about a 'hundred or so people with fixed opinions about conservatism whom no eloquence could move'.

Then there was the world of music which he had begun to explore and, as a member of the St John's Musical Society, he listened to the music of Mozart, Bach, Schubert, Chopin, Scriabin and Ravel, among others. One Sunday afternoon he went, as so many undergraduates have done, to King's College Chapel to listen to the music and the singing and to look at the stained glass, 'As a service it feels very far away and detached but it's quite nice to hear.'

All these activities, important to his development as they were, were peripheral to his main interest of science. He was a member, and later, Treasurer of the Mathematical and Wireless Societies and in his second year he read a paper to the latter on the 'photophone'. In the early days of radio, or 'wireless' as it was then known, the microphone consisted of a telephone mouthpiece and was liable to make distorting noises when a musical note clashed with its own natural frequency and one attempt, not wholly successful, to solve this problem was the photophone. Afterwards he described how, in the lecture, 'I managed to retain my wits quite well this time and did bits without reading from my notes. I think one improves in these matters.' He later became a practised lecturer, quiet (alas, at times inaudible), factual and persuasive, particularly in his later years when he tried to inform the layman of the advantages to be gained from nuclear power. In the Mathematical Society a typical example of a subject discussed was the ratio of boys to girls in a family, in which a mathematician, a biologist, a theologian and a statistician took part; the consensus of opinion seemed to be that there were 'a greater number of "all boys" or "all girls" families than could be accounted for by pure chance'. He also formed on his own a small study circle which met in his rooms and to which he read a paper on 'Apprenticeship for Industry', drawing on his experiences at Metro–Vick. 'I really knew very little about the subject, but collected a little book by A P M Fleming and rehashed a good deal of it.'

Sport continued to attract him; he played football, cricket and hockey for St John's, took up tennis and joined the mountaineering club; he spent part of his second Long Vacation climbing in the French Alps with Peter Reilly, another member of his college, and sometimes he would take long walks on his own in the countryside round Cambridge.

His second year at Cambridge (1923/4) was financed by the St John's

Sizarship and Exhibition, the support from his aunt, the Metro–Vick grant and by a £100 scholarship from the British Electrical and Allied Manufacturers Association for which he had been given a recommendation by Fleming. It was now that he felt he could devote some time to attending classes at the Cavendish Physical Laboratory. Miles Walker had given him a letter of introduction to Rutherford, then Professor of Experimental Physics. The Laboratory in Free School Lane was only about five minutes' bicycle ride from St John's; it had been opened in 1874 by William Cavendish, seventh Duke of Devonshire, a leading industrialist of the day, distantly related to the great scientist, Henry Cavendish. Entrance was through a dark, archaic-looking gateway, surmounted by an effigy of the Duke, and closed by oak doors on which were carved in old English letters the second verse of the 111th Psalm in the Latin of the Vulgate version: 'The works of the Lord are great, sought out of them that have pleasure therein'. Inside was a small courtyard filled by a number of sheds and surrounded by laboratories and lecture rooms. On his first visit, Cockcroft found Rutherford in one of the laboratories,

> sitting, as he so often did, on a stool. He received me very kindly and gave me authority to devote such time as I could spare from mathematics to work in the advanced practical class, then, looking at me with those penetrating eyes, he promised to take me into the Cavendish *if* I got a 'first'[13].

Here he learned how to conduct experiments. In those years, evacuated glass containers were used for much of the experimental work; they were, as he told Elizabeth, 'one of the few things that will keep a really good vacuum', and it was necessary for students to master the art of glass-blowing. Sir J J Thomson's assistant, Everett, offered glass-blowing lessons to students at two guineas per term and he also sold 'Everett's wax' for sealing vacuum apparatus, at one shilling per stick 'all to be paid for out of our pockets'. Eventually he became

> fairly proficient. I must have made at least a dozen attempts at a particular piece of apparatus I've been constructing. You get one nicely finished, a really beautiful production and let it cool down gently—as you think—when there's an ominous crack and the thing goes to bits.

He became proficient enough to 'cut a thick tube into nice little pieces with clean edges which is the first stage in the game I'm playing'.

Sometimes on his way to his bench he used to see the celebrated Sir J J Thomson (Rutherford's predecessor in the Cavendish Chair, but by now Master of Trinity College),

> standing at his little desk looking over the results of Everett's experimenting or peering through his spectacles at the mass of glass tubing which formed his experiment. He was a much loved figure, always giving us a cheerful grin on passing and always full of talk on topics other than physics[14].

As Cockcroft had to combine classes at the Cavendish with his mathematical lectures, the only time available for the former was the lunch hour, when he 'chewed chocolate' as he worked and he returned for another hour before the Laboratory closed at 6 PM. As he confessed to Elizabeth,

> The trouble now, as always, is to find time to do everything, and I feel always
> I have hours and days too little. We shall have to do as Bernard Shaw suggests
> in his latest play—expand the span of human life to 300 years.

Rutherford had evidently already begun to take some notice of Cockcroft and, in the autumn term of 1923, he was invited to one of Lady Rutherford's parties for graduates and undergraduates and their wives or girl friends. She herself at that time took no interest in science, leaving her husband to organise competitions of a 'scientific nature'. Music was provided, but Cockcroft reported that most of the guests 'spent their time talking' until the end of the party at 11 PM.

In June 1924 he sat for the Tripos, reporting to Elizabeth on the 12th.

> I did immoderately or fairly well, doing about six quite good complete ques-
> tions, three with bits left out and three or four halves. A sufficient condition for
> a 'B Star' is seven *complete* questions... it is not, however, a necessary condition
> —a most important difference as any mathematician will tell you and if you
> can't get the separate number of complete questions they begin to count up bits,
> two good bits = 1 question, 5 bad bits = 0 and so on; so that I just take a chance
> and no more. We had the ordeal in the Senate House where all the historic
> battles of the Maths Trip have been fought. Kelvin, Maxwell & Co all graced
> the seats—and it is quite an imposing place but very noisy as the street abuts
> on to its sides and one can hear quite a lot of the small talk of the passers-by.

Cockcroft achieved his B Star as a Wrangler in Mathematics. He had always intended to return to Metro–Vick and the salary offered would enable him at last to marry Elizabeth. Cambridge, as he said, had 'a way of running off with money' and £330 a year would enable the young couple to live reasonably comfortably in Manchester. But his academic success inclined him to becoming a post-graduate research student at the Cavendish. This would again depend on financial support from Metro–Vick.

> If they don't go far enough the best thing would be to fix the date definitely for
> the following year [1925], by which time I should have finished at Cambridge
> and, by which time, I should have saved enough to start with some hundred
> pounds or so in hand towards any house purchase we might have decided on.
> By the later date you would be 26 still and I 28 so that by the time our offspring
> grew up I should still be able to introduce them to the joys of mountains and
> other strenuous pursuits.

Metro–Vick was prepared to offer a grant of £300 a year, on condition that Cockcroft continued to carry out some mathematical and scientific work for their research department and he was awarded a State Scholarship[15].

He calculated that, if they married, lodgings, heating and food would cost them about £370 a year and College bills, subscriptions, insurance, travel, etc would add another £150 to their total expenditure. Feeling that they would soon be able to get married, Cockcroft registered for his PhD on *The condensation and reflection of molecules from surfaces* and returned to Cambridge in time for the Michaelmas Term of 1924, and later, his own College awarded him a Strathcona research scholarship worth £200 a year.

CHAPTER FOUR

CAVENDISH RESEARCH STUDENT

In the spring of 1924 Rutherford had been Cavendish Professor for almost five years. When he arrived in Cambridge he had asked the authorities for permission to expand the laboratory and to increase his staff in order to fulfil his proposed programme of work, but nothing had been done. On 12 March 1924 he decided to remind Sir Frank Heath, Secretary of the Department of Scientific and Industrial Research (DSIR), which administered a fund to promote industrial research, about an offer made by the latter to help to pay for an Assistant Director of Research who would relieve him of the large amount of routine work and also be able to help in the training of research students[1]. The candidate he had in mind was James Chadwick, one of his most promising Manchester students, who had come to Cambridge shortly after Rutherford in 1919 supported by a Wollaston Studentship, and later a Fellowship of Gonville and Caius College. The University accepted the offer of the DSIR and Chadwick took up his new appointment that autumn. The DSIR next agreed to offer a grant of £500 to the Cavendish for the next three years on the grounds that Rutherford's research into radioactivity was extremely important from the point of view of defence. Again, the University gratefully accepted the offer; at that time it was sustaining the Cavendish with an annual grant of around £2000 a year[2]. The Assistant Secretary of the DSIR responsible for these transactions was Henry Tizard who had made a name for himself in experimental work in the Royal Flying Corps in the war and who was to be closely associated with Cockcroft's work in defence and atomic energy in the future.

Research work at the Cavendish for the next six years may be summarised as follows. (1) The transmutation of the lighter elements begun by Rutherford at Manchester was continued in close collaboration with Chadwick. (2) The study of fields of force around atomic nuclei, another major interest of Chadwick and C D Ellis. (3) Investigations into radiations from radioactive substances, continuing Rutherford's research at Manchester into alpha-particle and beta-particle spectra. (4) The resistance of metals in strong magnetic fields. (5) Reflection of radio waves from the ionosphere, following the experiment of Appleton and Miles Barnett in December 1924. The first three greatly benefited by improvements made on the one hand to the Wilson Cloud Chamber which enabled the tracks of alpha-particles to be seen, and, on the other hand, to electronic devices which counted fast moving particles. Although (4) and (5) were outside Rutherford's main interest he always gave them strong support.

Cockcroft had selected for study for his PhD degree the behaviour of metal atoms as they were deposited on a surface *in vacuo*, work following upon some arresting discoveries by Otto Stern and colleagues in Hamburg, work for which Stern later received the Nobel Prize; but he also occupied his time in helping to build the equipment to be used for generating intense magnetic fields. It was only after his PhD degree had been awarded in 1928 that he began the work on accelerating atomic particles, leading to nuclear disintegrations, which in another four years brought him fame.

First he had to be initiated in Chadwick's Beginner's Class in the Attic held during the Long Summer Vacation. It was customary in those days for all new entrants into the Cavendish Laboratory to start by learning the rudiments of experimental work using radioactive sources, by acquiring some expertise in glass-blowing and learning the techniques of evacuating apparatus and measuring very low pressures. Usually two beginners worked together as space was at a premium and there was generally insufficient apparatus to go round. His colleague was Joseph Boyce, a young American research student, who later wrote,

the accident that I was assigned as Cockcroft's partner in the Cavendish training course in radioactive measurements in the summer of 1924 did much to augment my year in Cambridge and developed into a life-long friendship which I valued greatly[4].

Cockcroft referred to him in a letter to Elizabeth:

I count the flashes I see by looking through a microscope at a screen. Every time the radium atom fires out a bit of its inside, it hits the screen and gives a flash. Two of us look at the screen together and when we see a flash, press a key and mark a tape machine outside. The game is to find out how many each miss and it appears I miss about one in ten and Boyce about 16 in 100.

It was arduous work and on 9 October 1924 he wrote: 'I have had a hectic day with my electroscope. To-day I've been at it 1.0 to 6.0 PM'.

Boyce remembered how

each member of the training course was made to construct a simple electroscope. He would measure the ionisation produced by the alpha, beta and gamma rays emitted by a radioactive substance; their ranges varied in their penetration of air, paper and sheet lead, and could be sorted out, one type from another, by quite simple filters. This became an object lesson in how much could be learned with simple apparatus[5].

There was a General Election in the autumn of 1924 and Cockcroft took Boyce along to the Union to hear the returns. The Conservatives won and the Liberals were replaced by the Labour Party as the main Opposition. Boyce remembered that it 'was not a happy evening for a Manchester Liberal, nor for that matter, for a Wilsonian Democrat from the US'.

Chadwick must have recognised Cockcroft's engineering flair for he asked him to devise a way of counting rather large numbers of alpha-particles coming from a strong radioactive source, and Cockcroft produced an elegant solution which he described to Elizabeth in the following terms,

> You can't count the flashes when they come too quickly, so that you arrange a motor to drive a wheel with a hole in it and only count every time the hole comes round and lets you see the screen.

By the beginning of November he had been 'turned out of the training course as semi-proficient—or at any rate as having wasted enough time here'.

He had by then caught the eye of Peter Kapitza, a Russian electrical engineer in charge of the magnetic laboratory. Kapitza's father had served in the Tsar's army as a General in the Engineers and Kapitza had been a lecturer in electrical engineering in the Petrograd Polytechnical Institute from 1919 to 1921. He was not unsympathetic to the new regime and was sent to England in 1921 to purchase scientific equipment. He took the opportunity to visit Rutherford at the Cavendish and was so impressed that he applied to become, and was admitted as, a research student in July 1921. The Soviet Union doubtless appreciated that what Kapitza would learn at Cambridge would ultimately be of value to them and allowed him to stay. He enjoyed strong support from Rutherford who considered him to be 'a man of marked skill, exceptional ability and great originality of mind, who has very unusual qualifications for pioneer work of this character'[6].

Kapitza's aim was to produce extremely high magnetic fields to ascertain if, and how, they might modify electron orbits and movements in atoms arranged in a well defined atomic lattice in a crystal of a metal. To generate a high field, he first constructed a very large battery which he discharged through a copper coil but this did not produce a large enough field at the centre of the coil so he conceived the idea of short-circuiting a large alternator —an AC generator—for a single half-cycle (one hundredth of a second) through the copper coil, the energy for the field coming out of the stored energy of the rotating armature of the machine. It was probably Cockcroft who suggested to Kapitza that the Metro–Vick Company made such machines and he, together with Miles Walker, drew up a specification and Metro–Vick were asked to tender. The DSIR gave a grant of £8000 to be spread over the next four years and also paid for the machine[7]. Cockcroft calculated the forces in the coil when subjected to the very high transient currents and all in good time a field of 300 000 gauss† was created at the centre of the coil without accident; it was the highest field ever made by man up to that date.

Kapitza became one of the very few close friends of Cockcroft who in 1924 described him to Elizabeth 'as a grand fellow with eyes like your Uncle Joshua [Crabtree] and he speaks a very broken sort of English; he thinks he will be able to avail himself of my services if they come off and Rutherford agrees'. Rutherford did agree and early in 1925 the plans for the dynamo were approved. Kapitza drove Cockcroft to Trafford Park to inspect the progress of the machine; they stayed at Birks House and after supper sat round the table discussing the problems that had arisen during the day's work.

†Gauss was the unit of magnetic field at that time.

Figure 2 Sir Ernest Rutherford and Cockcroft in the Magnetic Laboratory.
(Courtesy: Churchill College, Cambridge)

In May 1925 the switchgear began to arrive and the Cavendish staff in shirt sleeves set about shifting the packing cases, each weighing one ton, with rollers and levers. Next came the generator accompanied by Metro–Vick mechanics to assemble it. Cockcroft wrote a long account of this to Elizabeth, telling her,

> It took two or three hours to get it off the truck and the men were lubricated by three gallons of beer, the Professor paying for the second instalment and sampling it himself. By mid-July the machine was running and the 'Crocodile' [Kapitza's nickname for Rutherford—in Russia there is a tradition that a crocodile never goes backwards] and F W Aston—sometime Nobel Laureate— came to look at it in action, almost with awe. Kapitza is rather nervous about it yet, I think, as he's not used to running high-speed machines. I got over a good deal of it when I was at Metro–Vick and feel fairly calm in running it up to speed. It should extend the region of knowledge of atomic physics very considerably, if everything goes well, and it is for this reason that I am so lucky in getting in with the work. What we have to do with it is to make magnetic fields just about as strong as those holding in the outer shell of the atom, and we can disturb this shell very considerably when we switch on our current. Whilst it's disturbed we take photographs and do experiments to find out how it's disturbed and then knowing this we shall know much more about the atom.

By October 1925 most of the equipment was installed in a shed in the Cavendish courtyard formerly used by chemistry students and this new Magnetic Laboratory was formally opened by the Chancellor of the University, Lord Balfour, on 9 March 1926.

In the meantime Cockcroft had been officially nominated as one of Kapitza's assistants and the DSIR was asked to provide a stipend.

> Cockcroft [wrote Kapitza to the Secretary of the Research Board] is keeping all the accounts and takes over a good deal of the correspondence with firms. Moreover, I put into his hands the supervising of the wiring of the place and the erection of the foundation of the dynamo. The second job is already accomplished, and I was highly satisfied with the way he helped me with this. He saved us a lot of time and money by his quick making of working drawings. There are also many other cases in which he has helped us[8].

After due consideration the DSIR approved a salary of £1 a week, a sum not commensurate with the amount of time he devoted to the Magnetic Laboratory.

In addition, Rutherford asked him to supervise the rewiring of the remainder of the Cavendish, it had not been done for 30 years apparently and was getting into a very bad condition. This extra work helped to bring in more money, so important if he was to marry that summer. As Rutherford was not interested in practical details, Cockcroft went for advice to Lincoln, in charge of stores, 'a most important man in the lab who controls all the stores and gets everything done, a man with a good sense of humour and a wonderful Old Bill moustache and we get on well together'. Rutherford's well known insistence on economy was now borne home on Cockcroft. One example was Kapitza's request for an office telephone.

> The Prof is a great economist and he's continually having tiffs with Kapitza on

this score. He told Kapitza the other day that he was an 'expensive child'. To this Kapitza retorted that 'if you bring a child into the world you must educate it'. And so he got his telephone.

At later dates he was also useful to Rutherford, again in his capacity of 'spare-time, honorary electrical engineer to the Laboratory', as he later described it, when Rutherford and three of his students—Wynn-Williams, W B Lewis and Vivian Bowden—were engaged in analysing alpha rays by an annular magnetic field. 'For this experiment', Cockcroft explained, 'I designed a new kind of "bun-shaped" magnet and the accuracy of relative velocities was improved to about 1 in 5000'[9]. A feature of this electromagnet was that it used a much smaller weight of steel compared with a similar one operating in Paris and needed only a few hundred watts, obtainable from a battery, to energise it. Cockcroft also designed, in company with C D Ellis and H Kershaw, a permanent magnet with an adjustable field for beta ray spectroscopy using, at the suggestion of Kapitza, bars of cobalt steel with the yoke and pole pieces of mild steel[10].

While Cockcroft with his mathematical ability was able to help Kapitza, Kapitza in turn sharpened Cockcroft's intellectual powers for he was a man who had wide interests, was extremely sociable and enjoyed discussion. While he had great respect for the Cambridge tradition, he found the undergraduates, on the whole, tended to be treated too much like schoolboys, and when abroad he had observed that young English research workers, who were usually more talented than their continental contemporaries, were afraid to express opinions for the fear that they would appear ignorant or stupid[11]. Kapitza therefore founded what became known as the 'Kapitza Club' which met every week during term in one of the colleges. On the first occasion Kapitza broke down the silence by deliberately making howlers so obvious that even the shyest young research worker put up his hand to correct them. In this way Kapitza raised the 'standard of general discussion of physics and engendered a freer exercise of the scientific intellect'. Speakers at the Club, apart from Kapitza and members of the Club, included distinguished visitors such as Bohr, Franck, Langevin, Born, Ehrenfest, Schrödinger, Karl Compton, and G N Lewis. Cockcroft was elected a member in 1924. In a description to Elizabeth he wrote:

> It consists of 12 members—all the bright young sparks of the Cavendish, and they read papers to each other, weekly, on recent work in physics. When no-one reads a paper they have what is diabolically known as 'five minutes'. You go round the alphabet and have to get up and talk for that space of time in turn. I got caught first night with very little to say. However, I said something and saved my bacon.

Between 1924 and 1933 he spoke or read a paper on at least 20 occasions, the subject generally relating to electrodynamics, though he also gave an account of one of his American tours. The topics discussed were usually devoted to the latest advances in physics, but the proceedings were conducted in a light-hearted atmosphere. On 6 November 1925, for example, there is an entry in the Minute Book signed by Cockcroft[12]. 'A determination was made of the mental characteristics of the Club. The results of the investigation are as follows:

Outstanding capacity	nil
Above (?) normal	4
Degenerate	1
Alcoholic degeneracy	1
Normal	4
Inferior	2
Vulgar	1'

Cockcroft was also invited to join another select society known by the mathematical symbols $\nabla^2 V$, a club of experimental and research physicists of long standing which met twice a term. 'It consists of 25 members and I was very fortunate to get in for there were only six experimental vacancies and nine nominations, Boyce also got in'.

Whilst studying for his mathematical tripos he had extended and written up the work he had been doing with colleagues in the Manchester College of Technology under the direction of Miles Walker. This paper had been accepted by the Institution of Electrical Engineers and the authors were invited to read their paper before the Institution on 6 November 1924. It was, his friend, Mark Oliphant, the Australian physicist, wrote after Cockcroft's death,

> an account of the application of the electronic valve oscillator, as a generator of a pure sine wave of variable frequency, to the dynamometer method of harmonic analysis of voltage and current waveforms at commercial power frequencies. The very complete analysis of the system and its limits of accuracy foreshadows the thorough approach to any problem which was to be so characteristic of the man[13].

Conscientiously he went to a lecture at the Institution before November to see how things were done. The remarks he intended to make on presenting the paper in the Institution were written whilst he was studying the decay of radioactive materials, 'watching the transmutation from radium to lead as interpreted by my electroscope and gold leaf'; having to go and help Kapitza; or clearing up after an accident in setting up a glass apparatus; but, as he said philosophically, 'Research is a story of such accidents—that and making things go right that jib'. The lecture was evidently a success and to celebrate he and Boyce and the latter's mother—a widow then living in London while her son studied in Cambridge—went to the cinema to see Douglas Fairbanks in *The Thief of Baghdad*. The following morning they packed up their apparatus and, before returning to Cambridge, Cockcroft spent an hour in the British Museum which he described as a melancholy place.

He started the work for his PhD thesis towards the end of 1924 after completing the course in the Attic; he had first to produce beams of different atoms or molecules *in vacuo* and then deposit them as thin films on surfaces cooled to low temperatures. This involved making up fairly complicated glass apparatus in the way he had been trained in the Attic but he was never good at glass-blowing, he never learned to anneal the joins adequately so that they cracked repeatedly and set his progress back again and again. The phenomena were studied in three separate series of experiments. Cockcroft concluded that:

> The extreme sensitivity of the boundary of the deposits to changes in stream density may be a valuable tool in experiments on the reflection of atomic streams from crystal and other surfaces where it is desirable to obtain information on the symmetry of the reflected beam and it is hoped to use this property in experiments now in progress.

He finally took his PhD on 6 September 1928.

Knowing his close association with Kapitza, then living in rooms in Chesterton, Elizabeth was apprehensive lest John became too preoccupied with scientific work. John reassured her. It is, he declared,

> often necessary for people of my age to work three or four hours in the evening at home, not every evening of course, but anyway half and you mustn't grumble, because without work of this intensity it's impossible to get anywhere. If you look at any of the people who are in good positions you find this holds. I've hardly met an exception. It doesn't, *of course*, mean that I appear only at meals or am absorbed all the rest of my working life—Heaven forbid!

In college he had occasionally been distracted from his work. Once, one of the livelier Johnians tried to persuade him to climb the outside of the chapel tower. Cockcroft, then living on 'D' staircase in the third court, and, being of more mature years, declined. A policeman on beat duty in the street below

a)

b)

Figure 3   a) 'The Crocodile'   b) 'The Little Crocodile' (James Chadwick) with Kapitza at Chadwick's wedding at which Kapitza was best man.

frustrated the attempt by shining his torch on the climbers. In February 1925 Chadwick, known as the 'Little Crocodile', being Rutherford's deputy, asked Cockcroft to prepare a paper on the rotor ship for the Wednesday afternoon meeting of the Cavendish Physical Society. A German experimental ship using rotors driven by a small electric motor had recently been built, the spinning of the rotors in the wind created high and low pressure zones, so propelling the vessel and Cockcroft discovered that the aerodynamics had been worked out in 1746 by one, Rollins, who appreciated that cannon balls could be deflected by a rotor action. During that month he attended the University Sermon preached by the famous Dr Inge, the 'gloomy Dean' of St Paul's.

> He was busy throwing away a lot of the old dogmas of religion such as the idea
> of eternal hells and heavens, resurrection in the flesh, etc. There must have been
> a record attendance.

By the Spring of 1925 the financial prospects for John and Elizabeth looked reasonably bright. He had had to practise the utmost stringency in his way of life, existing on his research scholarship, the Metro–Vick grant and the small stipend from his work in the Magnetic Laboratory. That Easter Boyce and his mother acted as chaperons to the engaged couple when they all stayed at the Lodore Hotel, near Keswick in the Lake District. Boyce remembered that on Easter Monday they walked to the top of Scafell Pike, and 'After the week-end, John drove us to Todmorden where Mother spent the night at the Crabtree house; I was a guest at the Cockcroft home'[15]. For the past year Cockcroft had been house-hunting and on 8 August 1925 settled on 87 Grant-chester Meadows, a little way outside Cambridge.

After nine years of waiting and planning, John and Elizabeth were married at Bridge Street United Methodist Church, Todmorden on 26 August 1925. It was a family occasion. Kapitza immersed in his work, was, to his great sorrow, unable to attend, he gave the couple a piece of Russian peasant furniture—a small hand-painted oak cabinet and the Rutherfords made them a generous gift of £50. Their honeymoon was spent travelling in Holland and Germany, after which they returned to Cambridge to prepare for the Michaelmas Term. Chadwick married just before it began, and on this occa-sion Kapitza was best man, borrowing for the purpose R H Fowler's top hat. Writing to Rutherford, who was abroad, a few days later, Kapitza noted in his idiosyncratic spelling, 'The numeroux newly-married couples are spend-ing there [sic] time more in making their nests as on scientific investigations. But this is indeed temporary'[16].

The Cockcrofts only spent a year at 87 Grantchester Meadows. Towards the end of 1926 they moved into 11 Little St Mary's Lane, much more conveni-ent, as it was only a few minutes walk from the Cavendish and no distance from St John's. Here their first child, Timothy, was born on 19 January 1927. He was not a strong baby and suffered more than most from ailments common in early years, but there seemed to be no cause for undue concern. John and Elizabeth settled into a domestic routine though he did not allow this to distract him from his work.

On 28 April 1927 Kapitza, whose first wife had died from privations in the difficult years following the Revolution, married again unbeknown to his colleagues, his 24 year old bride, Anna Krylova, being a Russian emigrée studying archaeology in Paris where the wedding took place. Kapitza belatedly discovered that his wife would require a visa in order to enter England and he wrote to Rutherford requesting him to send the document to Paris.

> What do you think about the marriage??!! I fear you are rather angry. This is why I propose to have no honeymoon and bring my wife in a few days to Cambridge. I hope you understand I am a victim of my own 300 000 Gauss and I have to confess that the dose which I received is rather a strong one.[17]

Inevitably the official wheels took time to turn while the Kapitzas waited impatiently in France, a fortnight elapsed before the visa was sent to Paris. In an accompanying letter, Rutherford, who had been bombarded with telegrams and letters by Kapitza, told him that he must 'suffer in delay for his sins of commission and omission'[18]. The Kapitzas, after spending some time in the Cockcrofts' first home in Grantchester Meadows, built a house in Huntingdon Road. C J Milner, later to become Professor of Physics at the University of New South Wales, remembered discussing with Kapitza, who had a reputation as a car 'buff', his bullnose Morris which he had just bought for £3.10s.

> Just then Cockcroft dropped in. 'Hey John', said Kapitza, 'what did you pay for your old Morris?' '£5' said Cockcroft. 'Why John, you've been done', said Kapitza. 'Milner has got one just like yours and he only paid £3.10s for it'[19]. 'Oh', said Cockcroft, 'I've seen Milner's car on the road, and it runs on a sinusoidal course, I paid extra for mine to go straight'.

From 1927 to 1929 Cockcroft made several visits to Germany. On the first of these he went to Berlin and in the train 'sat opposite a bewitching German Fraulein travelling from London. So you see it was worth it', as he teasingly wrote to Elizabeth. He had an hour's talk with Lise Meitner, then working with the chemist, Otto Hahn at the Kaiser Wilhelm Institute at Dahlem outside Berlin, both of them had been in Cambridge the previous summer attending the conference on beta and gamma rays. He spent some days at Göttingen, centre of German atomic physics; 'Lectures start at 7 AM. Think of it!' [he wrote to Elizabeth]. 'And they go on to 7 PM.' In company with the theoretical physicist, Nevill Mott, and another Cavendish colleague W H McCrea, he was taken round the famous Hydrodynamic Institute where there were 'a lot of side shows that would put Midsummer Common [the annual fair in Cambridge] to shame. Wind tunnels that we walked across in a 40 mph gale issuing from a 7 ft nozzle, a rotating room where we were turned round at 20 rpm.' He went to a performance of The Flying Dutchman and the next morning 'caught the train for Cologne and Aachen with 5 min to spare' (such tight schedules for journeys became characteristic of him). At Aachen he saw the Aerodynamic Institute and 'collected some information for George [G T R Hill, brother of the physiologist, A V Hill] on German gliding clubs and went to see the place where they make the gliders. One man flew for 110 km but this is exceptional.' He called on Professor Stern whose work had inspired his own on molecular beams. On another visit to the Reichsanstalt, Berlin, he met Ernst Gehrcke, an authority on optics and a notorious critic of Einstein's theory of relativity, and also Walter Bothe who was working on radioactivity. The physical section of the Reichsanstalt he noted was 'rather ancient and a little musty like the Cavendish'. He had become a friend of the Hungarian physical chemist and pioneer in the use of isotopes, George von Hevesy, then working at Freiburg, and stayed with von Hevesy and his Danish wife, who spoke English fluently. One afternoon he was taken to see a riding display, and recalling his experience in the army, he watched critically. The riders in red coats attempted to jump over gates and fences

> considerably lower than those through which we at Weedon used to urge our retired cob horses. After this they all rode by headed by an old general [a friend of the von Hevesys] who *could* ride. The proceedings ended with the singing of *Deutschland über Alles*.

He wrote three papers in the course of the following two years apart from his PhD work; one was on the design of the coils in which the very strong magnetic fields had been produced and it says much for the excellence of his calculations that no coil ever suffered damage from the enormous forces imposed on the turns. Indeed, had there been an accident the consequences might have been very serious. Two papers were written on problems posed by design engineers in the Metro – Vick Company, the effect of curved boundaries on the distribution of electrostatic fields around conductors and on the skin effect in rectangular conductors in which high frequency currents are flowing; the work was so well done that it has stood the test of time and it fully justified the small stipend which Mr Fleming had given him.

CHAPTER FIVE

ARTIFICIAL DISINTEGRATION OF THE ELEMENTS

It was in 1919 that Rutherford first disintegrated the nucleus of an atom, nitrogen, by bombarding it with alpha-particles from a radioactive source, the first artificial disintegration of an element. The alpha-particle is the nucleus of a helium atom travelling with an extremely high velocity, a velocity when it leaves a radium atom which could only be equalled if it were to be accelerated through an electric potential of, say, eight million volts. In the following four years he and Chadwick succeeded in disintegrating several other elements and the idea became well established that nuclei of the heavier elements were probably composed of those of hydrogen and helium together with particles having no electric charge, neutrons. This concept had been well expounded by Rutherford in his Bakerian Lecture to the Royal Society in 1920.

One of the present authors (Allibone) who had a Metropolitan–Vickers scholarship to work on the preparation of metallic zirconium and its alloys in Sheffield University heard, in November 1925, Dr C D Ellis from the Cavendish Laboratory lecture on these transmutation experiments of Rutherford and Chadwick, and, after the lecture, he asked Ellis about the possibility of getting a post-graduate scholarship to Cambridge. Allibone had already learned about Dr W D Coolidge of the General Electric Company of America generating a voltage of 300 000 volts and applying these to an x-ray tube, and, as he had some experience of high-voltage work in the Metro–Vick Company he suggested to the Director, Mr A P M Fleming, that he might go to Cambridge and try to produce disintegrations with particles accelerated to 300 kV or more in a vacuum discharge tube. He made his application to Sir Ernest Rutherford and was invited to meet him on 29 March 1926 at the Cavendish. After listening to Allibone's proposals for building a very high-voltage generator and discharge tube Rutherford took him down to the 'biggest room we have', big in linear dimensions and higher than any other room in the Laboratory. There he was introduced to John Cockcroft working in one corner and to Leslie Martin, the Australian, in another. 'Is this room high enough for you?', barked the Old Man; Allibone could only reply that he would try to generate the highest voltage possible in that height, about 500 000 volts, and that he would need half the room to accommodate the apparatus with sufficient clearance for safety.

In due course, Rutherford accepted him and he entered the Cavendish in October 1926 on the strength of a Wollaston research scholarship at Caius College augmented, like Cockcroft, by financial support from Fleming who also offered to help in the supply of some of the apparatus. Allibone consulted his colleague in the Works, Brian L Goodlet, head of the High Voltage Laboratory, with whom he had worked for a short time, and Goodlet recommended the construction of a Tesla transformer for 500–600 kV, being far smaller and lighter than a power frequency transformer of the same voltage. Rutherford had suggested that electrons should be accelerated in the discharge tube as, at that time, he considered that it was not possible for positive ions of modest energy to get near to a nucleus whereas electrons might enter a nucleus.

By the autumn of 1927 Allibone had built the Tesla transformer and was experimenting with a discharge tube able to withstand several hundred kilovolts. This led Rutherford, in his Royal Society Anniversary Address on 30 November 1927[1], to indicate a new line of research, though he did not refer to Allibone by name. A supply of electrons and atoms capable of being artificially accelerated to very great speeds, he concluded,

> could not fail to give us information of great value, not only on the constitution and stability of atomic nuclei but in many other directions; it has long been my ambition to have available for study a copious supply of atoms and electrons which have an individual energy far transcending that of the alpha- and beta-particles from radioactive bodies. I am hopeful that I may yet have my wish fulfilled, but it is obvious that many experimental difficulties will have to be surmounted before this can be realised, even on a laboratory scale.

These remarks apparently spurred several scientists, especially in the USA, to think about accelerating electrons and positive ions.

The Tesla transformer was a very convenient source of high potential in the Cavendish but the rotary sparkgap used in the primary circuit made an extremely loud and unpleasant noise and the radio-interference was intense, so intense indeed that it was necessary to work out a timetable of operation to avoid spoiling experiments in the radio laboratory not far away, and, all in good time, to avoid spoiling experiments conducted by Ernest Walton, of whom more anon; fortunately there was no interference with the Cockcroft's molecular beam experiments though the noise was most disagreeable to all. It was thought advisable to find out whether a frequency of 100 000 cycles per second (Tesla frequency) was as lethal as the 50 cycles of the mains, unlike very high frequencies which were known to be therapeutic. It was decided to experiment on a rat but the work had to be supervised by a medical man to keep on the right side of the law. Cockcroft got Professor J Barcroft to supervise while Allibone operated the Tesla coil. According to Martin, who was watching with Cockcroft, Allibone passed a spark through a rat to earth, boring a hole half an inch in diameter. Rutherford himself was another fascinated spectator who 'loved to edge closer and closer to the HT electrode, holding a vacuum tube at arm's length in an attempt to increase the brilliance of the electrical display. These visitations scared us.' Rutherford liked the direct approach, 'but his visits became less frequent'[2]. Eventually, after a great deal of trouble (everything had to be made by hand), Allibone constructed a suitable discharge tube and began to obtain results from scattering of electrons using targets of aluminium, copper, gold and tin foil.

Leslie Martin left in 1927 and his corner of the room was taken by Ernest Walton who arrived on 9 December 1927. He was six years younger than Cockcroft, son of a Methodist minister, born in County Waterford and educated, first at the Methodist College in Belfast and then at Trinity College, Dublin where had had obtained a degree in mathematics. He had obtained an 1851 Exhibition Overseas Research Scholarship and arrived at the Cavendish in October 1927 from Trinity College, Dublin. Like Allibone, he wanted to produce fast particles, electrons or positive ions. He was an extremely likeable man, full of humour and of original ideas, exceptionally clever with his hands and quite capable of making spare parts for watches. Describing his work at this time, some fifty years later, he wrote:

> Knowing that the potentials required to produce particles likely to be energetic enough to disrupt nuclei would be impossible, there and then, I suggested a method for accelerating electrons in a circular electric field. Rutherford immediately suggested a more practical method of producing the circular field. It was really the method being used at that time in the laboratory by J J Thomson in his study of electrodeless discharges in gases,[3]

a method later to be developed successfully by Professor Kerst in America, the apparatus being called by him a 'Betatron'.

Towards the end of May 1928 Walton realised that Rutherford's suggestions for producing fast electrons by an indirect method was not going to work and he turned to thinking about alternative indirect methods. In the middle of 1928 he suggested to Rutherford the method of accelerating positively charged particles which in due time became known as the 'linear accelerator'. He proposed using caesium ions 'as they were easy to produce in a good vacuum and their high mass eased the problem of producing high voltages at high frequencies'†. The idea was new to Rutherford who, after making a few quick, simple calculations, agreed that the method was feasible and worth trying. Walton then began to set up an apparatus, Cockcroft helping to solve the engineering problems. The experiment was much influenced by a paper published earlier by R Wideröe, the German physicist who had used a similar arrangement to produce high-speed positive ions. Unfortunately Walton met several obstacles:

> (1) my high frequency source was a quenched-spark generator, and
> (2) very little was known about the focusing of ion beams. Indeed, I had unwittingly destroyed the focusing action between the cylinders by covering the ends with gauze to secure a field-free space inside them.[4]

---

†To produce ions of a given energy in a linear accelerator of some specified length, the lighter the ion, the larger must be the voltage applied between successive electrodes; in those days it would not have been possible to give hydrogen ions a large energy in such an accelerator.

Another overseas scientist who arrived at the Cavendish in October 1927 was Mark Oliphant, who later described himself as 'a raw young Australian physicist who, with his wife, was befriended by a man [Cockcroft] who was also a research student although a little senior in status'. He became one of Cockcroft's handful of lifelong intimate friends. Oliphant had a gift for designing apparatus and 'set to work on the properties of positive ions' devising ways by which beams of positive ions of different elements could be accelerated through modest voltages.

In America at the Carnegie Institute in Washington Professor Merle A Tuve had developed a suitable vacuum discharge tube energised from a Tesla transformer in 1928 and in that same year Charles Lauritsen who, at the California Institute of Technology, had built a large transformer to test power lines and power-line components used this to accelerate electrons in a vacuum tube to produce x-rays. Dr Robert Van de Graaff, working under the auspices of the Massachussetts Institute of Technology had in that same year, invented a new method of generating a high voltage. He sprayed an electric charge on to an endless paper belt travelling at a high speed, carrying the charge from the ground up to a large sphere mounted on an insulating column but his very large machine did not operate until 1931. In 1928 Tuve's boyhood friend, Ernest Lawrence, who had become Professor of Physics at Berkeley a year after his first visit to Cambridge, was thinking of a completely different method of accelerating positive charges; it began in a manner similar to Walton's 'linear accelerator', but then he conceived the idea of deflecting the beam of particles into a circular orbit by means of a magnetic field and giving them a boost of energy by a small electric field twice per revolution; this device he called a cyclotron and it began to operate in 1932. High-voltage experiments were also taking place in Germany, Russia, Poland and the Netherlands and there was a flow of information through the scientific journals and through inter-laboratory visits all concerned with ways by which electrons and positive ions might be endowed with very high velocities—just as Rutherford had wanted.

It was a Russian theoretical physicist, the 25 year old George Gamow, who enabled the great forward step to be taken. Finding himself out of favour with the Soviet authorities, he had rowed himself across the Black Sea, and eventually joined Niels Bohr at Copenhagen. In the middle of 1928 he published in German a new explanation of the Geiger–Nuttall law (1911–12) which related the range of an alpha-particle to the half-life of the parent radioactive nucleus; the shorter the half-life, the greater the energy of the alpha-particle. His explanation, based on the relatively new wave mechanics of those days, was that the alpha-particle in the nucleus escaped not by *surmounting* the energy barrier surrounding the nucleus, but by penetrating *through* it, and the probability of escape depended on the energy of the particle within. Then he applied this theory in converse manner, reflecting on why Rutherford's alpha-particle had entered into the nucleus of a nitrogen atom (the 1919 experiment) and in a manuscript he sent to the Cavendish Laboratory in December 1928 he calculated the probability of a particle from outside penetrating *into* the nucleus even though its own energy was too small to surmount this barrier round the nucleus. Cockcroft saw this manuscript and realised that if Gamow were right, it would be *unnecessary* to accelerate particles by means of excessively large voltages to enable a nucleus to be penetrated. At some date which has not been ascertained (probably between December 1928 and January 1929) he wrote a memorandum to Rutherford summarising his own calculations; protons with an energy of only 300 000 volts should be able to penetrate into a boron nucleus with a probability of about 6 in 1000, and he therefore suggested to Rutherford that he should build equipment to accelerated protons through 300 000 volts. This famous memorandum did not see the light of day until Oliphant unearthed it from Rutherford's papers after his death[5], it was then 'lost' again in the Cockcroft files and has recently been found by one of the authors (see figure 5).

Figure 4 Dr George Gamow and Cockcroft, January 1929. (Courtesy: Churchill College, Cambridge)

He started immediately to collect apparatus together to build an accelerator tube like Allibone's and acquired the largest induction coil in the Laboratory: he stopped his work on the deposition of metallic vapours on surfaces cooled to liquid-air temperatures, having obtained his PhD on this work in the autumn of 1928. At the end of 1928 Gamow came to Cambridge on a Rockefeller Fellowship and at the Kapitza Club on 22 January 1929 he described his new work, putting on the board the formula for the probability

The Probability of artificial Disintegration by protons.

On Gamow's theory, the probability of an α-particle entering the nucleus after coming within the effective collision radius r_m is

$$W_1 = e^{-\frac{16\pi e^2 Z}{hv} J_K}$$

Z being the atomic no. of the bombarded material, v the velocity of the α-particle and J_k being a function of

$$k = \frac{m\, r_m\, v^2}{4\sqrt{3}\, e^2\, Z}$$

given on the appended curve. r_m is taken to be the radius at the peak of the potential energy curve of the α-particle in the field of the nucleus, and is taken as $1.21\ 10^{13}\left(\text{Atomic Wt}\right)^{\frac{1}{3}}$.

For a proton disintegration taking account of the half charge the probability becomes

$$W_1 = e^{-\frac{8\pi e^2 Z}{hv} J_k'}$$

J_k being modified by an increase of $2\sqrt{2}\, \text{&}\, K$ to take account of the half charge.

The calculated probabilities are given below.

Volts.	α-particle Al.	Proton Al.	Proton Boron.
3.10^6	0.20	1.00	1.00
1.10^6	10^{-8}	0.062	0.55
5.10^5	10^{-15}	10^{-5}	0.055.
3.10^5	10^{-26}	10^{-8}	0.0059
2.10^5			$2.27.10^{-4}$

Thus a 300 k.v. proton should be 1/30th as efficient as a Polonium α-particle. The range of a 300k.v. proton is 5mm in air, taking the no. of disintegrations in Al. by Polonium as 10^{-6} of the incident α's we should expect $1.8\ 10^6$ disintegrations per microampere of protons, per mm of air equivalent.   J.C.

Figure 5   Memorandum written by Cockcroft to Sir Ernest Rutherford giving the probabilities of 300 kV protons entering into the nuclei of aluminium and boron atoms, based on the new Gamow theory. Undated, but probably late December 1928.

of nuclear penetration. Allibone and Walton had not previously seen this formula; they went with Cockcroft back to their laboratory and watched him repeat the calculation of his memorandum, putting into the equation 1 microampere of protons accelerated to 300 000 volts striking a target of boron; this yielded a probability of disintegration which was quite acceptable, especially when it is remembered that a microampere of positive ions is equivalent to very many millions of protons per second[6]. Rutherford decided that Walton, who in his opinion, was 'an original and able man [who] had tackled a very difficult problem with energy and skill'[7] should abandon the indirect methods of producing fast electrons and protons and that he and Cockcroft should collaborate and build a positive-ion source, similar to Aston's or Oliphant's to produce protons, and a vacuum tube to work at some hundreds of kilovolts to accelerate these protons before they struck targets of different elements.

Cockcroft then decided that to energise his discharge tube he would generate a steady DC high voltage in preference to the Tesla high-frequency or the induction coil transient type of voltage; these two forms last for only a small fraction of a second per second of operation, so the discharge tube connected to the generator would therefore produce far fewer protons than if the voltage were steadily maintained. He persuaded Rutherford to ask the University for a grant of £1000 with which to buy a transformer for 300 kV and the ancillary equipment to rectify this and deliver DC to the discharge tube[8]. This was an extremely fortunate decision, for without the DC generator it is very unlikely that the disintegration experiments would have yielded enough particles to be detected unambiguously. For the next three years the two young men developed by trial and error the techniques that were to bring them fame in April 1932.

Cockcroft had already begun to acquire a reputation for pursuing two, sometimes more, jobs simultaneously. On 5 November 1928 St John's elected him a Fellow, this appointment being renewed on 23 January 1931. The College had asked him to advise on rewiring the interior and at the Cavendish he continued to help Kapitza in the Magnetic Laboratory. In 1930 he was appointed a University Demonstrator and lectured on electrodynamics to third-year physics students; lectures according to C J Milner, who attended them, 'amazingly time-efficient, like everything else he did', and which were Milner's stand-by on 'many occasions for more than 40 years'[9]. 'The general impression was', continued Milner, 'that this man was performing *very satisfactorily* about 2½ fulltime jobs.' Although modestly remunerated (in 1935 his gross income from academic work amounted only to £450) it helped him to provide security for his family.

Because there were so many calls on Cockcroft's time Walton had to take the larger share of the construction work on the apparatus.

> I liked this [he remembered] as I was fond of working with my hands. I had a lathe at home and had collected quite a number of tools. So I probably had more workshop experience than the average research student. John was very good at listening to what others had to say. He would rarely interrupt and eventually would give his opinion or make a note to look into the matter further. It was very pleasant to work with him. We had many happy discussions about our

work. I cannot recall a single occasion when there was any sign of discord between us.

Cockcroft, Walton continued, was

> very good at locating unusual apparatus needed for our work. His background of mathematics and engineering was very valuable. Samples are his calculations on the design of magnets required by Rutherford for the study of alpha rays and by Ellis for the study of beta rays. The former was like a bun or 'double mushroom' with a central yoke around which the energising coil was wound. Compared with other types, it was far lighter and needed only a few hundred watts from a battery to give the necessary energy. He was on various committees —how many I don't know, as he seldom talked about his other commitments. I recall one incident which arose because of the time he was devoting to other matters. He was given the task, very appropriately, of supervising an American student who had come to do research in 'theoretical engineering'. The student made several unsuccessful attempts to find him in the lab, but eventually succeeded. Immediately afterwards, Cockcroft mentioned to me how sorry he was not to have been able to help the student. The position was he just did not have the time to study the problem given to the student.[10]

Often his own work suffered; as Allibone asserted 'I saved his apparatus time and time again when he switched on, then dashed out to do something and forgot to turn on the cooling-water for the pumps'.

Allibone designed for Cockcroft and Walton the rectifiers to convert the alternating voltage of the transformer into a steady direct current source of power; they consisted of three large vacuum tubes rather like those he had been using; they were evacuated by diffusion pumps which used a special oil as the operating fluid instead of the commonly-used mercury. This oil, called 'Apiezon oil' had been produced by another Metro–Vick engineer, C R Burch, and some had been supplied to the Cavendish workers before it was available commercially. B L Goodlet designed a specially small transformer to fit into the room; it had to be assembled there as it was too large to be taken through the various doors of the Laboratory, and two engineers from the Research Department of Metro–Vick completed the assembly and tests of the transformer in December 1929. Meanwhile the rectifiers had been assembled and vacuum tested, and their electrical characteristics were determined, taking a lead over the room from Allibone's Tesla. They were operated with the Goodlet transformer in February of 1930 (see figure 6).

In the autumn of 1929 the Cockcrofts' domestic life was clouded by tragedy. On 11 October, just after the start of term, Timothy died suddenly from a severe attack of asthma. He had never been very strong, but had what Elizabeth's Uncle, Joshua Crabtree, described as 'a grave and winsome beauty'. The shock to them both took a long time to get over. The effect on Cockcroft was to make him concentrate on his work even more intensely than before. Joy Stebbing, who was his secretary at the Cavendish, remembered 'vividly how desperately sorry everyone was, though Dr Cockcroft was not a man to whom it was easy to say any words of sympathy'[11]. Joshua Crabtree asked John to come and have a talk with him if he felt inclined. But it is doubtful whether he did. By a strange coincidence, both Oliphant and Walton were to lose sons, Oliphant in September 1933 and Walton in December 1936.

Oliphant was travelling on the continent with his father at the time, and it was due to Cockcroft that they heard the sad news from an appeal made through the Brussels radio station.

In 1929 the Cockcrofts moved from Little St Mary's Lane to 31 Sedley Taylor Road on the south-east side of Cambridge, then quite rural in character. H C Hughes, an enterprising local architect commissioned by Cockcroft to carry out restoration work at the College, designed it and he also designed houses for Kapitza and Oliphant, the latter's in Conduit Head Road being the most *avant garde* in appearance. One of the features of the Cockcrofts' house, intended for Timothy, was a large bow window in the drawing room designed to admit ultraviolet rays, considered at the time to be beneficial to health. There was room for a tennis court at the back and the Cockcrofts were constantly entertaining, their warm hospitality welcomed colleagues, students, scientists from abroad and many others; Mrs Allibone, then newly engaged, stayed in No 31 for May Week. It was a most friendly house.

On 28 February 1930 amid a gathering of eminent engineers and scientists including seven actual or potential Nobel Laureates and a bevy of Fellows of the Royal Society, Rutherford opened the new Metro–Vick High-Voltage Laboratory, of which Allibone took charge that June. Surprisingly, Rutherford spoke about 'many millions of volts' being required to disintegrate atoms[12] instead of pointing out that it might be possible to penetrate nuclei without having recourse to high voltages. Allibone believed that he never accepted the forecasts of theory gladly, his motto was 'Well, try it and see,' and although he had given permission to Cockcroft and Walton to look for disintegrations of elements by protons accelerated to a modest few hundreds of thousands of volts, he probably never believed that they would be successful. Indeed, he had been encouraging Goodlet and Allibone to design a Tesla transformer and a discharge tube wholly immersed under oil, hopefully to produce beams of particles at two million volts.

During the last months of 1929 Cockcroft and Walton had constructed a discharge tube large enough to withstand the 300 kV which the transformer/rectifier combination should be able to supply and all was ready for test on 17 March 1930. At the top of the tube they had placed the small glass chamber in which low energy positive hydrogen ions, protons, were produced; these entered the high-voltage discharge tube in a very fine beam and after acceleration they appeared at the bottom of the tube still bunched into a fairly narrow beam which could then bombard any target placed in their path. First, it was necessary to analyse this beam to determine what fraction of the ions were protons and what fraction were molecular hydrogen ions. This they had done by June and they started the critical experiments, bombarding targets of lithium, beryllium and lead. They had expected that gamma rays, rays not unlike x-rays would be produced in the targets so they used a goldleaf electroscope to detect the rays; they found no convincing evidence of any nuclear transformation up to the limit of 280 kV. In August the transformer failed internally so they sent an account of their work to the Royal Society in a paper entitled *Experiments with High velocity positive ions* and reported that a 'non-homogeneous radiation was produced, the intensity being one ten-thousandth of that produced by a similar electron source at the same voltage'[13].

In June 1930 Walton's scholarship from the 1851 Exhibition Commissioners expired. Fortunately the DSIR agreed to support him for the next four years with a Senior Research Award. He also won a Clerk Maxwell scholarship. Had it not been for such financial aid (the country was then deep in the Depression) neither Cockcroft nor Walton would have been able to complete their joint experiment.

It was probably the failure of the transformer and the inability to generate more than 280 kV that prompted Cockcroft to think of a way of producing a high DC voltage from a modest AC voltage using a 'voltage-multiplying' circuit, a circuit which could step up a voltage V to $4V$, $6V$, $8V$ etc a circuit which, unknown to Cockcroft had in fact been invented 30 years earlier. He calculated the full characteristics of such a circuit, calculations which have been invaluable to later users of the circuit, and then he and Walton erected a column of four rectifiers and condensers to produce a DC voltage four times the transformer AC voltage. All worked well and once more they bombarded lithium with 250 kV protons but it was a race against time because their room was required by the Physical Chemistry Department and it had to be vacated in May 1931.

They moved into the Balfour Library from which the seating and other fittings had been removed, and, having now much more height and space, they decided to build, with the help of £600 worth of grants, a generator and

Figure 6 Two thermionic rectifiers and the Metro–Vick 300 kV transformer used to supply direct current to the first accelerator tube. (TEA)

new tube to operate up to a much higher voltage, 500 to 700 kV, thinking that the ions which previously had been accelerated up to only 300 kV had insufficient energy to cause any disintegrations. The column of four rectifiers stands to the left of figure 7 and the new discharge tube of two glass cylinders is shown on the right, both columns being continuously pumped by Burch's Apiezon oil pumps, the bottom end of the tube being a few feet above the floor.

> I have never regarded the move to the larger room [wrote Walton] as anything but fortunate. The higher voltage enabled us to investigate immediately elements up to about fluorine. For most work we could produce far more disintegrations than we could cope with. This meant that we were operating the apparatus mostly well below its limits, which meant that breakdowns were not very frequent. If we had remained in the old room with its low ceiling, observations would have been difficult. Indeed we would have had to lie down on the floor to see the scintillations—not a very relaxed position for reliable counts[14].

When the apparatus was completed they continued to look for gamma rays with their electroscope; Walton's reference to 'scintillations' quoted above will be explained shortly. Progress was slow, indeed Cockcroft had an extremely busy summer and autumn with various commitments and not till almost the end of the year was much experimental progress made.

During the vacation Cockcroft paid his first visit to the USSR. An international congress on the history of science had been held in London in June and a large Soviet delegation flew from Moscow for the event causing a stir by their mode of travel. After the conference, J G Crowther, the left-wing scientific correspondent of the *Manchester Guardian* arranged two tours to Russia in conjunction with the Society for Cultural Relations with the USSR. The first five-year plan had just been launched and there was a good deal of curiosity about the progress of Russian industrialisation.

Cockcroft and Allibone had arranged to go together on the first trip, their fares being paid by Metro–Vick, but Cockcroft found that the dates were inconvenient and Allibone could not change to the second. Julian Huxley was the only Fellow of the Royal Society in the first party of about 40 doctors, writers and a handful of scientists, including Allibone, who visited the famous Russian physicist, A F Joffé at the Institute of Sciences in Leningrad.

On 13 August, Cockcroft sailed from London in a Russian ship for Leningrad. His companions included John Pilley a science historian, N W Pirie a young Cambridge biochemist, H D Dickinson a lecturer in economics at Leeds and Glen A Millikan a crystallographer and son of the famous American physicist R A Millikan. Apart from meals, there was practically no service on board, which led to a discussion on whether or not there should be a collection for the crew.

> A very militant interpreter proposed that the amount collected should be written down and posted up in the ship for all to see and a young law student from Cambridge objected and wanted a box passed round; also Dickinson got up and said that in a Soviet ship there was no more reason for the passengers to tip the crew than the crew to tip the passengers![15]

A party of workers emigrating to the Soviet Union was also on board and they passed the time in vigorous political discussion. Cockcroft took with him the recently-published Macmillan Report on British finance and industry and quoted statistics, while Dickinson assisted a vehement Clydesider when he floundered during an argument (the economic crisis was at its height and a National Government about to be formed in Britain). 'The physics party', wrote Cockcroft, 'held the balance between the Tories and the others.' Crowther, who accompanied both tours, later provided a vivid vignette of Cockcroft.

> When the party of scientists arrived in Leningrad and was taken to the Europa Hotel, there was a long wait in the lobby, while rooms were allotted. Cockcroft sat down on a large chair and pulled out a sheaf of papers. On one was a graph of a curve; he pondered this, and then began to write out underneath it calculations in very neat numbers and words. Presently he was told the number of his room, and no time had been wasted[16].

In Leningrad he visited Joffé's laboratory where Chariton, a former Cavendish student worked, and also called on the Metro–Vick office which since 1922 had been the headquarters of a team of engineers engaged on erecting Metro–Vick turbines in Russia and instructing Russian design engineers in the design and manufacture of their own turbines. He was, however, more impressed with Moscow because of its greater activity and he went to see the well equipped high-voltage laboratory, at the Krzhizhanowsky Power Engineering Institute, housed in a disused church, a church now known to have been the one in which Pushkin had been married (and now, in 1982, being restored to commemorate Pushkin's life). He also went to meet Kapitza's mother, a scholar deeply versed in Russian folklore.

But the highlight of the trip was his visit to Dneiprstroi where the great dam, under the guidance of the distinguished American civil engineer, Cooper, was being built for hydroelectric power.

> As we approached, the whole horizon was a glow of lamps where the work goes on day and night. We stayed in a hotel of which only the top floor was finished and that not too well. We dined out in a modest restaurant full of young workers from the dam and ate a salad with eggs in aspic and black bread.

Cockcroft was impressed with the way the dam was being built in sections.

> There is a continual shriek of locos trundling trucks of cement from the mill. High cranes pick up five-ton loads and lower them on to the depths below. Down there, girls and youths tread the concrete into place with jackboots and the walls rise steadily. Almost all the workers are young—under thirty, I should say. The whole countryside is dotted with their bungalows.

On leaving Kiev, the party split up and Cockcroft returned to England via Austria and Germany, staying a few days in Vienna where he attended several concerts.

Summarising his impressions in a report to Metro–Vick, Cockcroft found some of the laboratories cramped for space and badly designed. Because there was little contact with the outside world, research was several years behind the best British and American laboratories. But he was impressed with the enthusiasm and drive of the Communists, though 'whether the final result will bear any resemblance to the Marxian communism is one of the most interesting questions for the future'[17].

On his return, Cockcroft took up his duties as Secretary organising the celebrations for the centenary of the birth of James Clerk Maxwell, the first Cavendish Professor of Experimental Physics. This was in itself a major task though recently he had acquired secretarial help. Hitherto, Rutherford had used one of the laboratory assistants whose sole qualification for the job was, according to Vivian Bowden, then a research student (later to become Principal of Manchester Institute of Science and Technology), 'that his hand was no longer steady enough to do any experimental work. The arrival in the Cavendish of a competent shorthand typist who was, furthermore, very good-looking and very nice had a dramatic effect on the whole organisation'.[18] Joy Stebbing (later Mrs Clarke) had the equivalent of what now would be called A-Level physics and had replaced two, more senior, girls from the local agency who had found the writing of Cockcroft and Kapitza incomprehensible and were unable to cope with the scientific terms.

The celebrations in Cambridge were preceded by the unveiling of a tablet commemorating Faraday and Maxwell in Westminster Abbey on 30 September and Cockcroft was one of the University delegation headed by the Vice-Chancellor. At Trinity College Sir J J Thomson, gave a dinner for over 200 guests, Planck, Zeeman, Bohr, R A Millikan and Marconi being among the luminaries present. There were lectures and conducted tours round the laboratories.'Never before', recalled Mrs Clarke, 'had so many famous scientists circulated in the Victorian rabbit warren of the Cavendish.' Niels Bohr was one of those who addressed the delegates. Cockcroft and his secretary had to record it for publication, 'he doing what he could in long hand', while she 'struggled with shorthand ... it was largely mathematical equations on the blackboard accompanied by a very broken English discourse and even our combined efforts did not produce anything very coherent and I don't think anything came of it'[19].

At last he was able to resume his research work, the apparatus, looking not unlike Bowser petrol pumps with two long glass cylinders, was completed. The inevitable teething problems ensued and much time was spent by Walton and their invaluable laboratory assistant, Willie Birtwhistle, who had joined them that June, perched on a ladder sealing the joints with a special plasticine supplied by Burch. There were so many joints, many not too well made, that getting a really high vacuum in the column of rectifiers and the discharge tube was, to say the least, tricky; moreover, all the internal electrodes were 'dirty' in the high vacuum sense, that is to say they were covered with an oxide layer and almost certainly with body grease due to being handled during assembly, so lengthy periods of 'de-gassing' were necessary to remove these contaminants. In achieving a good vacuum

Success was indicated [recalled Cockcroft] by a discharge tube mounted on top of the first stage of our oil diffusion pump showing first pink, then green and finally black. We out-gassed the tubes by repeated discharges until they were hard. The DC voltage on the accelerating tube was measured by the spark length between two large aluminium spheres and checked by a magnetic deflection of the protons after acceleration—the highest energy being about 500 kilovolts[20].

His word 'hard' is the physicist's way of saying that the gas pressure in the apparatus is so low that an electric discharge cannot take place between two electrodes stressed at different voltages.

They recorded their progress with the new apparatus in a note headed *Artificial production of fast protons* published in *Nature* on 13 February 1932.

> The maximum energy of the protons produced up to the present has been 710 kilo-electron volts. We do not anticipate any difficulty in working up to the 800 kilo-electron volts.

So far they had continued to look for gamma rays rather than for alpha-particles.

> We had [wrote Cockcroft to the American physicist, Karl Darrow, six years later] the fixed idea that the gamma rays would be the most likely disintegration products[21].

According to Walton, the reason for looking for gamma ray emission first was that there was speculation about the penetrating radiation produced by alpha-particle bombardment of beryllium and boron. It was also a very simple thing to do as they had a considerable amount of experience in using a goldleaf spectroscope, This speculation had arisen from reports by the Curie–Joliots in Paris that when an alpha-particle bombarded beryllium a gamma ray was emitted, an observation which Chadwick put to the test in January 1932 and discovered that instead of a gamma ray emission a particle of mass equal to the proton had been omitted having no electric charge, the 'neutron' forecast as long ago as 1920 by Rutherford.

Walton's recollections of what happened in February and March 1932 were quite vivid as recorded five years later. They continued to experiment using beryllium as the target material and then had trouble with the rectifiers. On 10 March they 'tried the effect of putting helium in the discharge tube'. Then they re-introduced hydrogen and 'on 14 March we investigated the nature of our ion beam [as it emerged from the tube through a thin mica window] deflecting the beam using a magnetic field. This seems to have been continued after the Easter holidays until 12 April'[22]. It must have been about this time that Rutherford and Chadwick, getting impatient with no results, told them to get a move on. Allibone recalls that Rutherford had told them to 'stop messing about deflecting the beam'; Walton remembered that

> Rutherford came in one day and found us doing magnetic deflection experiments and told us that we ought to put in a fluorescent screen and get on with the job, that no-one was interested in exact range measurements of our ions[23].

Now the point of using a fluorescent screen was that such a screen, a piece of paper or card coated with very fine crystals of zinc sulphide, was that it provided the very best way of detecting alpha-particles, indeed, such screens† had been used by Cockcroft and all the beginners in Chadwick's class in the Attic. Rutherford must have felt 'in his bones' that when a proton bom-

---

†The alpha-particle traversing a crystal of zinc sulphide modifies the electron orbits in the atoms and molecules of this mineral causing them to emit a green light which persists for a few seconds after the alpha-particle has struck the screen.

Figure 7   The Cockcroft–Walton accelerator showing Walton seated to observe scintillations, April 1932. (Courtesy: The Cavendish Laboratory)

barded a lithium atom an alpha-particle *must* be produced; wasn't that just what Gamow had suggested, and wasn't that what Cockcroft's 1928 Memorandum had been all about, so with his innate reaction 'Try it and see', no wonder he was impatient with Cockcroft and Walton 'messing about with gamma rays'!

On 14 April they put a target of lithium in the tube. While Cockcroft was in the magnetic laboratory helping Kapitza, Walton waited until the tube was supporting a reasonably high voltage before looking for scintillations. Then he crawled into the little cabin underneath the bottom of the accelerator tube where observations were made. Immediately he saw scintillations on the screen. He phoned Cockcroft who came and confirmed that they were genuine alpha-particles. Rutherford was then summoned and manoeuvred with some difficulty into the cabin. Walton recalled that after looking at the screen he

> shouted out such instructions as 'Switch off the proton current! Increase the accelerating voltage!', etc but he said little or nothing about what he saw. He ultimately came out of the hut, sat down on a stool, and said something like this: 'Those scintillations look mighty like alpha-particle ones. I should know an alpha-particle when I see one for I was in at the birth of the alpha-particle and I have been observing them ever since.' I have since thought that he might have added that he was also in at their christening![24]

Rutherford wisely swore both Cockcroft and Walton to strict secrecy so that they could analyse the effect of the disintegrations without any interruptions from visitors. (The story that Cockcroft went skimming down King's Parade and saying to anyone whose face he recognised: 'We've split the atom! We've split the atom!' was as Cockcroft himself wrote many years later 'much more fancy than fact'[25].)

On the evening of 16 April they went round to Rutherford's home and reported the results. There and then they prepared a letter for *Nature* which was published on 30 April. In it they asserted that

> the lithium isotope of mass 7 occasionally captures a proton and the resulting nucleus of mass 8 breaks into two alpha-particles, each of mass four and each with an energy of about eight million electronvolts. The evolution of energy on this view is about sixteen million electron volts per disintegration[26].

The full atomic equation for this first man-made artificial disintegration of any atom may be written as

	Lithium	+	Hydrogen	=	two atoms of Helium	+	some energy.
	Li	+	H	=	He	+	He	+	17 MeV.
atomic weight	7.0146	+	1.0078	=	4.003	4.003	+	.016
nuclear charge	+ 3		+ 1	=	+ 2	+ 2		

and the energy released, corresponding, according to Einstein's equation $E = mc^2$ (where E is energy, and m is mass and c is the velocity of light) was equal to the difference between the masses of the original atoms lithium and hydrogen, and the masses of the product atoms, helium. The energy released was given to the two helium nuclei and amounted to about twice the value given to an alpha-particle as it leaves the radium atom; thus these particles from the reaction, hitting zinc sulphide crystals smashed them and caused the scintillations which Walton had seen. Rutherford was as elated as were his pupils, and indeed as were all members of the Cavendish; there is a photograph extant, (figure 8) showing the three in happy mood. On 28 April they went with Rutherford to the Royal Society where the great discovery was announced and afterwards Cockcroft and Walton dined as Rutherford's guests at the Royal Society Dining Club; a very great day for them all.

Figure 8 The Atom Smashers: Walton, Rutherford and Cockcroft. (Courtesy: E T S Walton)

Subsequently it provided the headlines in the world press and was a welcome relief from the sombre economic situation that was currently the fare of newspaper readers. A cartoon in the *Daily Mail* depicted the figure of Taxation lying on an anvil. Another figure, 'Poor Old Alchemist (Fate)' was shown addressing Cockcroft and Walton: 'That's all very well but here's an atom I bet you fellows cannot split!' Although a section of the popular press hailed the so-called 'splitting of the atom' as being perhaps the beginning of a development which would mean according to *Reynolds News* 'nothing less than the complete abolition of irksome manual labour and a new era of prosperity for all', Rutherford was quick to discount the likelihood of any practical application of the experiments. He continued to emphasise the importance of extending the boundaries of knowledge by direct experiment in the laboratory. Such information, he said in a broadcast later, 'cannot but widen our outlook on the nature of matter, but must also have a direct bearing on many problems of cosmical physics'[27].

Ritchie Calder, the young science correspondent of the *Daily Herald*, visited the Cavendish and published a graphic account of the accelerator in action on 27 June 1932. Some years later, he remembered Rutherford telling him that the atom will always be a sink and never a reservoir of energy.

> I still remember Cockcroft saying, 'Prof, you can't say that.' And, in fact, of course, Cockcroft was right. What Rutherford was talking about was the fact that you were using all this energy to get a relatively small return, but he did not foresee that by 1939 his old student, Otto Hahn, would have discovered uranium fission, [from which flowed] the whole story of the release of atomic energy as we know it. This was one of those moments in history when the new generation was facing the guru, and I had a great respect for Cockcroft at that moment[28].

Cockcroft himself had his first experience of newspaper publicity. Unfortunately, Crowther, whom Cockcroft was relying upon to write an article, was not available, with the result that *Reynolds' News* published a

> very garbled account from someone at Bristol and the rest of the Press followed suit. However one tries to put things right [he wrote to Crowther] short of writing an article oneself, one only seems to make it worse.[29]

Later, during and after the war, Cockcroft became quite expert at handling the press.

By coincidence a sombre and prophetic note was struck by a play which opened in the West End of London at the same time as the Cockcroft–Walton experiment was reported in the Press. Called *Wings over Europe* and written by the poet Robert Nichols and the actor – producer Maurice Browne, it was based on the splitting of the atom by a young scientist who was an ardent pacifist. He was determined that the fruits of his discovery should be the property of mankind and never be exploited by a nation or a class. But this brave gesture was doomed to failure and Desmond MacCarthy concluded his review of the play in the *New Statesman*, 'it looks as if we might soon be faced by problems not different in kind from those which the Cabinet on the stage of the Globe Theatre fails so humiliatingly to solve'[30].

Whatever the popular view might be, there was no doubt that the scientific world appreciated what had been done. One of the first notable physicists to congratulate Cockcroft and Walton was von Hevesy who wrote: 'It is a great step forward. We begin to understand how elements get synthesised[31].' Ernest Lawrence, then developing his first cyclotron, told them that he was trying to corroborate their experiments. 'Unfortunately our beam of protons is not nearly as intense as yours although of higher voltage[32].' However, by September he had succeeded in disintegrating lithium. In his reply to Lawrence, Cockcroft explained how they had no space for increasing the voltage beyond one million. He reported that they had since obtained scintillations from magnesium but not from gold or chlorine.

Gamow who, since leaving England, had been kept informed by Cockcroft about the Cavendish work, congratulated him on

> the splendid results you have obtained in the proton bombardment. But the bad thing is I cannot understand the theoretical possibility of those for the heavier elements. Recently I have done some calculations based on the usual formula for penetrating through the barriers. Can the resonance hyphothesis help us? It is very pity [*sic*] but it can't[33].

Cockcroft, who appreciated Gamow's sense of humour, replied:

> I am most disappointed in you. I always believed it possible for a really good theoretical physicist to explain any experimental result and now you fail me at the first test[34].

Gamow thought the explanation for the unexpected number of scintillations they had reported for the bombardment of uranium and other heavy elements by protons, carried out since 14 April, was due either to neutrons in the beam or, less likely, due to impurities; in the event the impurities proved to be the source of disintegrations ascribed by several scientists to other nuclear reactions, as will be further described in the following chapter. Ludwig Wertenstein, the leading Polish nuclear physicist who had spent a year in the Cavendish, sent a telegram which read 'hurrah for the two alphas'[35] and the Physical Research Institute of Moscow University congratulated 'the research workers of the famous Cavendish Laboratory on their new important achievement on the way to the solution of the fundamental problem of the atomic nucleus'[36].

During the following months they bombarded many other elements with protons with varying degrees of success and sent two papers to the Royal Society in 1932; a most profitable year. Great as their discovery had been, it was overshadowed scientifically by the extremely important discovery of the neutron by Chadwick only two months earlier, as already mentioned; that discovery had attracted hardly any attention from the outside world. In his Bakerian Lecture to the Royal Society in 1920 Rutherford had speculated on the possible existence of a neutral particle formed by a combination of a proton and an electron, and he and Chadwick had discussed this possibility repeatedly over the years. Chadwick had actually searched for it experimentally with no success until the Curie–Joliot article gave him the clue and in the space of a week or two he had done the crucial experiment which enabled him to announce the discovery of a neutron in February 1932. It was a discovery having a profound effect on the understanding of nuclear physics and it came as no surprise that Chadwick was awarded the Nobel Prize quickly, in 1935.

The year 1932 was, indeed, as Eddington aptly named it, an *annus mirabilis*. For in addition to the work of Chadwick, and of Cockcroft and Walton in England, Fermi in Italy published his theory of radioactive beta decay which demonstrated the existence of another interaction between elementary particles; while Carl Anderson and Seth Neddermayer in the USA discovered the positron, the particle having the same mass as the electron but carrying a positive instead of a negative charge, a particle which had been forecast by

Dirac who, like Cockcroft, was a Fellow of St John's. This extraordinary surge forward of knowledge was summed up nearly 40 years later by Victor Weisskopf, the Viennese theoretical physicist, and later Director General of the European Organisation for Nuclear Research (CERN), as 'the beginning of a new type of physics dealing with the structure of the nucleus and its constituents, and working with hitherto unknown forces and interactions'[37].

Official recognition, however, of Cockcroft and Walton's scientific engineering advance in nuclear physics was not immediately forthcoming. Cockcroft, then 39 years old, was elected a Fellow of the Royal Society in 1936 and in 1938 he and Walton were awarded the Royal Society Hughes Medal jointly for their work on atomic disintegrations. It was also accompanied, as C T R Wilson originally pointed out, 'by a nice little cheque—and a free anniversary dinner'[38]. But they had to wait 19 years before they became Nobel Laureates after developments in nuclear physics had changed the course of history. It was a fair and correct appraisal of what had been essentially a mutually-dependent partnership. Cockcroft, with all his other commitments, could not have done the experiments on his own; temperamentally, he was not a good experimental physicist and tended to be slipshod and forgetful. Walton, on the other hand, had a fine brain, was capable with his hands and had perserverance, and in that respect, he made the experiments of 1931–32 the success that they undoubtedly were. Cockcroft himself wrote five years later that 'those of us who knew Walton are quite clear about his contribution to our joint work'. Certainly there were many scientists who considered that this great experiment which heralded a new era was more worthy of the Nobel Prize in Physics than some of the others awarded during those 19 years. When one reflects that, on simple atomic theory the nuclei of almost all elements contain more neutrons than protons, Chadwick had discovered the 'material' of which more than half the whole universe is composed. But the Cockcroft–Walton experiment also led to a greater understanding of nuclear physics; the acceleration of charged particles became a science in its own right needing the design of enormous machines costing millions of pounds and particle acceleration led to the discovery of new elements, even the proton bearing a negative instead of a positive charge. That original experiment of 1932 has every right to stand four square with the neutron discovery in heralding in the new age of atomic power. Reflecting on the matter fifty years later, it seems surprising that the Jubilee of the neutron was celebrated with much acclaim whereas that of the Cockcroft–Walton experiment has had but scant attention.

In a way, Cockcroft and Walton were lucky in being the first to produce artificial disintegrations. They had a good start with rectifiers and discharge tube but they took a long time, three and a quarter years from early 1929 to April 1932 to achieve success. The whole apparatus was working well early in 1930, yet still another two years passed before they even made the crucial experiment. They were lucky too in that none of the other physicists who must have read Gamow's second paper reacted as Cockcroft had reacted, for he had done the calculation *immediately* which foreshadowed possible success with relatively slow protons; the other investigators pressed on applying higher and higher voltages to their tubes (in Lawrence's case using circular orbits) and never stopped to do the 'crucial' experiment until the Cavendish pair did it. But in this way are Nobel Prizes won.

1932 was also rounded off by a happy domestic event when a daughter, named Dorothea, was born to Elizabeth in October, a birth which did something to mitigate their sadness over the loss of Timothy. Meanwhile, since the death of his father in 1927, management of the mill had passed to John's younger brothers, Eric, Keith and Leo though John kept his seat on the board of directors. Despite all the calls on his time, he continued to give advice when decisions were called for changes in policy, or for the purchase and installation of new equipment. By specialising in its products and by building up export sales to the Commonwealth, the mill managed to survive the bleak years of the depression of the 1930s. Up-to-date machinery was put in, including a water turbine to drive the looms; and, in 1936, when lack of floor space was proving a handicap to expansion, the Cockcrofts acquired the rundown Derdale Mill in Todmorden.

CHAPTER SIX

THE NEW PHYSICS

The success of Cockcroft and Walton's experiment indicated to Rutherford that some nuclei might be disintegrated by protons with lower energies than used by them; at last he really believed in Gamow! He wanted to be personally involved in this exciting chase and decided to build a 'low voltage' ion accelerator; he calculated that, on the Gamow theory, with an ion current perhaps a thousand times greater than the Cockcroft–Walton ion current he might get disintegrations at a mere 200 000 volts. Throughout his later career he had, at times, worked with one or more collaborators, inviting them to join him if they had techniques they could contribute to his ideas. He persuaded Mark Oliphant who had been developing extremely good strong positive ion sources to relinquish the work and join him in building the accelerator. He got Cockcroft to phone Allibone at Metro–Vick in May 1932 to enquire about a powerful low DC source consisting of two 75 kV transformers and rectifiers to give 200 kV DC and he followed this up with a letter on 18 June.

> In our experiments on atomic disintegration I would like to have one of those transformers, we want the weight to be reduced to a minimum and an output of 100 milliamperes. I want to get it as quickly as possible.

Allibone replied the next day offering a 75 kV or a 100 kV transformer suggesting a voltage-doubling circuit and received a handwritten reply from Rutherford's cottage in Wales 'The 100 kV transformer would give 200 kV which is sufficient for my purpose. What is the price?' followed up on 30 June 'I want the transformer *at once* for 100 000 volts; I note the price, send it to the Cavendish as soon as you can, our work is held up until we get it'[1]: he got it very quickly.

When Allibone was next in Cambridge Rutherford grumbled about the price of £100 which Metro–Vick had charged. Allibone replied that it was only one farthing per volt, whereas a flash-lamp battery cost two or three pence per volt and died within the year. Rutherford laughed and accepted the reproof. Within the year he and Oliphant had done a remarkably good piece of work. They built a simple single-stage ion accelerator which operated at 160 000 volts and they produced copious disintegrations in lithium and boron even at as low a voltage as 40 000, publishing these astonishing results early in 1933. In Oliphant's Biographical Memoir on the life of John Cockcroft he tells us

> Cockcroft welcomed this expansion of such investigations and, with characteristic kindness, helped in every possible way to bring the new, lower voltage equipment into operation[2].

Now, as already reported, Rutherford had suggested in that famous Bakerian Lecture of 1920 that a form of hydrogen might exist in which the nucleus had a mass of two, being composed of one proton and one neutral particle (the neutron) having the same mass. In 1932 his theory was confirmed by Harold Urey of Columbia University, New York who called the element deuterium and its nucleus a deuteron. Shortly after, Urey appreciated that it might be possible to concentrate deuterium by the electrolysis of water and Gilbert Lewis at Berkeley produced deuterium by this method for the first time in 1933. The water molecule composed from deuterium D_2O has an atomic weight of $4 + 16 = 20$, compared with ordinary water, H_2O with a molecular weight of $2 + 16 = 18$ and the former was thus called heavy water. The use of deuterons in disintegration experiments now became extremely attractive and Lewis gave a cubic centimetre of heavy water to Rutherford when visiting Cambridge shortly after making the first concentration. He had given some also to Ernest Lawrence who reported early in 1933 that, with colleagues, he had accelerated deuterium ions in his cyclotron up to the equivalent of 1.2 million volts and had obtained disintegrations of a very large number of elements.

Early in 1933 Cockcroft was invited to attend the American Association for the Advancement of Science meeting at Chicago in mid-June being held at the same time as the World Fair. His journey was to be subsidised by the Rockefeller Foundation and by medical research organisations in London interested in the production of radio-isotopes for the treatment of cancer. His appetite had been whetted by Boyce's account of the experiments of Robert Van de Graaff, C C Lauritsen, M A Tuve and, above all, Ernest Lawrence, with his cyclotron at Berkeley where, according to Boyce, 'things are really going on'[3]. On 13 March 1933 Cockcroft wrote to Lawrence that he hoped to visit the States that summer and asked whether he could see his laboratory. Lawrence was delighted, informing Cockcroft on 2 June that they had obtained 'so many disintegration effects that it is impossible for me to keep them all in mind', but mentioning aluminium, magnesium and ammonium nitrate[4].

Leaving their ten-months old daughter, Dorothea, at Todmorden, the Cockcrofts crossed the Atlantic in the *Majestic*. While Elizabeth went to visit relations in New England, he was thrown into an 'almost continuous round of lab visits, talks, motor trips and otherwise exhausting dissipations'. He first visited Van de Graaff at Boston and was taken to see his giant high-voltage generator installed in an airship hangar at Round Hill alongside the old Whaling Station. Describing it in a letter to Dee and Walton, he wrote:

> I fancy they will have grave trouble with roof-sparking due to dust, bird droppings, etc. The belts are made of a very stout paper. They are just beginning to construct a vacuum tube. Van de Graaff says he would not get money for developing the vacuum tube idea but could get cash for producing vast sparks.

> It seems to me that the whole future of this method (Van de Graaff) depends essentially on how many volts one can get straight on to a tube by sub-dividing it.[5]

By this he meant that, whereas in his Cambridge apparatus the discharge tube was built in sections and each section was cross-connected to a corresponding tapping-point on the rectifier column of the DC set, thus ensuring a uniform voltage distribution over the length of the tube, in the Van de Graaff generator there were no intermediate tapping-points so there was no assurance that the voltage on the tube would be uniformly distributed and spark-over might well take place at an unacceptably low voltage.

The Chicago conference was the first time that Cockcroft had spoken to an international assembly which included scientists like Niels Bohr and Enrico Fermi. Lawrence attended the session on the transmutation of elements and was impressed with Cockcroft's contribution. Unfortunately Bohr 'got up to open the discussion and talked for about an hour thereby squashing any chance of a useful discussion which is rather a pity', John wrote to Elizabeth, 'On Thursday afternoon I went to hear Bohr give a lecture I seem to have heard many times before and which not one per cent of the audience would comprehend.' Alas, Bohr was so frequently like this, inaudible, incomprehensible and totally unaware—because scientists lionised him *as* a scientist—of what a complete failure he was as a speaker. Kenneth Bainbridge, a young physicist from Swarthmore, Pennsylvania, who had developed a spectrometer for the accurate determination of atomic masses, also spoke well, according to Lawrence. Bainbridge became a lifelong friend of Cockcroft and was awarded a Guggenheim Fellowship which took him to the Cavendish that autumn. Cockcroft thought Tuve's paper was 'not at all convincing and gave the impression of great enthusiasm but too much hurry'.

Outside in the heat the scientists discussed mutual problems by the lagoon in the World Fair. One evening, Cockcroft was one of a party which included F W Aston, the Bohrs, the two Comptons, A V Hill, Fermi, and their wives who were to be the guests of one of Chicago's wealthy people whose Georgian-style house was adorned with paintings by Old Masters and with Ming vases. 'To crown Aston's day they brought us home in a Rolls Royce!' Cockcroft and Aston then went on to Washington to call on Tuve, L R Hafstad and O Dahl working in the Department of Terrestrial Magnetism at the Carnegie Institution. They had started working with a Tesla coil for generating 1 MW but had abandoned it in favour of a Van de Graaff. 'This was at first built outside but was too much plagued by insects, so after that the Van de Graaff was rebuilt inside a laboratory'.[6] The first results had recently been reported at the Washington meeting of the Physical Society and had confirmed the Cockcroft–Walton lithium disintegration results and had also concluded that the alpha-particles emitted on bombardment of heavy elements were due to impurities. Cockcroft was impressed by O Dahl's characteristic Norwegian use of fishing line for controls of the ion source situated at the top of the high-voltage discharge tube.

From Washington Cockcroft travelled by way of the Sante Fe railway, through Meteor crater, Flagstaff and the Grand Canyon to Pasadena. At the

California Institute of Technology he met Charles Lauritsen and saw his

> 1 MW transformer and a double-ended x-ray tube which looked rather similar in construction to our Cambridge tubes. Soon after my visit they turned over from accelerating electrons to deuterons and studied the production of neutrons by deuteron bombardment of lithium and beryllium[7].

He spent a day on Mount Wilson at the observatory and was shown by the Director, Edwin Hubble, the 100 inch telescope through which he saw a 'new cluster of 10^8 light years away, a spiral nebula and Jupiter—it is certainly the most impressive piece of physical apparatus in the world'.

Lawrence was unable to greet him at Berkeley, but had given instructions that he was to be shown round thoroughly. The 11 inch cyclotron had been in operation for just over a year and Cockcroft learned from Lawrence's colleagues how to make adjustments. He was particularly impressed with the method of operation,

> The experiments were divided into shifts: maintenance shifts and experimenters. When a leak or fault developed in the cyclotron (which happened quite often) the maintenance crew rushed forward to plug the leaks by melting the numerous wax joints and fixed the fault, when the operating shifts rushed in again.[8]

With deuterium ions in the cyclotron they had disintegrated lithium as Cockcroft and Walton had done. He wrote to Rutherford:

> At present, using molecular ions of about 3 million volts energy about 10 kW are required to operate the magnet. This will have to be increased very considerably to get up to the full energy of the ions—10 million—which Lawrence hopes for.[9]

While at Berkeley Cockcroft received an urgent telegram from Oliphant asking him to bring back a can of heavy water for the experiments he was conducting with Rutherford. Cockcroft purchased 10 dollars worth from Lewis and with some difficulty got it past a curious Customs officer who could not understand why a liquid resembling water should be brought into the United Kingdom. On arrival in Cambridge Rutherford told him that he had spent too much money on it and should have first obtained his permission to buy it! He also brought back some polonium for Chadwick, to enable him to bombard light elements; this came from a New York Hospital where G Failla, a radiologist,

> had been collecting old radium tubes [filled with radon† which, after disintegration, produced polonium] for 15 years and still had some up his sleeve in spite of immediate requests to which he is now turning a deaf ear[10].

Cockcroft was very impressed with the lavishness of the equipment at Berkeley and wrote home enthusiastically about the possibility of producing isotopes in the accelerators he had seen, 'We are really too slow in develop-

---

†Used for gamma-ray therapy in treatment of cancer.

ment of such things at home. We have the knowledge and technical ability but not enough appreciation and drive at the top.'[11] It was an observation that he was to make frequently in the critical years to come, but it is not immediately obvious why he made this comment; his was the only high voltage generator in England doing disintegration work and it had only been operating for 12 months; the Berkeley cyclotron had only just started to work and could hardly be said to be a proven instrument of great value (which of course it was, all in good time) so what 'drive' was he looking for? Rutherford had allowed Kapitza to drive ahead with the large machine and with low temperature work—ahead of the Clarendon Laboratory in Oxford, it should be noted—and he had allowed Cockcroft and Walton to build a generator for as high a voltage as they had wanted to do. Allibone had had discussions in Metro–Vickers as to whether the Company should start work on similar lines to the Cavendish and the Director had decided, with Cockcroft's agreement, that it would be inappropriate to do so, the Company's function should be to support Cockcroft, not to compete with him.

He concluded his tour with a visit to universities in Canada, including McGill in Montreal where he 'gazed with appropriate reverence on the rooms where Rutherford made his reputation 25 years ago or so'. Before leaving America he stayed in the Boyces' log cabin in the Adirondacks and made the acquaintance of one of their neighbours—Miss Mary T Cockcroft—then in her late 70s and whom he was to visit on several occasions in her New York apartment before and during the war. She was, as described in chapter 1, a descendant of Colonel Cockcroft who went to America in 1750 to fight in the Indian Wars and subsequently made his home there.

During Cockcroft's absence Professor Rutherford, Oliphant and B B Kinsey had accelerated deuterium ions obtained from the small quantity of heavy water G N Lewis had presented to the Professor. They obtained far many more disintegrations than they had had with a proton beam in their low voltage accelerator. Walton too had been busy finding that spurious effects could arise if the target materials were not extremely clean. This was the situation when the leading physicists of the world met in Brussels in October at the Seventh Solvay Conference, the theme this year being, inevitably, 'the examination of questions relative to the constitution of matter.' A strong delegation from the Cavendish led by Rutherford and Chadwick included Cockcroft, Walton, Blackett, R Peierls and C D Ellis. Other celebrated physicists present were Einstein, Bohr, Fermi, Gamow and Lise Meitner. Prior to the conference Ernest Lawrence wrote to Langevin, the President about two points he intended to raise concerning some comments he had met in the pre–conference release of Cockcroft's paper entitled *Transmutation produced by high velocity ions*. One concerned the disintegration products when targets were bombarded by the new ion of deuterium. The Berkeley school had bombarded many targets with deuterons accelerated to very high velocities in the cyclotron and in many cases protons and neutrons were emitted as products of the collision with target atoms; from this Lawrence deduced that the deuteron had itself broken into a proton and a neutron as it collided with the target nucleus, whatever it might be. The second point concerned Cockcroft's remark that the cyclotron could only generate small currents. At

Figure 9 The Solvay Conference, October 1933. (Courtesy: The Cavendish Laboratory)
  Standing from left to right: E Henriot, F Perrin, F Joliot, W Heisenberg, H A Kramers, E Strahel, E Fermi, E T S Walton, P A M Dirac, P Debye, N F Mott, B Cabrera, G Gamow, W Bothe, P Blackett, M S Rosenblum, J Errera, Ed Bauer, W Pauli, M Cosyns, J E Verschaffelt, E Herzen, J D Cockcroft, C D Ellis, R Peierls, August Piccard, E O Lawrence, L Rosenfeld.
  Seated from left to right: E Schrödinger, Mme J Joliot, N Bohr, D Joffé, Mme Curie, P Langevin, O W Richardson, Lord Rutherford, T de Donder, M de Broglie, L de Broglie, Mlle Meitner, J Chadwick.

the Conference Lawrence found the Cambridge school were almost united against his suggested dissociation of the deuteron; Chadwick arguing that such was energetically unlikely, Cockcroft and Walton believing that the effects observed might be due to impurities on the target. Lawrence was meeting Rutherford for the first time and tried to persuade him to instal a cyclotron, but the latter was quite content to go on using Oliphant's 190 kV accelerator which had been doing such useful work. Rutherford explained that it was one of his principles that the apparatus used at the Cavendish should be developed and, if possible, made there, to which Lawrence replied, 'Sir, you use spectrometers in the lab every day but they weren't invented there, were they?'[12] Cockcroft, although appreciating that Lawrence's cyclotron had shortcomings, agreed with Lawrence that the Cavendish should have one.

After the meeting, Lawrence went to stay with the Cockcrofts in Cambridge and they continued to discuss the results of bombardment with deuterons. Cockcroft continued to believe that the instability of the deuteron deduced by Lawrence was more likely to be due to transformation of some contaminating material on the targets under bombardment. That winter he and Walton, using the heavy water that he had brought back from America, analysed the protons emitted by various elements, after bombardment by deuterons. They discovered that although iron gave a small yield of protons, none were observed from copper, gold or copper oxide. Although they had not worked at very high voltages, Cockcroft believed that the evidence was against Lawrence's interpretation of the break-up of the deuteron. In February 1934, using a higher concentration of heavy water, he and Walton discovered that from a number of metals they were getting three groups of particles of the same range as reported from Berkeley. One of these three groups, with a range of 13 cm in air, was believed by Lawrence to be due to the instability of the deuteron. At the end of that month Cockcroft wrote to Lawrence:

> It seems clear that these three groups cannot all be due to this break-up, and we therefore feel strongly that the alpha-particle group and the 7-cm proton group are at any rate due to an impurity which is probably oxygen. We are not yet certain about the 13-cm group, but are carrying out experiments with white–hot tungsten targets which I hope may finally dispose of this possibility.[13]

At the end of this letter he added a postscript to the effect that they had just found that when they boiled tungsten in caustic soda the smaller groups disappeared on heating and reappeared on oxidation, which indicated that they were due to oxygen.

Lawrence replied on 14 March, readily admitting he had made a wrong assumption and that the instability he had observed was due to contamination of the targets,

> These recent experiences [continued Lawrence] have impressed upon us forcibly the fact that much of our work has been of too preliminary character to be of value. I regret very much that the question of deuteron instability involved you in so much work, and I want to thank you very much for stepping in and clearing the matter up so effectively, and so promptly.[14]

Just over a month later Cockcroft was writing to Tuve:

> The fact is that it is not possible to proceed quickly in this work and get results
> which are certain. We had our first lesson in the impurity effect for protons in
> heavy elements; Lawrence has now had his, and the German workers have so
> far been wrong as often as right, owing to their apparent lack of appreciation
> of statistics. There is a real danger of the subject getting into a mess, and I feel
> that the only thing to do is to delay publication until we are reasonably sure.
> With these sentiments I know you are in agreement.[15]

Just to complete the story of this baffling problem of possible contamination, we can turn to work which Rutherford and two assistants were doing
that autumn. With his 200 kV accelerator, deuterium was used to bombard
a target containing deuterium; two new reactions were discovered, either the
deuterium ion picked up a proton and thus became an ion of helium having
a mass of three, or it picked up a neutron and became an ion of hydrogen
having a mass three. These very two combinations had been forecast in that
1920 Bakerian Lecture, so it was very fit and proper for their discoverer to
be the man who had forecast their existence; Rutherford was overjoyed. It
now provided the keystone to the Lawrence–Cavendish controversy;
whenever deuterium was used to bombard targets of other elements, those
targets were *almost bound to be contaminated* by heavy-hydrogen molecules so a
deuterium-deuterium reaction occurred to complicate the reactions of
deuterium with the target material being investigated. His letter to Lawrence
includes the following:

> I think you will have heard from Cockcroft about some of our observations—
> Oliphant and I have been particularly interested in the bombardment of D with
> D ions, I believe there can be little doubt that the hydrogen istotope of mass 3
> is produced. The evidence for the helium isotope of mass 3... looks to me not
> unlikely.—We suggest, very tentatively, that your results may be explained as
> due to the bombardment of films of D and of D compounds[16]

to which Lawrence replied,

> Your experiments on deuterium ions together with Cockcroft and Walton's re-
> cent work have certainly cleared things up in a beautiful fashion. There can be
> no doubt that our observations which we ascribed to deuterium break-up are in
> fact the results of reactions of deuterium ions with each other. Dr Cockcroft
> might be interested to know that we are gradually increasing our currents in the
> cyclotron and are now regularly working with several microamperes.[17]

Events in the history of nuclear physics were moving rapidly. Early in 1934
Professor Joliot and his wife Irène Curie had discovered artifical (or induced)
radioactivity when they bombarded boron with alpha-particles and found that
radioactive nitrogen was produced, that is to say, atoms of the target, in this
case, nitrogen, did not all disintegrate at once, the atoms disintegrated at
different times, just as the element radium emits alpha-particles over a very
extended period of time and for that reason was, way back in the early years
of the twentieth century, called 'radioactive'. The product of that radio-

activity might be an electron, a proton, an alpha-particle, a gamma ray or even some other nuclear constituent, as will be observed in a later chapter.

On 1 March 1934, Cockcroft, Walton and a new collaborator, C W Gilbert, obtained similar results with carbon, they were able to detect the radioactivity, in this case a gamma ray and a positive electron, with a Geiger counter belonging to Bainbridge who had been working in the Cavendish for the past five months. 'It was the first example', said Cockcroft recalling the experiment, 'of a nucleus being captured and emitting surplus energy by gamma radiation, though I ought to say we did not detect the gamma rays at that time!'[18]

A few weeks later he heard from Boyce that Lawrence had been bombarding 12 elements with deuterons, all of which had produced radioactivity. 'Somehow I suspect', continued Boyce, 'impurities in some of such a long list of elements[19].' In June 1934 Tuve and Hafstad wrote to the *Physical Review* and queried Cockcroft's and Walton's recent claim that 'when carbon is bombarded with protons a radioactive element is produced which has a decay period the same as that of the radioactive element produced when carbon is bombarded with deuterons'[20]. Cockcroft repeated the experiment to check the purity of his beam and obtained his original results. Then he wrote to Lauritsen, who had reached similar conclusions to himself, and told him that he believed that Tuve had made a mistake in his results. In due course, Hafstad admitted that they were indeed wrong; 'even if we had been correct our results should have been presented in a different light.. We meant well but slipped into the old error of jumping to the most obvious conclusion'.[21]

All this work was discussed at an important international conference on physics which began in London at the Royal Institution on 3 October 1934. Nuclear physics dominated the agenda. Rutherford gave a survey of current research and papers were read by Professor Joliot and his wife, Fermi and R A Millikan. The conference then moved to Cambridge where Chadwick, Cockcroft, Oliphant, N Feather, Max Born, Gamow, Lauritsen and H R Crane revealed progress in the 'artificial transformation of atoms and on the constitution of atomic nuclei'. Cockcroft's contribution was entitled 'Transmutations produced by high speed protons and diplons' (another name for deuterons). He described his earlier experiments in disintegrating lithium, boron, carbon and oxygen by protons and deuterons and concluded by pointing out how effective deuterons were compared with protons in penetrating and disintegrating atomic nuclei.

This meeting marked the climax of the work of Rutherford's brilliant generation of the early 1930s. The disciples now began to leave the master to pursue their individual bent. From 1935 onwards, Chadwick, Oliphant, Walton and Ellis, among others, were to leave the Cavendish and establish themselves in other university laboratories. Cockcroft, though remaining in Cambridge, no longer had time for experimental work. For one thing he had become very preoccupied with college affairs. There were times, according to Allibone, and he was not the only one to notice them, when Cockcroft came to the laboratory to start up his apparatus and then cycled back quickly to college to supervise some work there and then dash back again

often to find parts of his apparatus in ruins because he had forgotten to turn on the water supply or something had got too hot and had melted. It was surprising that with his good memory he could be so forgetful of these small details; in fact, he was a better engineer than an experimental physicist.[22]

His last two papers were published in the Proceedings of the Royal Society. They were 'The production of induced radioactivity by high velocity protons and diplons' described jointly by himself, Walton and C W Gilbert, published in 1935; and 'Further experiments on the disintegration of boron' published in 1936, this time in conjunction with W B Lewis whom he described as 'a great hand at counters. ... and can smell which valve or resistance in a set is giving trouble'[23]. His partnership with Walton had ended in 1934, the latter returning to Trinity College, Dublin where he had been offered a Fellowship in experimental physics.

It was in 1934 that Enrico Fermi, the Italian physicist, and his students discovered the great increase of effectiveness of neutrons in causing disintegrations if they were slowed down to a small velocity. This slowing down by collision with light elements was patented and Fermi's representative came to England in 1936 to offer the patent to Metro–Vick. Allibone went to London to meet him and asked Cockcroft to join him. After the meeting, Allibone and Cockcroft calculated the probable cost of producing a million-volt tube to accelerate deuterons and create an intense source of neutrons from a double deuteron reaction, slowing the neutrons produced by passing them through heavy water or graphite, and then bombarding a target to make it emit gamma rays. The cost was far higher than that of producing gamma rays from a radium bomb, usually one gram of radium. Metro–Vick offered Fermi certain terms with which Cockcroft agreed but they were not accepted and the patent went elsewhere. It became the master patent of the graphite 'pile' or uranium reactor of the 1940s and therefore royalties were due on it for the first American reactors and the first two research reactors later built at the Atomic Energy Research Establishment at Harwell. However, Allibone found that there was an error in the British patent which rendered it invalid.

Rutherford had long appreciated the need for a new Cavendish wing which would include a high-voltage laboratory in view of the importance of the disintegration work. In 1934 he appointed Cockcroft and Oliphant members of a building committee, the former being obviously invaluable because of his engineering knowledge and his contacts with Metro–Vick. An appeal for funds was launched and Cockcroft sent letters to likely donors. Cockcroft was made responsible for the design of the high-voltage laboratory and during that year he and Oliphant visited a number of continental laboratories to discover what features should be incorporated in the new building. They were particularly impressed by the Philips Laboratory at Eindhoven; Cockcroft believed that it was superior to similar buildings in America. His conception of the new high-voltage laboratory was that it should be about 45 feet high and 45 feet broad in order to house an apparatus capable of generating two million volts. The generator would be used for x-rays and for positive-ion work with counters and Wilson cloud chambers.

By the summer of 1935 the design for the high-voltage laboratory appeared to Oliphant to be getting out of hand; instead of Cockcroft's 'optimistic' original estimate of £6000 it had already more than doubled. He wrote to

Rutherford, then on holiday, and told him that, due to Cockcroft, the plans were too elaborate; all that was required was a simple structure more like a hangar which could easily be adapted to any purpose. He further suggested that much of the planning had taken place without being discussed by the building committee which had only met on a couple of occasions; while Cockcroft had been too busy with college buildings (in his capacity as Junior Bursar at St John's) to give it all the attention it required[24].

But once he became absorbed in a particular job he *did* give it all his attention as recalled by Rudolf Peierls, one of a number of young scientists who had left Germany on account of the Nazis' anti-Jewish campaign, and who had recently joined the Cavendish staff as a lecturer.

Cockcroft was working in my room because there was a drawing board, on which he was busy with some kind of drawing. And, while he had his head over the drawing board, the secretary came in and said: 'The architect is on the phone. He wants to know whether the electric light switches in the high voltage laboratory should be black or brown.' [In those days, you may remember, light switches were either black or brown.] This is just the kind of question where, since the answer did not matter, I think almost everyone of us would have said, 'Let me see, it really does not matter, but should we have it either black or brown?' Not Cockcroft; without lifting his head from the drawing board he said 'brown' and went on drawing. I felt at that time enormous admiration for that way of not letting a trivial detail bother you.[25]

There was a good deal of discussion over the type of high-voltage generator to be used. Allibone had designed a very powerful generator using continuously evacuated rectifiers which would take up a lot of space. Oliphant, however, thought that home-made rectifiers should be installed, immersed in a tremendous tank of oil but Cockcroft disliked this idea on the grounds that it would frequently have to be dismantled for maintenance. Eventually the proposal for the Metro–Vick generator was abandoned as it was too large and instead two generators using small sealed-off rectifiers were to be bought from Philips of Holland, the accelerator tubes being made in the Cavendish. By the end of 1936 the new high-voltage laboratory was ready and the first 1.2 million-volt generator with its accelerator tube was erected in one corner; at a later date the second designed for 2 million volts was erected in the centre of the laboratory but difficulties were experienced with the home-made accelerator tube, sparkover to the walls occurred and the apparatus never worked at its full designed voltage.

The balance of the Cavendish wing had yet to be designed and built and, as a member of the Cavendish Building Committee, Cockcroft was also concerned with the selection of an architect for the new wing. Eventually Charles Holden was selected, an architect responsible for the 'elegant tube stations of North London'[26] and later the headquarters of London Transport in Westminster and the central tower of London University in Bloomsbury. Fortunately money for this ambitious project was provided by Sir Herbert Austin, the motor car manufacturer, who took a keen interest in the work of the Cavendish and was a friend of Stanley Baldwin, Prime Minister and Chancellor of the University. On 29 April 1936 he offered £250 000 towards the new wing which was named after him; it was completed in 1940.

By the spring of 1936 Rutherford was still adamant that the Cavendish did not need a cyclotron but, nevertheless, Cockcroft went ahead with a design based on a magnet with a maximum field of 17 000 gauss; he sent details to Lawrence who then wrote to Rutherford explaining how he had improved his machine and could now deflect the beam of hydrogen or deuterium ions as it emerged from the vacuum chamber. The advantage of this was firstly, that it enabled the scattering experiments to be carried out more effectively, and secondly, the experimental region was far removed from any neutron background produced by the circulating ions in the chamber striking various parts of the accelerating system. 'I think we now have', Lawrence continued, 'an apparatus which closely approximates one's desires'. He and his colleagues had 'got quite a thrill out of seeing the beam of six million volt deuterons making a blue streak through the air for a distance of more than 28 cm.'[27]

The matter came to a head early in June. Chadwick came down from Liverpool University, whither he had gone after leaving Cambridge, to examine for the Tripos and stayed several days with Rutherford. He took the opportunity to press the latter about Cambridge's need for a cyclotron. Rutherford would not give way and the subsequent estrangement between the one time master and pupil was not healed before Rutherford's death just over a year later. However, by the end of that month Rutherford gave permission to Cockcroft to go ahead and put him in charge of the design. The latter was already making use of the drawings that Lawrence had sent him and further help came when B B Kinsey, one of Lawrence's staff, returned to Cambridge. On 16 November 1936 Cockcroft told Lawrence that the new high-voltage laboratory was nearing completion and that the fabrication of the magnet was in hand in Sheffield.

An opportunity to gain experience using Lawrence's third, and more efficient, cyclotron was provided in 1937 when Cockcroft was invited to give a course of lectures on low temperature physics and the transmutation of elements at Harvard by Theodore Lyman, director of the physics laboratory. Cockcroft eagerly accepted the invitation which had the support of the President of Harvard, James Conant[28]. Elizabeth was again able to accompany her husband and they crossed the Atlantic in the recently completed *Queen Mary* at the end of March. While John lectured, Elizabeth stayed with friends at Salem, Massachusetts, afterwards rejoining him for a few days holiday with the Boyces. Boyce recalled that Cockcroft asked to see Williamsburg, Virginia, as he had read about the restoration of its colonial buildings, and he also visited at Charlottesville, the University of Virginia with its Jeffersonian buildings and the laboratory of J W Beams[29]. When not lecturing Cockcroft enjoyed 'hearing about other people's work and being lavishly entertained'. He and Conant liked each other and the latter offered him a professorship in nuclear research—a tempting offer as he would have had 'an absolutely free hand as director'. But he decided, after some hesitation, to turn it down on account of his important commitments in Cambridge, much to the disappointment of Bainbridge and his other friends at Harvard[30].

After more lectures in Chicago he met Sir James Jeans, the famous astronomer, and his Austrian wife, Susie Hock, the organist, who was giving

Figure 10   Dr A E Kempton and Cockcroft together with the 37 inch cyclotron in the Cavendish Laboratory. (Courtesy: The Cavendish Laboratory)

recitals. But the highlight of his tour was the four days spent at Berkeley where he stayed with Donald Cooksey, Lawrence's deputy. The first day he spent 'getting the hang of the cyclotron' and watched the beam come out as already described. 'You'll probably hear', he wrote to Elizabeth, who had returned to the East Coast to stay with her relations, 'a lot more about beams coming out in future'. The next day Lawrence taught him how to throw the apparatus out of adjustment and then put it right. In the evening they relaxed in a restaurant in San Francisco, looked at the great new bridge spanning the Golden Gate, and then returned by the ferry across the Bay to the laboratory 'to play with the machine for three hours'. 'I am very glad I came here', he wrote, 'the experience may save endless trouble in the future'. Lawrence also granted leave to D G Hurst who had obtained an 1851 Exhibition Overseas

Scholarship to join Kinsey at Cambridge and help with the building of the cyclotron, which had been proceeding slowly, most of the components at last arriving by the midsummer of 1937, the magnet being installed by the end of the year. By October 1938 Cockcroft was able to report to Boyce that it was giving some 12 microamps of 5 MeV protons. Although there had been teething problems he hoped to bring it up to 10 MeV. However Oliphant recollected that he thought the cyclotron was too small and when he was in Berkeley in 1938 he found that Lawrence was of the same opinion, they both agreed that the energies likely to be produced would be insufficient to enable the Cavendish to compete successfully with the Americans: Cockcroft was not convinced. Many years later he defended his choice, contending that the high voltage laboratory under Dee's leadership 'produced a very interesting series of results on proton experiments, particularly resonance capture of protons'. The cyclotron also proved 'to be very useful in the war years when left in the hands of Feather and Bretscher to carry out work for the atomic energy project and it continued to produce good results until dismantled in 1960'.

Construction of two other considerably larger cyclotrons in Britain was under way in 1938, one being the responsibility of Chadwick at Liverpool University and the other under Oliphant at Birmingham University. In December 1938 Oliphant spent a month with Lawrence at Berkeley learning how to operate his cyclotron, but shortly after returning home he became involved in research on radar. While in California he told Cockcroft 'the centre of physics has crossed completely to this continent'. This was because even with the two larger cyclotrons under construction Britain was only catching up with Berkeley and other American laboratories, whereas they were now forging ahead with new concepts.

Cockcroft's domestic life in the later 1930s had been enhanced by the birth of a further two daughters, Jocelyn in 1934 and Elizabeth in 1936.

> We shall soon need [he had written to Bainbridge, by then back at Harvard, on 14 December 1934] an extension of the house to give the family room to move about in. I shall have to sell this to Dee and build another—I think it would be rather fun after the experience we have now—the main problem is that Dee wants to build a 16th century Cotswold house with lots of secret passages and corners—he's incurably romantic. This week he's been preparing a broadcast for the Cavendish Dinner. The first item 'Foundations of Music' is played as Rutherford takes the chair—'Who's afraid of the big bad wolf!' There is then a conducted and highly libellous tour of the lab and a birthday gift series. I was myself told that if I looked inside my file I'd find a lovely gift of a pound of plasticine and a pint of M grease! However, as Oliphant appreciated the joke so much it has been transferred to him and they've got another one on me, not yet communicated.

Eventually, an extension was added to the Cockcrofts' home but, owing to the possibility of war from 1937 onwards, and Cockcroft's commitments, all plans of building a new house had to be abandoned.

CHAPTER SEVEN

THE MOND AND FELLOWSHIP OF ST JOHN'S: WAR CLOUDS

In the late 1920s Kapitza had been investigating the effect of his very strong magnetic fields on the electrical resistance of some pure metals down to the temperature of liquid air and he now wanted to extend his measurements to much lower temperatures, the temperatures of liquid hydrogen and then of liquid helium, very near to the absolute zero of temperature. With the aid of Cockcroft and the Canadian, Dr W L Webster, he designed a liquid hydrogen plant comprising a compressor and liquifier with funds provided by the DSIR. By May 1930 this plant was operating satisfactorily and his mind turned to a helium liquifier.

No low temperature research laboratory then existed in Britain and nothing had been done in this field since the work of Sir James Dewar before 1914. After discussing the matter with Rutherford, Kapitza wrote him a note pointing out that as low temperatures were 'one of the most powerful tools for physical research'[1], Cambridge ought to have a cyrogenics laboratory to house the necessary apparatus. Considerable support was provided by the Royal Society of which Rutherford was still President; not only did it make a grant of £15 000 towards the building of a new laboratory, but in August 1930 Kapitza was awarded a Royal Society Messel Professorship. The building was to be called the Royal Society Mond Laboratory after Sir Alfred Mond, an early supporter of Dewar. Trinity College had elected Kapitza a Fellow in 1925 and there was some grumbling in the Cavendish, though more outside Cambridge† where he was only known by his published work—which was considered by some to be not particularly impressive—that he was receiving undue attention from Rutherford. Whether or not there was any justification for criticism, Cockcroft, for one, went on record years later, declaring that the Mond had 'been of tremendous importance in building up the school of solid state physics in Cambridge'. It is true that in 1929 Kapitza had been elected a Fellow of the Royal Society; he was a Soviet citizen and held a Soviet passport, going yearly to the Soviet Union. Now the few foreigners who were elected to the Society were elected as Foreign Members,

---

†One of them was T H Laby, the Australian physicist elected FRS in 1931, as recorded by Andrade in his book on Rutherford.

being, generally, the cream of the community from whence they came; not so Kapitza, he was elected just as though he had been British and this had caused resentment, for his stature at that time would not have warranted his election as a Russian 'Foreign Member of the Royal Society'. However in those days the Bye-laws of the Society did allow a foreign scientist 'working in Britain' to be elected to the ordinary class of Fellows so the resentment was not justified.

In February 1931 the University accepted the Royal Society's offer and promised to provide £1500 *per annum* for the upkeep of the Laboratory, and the DSIR agreed to extend the annual block grant it was providing in support of magnetic research. The supervision of the plans and general arrangements became the responsibility of the Committee of the Magnetic Laboratory, from March 1931 renamed the Royal Society Mond Laboratory Committee. Rutherford was Chairman, Cockcroft was Secretary and other members who attended regularly were C T R Wilson, then Jacksonian Professor of Natural Philosophy, Kapitza and Sir Frank Smith, who had succeeded Tizard as representative of the DSIR. Joy Stebbing took shorthand notes and did the typing. Cockcroft she recalled,

> was a very reserved man and rather distant as an employer; he expected hard work and often kept me late, but I had a great admiration for him. He treated me like an intelligent human being and I enjoyed working for him, and was made to feel part of a team with him and Kapitza. He did not spare himself and always seemed to be taking on time-consuming tasks for other people. Lord Rutherford and Professor Kapitza were very different—full of jokes and fun, and treated me in a fatherly fashion.[2]

The new building would take the place of the shed housing Kapitza's dynamo and workshops, and by the summer of 1931 the Mond Committee had approved the estimates and specifications. H C Hughes, who had designed the Cockcroft home, was appointed architect and, encouraged by Kapitza, he was to design for the extremely limited space, a building, clean and functional in the manner of the post-war German Bauhaus School of Architecture†. Kapitza took a keen interest in the decoration of the building and invited the sculptor, Eric Gill, to carve two reliefs at the entrance, one to represent a crocodile—symbolic of Rutherford, and the other was to be a portrait of the great man. Gill took more licence in portraying the Professor's nose than was acceptable to the Cambridge academics. They considered it was too semitic in character (the Jewish exodus from Nazi Germany was much in the news); while Rutherford thought it made him look like an Assyrian! Gill explained to Kapitza that the characteristic feature of a Jewish nose was not the bridge but the beak; 'a prominent bridge', he wrote, 'is rather Roman and the classical people ought to have been pleased'. In order to settle the matter, Rutherford asked Bohr, who was also a collector of modern art, to adjudicate. Although Bohr only had a photograph to study,

---

†Compared to the antiquated and barn-like laboratories surrounding it. It had vibration-damping walls and sleek steel and scarlet furniture in the Director's office.

he told Kapitza that he thought the portrait 'both thoughtful and powerful'[3] and asked for a replica to be made for his laboratory in Copenhagen.

While Cockcroft at this time was occupied with developing his accelerator and, as will be seen, was supervising the restoration of St John's College, he concerned himself with ordering the apparatus and with the minutiae of the interior design of the Mond. When Hughes wrote to congratulate him in 1932 on the disintegration experiments, he concluded:

> The way in which you keep a hold on the multitudinous changes and chances of the Mond Lab in the midst of your other so engrossing works strikes me as nothing short of marvellous. I owe a great deal to your clear and calm head and it is amazing to think you are doing world-shaking researches all the while.[4]

The opening ceremony was performed by Mr Stanley Baldwin, then Lord President of the Council and Chancellor of the University, on 3 February 1933, and the event received a fair amount of attention in the press. There is an amusing little known story of this. Rutherford had written the draft speech for Mr Baldwin—presumably some considerable time beforehand— and when he came to write his own speech he had substantially forgotten the words he had already written. Rutherford spoke first, a fine vigorous speech, and then Baldwin rose. He had no alternative but to read what was in front of him, and lo and behold many of the words and format were identical with what had just been heard.† A centre page article written jointly by Rutherford and Cockcroft was published in *The Times*, they pointed out that:

> Thirty years ago the most important researches in the Cavendish were carried out with sealing wax, glass and wire; a glimpse of the heavy electrical machinery, compressors, high voltage apparatus and elaborate electrical recording instruments which form part of the new Cavendish and its new offspring is sufficient to show how far we have moved from those days of simplicity.

They explained the significance of the great generator which enabled the time of the duration of experiments 'to be reduced to a fraction of a second, in this way very heavy currents may be used without increasing the temperature of the coil beyond a safe limit'.

The helium liquifier had been approved by the Committee at the end of 1931; it was of a very original design, entirely Kapitza's though Cockcroft as usual was very much concerned with the minutiae. On 18 April 1934 Kapitza had obtained his first liquid helium in the presence of Cockcroft; it was to be the last thing he did at Cambridge. He had been in the habit of returning to Moscow in the long vacations to visit his mother and other relations. That July, accompanied by Anna, he went as usual to Moscow, later he gave a course of lectures in Kharkov and attended a congress held in honour of the great 19th century Russian chemist, Mendeléev. A few days before he was due to return to England he was summoned to Moscow and requested to undertake work of an unspecified character in the Soviet Union. As he already had a return visa, Kapitza demanded to return first to Cambridge. He was

†The author TEA was present and Cavendish colleagues enjoyed the fun.

then deprived of his passport, though Anna was allowed to return to look after their two young sons who were of British nationality by birth. Anna subsequently decided not to return to Moscow until 1936.

Although Rutherford made several protests to the Soviet Embassy in London, he met each time with a rebuff and by April 1935 it was clear that Kapitza would be unlikely to return to Cambridge. On 30 April a statement was made by the Soviet Embassy to the effect that scientists were badly needed to help with the development of the national economy of the Soviet Union, making it necessary for the Government to recall Soviet scientists working abroad;

> Dr Kapitza belongs to this category. He has been appointed director of a new institute for physical research under the Academy of Sciences. This institute has been specially founded for him by the Soviet Government and large sums have been set aside for the building and its equipment under the directorship of Dr Kapitza, and in accordance with his desires and requirements. As far as his personal life is concerned, he is very comfortably situated and receives a good remuneration.[5]

In response to the news of Kapitza's detention in the USSR, Rutherford insisted that the Soviet Union had every right to call upon Kapitza to work within his homeland, although he agreed that to isolate a scientist from his original work and from his family would not turn him into a great physicist. Rutherford's opinion of Kapitza was that

> if not a genius [he] had the brain of a physicist and the ability of a mechanician, a combination so rarely wedded in one brain that it made him something of a phenomenon[6].

This ability had undoubtedly led to his two great achievements in Cambridge, the great dynamo and the apparatus for liquifying helium.

Rutherford had taken charge of the Mond during Kapitza's absence, but as Cockcroft was so closely associated with low temperature research he was appointed Assistant Director of the Laboratory in May 1935, although the post carried no emolument. He was to play the leading part in the events now to be described. During that summer two friends of Kapitza, Professor Adrian, the physiologist, and Dirac visited him in Moscow and the latter spent some time discussing his plans for continuing his research with intense magnetic fields. In August, as a result of these talks, Kapitza wrote to Rutherford suggesting that the Soviet Government would be prepared to buy the bulk of the equipment, or duplicates, that he had been using in the Mond. Rutherford was shortly afterwards informed by the Soviet Embassy that they had been authorised to negotiate a settlement.

A special meeting of the Mond Committee was held on 11 October 1935 chaired by the Vice-Chancellor and attended, among others, by Rutherford, Cockcroft, R H Fowler and Dirac[7]. Sir Frank Smith said that there was nothing to stop the University from buying the Mond apparatus which had been supplied before 1926 and bought with funds provided by the DSIR; the large generator and ancillary equipment. Cockcroft then explained that new methods had been developed to produce extremely low temperatures making use of a very strong magnetic field instead of a helium liquifier; the field necessary was not as strong as those produced by Kapitza's generator, in fact it could be created by a moderately large electromagnet which might cost around £5000 and this same magnet could also be used in nuclear research to deflect beams of high speed particles; it would therefore be better to buy an electromagnet and let Kapitza have his generator.

The Committee agreed that the Mond should not continue the same kind of work that Kapitza had initiated, and that therefore all the apparatus which could not be used for nuclear research should be transferred to Russia immediately. The apparatus currently being used for low temperature research which was being carried on under Cockcroft's direction could, without difficulty, be duplicated and in this way it would be possible to continue the work at the Mond and, at the same time, enable Kapitza to pursue his studies in intense magnetic fields at low temperatures. Provided that the various parties involved, such as the DSIR and the Royal Society, approved these arrangements, the Soviet Union should be asked to pay to the University a suitable sum for the equipment they were going to receive, a sum finally settled at £30 000 and, again, it was Cockcroft who was principally engaged in the negotiations. The Russians also reimbursed the Royal Society for the stipend due to Kapitza during the period of his absence in the USSR. This money provided a fund for the upkeep of the Mond Laboratory. Kapitza's two technical assistants, Pearson and Laurmann, were given leave of absence to join him in Moscow and help him to set up the equipment. Most of it was transferred to the Institute of Physical Problems in Moscow during the winter of 1935/36 under the supervision of Cockcroft, the generator had had to go via Archangel in midwinter.

As a token of their gratitude, the Russian Academy of Sciences invited the Cockcrofts to visit the new Institute that September, and Kapitza invited them to accompany himself and Anna on a holiday in the Crimea and the Caucasus. They travelled to Russia by sea, breaking the journey to stay with the Bohrs in Copenhagen. At Leningrad they were met by Kapitza, who seemed to be in a position of some power, with an Academy car. After staying a few days in Leningrad, which was more prosperous than when Cockcroft had seen it five years before, sightseeing and going to the opera, they travelled to Moscow[8]. Cockcroft found the Institute fully equipped with the Cavendish machinery, though there were 'innumerable defects' being put right by the erectors. The laboratory itself bore traces of Kapitza's 'strong-willed methods'; doors which did not fit were chopped down; concrete which was not level had been hacked up. Compared with the Mond, the Institute had 'bigger workshops, many more staff and a house, not quite ready, for the Director'.

The Kapitzas and Cockcrofts then left for their holiday in the south. At Sevastapol Anna and Elizabeth rode from the station to their hotel 'on top of the luggage in a 1908 Ford' while Kapitza and Cockcroft 'followed in an equally antiquated tram'. Unfortunately Cockcroft caught a cold which developed into bronchitis and the trip to Batumi and Tiflis which they had planned had to be abandoned. The Cockcrofts returned home via Stockholm. While in bed recovering, Cockcroft summarised his impressions of his second visit to the USSR in a letter to his mother. Due to their five year plan the Russians had made great efforts to solve their many problems which were hardly understood by the west.

> I believe [he wrote] that the people who write for the Northcliffe papers about Russia are simply burying their heads in the sand and unwisely ignoring hard facts. There is little here that compares to popular notions of Russia. Incomes, far from being equal, vary in the ratio of 20 : 1 according to ability. Private personal property is encouraged provided that it is put in land or factories or 'means of production'. There is real enthusiasm amongst the manual workers as they could now make the natural progress one can see. There is, too, a great deal of ability at the top. The worst things are the excessive red tape and bureaucracy and the lack of personal cleanliness engendered by bad housing and in the hotels, very bad building.[9]

So the transaction between the Mond and the Institute of Physical Problems was satisfactorily concluded. Its success was due to a combination of Rutherford's good sense in not allowing political prejudice to cloud his judgment, while credit was due to Cockcroft for the business-like way in which the transaction was carried out. Contact with the Russians was maintained, and in 1937 Rutherford allowed David Shoenberg, one of Kapitza's students in the Mond, to continue to work under him in Russia for six months. Kapitza's Institute made a number of fundamental discoveries on the superfluidity of liquid helium, and with L D Landau as chief theoretical physicist, became a major centre of research in Moscow. Ex-Cavendish colleagues of those days were delighted when Kapitza was awarded the Nobel Prize in 1978 for his low temperature work.

Cockcroft and Kapitza did not meet again for 22 years, but they kept in touch by writing. After the war Kapitza fell foul of Stalin and was compelled to leave the Institute for a country dacha where he was, however, able to continue his researches to a certain extent. When Khruschev came to power he was reinstated and in due course became the Grand Old Man of Russian science. But he never forgot the halcyon years in Cambridge:

> What a wonderful time it was then at the Cavendish! [he wrote to Nevill Mott in 1964, two years before he and Anna returned to stay with the Cockcrofts in Churchill College.] The science belonged to the scientists and not to the politicians. Nowadays in spite of the terrific amount of money which is available for science we do not enjoy our work nearly so much as in the old days. The young generation will never know how pleasant the scientific work was in those days.[10]

When Allibone had lunch with the Kapitzas in 1971 he was offered a fine sherry, claret and a Cognac, no Russian wines! Kapitza had obtained Brezhnev's permission to issue a postage stamp to commemorate the centenary of the birth of Rutherford that summer, but Allibone had failed to get the British Postmaster General to do the same.

As Assistant Director of the Mond, Cockcroft developed his interest in low temperature physics and encouraged the growth of several new lines of research which later bore fruit. The fact that he had already, as Professor E C Stoner wrote, 'played an important part at several stages in the development of Kapitza's investigations'[22] made this a not unduly difficult task; and he had Rudolf Peierls at hand to advise him on future researches but he never became an authority on low temperature physics and never did any experiments in the Mond. Before going to the USSR, he attended the Seventh International Congress on Refrigeration at The Hague, and read a paper on the design and operation of the Kapitza helium liquefier. He was one of a large British delegation representing both scientific and industrial interests, and Professor Simon, D N Kurti and D Mendelssohn represented the Clarendon Laboratory, Oxford. It was also an occasion for the reunion of scientists who, because of their race or political views, had been exiled from Germany or Italy; and there were animated discussions beneath the sunshades on the beach at Scheveningen. Cockcroft wrote to Elizabeth:

> It has been interesting to meet so many new people, Dutch and Russian physicists principally so far. Tomorrow we pay an unofficial visit to Leiden to see experiments and talk to people there. I'll take a sideways glance at the Hotel du Commèrce [where they had stayed during their honeymoon] for old time's sake.

Cockcroft had, as noted earlier, become renowned for the number of jobs he undertook simultaneously. It was no exaggeration that when he was invited to deliver the course of lectures at Harvard, referred to above, Bainbridge should write in anticipation: 'I hope that the Prof can spare your aid, that St John's will run on its own momentum for a while and that the Tudor brick walls can remain unmolested'[12].

Like a number of the older colleges, the lighting system of St John's College was quite inadequate. Staircases were dimly lit by gas jets and at night, when returning to their rooms, members of the College had to grope to find the keyholes of their outer doors. Cockcroft had prepared a report during the winter of 1931–32 in response to a request by the College Council; he advised[13] rewiring of the Chapel and most of the rooms where electrical insulation was below the normal standard. Action was taken and the work spread over several years. The old gas lamp posts were removed with the exception of one kept as a reminder of the great engineer, Sir Charles Parsons, who had climbed it as an undergraduate following a bump supper. The most interesting part of the work was the lighting of the Chapel where Cockcroft enjoyed himself 'playing about with floodlights and different lighting fittings' in various parts of the building.

In October 1933 he was appointed Junior Bursar of St John's and as such was responsible for the domestic administration of the College, such as managing the staff and seeing that the buildings and grounds were properly maintained. Cockcroft's reputation, like that of Dirac's, in advancing the frontiers of science, was scarcely known to most members of the College, who were studying the humanities, but he quickly acquired a name for the conscientious way in which he set about his new job.

> I have been looking into College finances [he wrote on 30 December 1933] and finding out what our real financial strength is to satisfy myself that I'm not likely to bankrupt the institution.

He also found some allies among the young dons in the Senior Combination Room.

I sat down next to [one of the senior dons] in Hall. He talked continuously about the good old days and incidentally provided an additional motive to our moving one of the lesser and uglier Combination Room portraits by telling us what a rogue the old gentleman in question really was.

One of the young dons was Glyn Daniel, later Disney Professor of Archaeology, who after being elected Fellow soon after graduation wanted to keep his old undergraduate rooms. He turned to Cockcroft for help and in no time and with the minimum of fuss the latter had installed modern conveniences and converted the rooms into appropriate accommodation for a Fellow[14]. An older don, Sir Joseph Larmor, the celebrated physicist, found Cockcroft's attentions less welcome:

You would surely be better employed [he wrote on 17 August 1932] in cracking atoms or in exploding magnetic fields than in rooting up the floors of my room. It is my bedmaker, now on holiday until September, that is in control of such matters including the annual lifting of carpets which we had thought of foregoing this year... your people will doubtless consult me when she returns.[15]

As Junior Bursar the most exacting part of his duties were concerned with both restoration of the old buildings and with the construction of a new extension to the College. When his mother, in congratulating him on his appointment, hoped that the Bursarship would 'take you into the fresh air more instead of that dirty, stuffy sunless "lab" of yours', she did not foresee the numerous journeys that her son would make in search of architects or materials for restoration. Concern about the state of the buildings—to which little had been done for a number of years, apart from repairs to the roof of the 17th century library—had come to a head in 1927 when the ravages of the deathwatch beetle began to be discovered in the old woodwork. A standing committee was appointed and it had to submit a programme at the beginning of each Michaelmas term on the restoration work to be undertaken. As Junior Bursar Cockcroft became a member of this committee. One of the stipulations of the Governing Body of the College, made at the insistence of the great historian, G G Coulton, was that 'no portion of the carved as distinct from dressed stonework of the College and ornamental work should be removed without permission of the Council'.

The first major task was the restoration of the early 16th century Gate House and the First Court. When first discussed, the Fellows disagreed on whether or not the foundations were subsiding. Sir Joseph Larmor, who had passed through the gateway daily for the past 50 years, declared that they were; not so the Dean. Cockcroft in his practical way asked an American engineer, Dr Edmund Astley Prentis, then in England advising on the construction of the new Waterloo Bridge, to make an examination which confirmed Larmor's suspicions. Cockcroft then brought in the well known civil engineers, Sir Alexander Gibb & Partners, to submit a detailed report and recommendations. This was submitted on 7 May 1934, and in the light of it the College decided to rebuild completely in Tudor brick the two turrets facing St John's Street and strengthen them by steel stanchions built into the brickwork.

Bearing in mind Coulton's insistence on conservation, it was necessary to procure old bricks which were of the same period as the turrets. Cockcroft had, in the meantime, been looking for the source of the bricks in Second Court which needed refacing.

> I knew [he wrote to Elizabeth on 8 April 1934] it came from Stow but wasn't sure which Stow, so Meredith Jackson [who had been a fellow undergraduate and was then a University lecturer on law] and I set out after lunch in 'Jumbo' [a bullnosed Morris], going via Mildenhall and Brandon to Downham Market round which various Stows congregate. Sure enough at the first Stow we came to [Stow Bardolph], the parish church was buttressed up with Second Court brick of which we carried (sic) a sample. We then heard of an old brickyard which had been shut down 20 years and ran it to earth without difficulty. Here we discovered the remains of extensive excavations from which there is no doubt our brick came. Most of the cottages round about are sprinkled with it and many of the churches. We explored to find old derelict cow sheds, etc which we might try and pull down and made a good start by finding one which would do to repair two sides of Second Court with. I also heard of another brickworks near Lynn which makes homemade bricks so shall go again this week to see what they can do. We called on the way back at a manor house inhabited by a friend of Meredith's, built 1570, and there again were all our bricks!

Two days later he went on another expedition, this time accompanied by the Dean, combing the area from Ely to Lynn.

> I expect to go again and explore the slums of Lynn which appear to be built with the most delightful brick. There is a beautiful mansion called Middleton Towers which has a gate like the College. We walked in to see if it was for sale but found the family at home.

Oliphant also accompanied him on several of these trips which, as he recalled,

> often involved visiting cathedrals and other buildings of interest on the way. I never knew John to spend more than ten minutes in absorbing all the architectural and historical features of such buildings. One trotted around with him in a haze.

Another source of bricks was found at the Abbey Farmhouse on the Newmarket Road, so the College bought the building, demolished it, and used the bricks to face the gateway; they arrived in 200 lots and were stacked in the First Court. By August 1934 the two turrets were completely cut away from the gatehouse for reconstruction. Cockcroft was then asked to raise the roof of the south-east turret by four feet. This was accomplished by using the wooden shelving from the Old Acton Library, then being demolished, and refixing it in the turret. With the bricks he had discovered at Stow Bardolph the six eastern gables in the north wing of Second Court were rebuilt during 1934 at a cost of £119.

While the Great Gate was being restored, it seemed to be a good opportunity to restore to its former grandeur the painted coat of arms and other ornamentation over the entrance. Professor E E Tristram, the well known authority on medieval painting, was commissioned to supervise this work while it was executed by the College painter. During the preparatory cleaning of the stonework Cockcroft noticed that some of the ornamental stone was deteriorating. Examination revealed that a small quantity of washing soda in the lime pickle used to remove the old paint had caused a small caustic deposit which had penetrated the Caen sandstone. Copious washing to reduce the alkali content was recommended, but when Cockcroft consulted the Government's Building Research Station near London on whether new coats of paint would prove injurious to the ancient stone, he received a non-commital reply, being advised merely to ensure that the paint came from a reputable firm!

Cockcroft assiduously followed Coulton's injunction about ornamental stonework and when he discovered that the stone carver had, on his own initiative, carved two new small figures, he protested to the Dean. In the circumstances, however, it was decided not to pursue the matter any further; and the College History noted that the figures were charming[14]. Cockcroft's hand may be seen in several other aspects of restoration during those years which for him were busy enough in the high-voltage and the Mond laboratories.

At one point it seemed possible that he might even be able to combine scientific research and restoration when he proposed the application of high frequency currents to exterminate the deathwatch beetles ravaging the beams of the Hall ceiling. Metro–Vick, he had heard, were employing such a technique to destroy bed bugs in a slum-clearing operation. However, the scheme proved to be impracticable as it was found impossible to attach a generator to the beams, while the quartz crystals required to generate the high frequency power were too expensive.

During the latter part of 1935, the College approved a plan to build an extension to accommodate an anticipated increase in the number of undergraduates. Cockcroft took an energetic part in arranging for the drawing-up of alternative schemes to enable the Governing Body to make a decision. The plan, finally approved after a good deal of discussion, entailed the destruction of a number of old commercial properties in Bridge Street. In order to decide on the distance of the new building from the street, even in those days carrying a large number of motor vehicles, he arranged for measurements to be taken on the intensity of noise likely to be experienced.

The next problem was to find an architect to draw up a design which would be distinctive, functional and not too expensive, and Cockcroft was a member of a committee whose unenviable job it was to look at the work of 28 architects, a total of some 100 buildings. They then selected a short list of three architects including Sir Owen Williams, who had just completed the Pioneer Health Centre at Peckham, a local architect named John Murray Easton who had done work for several of the Cambridge colleges, and Edward Maufe, who had recently been commissioned to build the new Guildford Cathedral. Cockcroft described how he and his fellow members went to London to have another look at a students' hostel by Maufe.

Second views always seem to look worse than first as one develops more critical instincts and we came away thinking rather less of Maufe than before.

After this we travelled to London Bridge and there saw a bank by Hepworth which finally put him out of the picture. This done we went to Simpsons' and had lunch of saddle of mutton and jelly with cheese to follow—a most English and satisfying lunch. We then inspected Henry VII's chapel at the Abbey to observe the effect of the lime washing and then set out to Stanmore to look at work of Sir Owen Williams after having telephoned him in vain. After a slow journey in the gloom [it was December] we got there about 4.0 PM and set off in the fog to find the flats. After some vain efforts we hailed a gentleman in a large car and behold it was the architect himself.

The flats, they found, were ingeniously constructed out of concrete ribs and back panels.

Some months later they inspected the Friends' Meeting House in the Euston Road, and Holden's London Underground headquarters off St James's Park, and concluded by lunching with Sir Owen Williams who 'debunked the architectural profession'. Williams, in the event, dropped out of the running; Easton's design was unsatisfactory, and Maufe, despite their earlier doubts, was appointed in 1937. His daughter Catherine remembers being told by her sister how Father would build models of the extension to St John's on the sands at Hunstanton.

Cockcroft learned much from his experiences as Junior Bursar which were to stand him in good stead when he became responsible for the plans of the village at Deep River, Canada, accommodation for scientists at Harwell and, finally, the building of Churchill College, Cambridge. None of these schemes were plain sailing any more than at the Cavendish. But as Anna Kapitza assured him in an understanding letter early in 1939: 'The Cavendish is nothing compared to the College [St John's] to rebuild. All the styles to consider and all the Fellows to please. God help you!'[15] On 3 August 1937 Cockcroft drew up detailed proposals from which Maufe might prepare his designs, and by the end of that year work on the new building had begun.

In June 1937 the Paris World Exhibition had opened and in the autumn an International Congress of Science was sponsored by Professor Joliot and the younger French scientists, their intention being that it should inaugurate a series of international scientific conferences of a general character. Cockcroft was one of a strong British delegation including Blackett, J D Bernal, J B S Haldane, C H Waddington and W L Bragg, who all read papers. Rutherford had been unwell and was recovering from what was considered to be a minor operation. On 27 September he wrote from his Wiltshire cottage to Cockcroft to acknowledge the receipt of the latter's Paris lecture entitled 'Transmutation of Elements and Deuterons' which he generally approved.

> I am glad [he continued] you give a brief account of our new lab and apparatus and I think your estimates of probable yields of radioactive substances are very valuable at the present stage. There is a good deal of loose talk about intensities of artificial radioactive elements. Give my kind regards to Perrin, Joliot and Langevin. Find out the *practical* stage of development of the Paris high voltage arrangements. I have seen Joliot's presentation on the same.[16]

In mid-October, shortly after the Paris Congress, there was another meeting in Italy at which Cockcroft had been invited to give a paper describing recent low temperature work at the Mond; it was to celebrate the bicentenary of Galvani who had made outstanding contributions to the sciences of electricity and electro-physiology. The celebrations were held in Bologna, Galvani's birthplace. Cockcroft and the other British scientists found the atmosphere oppressive on account of the Fascists' stage-management of the proceedings.

> A lot of people [he noted in a letter to his mother] were very contemptuous of much of the Fascist behaviour, but they seem to think there was no likely alternative at present. It seems that they are catching the anti-Jewish complex from Hitler and that discrimination is just beginning. There was a great parade of ancient Italian physicists whose work is negligible. The young who are really good were not even invited to the official lunches, etc where there was room to spare for hundreds.

It was with some relief that he accepted the invitation of Professor Fermi, 'the real leader of Italian physics', to forego the opening of a library displaying relics of Galvani and drive to Ravenna and look at Byzantine churches. Later, Aston, included in the Cambridge delegation, 'told us that the King was specially concerned to talk to the English group and certainly wherever we went we were shown the greatest kindness'.

In the middle of the ceremonies Cockcroft received a wire from Dee to say that Rutherford had died suddenly on 19 October. Cockcroft immediately left for Cambridge. He later wrote several sympathetic obituaries of his Professor, but the tribute he penned on the train to his mother during the return journey to Calais gives a more spontaneous impression.

> Rutherford will be very greatly missed and it is a tragedy that he did not live till the end of his tenure. I was very fond of him. I have always had independence and freedom to work, relieved by his power and prestige from the necessity of struggling for means. Now I shall have to fend for myself and for the work we have built up in the Cavendish. Fortunately all the major developments of policy, the new high voltage lab, the cyclotron and the new lab building had been approved and put in hand during last year so that we can go ahead without delay.

> Rutherford was a really great character. In his later years he did not contribute directly so much to new ideas but he was a most shrewd judge of what development to back and what not, and on the value of alternative lines of work. He was, too, a most remarkably good judge of a man's capacity and always picked his people well. This was shown up most especially in the recent years when we have had such a drain of men away from the Cavendish, Kapitza, Blackett, Chadwick, Oliphant, Ellis. Most of all his judgment in large questions of policy was always first rate. There are certainly no other Professors in Cambridge with his combination of scientific distinction and administrative power. And it is certain that the next Cavendish Professor will not be his equal by many magnitudes. Who they will elect is difficult to say. He will have a hard task to follow in the succession of Maxwell, Rayleigh, J J Thomson and Rutherford. The most likely candidates are Appleton, now Jacksonian Professor at Cambridge, Blackett, just appointed to Manchester, and Chadwick now at Liverpool. Of these I prefer Blackett.[17]

Cockcroft's apprehension of what the outcome would be was reflected in a letter to Bainbridge on 27 December 1937.

> Appleton [who was the Jacksonian Professor of Physics] is in charge of the lab at the moment and is regarded by the local administrators and non-physicists

as the strongest candidate. I don't know much about the details of his work; I can only judge by his approaches to the work in nuclear physics or low temperature and from that I feel very disturbed at the prospects of his succeeding. W L Bragg has been mentioned but since he has moved to be head of the NPL I doubt whether he would come. He would be better from a personal point of view but the presence of a crystallographer and ionospherist in the principal seats mightn't be too good for nuclear physics... The electors have anyway a tough job in front of them.[18]

Bragg was elected. He was to change the emphasis of research from nuclear physics to solid state physics, to the crystal structure of complicated molecules such as the nucleic acids, and to radio astronomy.

But events were now to turn Cockcroft's attention from the comparatively parochial atmosphere of university politics to a wider scene—the defence of the country against sudden air attack. Possibly more than most sections of the community, scientists were aware of the implications of Hitler's rise to power in 1933, for foreign scientists in considerable numbers were being absorbed in the academic communities in Britain and America. Several of the younger generation of Cambridge scientists like Joseph Needham, Lancelot Hogben, J D Bernal and P M S Blackett tended politically to be on the left wing, indeed Bernal was an avowed communist, and in the early 1930s some of them had found an outlet in the Cambridge anti-war group, though later, with the onset of the Spanish Civil War, the mood changed to a campaign of non-appeasement of the Fascist dictators. Cockcroft was not a member of this group. He had seen enough as an impartial observer on his two visits to Russia not to be deceived by the promise of a new dawn in that direction. On the other hand, as a director of John Cockcroft & Sons (he continued to follow the fortunes of the family business), he disapproved of the government's economic policy and he was critical of the policy of Imperial Preference for the cotton industry which, since 1931, had entered a period of depression. He was content to be a tolerant, and sometimes amused, spectator of political activities. Once he went, during a visit to London, to a lecture organised by the Friends of the Soviet Union. 'I arrived just in time to hear Patrick Blackett holding forth—also Mrs Cecil Chesterton on the position of women—very enthusiastic and perhaps not very critical.'

While the intellectuals were demonstrating against fascism, or demanding air-raid shelters, a significant step had been taken by the Air Ministry. At the end of 1934 it had invited Tizard, who had left DSIR to become Rector of Imperial College, to head a small secret committee of scientists, including Blackett and A V Hill, officially called the Committee for the Scientific Survey of Air Defence, to discover whether recent advances in scientific and technological knowledge could help present methods of air defence. During the next three years it had been responsible for getting the Government to develop the science of 'radio direction finding', RDF, later called Radar, which had been pioneered by the researches of Watson-Watt and his colleagues at Bawdsey Manor on the Suffolk coast. Watson-Watt had attended an Institution of Electrical Engineers meeting in Manchester in the summer of 1936 and in the Research Department of the Metro–Vick Company he saw for the first time the continuously evacuated tetrode (4-electrode) valves made for the GPO operating at 6 kW; he had never seen so much C W (Continuous Wave) power before and at once got the Air Ministry to order a complete high-power transmitter for the first radar station at Bawdsey. When Allibone was in Cambridge early in 1937 Rutherford discussed these valves and asked him what kind of servicing was necessary for the many 250 kV, 500 kV continuously evacuated x-ray tubes and the 1000 kV tube Rutherford had officially inaugurated on Abdication Day 1936. Allibone explained that he had placed a technical assistant at each hospital to service the tubes and thus ensure 100 per cent utilisation; Rutherford thought that that might be necessary with the continuously evacuated high-power valves. The Metro–Vick Company contract was extended to a further 20 transmitters before the end of 1937, each of them giving 250 to 600 kW of power, and a chain of radar stations, called Chain Home or CH stations, was built first along the south-east coast to give early warning of the approach of hostile aeroplanes so that the fighters might be in the right place at the right time. There were, at that time, no sealed-off valves on the market capable of yielding the output of radio power needed, and by 1938 skilled operators were wanted to man these CH stations, operators well versed in high vacuum techniques to guarantee continuous operation.

Tizard appreciated that at Cambridge there was a potential supply of first class physicists, and some time early in 1938 he invited Cockcroft to lunch at the Athenaeum and told him about the secret radar stations. They agreed that it was important that scientists should play a part in air defence. At about the same time, the War Office was planning to expand its own small detachment of scientists at Bawdsey in order to develop methods of controlling anti-aircraft guns and searchlights by radar and Tizard may well have had in mind that Cockcroft should have a hand in this.

Cockcroft took the next step in concerning himself in the defence of the country when, on 20 July 1938, he responded to an invitation sent by Vice-Chancellors to senior university members 'with technical and other qualifications which might be useful in the event of war'. Their names were compiled in the Central Register of Scientists, and in Cockcroft's case this would lead to a senior appointment in the Ministry of Supply.

Meanwhile, Hitler's demands were increasing, culminating that autumn in his temporary appeasement by the British and French at Munich. For a few days war seemed imminent as Cockcroft found himself preparing the College against air raids. With his experiences on the Western Front in mind, he had already modified the designs for the new Maufe buildings to include an 18-inch thick concrete floor to cover part of the basement so as to make an air-raid shelter, with provisions for air locks against penetration by gas. As a contemporary College document made clear,

> Dr Cockcroft had the foresight to see the necessity of taking drastic air-raid precautions and an appreciable amount of the additional costs (of the Maufe building) are due to these extremely valuable additions and changes.[19]

Cockcroft's appreciation of the turn of events was indeed a good deal more realistic than those of a number of others such as Ernest Lawrence, who wrote to him from Berkeley expressing the belief that 'from now on the great powers will settle international disputes by peaceful negotiations'.[20]

> We have all had [replied Cockcroft] a big shake up with the war scare. I spent about two weeks doing nothing but preparing my College against air raids. We were expecting up to the Thursday of the Munich meeting to become a hospital, and this was changed at the last moment to orders to prepare for London children. If war had come we should have all gone over to defence research at once. I wish I could believe in Hitler's pacific intentions. I think it would be criminal folly if we did not push on with all possible measures to defeat the air menace, which has now become a most powerful method of political blackmail. I'm sure that if all the energy which has gone into nuclear physics since 1932 were turned on to this problem, it would be solved[21].

After Munich, Cockcroft and R H Fowler, Rutherford's physicist son-in-law, drove to Bawdsey where the high towers transmitting the radar beams were a landmark on that stretch of Suffolk coast, and were told about recent developments in both ground and airborne radar. On 1 February 1939 there was a meeting at Cambridge with Watson-Watt, the 'father of radar', who was now in charge of development at the Air Ministry. The meeting was inspired by Tizard who was still concerned about the urgent need for scientific participation at the stations of the radar chain then being extended along the east and south coasts.

A long list of young scientists from a number of universities was drawn up by Cockcroft at a meeting in the Cavendish chaired by Bragg, the newly appointed Cavendish Professor, and also attended by W B Lewis, J A Ratcliffe and P I Dee. They were then divided into eight groups, the intention being that each group should undergo a month's course under the RAF at a Chain Home station. This would give them some idea of the problems involved to help them in whatever war-work they would subsequently take up. Cockcroft took it upon himself to ask the selected scientists to serve, without revealing the nature of the work except that it had to do with short-wave radio; and he was also the link between them and the Air Ministry. The group leaders would go to Bawdsey to be let into the secret before the training began that September. Looking back years later, he believed that this was one of the most useful contributions he made to the war, as many of those he selected distinguished themselves not only in radar but went on to play an important role in the development of reactor physics and particle accelerators after the war.

During those last months of peace, Cockcroft made himself familiar with aspects of defence research other than radar through invitations to visit naval, air and army research establishments. By then he was visiting Bawdsey regularly and took part in the air manoeuvres held in August, only a few weeks before the outbreak of war, after which Air Chief Marshal Sir Hugh Dowding, Commander-in-Chief, Fighter Command, publicly expressed satisfaction with the 'various new methods' that had been tried out. On Sunday, 23 July, a cricket match took place on the splendid lawns of Bawdsey Manor when Cockcroft was captain of one side, including several Cavendish colleagues, and the other of Air Ministry scientists was led by the Superinten-

dent, A P Rowe, also a keen cricketer. Cockcroft's team won easily and he
increased the total score by 30 runs.

At the Cavendish he was accustoming himself to working under Bragg. His
main scientific interest was the cyclotron, which was then operating and as
Cockcroft reported to Donald Cooksey, 'getting quite a lot of nice results'[22].

Although no-one yet appreciated it, nuclear physics had already taken a
turn which would have repercussions far beyond the small circle of scientists
concerned. Late in 1938 two German chemists, Otto Hahn and Fritz
Strassmann, bombarded a uranium target with slow neutrons causing the
nucleus to split into two approximately equal halves. Two Austrian scientists,
Lise Meitner and her nephew, O R Frisch, confirmed and evaluated the
experiment, using the word 'fission' to describe the process. Cockcroft was
well aware of these developments, having tried unsuccessfully to find a haven
in Cambridge for Meitner, who had been forced to leave the laboratory in
Berlin where she had been working, and on 13 February 1939 received a long
letter from her in Stockholm describing recent events.† Shortly afterwards, he
discussed the significance of fission at a meeting of ex-Cavendish members
who used to foregather at regular intervals on Saturday mornings in London.
Harrie Massey, who belonged to this so-called 'Physics Club', later said:
'Everyone felt that here was something of the greatest importance even
though, if asked, no-one could have given explicit reasons for this belief.'[23]
Nevertheless, the awful significance of the fission of uranium was being
realised. Cockcroft was the first contributor to the discussion at the Institution
of Electrical Engineers on 13 April when Allibone read his paper on the one
million volt x-ray tube operating at the St Bartholomew's Hospital, and at the
dinner after the paper Cockcroft was his guest; he noted in his diary for the
day that he and Cockcroft had discussed both nuclear bombs and nuclear
power stations as distant possibilities. For the time being the Nazis' occupation of the Sudetenland and the likelihood of further demands by Hitler
overshadowed everything.

That March Cockcroft heard from Anna Kapitza who, with her children,
had readapted herself to life in the Soviet Union, in a letter characteristic of
that anxious time.

> Every letter which comes from England is full of war tales. Is it as bad as that?
> Here we are as if living in a different planet, and so we talk of different things.
> I begin to realise that 600 kilometers from the frontier is something to be
> thankful for[24].

That hopeful assumption would not hold good for much longer.

Academically, Cockcroft's pioneer work in nuclear physics was rewarded
that summer by his appointment to the Jacksonian Professorship of Natural
Philosophy in succession to Appleton. It was an appointment he was to hold
for the next seven years, during which time he would be serving his country,

---

†The possibility of inviting Meitner, then aged 61, for a year was considered. But as
war became imminent and nuclear physicists were earmarked for radar, Cambridge
no longer seemed to be the right place for her.

first as a war scientist, and then would be selected as director of the first civil atomic energy research establishment. On account of this, as he was to recall humorously, he 'delivered not a single lecture, a record probably unequalled even by the 18th century professors. I can only plead it was not entirely my fault and that I was in good company!'[25] His election was very popular; as Peierls wrote, 'For once an election about which everybody will be glad.' He resigned the Professorship on 30 September 1946.

CHAPTER EIGHT

A ROVING COMMISSION

By the 26 August, 1939 war looked increasingly imminent, and Cockcroft decided to move his family from Cambridge to Todmorden (Elizabeth was expecting another baby). He then drove to Bawdsey, only to find that the Air Ministry scientists were preparing to evacuate in view of the possibility of the Research Station being bombed. After discussing the situation over the phone with Watson-Watt, they arranged that his group should supplement the RAF personnel at the Rye Chain Home station. The other university groups, after being mobilised, were settling in at the other Chain Home stations on the south and south-eastern coasts. On Friday, 1 September, Cockcroft's group had arrived at the radar station '100 feet up with nice views and oast houses lending variety', when they heard the news that the Germans had invaded Poland.

At Rye, on that memorable morning of Sunday, 3 September, he heard Chamberlain announce on the radio that Britain was at war with Germany. His group studied the radar handbook under the eye of a competent flight sergeant in charge of the station, a humorous man with a fund of stories to tell against the Army and the Air Ministry. Cockcroft wrote confidently to Elizabeth assuring her that 'if we all do our jobs properly raids should soon become rare'. In the event, not a single enemy plane appeared and, apart from one or two false alarms, the scientists went down to swim from the pebbly beach or sat in the sun studying the manual. As the prewar organisation of scientists for an emergency had fallen on his shoulders, leadership of the groups attached to the neighbouring Chain Home stations also fell on his shoulders, and his quiet authority was soon needed to solve a variety of problems ranging from subsistence allowances to complaints that they were wasting their time and would be better employed back in their laboratories.

Cockcroft had been appointed Assistant Director of Research in the Ministry of Supply at the outset of war, deputy to H J Gough, a stolid 50 year old engineer, who was responsible for research and development of equipment for the Army. As Cockcroft was already familiar with radar from his visits to Bawdsey, his work lay mainly in this field, though it was soon to be extended to other items in the radar/radio programme, such as proximity fuses[1]; he was also to become responsible for liaison with French scientists, a duty for which he was well qualified because of his prewar acquaintance with European physicists.

Gough had intended that Cockcroft, in charge of his party of six Cavendish colleagues, should spend the early part of September at Bawdsey studying the problems of controlling anti-aircraft guns by radar, and then go to the Air Defence Experimental Establishment (ADEE), recently transferred from Biggin Hill to a decaying mansion called Bure Homage at Christchurch, Hampshire; they were now relieved from the manning of Rye. ADEE had been formed shortly after the First World War, since when its staff had been developing acoustic equipment for the long-range detection of aircraft. Inevitably, the development of radar had made much of their work obsolete, and the established staff found this hard to accept, while the intrusion of a band of young and rather undisciplined scientists enthusiastic about the new science hardly reconciled them to change.

In his capacity of Assistant Director of Scientific Research, Cockcroft became responsible for supervising the work of the ADEE and spent much time travelling between London, Cambridge and Christchurch. His experience as a soldier in the First World War made it easy for him to act as a bridge between the scientists and the military. The latter were led by the Commandant, Colonel Sylvester Evans, a Territorial Army officer and a scientist in civilian life, while the scientists were led by Dr D H Black, a New Zealander, a slightly younger contemporary of Cockcroft at the Cavendish. Black did not share Cockcroft's belief in the far-reaching possibilities of short-wave radar, and it thus fell to Cockcroft to convince the War Office staff responsible for radar that here was a powerful novel tool, though still untried and very much in the development stage.

Meanwhile, it was the Admiralty that made the first demand on Cockcroft's team. Vice-Admiral James Somerville, who had specialised in signals in the inter-war years, had become Inspector of Anti-Aircraft Weapons and Devices which made him, in effect, responsible for early warning systems. A radar set of some kind was required to be able to detect surfaced submarines likely to attack the Home Fleet's base at Scapa Flow. Somerville was the first Senior Service officer whom Cockcroft had met and the former's appreciation of what science could do ensured that the Admiral and the Jacksonian Professsor understood each other at once. In no time, Somerville had hired a submarine and trials were carried out with an army radar set which had been developed by the Australian physicist, W A S Butement, before the war at Bawdsey; this was able to pick up and follow ships at sea. On 15 September he and Cockcroft, who was impressed by the former's wide-ranging mind, watched Butement's set detect the submarine off Bawdsey. It was then agreed that Cockcroft should construct three sets capable of operating on a 1.4 metre waveband. One was to be erected on Fair Isle between Orkney and Shetland, one on the south end of Shetland, and one on the Orkneys, thus keeping the whole of the Pentland Firth under surveillance.

This was the sort of work in which Cockcroft excelled. His knowledge of the electrical engineering industry gave him a ready entrée. In order to save time, the components of a new set called the Coastal Defence Unit (CDU) were to be assembled by Metro – Vick (the transmitters) and Pye (the receivers). The time-base of the transmitter/receiver was assembled in the Cavendish by two members, M V Wilkes and J V Dunworth. Cockcroft supervised the work, which naturally entailed much travelling. He found it difficult to persuade the officials responsible for issuing petrol coupons that his work, which he could not describe in detail, was more important to the war effort than air-raid precautions. He also, for the first time, encountered Service bureaucracy when trying to obtain scarce electrical components. He described this to Elizabeth.

> You can have a ten-shilling phone call but cannot send a sixpenny telegram. The Establishment also suffers from being divided into three classes. (1) the people who know their stuff and don't work; (2) the people who don't know their stuff and labour; and (3) the very small class of people who do both. The sight of people of Kempton's and Wilkes's intelligence working with their hands was too much for people here.

In another letter he expressed his impatience with the Army component of ADEE. 'The military folk take such an unhurried attitude to jobs and the war. Since it's their life they're not in such a hurry to get it over as some of us.' As for Bure Homage, the Hampshire house, it 'has fallen sadly from its one-time estate, for it has no furnishings save the barest tables; even chairs are woefully inadequate. I wish I could have the running of the place for a week or so to stir up things.'

An outstanding exception among the 'military folk' was Colonel A V Kerrison, an artillery officer and a 'great mountain of a man, extremely intelligent, a good mathematician and a first-class designer' who had invented the independent predictor for the Bofors light anti-aircraft gun. He had been Army liaison officer at the Admiralty Research Laboratory, Teddington, and was now in charge of the fire-control group. Cockcroft's new CDU radar set required a mounting which could be rotated rapidly by hand. After discussing the problem with Kerrison, Cockcroft appreciated that the torque system used for the Bofors could be utilised for the CDU, and there and then Kerrison agreed to find the necessary parts. He arranged for the mountings to be made by a local firm and Colonel Evans paid for them out of the Establishment's Imprest Account. Afterwards, he explained to the War Office that this was

> highly illegal, but... whoever has to suffer in this matter, it should not be the contractor who, by providing the structures at very short notice, has been the sole means of Dr Cockcroft's work being got under way[2].

J A Ratcliffe, from the Cavendish, who had been detached from one of the Chain Home teams for the purpose, made a survey of possible sites in the Orkney Islands and in doing so had much impressed Admiral Somerville, who could not understand how a lecturer in physics was capable of doing a naval staff officer's job. By mid-October 1939, only one month after Cockcroft's meeting with Somerville, the sets were ready to be installed, the work being done by J V Dunworth and A E Kempton, both members of Cockcroft's Cavendish team, together with Donald Carmichael and A T Lewis, both of whom had brothers at the Cavendish, and who were anthropologist and civil engineer respectively, and G L Evans, a plant physiologist from St John's.

Cockcroft visited the remote island stations not long after they had begun to operate at the turn of the year. He travelled with Colonel W F H Miles, a retired Royal Marine with a keen interest not only in radio but in water divining, who had been made responsible for administering the stations. They flew to Scapa in a Scottish Airways plane, encountering a 50 mph gale. After landing, they 'spent a day walking up hills in snow blizzards and waiting for them to pass and bring out the sun, turning the Flow into a marvellous blue colour'. Next port of call was Kirkwall, Orkney where they inspected a site. Cockcroft was glad he was wearing a thick tweed suit, a cardigan and two scarves with a rug from the car over his shoulders. Reflecting on his experience of other Service scientists he

> came to the conclusion that I work as long as anyone in the Government service, for even the folks at Air Ministry Research Establishment [then located at Dundee] have their Saturday afternoons and Sundays off.

On a previous occasion he had helped to site a Chain Home radar station to cover the Firth of Forth, then sheltering units of the Fleet, and therefore an attractive target for the Luftwaffe. He described his experiences in a long letter to his family written by the fireside in his hotel lounge. The radar was sited on top of a hill 'down which a continuous sheet of water was pouring'. Another hotel at which he had stayed was 'a wonderful 1850 period piece, typical commercial/temperance, with cast-iron pillars, Scotch high tea, commercial room, but nowhere one could sit and talk'. This had followed a demonstration attended by 'air marshals by the dozen'.

Even after he had officially occupied his office at the Ministry of Supply in the Strand and had spent an hour or so reading 'some amusing files on hopeful inventions', he was more likely to be found at Christchurch or at Cambridge.His College had taken in RAF officer cadets and an odd assortment of institutions like the Commissioners for Lunacy, the Royal Society and the London School of Economics. In Cambridge, 'Expectant mothers walk about in droves. I believe they have red, green and blue labels according to the date of expectation!' On 12 October, College Audit Day, he made his farewell speech as Junior Bursar and shortly after, he signed the University Book as Jacksonian Professor. 'The war', he wrote to Elizabeth, 'still seems unreal, but the longer it is so, the better and the more prepared we shall be if it does break out.' On Tuesday, 17 October, after sitting down to dinner at the King's Arms, where he stayed in Christchurch, he learned that his fourth daughter, Catherine, had been born.

Since 17 September low flying enemy aircraft had been laying magnetic mines in the Thames Estuary and other approaches to ports on the east coast, causing heavy losses to shipping, but it was not until the discovery and analysis of an intact mine by naval scientists on 23 November that suitable degaussing measures could be introduced. Improvement of shortrange radar cover would not only make detection of low flying aircraft easier, but would enable mine sweepers to sail to waters where magnetic mines had been laid and shipping could be given adequate warning. Cockcroft discussed the prob-

lem with Air Vice-Marshal Philip (later Sir Philip) Joubert, the Assistant
Chief of Air Staff responsible for technical requirements. Even before the
advent of radar, Joubert had appreciated the importance of early warning in
air defence and, like Somerville, grasped the opportunity to use a practical
scientist like Cockcroft. The latter, in fact, became his unofficial 'scientific
adviser', often providing an opposite opinion to the official Air Staff view.
Some Chain Home, Low, (CHL) radar units were designed and were constructed by Metro – Vick; the wooden transmitting towers were assembled at
Christchurch. Cockcroft thoroughly enjoyed supervising the setting-up of the
equipment, and wrote several long descriptive letters to Elizabeth from
Margate while the work was in progress. One evening a convoy carrying the
wooden masts and other equipment from Christchurch was overdue and he
decided to look for them in his old Humber. He discovered the lorries near
Haywards Heath.

> They had been getting into bad trouble with the high framework catching the
> trees and so had taken four days to travel from Christchurch. I made them stop
> and reload all the timber for the masts on to the other three lorries which caught
> us up; and turned a large frame upside down. This work took us an hour and
> by then it was almost dusk. So we all pushed on to Uckfield and had refresh-
> ment. I came out hoping for a moon but was disappointed. And so I drove 80
> miles in poorish light through the twisting lanes of Kent. I got back about
> 10.0 PM and was glad to find a nice sole and chips. The lorries appeared next
> morning about 10.30.

Four days later he was helping the gang of erectors in a North Sea gale.

> We spent the best part of an hour holding on the ropes whilst part of our gear
> was being hoisted into the air. This was enlivened by the melancholy sight of
> a mined steamer sinking slowly and the rest of the convoy being turned back
> from our signal station to await new instructions.

Cockcroft had to urge on the civilian contractors to complete the job by 3
December. He wrote to Elizabeth:

> We had about 25 people on the go. By the afternoon it was blowing half a gale
> and causing us to pray for the safety of a rather flimsy-looking erection. I have
> been doing all manner of jobs, filing out holes, screwing up bits and pieces of
> wood and generally trying to keep everyone fully occupied. I have Ashmead,
> Fertel, Quarrington, Findlay and Vince plus three men from Pye and a gang
> of erectors and contractor's men.

When he visited the Fighter Command Operational Research Section at Stanmore several days later, he was pleased to discover that the CHL station at
Foreness Point under the supervision of E S Shire, one of Cockcroft's Cavendish team, had already begun to pick up low flying aircraft. They almost
invariably flew below 2000 feet, and the Operational Research Section
suggested that the point at which the radar track faded might be the area
where the mines were dropped. Although not infallible, this deduction often
gave results.

After getting the CHL set at Walton-on-the-Naze into action, Cockcroft
went to Shotton on the north-east coast, hoping to be in Todmorden for

Christmas Day with the family. But on Christmas Eve, he and Squadron Leader Gillam, from Joubert's staff, were arguing with a gang of erectors

> all equipped with turkeys and ready for home, that war needs had to take precedence over family reunions in 1939! So the CHL station was on the air by 27 December. From Shotton I went to Spurn Head and anxiously waited for apparatus, finally getting the station going by the New Year[3].

Fighter Command quickly appreciated that Cockcroft's low altitude sets could be used to counter the increasing number of dive-bombing attacks on coastal convoys. Seven more CHL stations were ordered to be erected along the east coast.

In the autumn of 1939 Dr C S Wright, Scientific Adviser to the Admiralty, asked him to take over the Admiralty Research Laboratory at Teddington, at a salary of £1400. But Cockcroft, though tempted, finally decided against it when he met Wright at a post-mortem conference on magnetic mines held at Teddington on 6 December 1939. He preferred to stay with his team of 'Cavendish irregulars', as he called them, making use of his engineering skill to improvise on the spot.

From the beginning of 1940 onwards, he became increasingly engaged in committee work. In order to stimulate new ideas for the Ministry of Supply and make the best use of scientists for research and development, an Advisory Council for Scientific Research and Technical Development was set up, composed of independent scientists of note as well as Government scientific advisers and chaired by Lord Cadman, the scientist and industrialist. Apart from Cockcroft, Appleton, Bragg, Harold Hartley, A V Hill, R V Southwell, G I Taylor and Tizard were members. They held their first meeting on 25 January 1940.

Cockcroft was a member, at one time or another, of eight of the committees which reported to the Council, dealing with fuses, proximity fuses of various kinds, field artillery observation, radar applications, radar-controlled guns and shortrange anti-aircraft guns and general physics. Although at the outset he shared Tizard's scepticism about the value of the Council, it survived the war and made a number of valuable recommendations on policy for radar, ballistics, fuses, metallurgy and structural engineering.

He used to stay, when in London, at the Blacketts' flat, 28 Tufton Court, Westminster, only a few minutes by bus from his office in the Strand. Blackett, who had been in the Navy in World War I, was then working on bomb sights at the Royal Aircraft Establishment, Farnborough, and his wife was a social worker in Lambeth. Cockcroft got on well with the Blacketts ('I always think most of Chadwick and Patrick in our generation', he confided to Elizabeth), and they used to have lively discussions on science, politics and the progress of the war after the day's work. Elizabeth and the children had, in the absence of air raids, returned to Cambridge in March 1940 and Cockcroft went to see them whenever his work permitted.

One of his preoccupations at this time was to remedy the lack of liaison with the scientists of France, then Britain's only major ally. For this reason he had visited Langevin and Joliot, who were similarly engaged on war work, in Paris before Christmas 1939[4]. He had, as he told Elizabeth, to impress on

Langevin 'the urgent necessity of seeing what scientists over here *are* doing'. Unfortunately the severe weather prevented Joliot from coming to London, but the Minister of Armament, Raoul Dautry, sent over Langevin and Pierre Auger, who was to play an important role in advanced nuclear physics after the war. They were accompanied by Lieutenant Jacques Allier, who worked for the Banque de Paris et des Pays Bas, and was now a technical intelligence officer. They passed on information about the latest advances in experiments relating to nuclear fission which will be described in chapter 11.

At the same time, Cockcroft was trying to get more use made of the remaining staff of the Cavendish and the Mond for projects which were not 'major war winners but ... may be important later'. He thought that obstacles were being created by lack of initiative and judgment, since 'our seniors won't move, we of humbler rank must do some stirring'. He had recently been elected a member of the Savile Club and here his friend Kenneth Pickthorn, historian and Member of Parliament for Cambridge University, introduced him to Colonel John Llewellin, Parliamentary Secretary to the Ministry of Supply. Cockcroft began to appreciate what could be done with 'backstairs influence. I shall probably need it in the end.'

Another point of contact with the younger scientists was the Tots and Quots (*Quot homines, tot sententiae*), a lively dining club founded by the anatomist and anthropologist, Solly Zuckerman, in 1931, at which a number of young scientists used to discuss topics relating to the impact of science on society. Although it was never intended that the convivial nature of the gatherings should be obscured, after Dunkirk there was a concerted effort to produce a paperback called *Science in War* castigating the authorities for failing to mobilise scientists in the crisis. Cockcroft was introduced as a member by J G Crowther, and at his first meeting sat with J B S Haldane, J D Bernal, Blackett, Hyman Levy, Lord Melchett, Solly Zuckerman, C H Waddington and the publisher, Allen Lane. Roy Harrod read a paper on post-war economic policy. 'There was a fierce discussion', wrote Cockcroft later, 'and it was rather fun.' Another topic discussed was the need to improve cultural relations with the French, following on Langevin's recent visit, and the possibility of forming an Anglo–French Society of Sciences.

In the spring of 1940 the 'phoney war' turned into real war when the Germans invaded Denmark and Norway. Next came their breakthrough in the Netherlands and the collapse of France.

The occupation of so much of Europe by the Nazis led Cockcroft to fear for the fate of his many friends abroad. But equally he was exhilarated by the urgency infused into the war effort by the new Prime Minister, Winston Churchill. 'All now depends on our plane output', he wrote to Elizabeth, who had returned to Todmorden with the children. 'We are suffering from the sins of omission of the last nine months and the incredible incompetence of some branches.'

After Dunkirk Oliphant sent his family back to Australia and urged Cockcroft to send Elizabeth and the children to Canada on the grounds that, knowing that those they cared for were beyond reach of the enemy, the men could concentrate on their work more effectively. Cockcroft did not agree; he drew moral support from his family even though he could only see them at infrequent intervals. There was also the possibility of being more permanently attached to ADEE at Christchurch, enabling him to rent a house. Gough and his deputy, E T Paris, were then engaged in trying to win a greater share in the running of ADEE, responsible to the Director of Engineer and Signals Equipment in the Ministry of Supply, Major General A C Fuller, a signals officer who had done outstanding work in World War I. Gough wanted Cockcroft 'to save ADEE from the military. They are trying to get rid of Black and the idea is that I should spend three days a week there to reinforce Black.'

The effective employment of dive-bombers by the Germans in advance of their armoured columns led Cockcroft to concentrate on the urgent need to make anti-aircraft guns more accurate. Experiments had already begun on various types of proximity fuse which would actuate a shell or rocket within lethal range of an aircraft and thereby eliminate the necessity of actually hitting the plane. One of these experimental fuses, which would be operated by radio in the proximity of the target, had been devised by Butement, Shire and A F H Thomson, a young radio physicist at Christchurch. The fuse depended on the use of extremely rugged valves and Cockcroft had discovered, by testing a German valve from a bomb which had been captured intact, that the valves could withstand the acceleration of being fired from a gun barrel. As the war continued, scientists appreciated that the accuracy of anti-aircraft weapons could only be improved by radar control and proximity fuses. Although Cockcroft favoured the development of Butement's fuse, the Ministry of Supply decided to investigate as alternatives other types of fuse using photoelectric or acoustic means of detonation.

While inspecting work on one of these projects in Manchester, Cockcroft and Blackett were told about an Air Ministry inspector at Metro–Vick who had a German girlfriend and was suspected of being a spy. Cockcroft described how the police took them to a house in Macclesfield where they

> found a wonderful collection of apparatus, but nothing very incriminating. I thought the evidence against the man was pretty strong and hope he gets put behind barbed wire for the duration.

The lack of anti-aircraft guns had stimulated efforts to develop rockets as alternative, though less accurate, weapons against the bomber. At that time experimental work was being carried out by a detachment of the Royal Aircraft Establishment under P I Dee at Exeter. Cockcroft kept the Ministry of Supply informed of progress and visited a number of trials in South Wales, during one of which Dee nearly hit an air vice-marshal. Rockets, aerial mines and cables attached to parachutes pre-occupied Professor Lindemann, who had become Churchill's scientific adviser at the outbreak of war, but Dee was sceptical about the efficacy of such weapons and related their shortcomings to Cockcroft in a series of caustic letters.

The accurate direction of searchlights was another problem exercising Cockcroft's mind. Oliphant, still in charge of the Physics Department at Birmingham University, accompanied him to watch trials of radar directed searchlights which, Oliphant recalled, would

> enable night fighters to locate a German bomber. These trials were at a place

named Stewponey, some distance from where I lived in Worcestershire. They were interrupted by an air-raid alert during which we drank horribly sweet cocoa from enamel mugs, and discussed the general problem. The idea was a failure because the bright light dazzled the eyes of the fighter crews. John was to stay the night with me, but we lost our way with blackout headlamps, a mist, no road signs, and very suspicious air-raid wardens of whom we asked the way, so that the sun was rising when we got to bed. I was irritated and cold, but John was quite unperturbed.[5]

The answer to many of these problems had, in fact, already been solved earlier that year in Oliphant's department by the invention of the cavity magnetron, a valve which, as Oliphant wrote, 'solved the immediate problem of large pulses of power' for shortwave radar. In mid-July 1940, he was sufficiently confident to propose to Cockcroft that magnetron frequencies should be standardised at wavelengths down to 10 centimetres.

What was now needed was an exchange of information with the Americans who, if they could obtain plans of secret British equipment, could manufacture it on a large scale and ship it across the Atlantic on what was to be called Lend-Lease. A V Hill, the scientific attaché in Washington, and Tizard at home, had urged over the past months the despatch of a scientific mission to the States. American scientists were also anxious to help the British in the crisis and give them the benefit of their advances in shortwave radar. Ernest Lawrence, no longer an isolationist, wrote on 22 May to Oliphant:

> There has been a good deal of progress in this country on microwaves, and I do not understand why Dr Hill has not been able to get the information you want. I think it has to do with the commercial aspects, and I have given him the best advice I could.[16]

While preliminary discussions on who should go with the mission were taking place early in July, Cockcroft was busily engaged in organising additional staff to help the rocket development team at Aberporth and, at the same time, trying to ease the friction between military and scientists at Christchurch. Hill, back from Washington, had already told him that the Americans had been asking for him, and Joubert proposed to Gough that he should represent the Ministry of Supply. But Gough replied that Cockcroft was indispensable and suggested that Andrade should go in his place. Joubert, rightly appreciating better than Gough how useful Cockcroft with his American contacts would be, wrote back on 6 July:

> The Mission is intended to go with full powers to explore and negotiate. It is not merely to survey the field, but to get things going as quickly and as widely as possible. In view of this, I sincerely trust that you will see your way to letting Cockcroft go.

Andrade would have been a complete failure; he did not have Cockcroft's engineering knowledge, nor his international reputation as a physicist, he also had the gift of quarrelling with people, even his fellow scientists.

There had also been difficulties with Tizard who, by general assent, was to lead the mission. His recent resignation as scientific adviser to the Air Staff on account of continuing difficulties with Lindemann was still reverberating, and Cockcroft had been too busy to attend a 'Lindemann must go' meeting which included Tizard himself, Blackett and Hill, but there was no doubt that his sympathies lay with Tizard. As he wrote about this time, 'I wish he were in charge of the war or had a powerful job. He always seems to have a very good judgment in strategical and military matters.' Later, with more experience of the direction of scientific policy, he expressed the opinion that Tizard was the most helpful of the 'real seniors—he is quite a magnitude above people like [Sir Frank] Smith† who skate agilely on the surface of things'. After the war, however, when he knew Lindemann (then Lord Cherwell) better, he stated that he believed

> his advice at the highest level often enabled important projects (like shortwave radar) to be developed in times that were miraculously short[8].

Although still not sure that he would go to America, Cockcroft set about collecting items of secret equipment, like the Kerrison predictor, proposals for a jet engine, and the priceless Birmingham magnetron for generating short waves. Most of them would be packed in a japanned tin trunk (the 'black box') which he had bought at the Army & Navy Stores, Westminster.

On 24 July he heard that Roosevelt wanted the British to come over and that American scientists like Vannevar Bush, Chairman of the National Defence Research Committee formed in June 1940 and Roosevelt's principal scientific adviser, J B Conant of the National Defence Research Committee, and F B Jewett, President of the National Academy of Sciences, had begun to organise themselves for defence research. Gough continued to raise objections to Cockcroft leaving the country—he had even spoken to Herbert Morrison, Minister of Home Security, then concerned about air defence—and now proposed that Cockcroft should spend half the week at Christchurch to 'reinforce Black'.

But American approval spurred the Government to take action. On 1 August Tizard, whose appointment as leader had finally been confirmed, went to see Churchill and obtained a *carte blanche* to give the Americans all the information they required, and at the same time he insisted that Cockcroft should go as his deputy. On the following evening, Cockcroft wrote to Elizabeth that Tizard had told the Ministry of Supply

> that he must have myself. And there it stands. I hate the idea of leaving you for six weeks but it is a big job and I shouldn't want to turn it down. Nor would you want me to, I know.

Final arrangements were made by Tizard and Cockcroft when they met at Oriel College, Oxford, on 4 August. Officially described as the British Technical and Scientific Mission, it included Captain H W Faulkner RN, Lieut.-Col. F C Wallace from the Army, Group Captain F L Pearce RAF, who had experience of recent fighting, and E G Bowen, the pioneer of airborne radar.

On 14 August 1940 Tizard left by air in advance of the main party to

---

†Sir Frank Smith was then Director of Instrument Production in the Ministry of Supply. He became chairman of the Advisory Council on Scientific Research and Technical Development after the death of Lord Cadman.

prepare the way. A fortnight later Cockcroft and the other members of the mission boarded the *Duchess of Richmond* bearing with them the precious black box. They were accompanied by a large detachment of sailors who were to man the fifty American destroyers provided by Roosevelt in exchange for American use of British naval bases in the West Indies. During the voyage Cockcroft digested the voluminous official papers and for relaxation read Steinbeck's *Grapes of Wrath*, a history of the USA, Maurois's *Ariel*—a biography of Shelley, and Drinkwater's *Charles James Fox* which complemented the American history. To entertain the sailors on the week's voyage he was asked to give a lecture. Obviously he could not talk about radar or any of the other contents of the 'black box'. Instead he chose, ironically, to talk on atomic energy. His audience was greatly impressed when he calculated that the potential amount of atomic energy in a cup of water could blow a 50 000 ton battleship one foot out of the sea.

On 8 September Cockcroft and his party were welcomed by Tizard at the Shoreham Hotel in Washington. Tizard had encountered an 'atmosphere of gloom and defeatism' on account of the exaggerated reports of the damage caused by German air attacks on Britain, but Cockcroft's party introduced a feeling of confidence. For the next two and a half months he drove himself almost without a break to establish scientific cooperation between the two countries, one of them still officially neutral.

Inevitably, the Americans were, at the start, suspicious as to whether the British were withholding information, but Cockcroft's friendship with leading American scientists like Arthur Compton, Merle Tuve, Alfred Loomis and Richard Tolman, who even at this stage had begun to work on war problems under the able direction of Vannevar Bush, an electrical engineer and founder of the National Defence Research Committee (NRDC), soon created an atmosphere of warmth.

After a week Cockcroft was able to write home: 'There is a burning desire to give us all the help possible in everyone I've met so far and I hope we shall be able to make use of the feeling.' Probably the most important discussion took place at the Waldman Park Hotel, Washington, in the presence of Compton, Loomis, a former New York lawyer and amateur scientist now working on shortwave radar, and Carroll Wilson, Bush's Executive Assistant, and naval and military officers. They agreed that an American team should start at once on the development and eventual production of 10 cm radar based on the magnetron to be used on the ground and in the air[9]. Development was to take place in commercial or university rather than in service laboratories. Loomis was to head a committee to direct the work.

Several weeks later Cockcroft visited Loomis's laboratory at Tuxedo Park, New York. After watching a demonstration of an aircraft being detected at a range of two miles, he produced the magnetron which was carried around in a wooden box, the lid being fastened by thumb screws[10]. In Loomis's sitting room he spread out the blueprint on the floor, and convinced Carroll Wilson and service officers that the magnetron was superior to the klystron, a large and less efficient valve then being developed in the USA. He later declared that 'our disclosures had therefore increased the power available to US technicians by a factor of 1000'[11].

Another important meeting took place at the home of Merle Tuve who, with Hafstad and other members of his laboratory, had turned their attention from nuclear physics to developing a proximity fuse. Cockcroft, accompanied by R H Fowler, the British scientific representative in Canada, revealed details of the radio operated fuse being developed in England. This meeting led to the prolonged development and production of American proximity fuses, the British appreciating that they could not compete in this area as they were already committed up to the hilt with producing less complicated items of equipment. There is no better account summarising what he accomplished in the forthcoming weeks than the letter he wrote to Gough on 30 September.

We have now completed three weeks' work and since Tizard returns this week, I must write to report progress.

The first two weeks were spent almost entirely in conference in which we described our goods. The US representatives showed great interest and are now in the throes of digestion. It is clear, however, that we have produced a profound effect in making them realise how far they were behind. After this we had three days visiting New York and their Signal Establishment [in New Jersey]. Here we saw their longrange RDF which corresponds to our CH. It has range of up to 120 miles and is in many respects good—but I think we can do a good deal to help them to improve it without undue trouble. We also saw their equivalent to our GL [gunlaying set]. It works on the same general line as Shire's experimental 50 cm GL. But the wavelength is 150 cm and it suffers from the corresponding limitations—thus it will be good from 17° elevation to the zenith, whereas our set on the basis of their results should be good for 8°. Having seen their performance I feel all the more confident that our GLs should go ahead as quickly as possible.

Tizard has arranged that, if desired, our research groups can work in Canada and I suggest that we should seriously consider transferring the 50 cm GL group to set production going in Canada. The Canadian Government seems only too anxious to help. A special organisation/research enterprise has been set up by them to supervise production and expenses of our scientists will be met. Similar problems arise with Air Ministry production and Tizard is going to raise the possibility of transference of some of their groups. We are also taking up the question of production of some of the GEC [General Electric Company's Research Laboratory at Wembley] valves since they are superior to anything over here.

The most useful things we have discussed for our own work are receiving-valves for the Air Ministry 10 cm work. We also hope to get help from the Bell Laboratory on 50 cm receivers since they are reputed to have studied this extensively. We see them this week and we have also to visit Sperry and RCA (Radio Corporation of America) who are working hard.

Civilian research seems to have got under way rapidly in the last two months under [Vannevar] Bush's committee—the National Defence Research Committee. It is a powerful body and is taking energetic action to rope in the cream of the young physicists. Thus they are studying proximity fuses for rockets and shells, microwave technique, uranium, anti-submarine work and no doubt many other things.

We have made contact with two of their sub-committees so far and have a good deal more still to do. [He had agreed with Carroll Wilson (Bush's executive assistant) and other scientists that the Americans should start at once to develop 10 cm radar, and had disclosed to them the magnetron and the details of Butement's radio operated proximity fuse.] I think that in the long run we should benefit a great deal by passing the ball on to them. I spent this weekend with their microwave sub-committee and thought they were extremely good— but short of a little guidance which we have been able to supply.

This week we are visiting Ordnance establishments—Fort Monroe, Aberdeen and Watertown to see AA work; also work on rockets and on centrifugal casting among others. I have sent off a complete report on centrifugal casting. I hope it arrives safely.

After this week I have to spend some time visiting industrial research labs— RCA [Radio Corporation of America], Sperry and possibly GE [General Electric] at Schenectady. I have been asked specifically to spend several days in Canada. By that time we ought to have given the US authority time to digest our information and I expect we shall be faced with requests for arrangements to manufacture. This is to be dealt with by the BPC [British Purchasing Corporation] but they will probably advise. Also by then we hope to have released a number of items on which we have asked for details. So I reckon it will take till 19 October to clear up everything.

Amongst additional items of positive use which we have got are:
  (1) a simple oxygen producer for use in enclosed spaces and possibly for the gas mask of the future.
  (2) naval predictors and fire control.
  (3) bomb sights.

All this has taken, and will take, more time than was originally proposed. I have asked Tizard to see you and find out how the work goes at home and whether I may stay. I am extremely anxious to know how things are going—we read so much in the US papers and yet know so little[12]

On 20 October he arrived in Ottawa, accompanied by the two secretaries on the mission, Miss Geary and Miss King. His intermediary with the Canadians was C J Mackenzie, acting President of the National Research Council of Canada, who had been Dean of the School of Engineering at Saskatchewan University and who was well experienced in large civil engineering projects. His first impression of Cockcroft had been unfavourable; the latter had listened in silence as Mackenzie told him of what the Canadians could do to help, and was discouraged by Cockcroft's apparent lack of response. The next day, Cockcroft's manner had entirely changed. He was full of suggestions and ready to make plans[13]. The two were to work together, and four years later Mackenzie warmly approved Cockcroft's appointment as head of the Canadian atomic energy project. Cockcroft remained in Canada until the end of the month, visiting civil and defence laboratories and institutions for training scientists. He enjoyed being in Canada and wrote home:

I can see clearly how much more we might have got made here if some of us had come out early and got things going. They are extremely able and willing to help.

He had to return to Washington for further discussions on radar equipment. Tizard, after returning to England, had been full of praise for the way Cockcroft had impressed American service officers, and recommended that he should stay in Washington to maintain liaison. But Gough was adamant that he should return as the work at Christchurch 'had suffered in his absence and it would be difficult to release him again'. In any case he was exhausted after endless meetings and journeys. As he wrote on 13 November:

> we have done our set job—to get the US moving—and now Fowler and Bowen and Wallace [the Army officer accompanying the mission] can stay to mind it for a while.

He was gratified to learn after visiting Dr Loomis's laboratory that American firms had

> pushed ahead at a surprising speed and delivery of a large amount of gear for the first five experimental 10 cm airborne sets is expected by 23 November[14].

The re-election of Roosevelt had helped to increase sympathy for Britain, as had the beginning of the night bombing of British cities. 'We all felt terribly sad about Coventry and are thirsting for the time when our labours will stop all that.' After a party held in honour of the mission, he wrote: 'We have had the satisfaction of seeing a lot of my friends brought into defence, Ken [Bainbridge], Lawrence, Beams and many others.' For that reason it was essential that the exchange of information should not cease after the mission had returned home. He continued: 'this side of the Atlantic is going to be all-important in a year's time and we shall need to keep in closest touch.' Both he and the anglophile Carroll Wilson agreed that permanent offices for scientific liaison should be organised in London and Washington. It was through Cockcroft that the British Central Scientific Office was set up in Washington in February 1941 under the physicist, Charles Darwin, with Dr W L Webster, ex-Cavendish/Mond Laboratory, who had been working under Cockcroft in the Ministry of Supply, as Secretary. An American office under J B Conant was shortly afterwards established in London. Scientific liaison between the two countries has continued to this day.

Cockcroft spent the remaining three weeks of his stay in further consultations and visits to proving grounds, and a final visit to Canada. A meeting of what proved to be of far greater significance, took place at the National Bureau of Standards in Washington, when Cockcroft told the President's Advisory Committee on Uranium, the Briggs Committee, what kind of nuclear research was being done in England. Although nuclear research was, for the time being, less urgent than radar, it might have the greater significance for the future, and he felt there was the need to impress on the Americans the necessity of continuing their work in this field. On 14 November he visited Columbia University, New York, where Enrico Fermi, whom he had last met in Bologna in 1937, was investigating the possibility of producing a chain reaction using slow neutrons, moderating the neutron velocity by passing the beam through carbon. At the same time he met Louis Rapkine, leader of the scientists who had left France for America, and discussed how they might be integrated into the war effort. After a quiet weekend with his distant relative, Mary Cockcroft, now aged 91, at her country home in Connecticut, he went on to Ottawa. There he met George Laurence, an ex-Cavendish man engaged on nuclear research, similar to Fermi's, at the National Research Laboratory and was later responsible for Laurence receiving financial support from Imperial Chemical Industries [ICI] for his work. Before returning to the States he arranged for the Canadians to design and build their own shortwave fire-control radar set.

The reason for another return to Washington was the belated arrival from Britain of a Bofors anti-aircraft and a six-pounder anti-tank gun. He watched them being demonstrated with a party of American officers, who were impressed with the anti-aircraft gun's accuracy. It was later to be manufactured in the USA in large numbers together with the Kerrison predictor. He was due to sail from New York on 1 December, and R H Fowler and Bowen were present to see him board the *SS Excalibur* 'in a semi-miraculous way' just before she sailed, as he had been wrongly informed of the time of departure. He enjoyed a few days basking in the sun in Bermuda, before crossing the Atlantic. He arrived in Lisbon on 11 December, flew to England and reported to the Ministry of Supply in London, where he was briefed on the recent heavy night air raids. He spent the weekend of 22 December 1940 in Cambridge discussing nuclear research at the Cavendish and passing on information about similar work in the States, and then left for Todmorden to spend Christmas with his family.

CHAPTER NINE

A PERIOD OF FRUSTRATION

Some weeks after Cockcroft's return from North America, there was a reorganisation of the Ministry of Supply's arrangements for the control of the scientists at Christchurch, making it possible for Gough and his staff to have a greater share in the shaping of policy for future equipment. Early in 1941 Cockcroft was appointed Chief Superintendent of the Air Defence Research and Development Establishment (ADRDE) as Christchurch was now re-named, though still under the Ministry of Supply. Colonel Evans became exclusively responsible for research and development, leaving Cockcroft to be what was termed 'scientific overlord'. This meant, in practice, that he was responsible for the scientific work of the Establishment, at the same time allowing him 'to do as little office work as possible and get around'—an arrangment which always appealed to him.

While the Ministry of Supply was better organised to deal with research and development, there was no corresponding improvement in the War Office to assess and pass on the requirements of the Army until the belated appointment of Charles Darwin in 1942 as Scientific Adviser to the Army Council, and the formation of a Weapons Development Committee. Thus, during much of the period of Cockcroft's appointment, the Ministry of Supply had to deal with staff officers who, however willing, lacked scientific knowledge or appreciation, unlike their more technically-minded counterparts at the Admiralty and Air Ministry. One example of their ignorance was given by R V Jones, then in charge of Air Ministry Scientific Intelligence; he recalled being asked by one of the War Office radar staff officers for a cyclotron (not appreciating that, even if available, it would weigh several tons) to be sent to the War Office and put on his desk!

Cockcroft, luckily, was excluded from much of the decision-making which fell upon Edward Paris, formerly Gough's deputy and now Controller General of Physical Research and Signals Development in the Ministry of Supply. But Cockcroft did have to deal with the commercial firms executing orders for equipment and for ensuring that the highly specialised work was kept to schedule. Although at Cambridge he had taken advantage of his contacts with Metro–Vick, in general his academic career had not fitted him for negotiating with industry, nor for the cut and thrust at the committee meetings of the Advisory Council for Scientific Research and Technical

104

Development. The actual running of the Establishment was something else. Here he was on more familiar ground with his experience of directing the Mond Laboratory. He assumed his duties on 29 March 1941, installing himself at Bure Homage 'in some nice big rooms with a colonnade looking south and which was being wasted on mail clerks and Registry'. Sir Geoffrey Burton, the Director General at the Ministry of Supply responsible for the reorganisation, later told Cockcroft that he had brought on ADRDE 'an almost miraculous change in a matter of weeks'[1].

Previously there had been some inter-Ministry competition for Cockcroft, who had greatly enhanced his reputation as a scientific coordinator during his American trip. Beaverbrook wanted him to fill an unspecified appointment at the Ministry of Aircraft Production, and Hankey, chairman of the Cabinet Scientific Advisory Committee, asked him to form an operational research section at Headquarters Coastal Command to provide scientific advice in the U-boat war. Cockcroft admitted to Elizabeth that it would be

> rather fun to be King of the submarine war—better than being King of ADRDE, but it would require much diplomacy—much more diplomacy than science.

The Ministry of Supply was determined to keep Cockcroft, and Hankey told him that 'I ought not to settle down for too long a job but be prepared to be directed to wherever the need was greatest'. Blackett was chosen for Coastal Command and Cockcroft, in the event, was to direct the Army radar establishment until the spring of 1944.

The role of ADRDE continued to be the development of equipment for controlling anti-aircraft guns and searchlights and acoustical equipment for artillery ranging; later the research and development of radio-operated proximity fuses was included. Small groups worked on each of these topics, usually led by a scientist of Cockcroft's choice and who, once appointed, was left to get on with the job. H W Forshaw, R G Friend and Dunworth, for example, were in the fire control team. Another key officer was Captain G W Raby, in peacetime Assistant General Manager of the English Electric Company and a Territorial Army officer who was in charge of Development and Works and constructed the prototype radar sets in the Establishment workshops to Cockcroft's requirements. During the blitz, Lord Cherwell, as Lindemann had now become, used to insist that new equipment be ready by the 'next moon phase'—usually a quite unrealistic demand.

In the early months of 1941, when not visiting gun and searchlight sites around the big cities, Cockcroft stayed at the Blacketts' flat in Westminster. Bombs held no fear for him, as might be expected of one who had served on the Western Front. He was constantly in demand by Churchill. It was necessary for their meetings to take place without the knowledge of Cherwell, who did not approve of the Prime Minister seeking advice from another scientist. He used to accompany Churchill on his visits to blitzed cities. After going through Manchester he wrote to Bainbridge:

> the damage is more concentrated in the centre of the city—as it has been in Sheffield and Coventry. But even so we were able to travel through the city on Boxing Day evening and to take a train with sleeper out punctually on time.

Figure 11 Cockcroft, on leaving ADRDE for Chalk River, with members of his staff, Malvern, 12 July 1944. Back row from left to right: Mr Parker, J A Henley, J V Dunworth, G C Rowe, H K Reed, J Ashmead, Capt. Gibson, R S H Boulding, E C Slow. Front row from left to right: R G Friend, Capt. T G Hodgkinson, C W Oatley, Prof. J D Cockcroft, Col. C H S Evans, E S Shire, E W Chivers. (Courtesy: Churchill College, Cambridge)

Travelling by day is quite normal, but if one moves over into night, delays of one or two hours are quite common. The best thing is to take a sleeper for night journeys. I had a near bomb my first night in London [after returning from the USA] and it blew out all the windows of our offices. But they tacked muslin over and we were not seriously inconvenienced. Before that our previous offices had been hit but with no casualties save to files. In general, life in Government offices is perfectly normal. This is an unduly pleasant picture of life, for in the big cities, night raids have obviously been pretty bad. But I think we shall survive these to hurry up with everything we want and will be ready for them.[2]

After a heavy raid on the East End of London, he wrote to Elizabeth:

I admire the pluck of those who stay near to the river in ramshackle houses which are blown down by the score by nearby bombs. A good thing if the whole area was rebuilt. But it means a lot of casualties, I fear.

Cockcroft had two objectives at this time, firstly to improve the operation of existing radar equipment, and secondly, to improve the quality of the radar sets by introducing shorter wavelengths which resulted in higher accuracy.

The training of radar operators was taken on by J A Ratcliffe, who had won a reputation at the Cavendish for being a lucid and stimulating lecturer; he was seconded from the Air Ministry Research Establishment to form the Anti-Aircraft Command Radio School at Petersham on the edge of Richmond Park. Due to the lack of physicists, many biologists and schoolmasters who had the necessary scientific background were indoctrinated in the principles of radar during a short course and were then sent to the gun sites to supervise the handling of the somewhat temperamental equipment[3].

Cockcroft took a close interest in the School and used to pay regular visits on Saturday mornings with General Pile, Commander-in-Chief of Anti-Aircraft Command. Other regular visitors were Blackett, who had formed a small operational research group to work for Pile, and Nevill Mott, who applied his theoretical knowledge of physics to increasing the accuracy of searchlights. On Cockcroft's first visit he found Ratcliffe 'in his element' supervising 60 pupils who had 'settled in the Parish Hall very comfortably'; later moving into a large Victorian vicarage and a collection of Nissen huts. In time, the Saturday meetings grew into colloquia, ending up with lunch at the Dysart Arms.

Pile was another senior officer who formed an admiration for Cockcroft, and when the war was over sent him a copy of his Despatch dedicated to

The greatest and most helpful of all scientists[4].

Like Air Marshal Joubert, he treated Cockcroft as an unofficial adviser after Blackett went to Coastal Command, inviting him to conferences at Stanmore, an action which did not meet with the approval of the Ministry of Supply. Cockcroft, for his part, thought Pile was 'a very nice quick-witted Irishman. I wish all our generals were equally intelligent.'

On Sundays, having spent the night at the Star and Garter Hotel on Richmond Hill, Cockcroft would drive to Swanage where the Air Ministry Research Establishment, now called the Telecommunications Research Establishment (TRE), under A P Rowe, was located. Cockcroft used to take part in Rowe's celebrated 'Sunday Soviets' at which senior officers and civil service officials, scientists and aircrew straight from operations, could discuss the shortcomings of equipment in a free-for-all atmosphere. Joubert, who had a house nearby, was often there, and the more Cockcroft saw of him, the more he found that he was 'the most approachable of senior officers'.

It was a pity that Cockcroft never adopted the 'Sunday Soviet' for his own Establishment. One reason was, as already described, that not enough senior Army officers were conversant with technical problems, while Cockcroft himself preferred other methods of persuasion, usually demonstrations. This method had its value, particularly when Cockcroft was in the States, but it tended to raise expectations of the early arrival of the equipment on trial. The path from prototypes to production model was a hard one and full of snags.

At least he persuaded the War Office of the value of operational research. In 1941 he reinforced Ratcliffe's school with a small group of scientists from Christchurch to work on Army operational research problems. When Ratcliffe returned to TRE in June 1941 his place was taken by Cockcroft's old Cavendish friend, Basil Schonland, the South African, who had recently established a coastal radar chain for the South African Army. By January 1943, Schonland's group had been expanded and was called the Army Operational Research Group†, under control of the Scientific Adviser to the Army Council, then C D Ellis. It covered tank warfare, army/air cooperation and airborne operations.

Cockcroft summed up its achievements to date in a lecture given to staff at the Ministry of Supply. He explained that there were two aspects of operational research:

(1)   the training of personnel to operate fairly sophisticated equipment;

(2)   mathematical analysis of operations by which it was possible to assess, for example, the rate of aircraft destroyed to the number of shells fired. Finally, he said how important it was for the scientists to give the impression of wanting to help rather than merely to find fault.[5]

He had a more difficult task to introduce a shortwave fire-control set for the anti-aircraft guns. The introduction of a shortwave airborne radar set made it easier to shoot down enemy aircraft in the air. At the same time, the inability of Bomber Command to locate and bomb targets in Germany accurately had led to an intensive effort to improve navigational and bombing aids. Similarly, in the war at sea, shortwave radar was essential for detecting U-boats both from the air and from the sea. The requirements of the Army, therefore, were inevitably placed on a much lower priority than those of the RAF and Royal Navy.

However, War Office policy was that development of a shortwave radar set, using the magnetron, called Gun Laying Mark III (GL III) should continue. The prototype of this set was first tested in June 1941, but slow progress was made because of the need for modification for overseas service. A further refinement was the beginning of the development of an automatic following

---

†On Cockcroft's suggestion. The War Office wanted to call it Army Operational Experimental Group.

device in 1942 which, after picking up a target, could follow it without human assistance, thereby eliminating crew fatigue and increasing speed and accuracy. Again, development suffered because of lack of clearcut policy from the War Office.

The Japanese attack on Pearl Harbour in December 1941, bringing America into the war, naturally increased the collaboration that already existed between British and Americans, as well as stimulating development of equipment in the States. Regarding the latter, since October 1940 an extremely accurate shortwave radar set able to track a target automatically for anti-aircraft guns had been developed for the US Army and a prototype was in operation by February 1942. It was called SCR 584. When Dunworth visited the States in September 1942 he saw a set in action, and reported home that it was far in advance of current British and Canadian fire-control sets and advised Cockcroft that the GL III set should be abandoned in favour of the SCR 584[6]. Such a proposal was anathema to the War Office, and development both of the GL III set and the automatic following device continued at a slow rate of progress. By May 1943, only 33 handmade pre-production GL III sets had left British Thomson – Houston's factory at Rugby[7] and that firm refused to accept a further order from the War Office of 30 automatic following sets on the grounds that it was too small to occupy their work force†[8].

In the summer of 1943 Cherwell challenged a paper by Cockcroft and Schonland which claimed the superiority of the GL III over the earlier GL II set. He produced statistics to prove that radar-controlled anti-aircraft guns were inferior to radar-equipped fighters in shooting down enemy bombers. He supported his argument by drawing attention to the more urgent claims of the Air Force and the Navy and to the limited labour force available to produce magnetrons. In August 1943, the Prime Minister, doubtless at Cherwell's insistence, ordered production of GL IIIs to cease, and that apart from the sets already in the pipeline, the Army's shortwave requirements should be met by Canadian production[9].

Faced with this decision, Cockcroft appreciated that the solution would be to try and obtain SCR 584s on Lend-Lease, as it was the only Allied fire-control set incorporating automatic following. The War Office, meanwhile, although aware of the option of ordering American equipment, had been unable to make up its mind. Cockcroft therefore decided in October 1943 on his own initiative[10], to obtain a set on lend-lease, and without obtaining War Office permission he arranged for a firing trial of the SCR 584 to be carried out on the Isle of Sheppey range that month. He found the set to be much more efficient than GL III; it could be operated with the British BTL electrical predictor, and an ATS crew, after a few hours training, could handle it. He recommended that the set should supplement existing equipment for the air defence of Great Britain[11]. On hearing this, the Director of Artillery in the Ministry of Supply, Major General W J Eldridge, was, in Cockcroft's words, 'very angry' and reprimanded him for his over-hasty action[12].

---

†They agreed, however, in September 1943, to develop and manufacture 50 sets, but there was no likelihood of early completion. A few sets were completed by the end of that year for directing searchlights.

By about the beginning of October 1943 Cockcroft had access to intelligence reports revealing the possibility of an attack on London by pilotless aircraft (flying bombs)†. They would present an almost ideal anti-aircraft gun target as they would fly at constant speed and in a straight line. Clearly, in this case the SCR 584s would be invaluable.

When, as will be described, Cockcroft went to the States in November 1943, he discussed with Vannevar Bush measures for defeating pilotless aircraft and the possibility of supplying the British with American shortwave radar which might be used with British predictors. Accuracy could be further increased by adapting American-manufactured proximity fuses to British shells. Cockcroft immediately cabled a recommendation for the War Office to ask for American sets[13] and followed this up on his return to England, persuading General Pile and Duncan Sandys, then Parliamentary Secretary to the Ministry of Supply and in charge of countermeasures against the 'V' weapons, to put pressure on the War Office. On 1 January 1944, General Sir Ronald Weeks, Deputy Chief of Imperial Staff, sent an urgent request for 134 SCR 584s to Washington[14].

Cockcroft's action was invaluable, as it turned out. After the start of the flying bomb battle, it was found that the SCR 584 with the BTL predictor was the 'only fire-control [even approaching] the desired performance against the [flying bombs] especially in foggy weather'. On 12 July 1944 an officer from headquarters Anti-Aircraft Command was flown to the States, taking with him a shot-down, but intact, flying bomb. After an interview with General Marshall, the American Army Chief of Staff, he succeeded in obtaining another 165 SCR 584s which were delivered in time to defend Antwerp in the autumn of 1944[15].

The success of the SCR 584 was inseparable from the proximity fuses, likewise supplied by the Americans to the British Army. In September 1940, American research and development under the direction of Cockcroft's old friend, M A Tuve, had gone rapidly ahead, and by mid-1942 the Americans were in a position to go into mass production.

Mistakenly, as time would show, the Director of Naval Ordnance and his colleagues decided not to rely on American production of proximity fuses, but insisted that Cockcroft's Establishment should duplicate development and British firms, like Electrical and Musical Industries (EMI), should manufacture fuses which would be used in naval shells for the defence of ships against dive-bombers and torpedo-carrying aircraft[16]. (The Admiralty Signal Establishment had neither staff nor facilities to undertake research and development.) In February 1942 work on fuses at the Projectile Development Establishment under Alwyn Crowe was transferred to Christchurch, and the proximity fuse group was put under C D Ellis, who soon discovered that as scarcely any of the features of the Projectile Development Establishment fuse were satisfactory design work would have to begin virtually from scratch[17].

In any case, the difficulties of designing suitable valves and batteries contained in a tiny instrument no bigger than a matchbox and subjected to high

†R V Jones in chapters 38 – 39 of *Most Secret War* gives a graphic acount of this discovery.

acceleration in a gun barrel were immense. Added to this was the lack of technical staff which, as Cockcroft recalled 'could be counted in twos and threes'[18]. The move of ADRDE, soon to be described, almost immediately to Malvern, finding suitable firing sites, and the time-consuming nature of the trials, all contributed to development being prolonged, not over months but over years. Ellis himself was transferred to the War Office to succeed Darwin as Scientific Adviser, and the work at Malvern lost impetus.

At last, in July 1943, after the chemist Dr H W Melville had arrived from Porton to take charge of the proximity fuse group, it seemed that fresh progress would be made. It was by then clear that production in Britain could not begin for at least another two years. At this point, the War Office staff, planning operations on the Continent, made a demand for proximity fuses to be used by field artillery[19].

When Cockcroft was in Washington in November 1943, he discussed with Tuve the possibility of adapting the American fuse to British shells to meet the flying bomb threat. Arrangements for adapting American fuses for British use were made by Wilfred Mann, a physicist on Gough's staff while temporarily attached to the scientific liaison office in Washington. When Cockcroft returned to England, the War Office was, he recalled, unresponsive and he had to approach General Pile who himself put the matter before the Chief of the Imperial General Staff, Sir Alan Brooke†[20]. This had the effect of adding to the demand for SCR 584s, a request for 150 000 proximity fuses (later increased to 640 000) for the British 3.7 inch AA guns. This reached Washington on 16 January 1944 in the nick of time[21]. A supreme effort was needed to convert fuses to fit British shells by May 1944, they had to be filled with a special explosive called RDX in Canada, but they were available to destroy 97 per cent of the flying bombs in late August/early September 1944, when it had been decided to move the AA guns nearer the coast. After the war, Cockcroft acknowledged the debt to the Americans when he wrote:

> Tuve undertook to develop fuses for the British 3.7 inch AA shell. The undertaking was faithfully carried out[22].

He, too, had played a not inconsiderable part. The inability to produce a British fuse in time was an acute disappointment to him, and led him to campaign after the war for more scientists to enter industrial research which, in his opinion, had so often failed to carry through original inventions.

Cockcroft's family had moved to Christchurch in June 1941, living in Regnell Cottage in Christchurch Bay Road. On clear days they had a fine view of the Isle of Wight, and they took advantage of the nearby beach to bathe in the sea. In January 1942 there was much joy when a long-awaited son, Christopher, was born.

But Cockcroft's absences from home were frequent. He used to go to Worth Matravers, not far down the coast, where TRE was experimenting with short-wave radar and which, Cockcroft remarked, 'included a great collection of talent, the intensity of argument exceeds anything that ever happened in the Cavendish'. Dover, then very much in the front line, was frequently visited

†Created Viscount Alanbrooke in 1945.

for demonstrations with shortwave sets able to detect enemy shipping and E-boats far out to sea. Much of this work was in charge of the 'quite indispensable' Kempton, who before the war, as already mentioned, had been a leading member of the Cavendish. A more powerful longrange ship detection set was installed on the Downs above Ventnor on the Isle of Wight. It was here in August 1942 that Cockcroft watched the passage of the ill-fated Dieppe expedition across the Channel. When Ronald Clark was gathering material for a short biography of Cockcroft, he asked him what his emotions were on seeing the armada go into action. Cockcroft could find no appropriate words, merely contenting himself with the remark that the equipment had come up to expectation. Another very accurate set was later used for the Normandy landings to record the numbers and dispositions of returning convoys, and Cockcroft recorded with satisfaction that this saved '40 per cent in turn-round time'[23].

Security on the coast had always been a problem for the scientists working in the open with their highly secret equipment. After the day's work was over, they used to dismantle it and put it under cover with an armed guard. The capture of a German early-warning set at Bruneval on 27 February 1942 led Churchill to be concerned for the safety of the two radar establishments on the south coast, and in May 1942 Cockcroft was instructed to move to Malvern whither TRE had already gone. He left behind Raby's Radio Production Unit which made small items of equipment and which continued to provide a valuable service, both for ADRDE and for the Signals Research and Development Establishment which occupied the vacated quarters at Christchurch and which, for a brief spell, was under Cockcroft's direction.

Malvern, noted in peacetime for its drama festivals and private schools, was a quiet Edwardian spa lying under the steep escarpment of the Malvern Hills. Rowe had installed TRE in the spacious buildings and grounds of Malvern College. Cockcroft found accommodation for his staff in a 'fine building' called Pale Manor Farm, a quarter of which was turned into living quarters, and laboratories were improvised in the huts which had recently housed an RAF officers training unit.

Rivalry between the two establishments (even extending to the wives of the respective staffs!) was inevitable. TRE, observed Cockcroft with some relish,

> got into terrible difficulties over billeting, and shelter billets only are now offered. So a state of revolt prevails!

He spent some time ensuring that his own staff were properly housed and that the canteen provided an efficient service. Elizabeth and the children were found a house with 'a well stocked garden' (useful in those days of rationing) close to the Worcester road.

His establishment seems to have been unfairly discriminated against by the local population. TRE was called 'priority camp' and ADRDE was known as 'Conchie Camp' because it was believed to have been hurriedly evacuated from bombing raids on the south coast. Some of Cockcroft's staff complained of being charged excessively high rents by local landlords.

Both Cockcroft and his staff were feeling the strain at this period of the war. He felt frustrated by the lack of progress being made by the Army shortwave equipment. So preoccupied did he become that Hankey and A V Hill, then a member of the Cabinet Scientific Advisory Committee, were concerned lest his scientific work should suffer. Hill wrote to Sir Andrew Duncan, Minister of Supply, warning him that

> a fine tool [like Cockcroft] ought not to be used improperly on work for which it is not suited, otherwise it will get blunted and [his] proper work will not get done.

At the same time Hill urged Cockcroft that he should not be too diffident

> because you would have unlimited support if you were to take a strong line in getting things put right, as you would like them[25].

His staff became restless at the long-drawn-out process of development which had induced a feeling of lack of urgency, especially as they were rarely told how their equipment had performed in the field. Possibly greater supervision of the groups by Cockcroft and the institution of 'Sunday Soviets' might have helped. Furthermore, the change for the better in the Allied fortunes made it unlikely that some of the anti-aircraft gun equipment under development would ever be used.

Some of this dissatisfaction was vented in a confidential report which Cockcroft asked J Ashmead to prepare; he had been one of the original Cavendish Lab team and was then in charge of the group dealing with radio research. It was entitled *A Study in Brown*, but was qualified by Ashmead who noted that it contained 'what people believe their grievances to be, not what they really are'[26]. The views expressed were probably those of only a minority. Whether or not Cockcroft took any action on the report before handing over to C W Oatley on leaving for Canada, is unknown. In February 1944 Black, who had been posted to Washington, informed Cockcroft about what was happening at Malvern

> Oatley is doing a good job...though they seem to be back on the double-rule principle† once more with Evans running the shops, drawing office, etc,

and there were complaints about the shortage of staff[27].

Not long after the move to Malvern, preparations by the Home Forces for a Continental campaign led the Establishment into new fields of research. Early in 1943 Cockcroft wrote: 'We now have contacts with Home Forces, airborne troops and tanks which may well grow rapidly'. One project was designed to help the gunners to improve their accuracy by observation of shell bursts—an adaptation of the shortwave equipment used at Dover.

> This [wrote Cockcroft] at once opened the prospect of directing accurate shooting on to the enemy columns at night and of ranging on to intercepted targets at night[28].

Like other schemes, it did not come to fruition before the end of the war. Other teams developed mobile early warning sets against an attack when troops were on the move. They were of limited value as they were unable

---

†Cockcroft was not replaced by another Chief Superintendent.

accurately to estimate height. One of Cockcroft's last actions before leaving the Establishment was to order a rangefinder for the Bofors gun. Some of these were available for use against the flying bomb.

Early in 1943 there were some high level discussions on whether or not to send a scientific mission to the USSR 'to promote the interchange of scientific and technical information directly connected with the war'. Cockcroft was one of those in favour as he had followed events on the Eastern Front from the start of the German attack, and when the Battle for Moscow began in October 1941 had sent on his own initiative the following message via the Russian Embassy in London:

> Greetings to Russian scientists and especially to Kapitza and my other friends in Russia who have worked with us in the past. Since the war began British scientists have devoted their entire energies to defeating the Nazi menace. We have for a year now been powerfully reinforced by the scientists of North America. With the further help of our Russian friends we will demonstrate that world science mobilised with a single objective can be one of the decisive factors in defeating the Hitler objective of a Nazi-controlled world slave state[29].

While the possibility of a mission was under consideration he sent a telegram to Kapitza on the occasion of the tenth anniversary of the opening of the Mond Laboratory. On 9 February 1943 he received the following reply from Kapitza:

> Very touched by your greetings 10th anniversary our Laboratory. Hope you are well and working hard for our common effort. Peter Kapitza[30].

On 13 July 1943 Cockcroft was informed that the Russian mission had been indefinitely postponed.

He had, of course, ever since his return from the States in December 1940 done what he could to promote the exchange of information with the Americans, for indeed it was of great importance for the Establishment's own work. The arrival of an American liaison team in England under J B Conant in early 1941 has already been noted. Cockcroft took them on inspections of work at Petersham and Dover. Bainbridge, then working on shortwave radar, was the next to arrive, and exchanged notes with W B Lewis at TRE, whom he knew from his Cavendish days.

Anglo–American scientific liaison followed a rather uneven course. Before their entry into the war, it was not always easy for the American scientists to get things moving in their own country. At the same time, the British Central Scientific Office in Washington found itself being upstaged by more powerful Service organisations like the British Admiralty Delegation† and the British Army Staff. In August 1941 Cockcroft wrote to W L Webster in the Washington office:

> I think it is essential from our point of view to maintain independent and adequate scientific representation in North America. Thus at the moment we are suffering from inadequate information about Tuve's work [on the proximity fuse], and this would have been cleared up if we had more staff with you[31].

---

†The US Navy insisted on exchange of information about proximity fuses taking place through this body rather than the BCSO.

But there were too few scientists for the work that had to be done at home, far fewer for overseas.

After the Americans entered the war, his friend W L Webster correctly foresaw that

> We will feel the change from the days when the US had everything to learn from the UK to new days when the American contribution of ideas is as large as that of Great Britain.

Cockcroft agreed, but thought that Britain should do her 'utmost to guide policy for such as we have the better war experience'[32].

When an American mission led by A H Compton and Lee A DuBridge, Director of the Radiation Laboratory in Boston, the American equivalent of TRE, arrived in England in March 1943, they spent three days in Malvern talking to scientists of the two establishments, and then Cockcroft went with them to Dover to see demonstrations of the latest equipment. Later that year, Tuve and Edward Salant spent some weeks in England providing information on the development of proximity fuses.

In November 1943 a mission led by Robert Watson-Watt, Director of Communications at the Ministry of Aircraft Production, went to the USA to discuss mobile radar sets for the forthcoming campaign in north-west Europe, how duplication of Allied radar equipment could be avoided, and to decide on radio and radar requirements for the Far Eastern theatre. The mission included Cockcroft, C E Horton, an Admiralty scientist, W B Lewis from TRE, Osmund Solandt, a Canadian scientist attached to the Army Operational Research Group, Colonel H M Paterson, Deputy Director of Artillery in the Ministry of Supply, who had been a tower of strength to ADRDE, and other technical officers from the Navy and RAF.

They crossed the Atlantic at high speed in the *Queen Elizabeth* and, on arrival in Washington, were met by R H Fowler. On 22 November they began talks with K T Compton, I I Rabi and US Service officers at the offices of the Combined Chiefs of Staff. The talks were interspersed with visits to the Radio Research Laboratory at Harvard, commercial laboratories at Princeton and Schenectady, the Army Signals Corps Laboratory in New Jersey connected with radio, radar and proximity fuse development, followed by fire-control and airborne radar demonstrations at Fort Monroe and Eglin Field, Florida[33]. The British party enjoyed eating steaks and fresh fruit again. At Palm Beach Cockcroft found time to 'splash about in the sea in the warm, soft air' and caught a 'small tarpon—the big fellows were evidently all asleep'. The visit ended after 'four solid days of conferences' punctuated by dinners and receptions, on 11 December. Cockcroft was gratified

> to be remembered from my previous visit which really started all the cooperation machinery. Major General Coulton [an American] told us feelingly that if I said a thing was so, his officers had instructions to ask no more questions. I hope I can keep up the reputation!

He sent a detailed report to Duncan Sandys on his return, re-emphasising the importance of Army shortwave radar necessary for the Far Eastern campaigns, noting, firstly, that when he had been at Brooklyn Navy Yard he had seen a cruiser, recently returned from the Pacific with five Japanese warships to her credit, due to radar fire-control, and secondly, a training film convincing him that the future of fire-control lay in 'auto-follow with visual following playing a very secondary role[34].

More significant than all this for his own future were his talks with Chadwick, then in charge of the British nuclear physicists in North America engaged in helping to make the atomic bomb or working in the Anglo-Canadian laboratory in Montreal where, as will be explained in the next chapter, nuclear research work begun by George Laurence in 1940, had been expanded. Cockcroft had already been sounded on the possibility of taking charge of that laboratory, and Chadwick, Oliphant and other British physicists in Washington persuaded him to visit Montreal and assess the situation for himself. Cockcroft was very doubtful about the chances of being released from Malvern.

After completing his business in Washington, which also included the important discussions with Vannevar Bush and Tuve on the British Army using American radar and proximity fuses, he left for New York on 15 December to stay with Mary Cockcroft. Next day he rejoined the mission in Canada where they visited defence laboratories in Toronto and Ottawa. On 18 December, before leaving for England, he talked with British, Canadian and Free French scientists at the Montreal Laboratory, though it is unlikely that he gave any indication that he might return as Director. Early the next morning he waited in the extreme cold with the rest of his party for the arrival of a converted Liberator bomber of British Overseas Airways Corporation, reserved for VIPs, in which he flew to Prestwick, the first of his many transatlantic flights. He described the flight in a letter to Elizabeth.

We left Montreal on Sunday morning—the party consisting of six of the Mission and three others, the Liberator was one of their best with seats and hot air unfortunately blown in past my neck. We took off in great style and climbed to 7000 feet and flew in between two layers of cloud till we struck the coast. After that it was clear and we could look down on the sea until we struck Newfoundland. It was barren dull rock with fjords running inland. Save for a lighthouse there was no sign of man for hundreds of miles until we finally saw a lake with a paper mill—then there was a railway, then a lake and a large airport with ice and snow-covered fields and railways. We came down in a nice landing and were whisked from the cold into a huge crammed hangar full of large aircraft—Fortresses, Liberators, etc.... We were due to leave at 8 o'clock (Canadian time) or 11.30 GMT but one engine failed to start and after two attempts it was 3 AM GMT before we took off. We climbed to 22 000 feet putting on our oxygen masks at 15 000 feet. It was a nice starry night and we flew steadily over the clouds. Time passed very slowly and it became light at 9 AM—then we could look down to the sea and by 10 o'clock we saw the coast of N Ireland with great joy. We sped across Ireland and soon crossed the sea to Glasgow seeing Ailsa Crag down below. From there we went quickly through Customs, etc and I was lucky enough to get on to a US Army plane carrying about 30 troops to Hendon. So we flew down over the Isle of Man and Shropshire in 2½ hours and I thus got home by 11 PM. It was a great day.

Cockcroft took some time to be persuaded that he should go to Montreal. The invasion of Europe was imminent and he was still trying to speed up production of the British shortwave fire-control sets and proximity fuses. There was another offer. A V Hill, recently back from India, told him that he was wanted as a scientific adviser to the Commander-in-Chief, General Auchinleck. 'It is a very high-level appointment—salary £2000', wrote Cockcroft to his mother. With the end of the war in Europe in sight, there was the strong pull of Cambridge, and Chadwick was informed that

> Bragg will certainly do all he can, either to keep Cockcroft in this country or to ensure he is not taken away at the end of the war in Europe at the latest[35].

But there were far more urgent reasons for him going to Canada, not the least of which was the likelihood that American cooperation and provision of raw materials to the Montreal Laboratory would depend on him becoming Director there. In those circumstances he could hardly refuse. In mid-April the British Government agreed that he should leave for Canada at once, reorganise the staff, and return briefly to hand over ADRDE to C W Oatley. On 16 April he drove from London to Malvern, passing through the orchards 'all ablaze with plum and apple blossom'. Three days later he was packing his bags. In nine days' time he landed in Canada in an American Douglas transport plane to take up his appointment as Director of the Montreal Laboratory.

His direction of work on Army radar was acknowledged shortly after D Day by a CBE in the King's Birthday Honours List. L H Bedford, who had developed the first anti-aircraft gun control set and was now a director of A C Cossor, the radio company, wrote on 12 June to congratulate him.

> You must have had some years of extremely hard work at ADRDE, not only on the purely scientific side, but also amidst the difficulties of user, the Ministry and even the manufacturer, and it is very gratifying to see your contribution officially recognised[36].

Oatley wrote to say how much he had enjoyed working for him for the past three years, but reminded him that the Establishment was once again suffering from a 'complicated Headquarters structure', though he hoped to 'get things straight quite soon'. Cockcroft finally severed his connection with Army radar in mid-June 1944, after watching, with Oatley and Rowe, convoys putting out to sea from Portsmouth with reinforcements for the Normandy beachhead.

Cockcroft's own feelings about the Establishment's value was that it had not been possible to do useful work until the scientists had gained control from the military in 1941 and, secondly, that the projects which had proved to be the most useful had been those suggested by the Establishment and not by the War Office or the Ministry of Supply; he believed that a future Establishment should be able to

> devote at least 30 per cent of its time to projects thrown up internally and to fundamental longterm work [37].

He might have achieved more if his work had been given higher priority; he might have coped better had he been more familiar 'with the real world of industry', and he was perhaps less successful than Tizard, Cherwell or Zuckerman at convincing the Services of the value of science. Zuckerman recounted how Cockcroft and Schonland once enquired why he was the only working scientist who was 'admitted into the inner planning circles,... I had no answer'[38]. Cockcroft's relaxed method of direction did not always produce results, as in the case of the proximity fuses. In committee he seldom spoke up clearly or strongly; he would, instead, remain almost speechless and then throw in a comment, always wise and often extremely valuable, but not as effective as if it had been expressed in more strident terms earlier in the discussion.

At the same time, his work was valued by his immediate superiors and by his colleagues. In January 1943 when he volunteered to join the abortive technical mission for exchange of information with the Russians Gough told him

> my own feeling in view of your present responsibilities balanced against what we may expect to get from the Russians for this country, you can best serve the nation by remaining its driving force at home behind your most important and wide field of research and development[39].

His own staff held him in high regard. Jack Ratcliffe, replying to a letter from Cockcroft early in 1945, expressed the belief that he should have been Chief Superintendent both of ADRDE and the Signals Reseach and Development Establishment, to the benefit of the latter, assisted by two deputies. Ratcliffe continued:

> As you say, all our devices worked very well indeed toward the end of the V blitz and never have the gunners had their tails up as they did then. Even the SLCs [searchlight control sets] claimed quite a few at night[40].

In September 1944, Schonland, by then attached to Montgomery's 21st Army Group Headquarters as Scientific Adviser, wrote from Belgium:

> All your particular babies have played their part; though AA was not called upon to do much here, it certainly paid dividends with Tim (Pile) who finished up in a blaze of glory, well deserved. One of the later things you started down on the Plain [possibly sound ranging] has done extremely well too... I want to tell you how grateful I am for letting me do something over here and for all the support and constant help and friendliness you have shown (I except the matter of a chief clerk in 1941!). I shall leave for South Africa [to return to civilian life] with a greater admiration for you than I had before and that is saying a lot[41].

CHAPTER TEN

BEGINNINGS OF ATOMIC ENERGY IN ENGLAND AND CANADA

Cockcroft was one of the handful of British scientists who, in the spring of 1940, agreed that the Government should investigate the possibility of making a uranium bomb. The application of nuclear fission to military purposes naturally came within his province as Assistant Director of Scientific Research in the Ministry of Supply. However, even before the war, he had been associated with developments following upon the experiments of the German scientists Hahn and Strassmann, published in January 1939, to which reference has already been made.

It should here be noted that atoms of uranium having different atomic weights exist in Nature, the most abundant—99.3 per cent—having an atomic weight of 238 (on the scale of hydrogen having the atomic weight of unity†) and written U_{238}, whilst only 0.7 per cent of the atoms have a weight of 235. At a theoretical conference in America on 26 January 1939 Professor Bohr discussed the exciting discovery of fission and suggested on theoretical grounds that it was the lighter atom, U_{235} which, having absorbed a neutron, split into two parts, and at that same meeting Professor Fermi suggested that at the moment of fission some neutrons might be released; if so, then they in turn might be absorbed by neighbouring atoms and produce further fissions, and thus a chain reaction might be set in train; whether they would do so would depend on how many neutrons were released and how many were then lost by escape or by being captured by atoms without producing fission.

There was tremendous activity in several laboratories in a very short space of time. In Paris Joliot with his colleagues Halban and Kowarski discovered that neutrons *were* released at fission, reporting this in *Nature* on 18 March, and on 22 April they further reported in *Nature* that the number released per fission was estimated to be 3.5. At Imperial College G P Thomson (son of 'JJ') with two colleagues, Michiels and Parry, had done a similar experiment, and on 29 April reported results similar to the French. This large neutron yield greatly enhanced the chance of a chain reaction proceeding in a mass of metallic uranium or possibly in a mass of oxide as oxygen has almost no affinity for neutrons, so the possibility of gaining atomic energy from such a

---

†Strictly speaking, the scale of atomic weight is based on the oxygen atom having the atomic weight 16.000; on this scale the atomic weight of hydrogen is 1.008.

reaction and also the dread possibility that a super bomb might be made, was obvious. Thomson was alarmed. He immediately suggested to Tizard, his Rector at Imperial College and Chairman of the Air Defence Committee, that Britain should lay hands on all the refined uranium oxide available to prevent it from falling into German hands. Tizard passed this message on to Blackett, and on 19 April 1939 Cockcroft received an enquiry from Blackett asking whether an arrangement could be made with the Belgian company Union Minière du Haut Katanga, which possessed a virtual monopoly over stocks of uranium in the Belgian Congo, to prevent them falling into the hands of the Germans. Neither Blackett, Tizard nor Cockcroft were convinced that a bomb was practicable, but on 31 May Cockcroft informed Tizard that he heard the

> German military authorities [were] taking uranium explosion very seriously and [were] making arrangements to make an immediate trial with 100 kg of uranium[1].

Thomson obtained one ton of uranium oxide for his next experiment, which was to try to obtain a chain reaction in a large mass of it; he knew that neutrons having a modest velocity, that is to say, somewhat lower than they have when released in the fission process, were strongly absorbed by uranium and did not cause fission, so he placed blocks of paraffin wax between the small wooden boxes in which the oxide had been delivered, thus making a 'pile' (like Galvani's 'pile' familiar to all schoolboys learning about electricity). With this arrangement, neutrons released from atoms undergoing fission would have to pass through the wax before encountering more uranium atoms, and as they threaded their way through the wax they would lose velocity by colliding with atoms of hydrogen or carbon; slow neutrons now colliding with uranium atoms would cause fission and the chain reaction might start. No reaction was found, so he changed the experiment by substituting water for wax; still no reaction was found. He concluded that it was not going to be easy to produce a chain reaction; it might be possible if metallic uranium were used in place of the oxide, or if the light isotope U_{235} could be used instead of the naturally occurring mixture of isotopes. To separate the isotopes was considered to be 'impossible' at that time; the only separation of isotopes which had been achieved on any significant scale was the separation of heavy hydrogen (mass = 2) from ordinary hydrogen (mass = 1). So the spectre of a super bomb receded, and on 10 May he asked Cockcroft whether the subject should be discussed at the British Association meeting at Dundee in August. Cockcroft actually drew up a provisional list of speakers, including Bohr, Frisch and Lise Meitner from abroad, and P I Dee and N Feather from the Cavendish, but the proposal failed to take shape as war became imminent in the following months and scientists were reluctant to publish results.

Work similar to Thomson's was being done in Paris by Joliot and his colleagues; they too had recognised that the velocity of the neutron must be 'moderated' before it could encounter another atom of uranium. They decided that instead of using ordinary water as moderator they would use 'heavy water' because, whereas hydrogen has a significant affinity for neutrons, deuterium does not, and they were anxious to avoid any unnecessary loss of neutrons. They were experimenting when war broke out and by the end of 1939 had considered that a chain reaction might occur in a large amount of uranium distributed in a large quantity of heavy water. Joliot therefore persuaded the French Government to buy up the total stock of heavy water belonging to Norsk Hydro, then the only company selling small quantities of heavy water to laboratories all over the world. Luckily, its financial assets were largely controlled by the Banque de Paris et des Pays Bas. Jacques Allier who it will be recalled, had already met Cockcroft in London, was instructed by the French Ministry of Munitions to move the Norwegian supplies of heavy water to France, and he successfully completed his task a few weeks before the Germans invaded Norway.

Professor Rudolf Peierls, working with Oliphant in Birmingham, had also read that account in *Nature* and, following another lead from the French, worked out the minimum size, the 'critical size', of a mass of uranium which might, under suitable conditions, support a chain reaction. He continued this work, as the war started, with Professor O R Frisch who had just arrived in England and was welcomed in Birmingham. By the beginning of 1940 they had written an extremely important memorandum on the possibility of making a super bomb using the light isotope of uranium U_{235}, and they gave precise details about size, detonation, the separation of the uranium isotopes and the effects of radiation released in an atomic explosion. Oliphant sent this memorandum to Tizard, who gave it to Thomson, who in turn discussed it with Cockcroft, Chadwick and Oliphant, but whether it was discussed with Professor Lindemann is not known. This group, together with Thomson and his scientific assistant Phillip Moon, became a subcommittee of the Committee for the Scientific Study of Air Warfare, and were to hold their first meeting at the rooms of the Royal Society in April 1940. Peierls and Frisch could not be invited to attend as, at that time, they were foreign nationals and as such had to be excluded from Government secret committes. Professors Blackett, Ellis and W N Haworth, the chemist, became members in due course.

On 10 April, the day after the invasion of Norway, Lieutenant Jacques Allier 'blew in' to Cockcroft's office in the Ministry of Supply and told him of the successful mission to remove the heavy water to France. Cockcroft took him to the meeting of the uranium subcommittee that day, where he reported on the latest work with heavy water in Joliot's laboratory and learned with dismay that the British and American stocks of heavy water were virtually nil.

Shortly after the invasion of France, an intriguing piece of information reached Cockcroft on May 15. This was a telegram from Lise Meitner—who had just escaped from Denmark to Sweden—to Sir Owen Richardson, Nobel prize winner and head of the Physics Department of King's College, London. It read: 'Met Niels [Bohr] and Margarethe [his wife] recently but unhappy about recent events please inform Cockcroft and Maud Ray Kent: Meitner'. Cockcroft had, it has been seen, recently tried without success to establish Meitner in Cambridge, but the implications behind the three words 'Maud Ray Kent' puzzled both scientists and intelligence officers[2]. Their immediate conjecture was that it contained an oblique reference to German research on a new secret weapon. Cockcroft took the matter sufficiently seriously to devote half an hour dictating notes on the theory put forward by intelligence officers that it was an anagram referring to the seizure of radioactive materials by the Nazis, though he himself, presumably because of his interest in radar, inclined to the view that it referred to some form of ray. Support for the latter supposition came from the rumour that the enemy had employed a 'death ray' during their assault on the Maastricht forts. Cockcroft suggested that the investigations be extended to Stockholm, and proposed that the scientist and well known writer on mathematical and other subjects, Lancelot Hogben, who had escaped to Sweden, should act as an intermediary. Nothing seems to have come of this suggestion and no-one seems to have thought of going to visit Lise Meitner to find out exactly what she meant. After the war it transpired that Maud Ray had been governess to the Bohr children†. She was then living in Kent and would naturally be concerned to know the Bohrs were not in immediate danger.

In June of 1940 the Committee for the Scientific Study of Air Warfare was disbanded, and the uranium subcommittee was taken over by the newly formed Ministry of Aircraft Production, acquiring the name of MAP Uranium Development Committee, rather ineptly contracted to MAUD, chaired by Thomson and Cockcroft, its task being to discover how uranium development could contribute to the war effort. The main urgent problems were to gather more accurate information about the passage of neutrons through uranium, a subject on which Chadwick and his assistant Dr J Rotblat had been working even before the setting up of the uranium committee, and to consider the ways by which the isotopes of uranium might be best separated. For these tasks the help of the Clarendon Laboratory under Professor Simon's leadership, and the Cavendish Laboratory under Dr Feather, were invoked.

After the German breakthrough in May 1940 the French stock of heavy water in Joliot's laboratory was moved to Clermont-Ferrand, but as the advance continued Joliot decided on 16 June—none too soon—that Halban and Kowarski should continue their researches in England, taking their cans of heavy water with them. Joliot, for various reasons of his own, decided to remain in occupied France. Escorted by the Earl of Suffolk, the British Science Liaison Officer to the French Government, who habitually wore a shoulder holster to the disapproval of officials in the Ministry of Supply, the French scientists and their families sailed from Bordeaux with their precious cargo, the world's stock of 180 litres of heavy water. On 18 June the Prime Minister reported to Parliament in those memorable words that

> the Battle of France is over and the Battle of Britain is about to begin.... if we fail, then the whole world will sink into the abyss of a new Dark Age, made more sinister, and perhaps more protracted, *by the light of perverted science.*

Was he thinking of the fearful possibility that the Germans might get the atomic weapon first? Only a week or so earlier Lindemann had been advised

---

†Though Wilfrid Mann, a member of the MAUD Technical Committee in 1941, had met Maud Ray at the Bohr's home in 1932.

by Professor Simon and Peierls that the possibility of producing an atomic bomb was now considered to be very real.

That day, the French scientists landed in England and left for London. Halban noted in his diary that Gough gave them a lukewarm welcome when they arrived at Paddington Station the next morning; he shook hands with Suffolk, glanced in the direction of the French, remarking 'Oh, is that the lot?' and departed. It was while they were temporarily incarcerated in the Great Western Hotel that Cockcroft appeared and made them feel more at home: 'I understood', Halban recorded, 'that he was going to do something'[3]. The heavy water, meanwhile, was lodged in Windsor Castle under the care of the Librarian.

Cockcroft became responsible for establishing Halban and Kowarski at the Cavendish where they could continue their experiments seeking to produce the chain reaction with heavy water as the moderator. Halban, who had a weak heart, was provided with a flat within walking distance of the laboratory, but Cockcroft allowed the Kowarskis, who had a small child, to stay at 31 Sedley Taylor Road until they found a place of their own. They began work on 15 July 1940.

The Cavendish team working for the MAUD Committee was led by Norman Feather, a rather austere physicist with a reputation for formality, and experimental work was in the capable hands of Egon Bretscher, a physical chemist who had been on the staff of the Cavendish for some years. It was not long before the differences of temperament and background of Halban and Kowarski made it difficult for them to work together. Halban, who came from the Viennese professional class, was an autocratic and polished man of the world. Kowarski, in contrast, came from a middle class Russian family with a Christian–Jewish background and had suffered from an insecure childhood, his large and rather ungainly appearance belied sophisticated tastes and a thoughtful approach to his work. Halban was the self-appointed leader for the French scientists in England and arrogated to himself all matters dealing with policy, treating Kowarski as a subordinate. As Halban became more and more absorbed both in the political and patent aspects of the project, Kowarski became personally concerned with the experimental work, and, in the end, proved to be the better scientist of the two. Furthermore, he had a more easygoing temperament which made him more congenial than Halban to his colleagues.

Most of the scientists working for the MAUD Committee in the Cavendish Laboratory came to look towards Cockcroft when they were in trouble rather than go to Feather. Nicholas Kemmer, then a junior member of the team recruited from Imperial College, described how Cockcroft would make a fleeting visit to Cambridge,

> a short part of which would include a private session with Kowarski in which Kowarski did the talking and Cockcroft would pull out his little note book and use about one square inch of it to summarise what he had learned. There was one occasion when Kowarski and I agreed that *I* had a valid point to make to Cockcroft. The only time left available for that was the taxi ride from the Cavendish to the station. I made sure that all I had to say was said then; the note book came out—so the 'meeting' was satisfactory[4].

On another occasion Halban tried to have a row with Thomson and was 'on the point of throwing his hand in', when Cockcroft arrived in Cambridge to intervene.

Cockcroft left England in August 1940 with the Tizard Mission, as has already been described, and had been asked by the MAUD Committee to disclose all the nuclear research work to the American nuclear physicists like H C Urey, Ernest Lawrence and Enrico Fermi but, in general, had found them sceptical of an immediate military application, and he did not think they were tackling the problem as wholeheartedly as they might. It was therefore all the more important that scientific liaison should be maintained. It is rather amazing that the American account published immediately after the war on atomic energy, written by H D Smyth, never mentioned the extremely important memorandum by Peierls and Frisch: there is merely a statement that there was some interchange of information with the British beginning in 1940. In June of this year, two of Lawrence's colleagues in Berkeley, Edwin McMillan and Philip Abelson, published a paper revealing that while bombarding uranium with neutrons, they had observed the production of new elements heavier than uranium. The uranium was converted to an element of atomic weight 239 and was strongly radioactive, changing quickly into another element of similar atomic weight which was almost a stable element. This they named plutonium. In Liverpool, Chadwick and Rotblat decided on theoretical grounds that this element should be fissionable when bombarded by neutrons, but they could not make the element to put their ideas to the test[5]. Likewise in the Cavendish group, Feather and Bretscher came to the same conclusion, that such an element would be suitable to make an atomic bomb and that it would be easier to make this element and to separate it from the parent uranium by chemical extraction than to separate the uranium isotopes to isolate the U_{235}, so on his return from America Cockcroft cabled R H Fowler in Washington on 28 December 1940, urging Ernest Lawrence to study the fissile properties of plutonium which he would be able to make in the large Berkeley cyclotron; early in 1941 this was done, and Glenn Seaborg proved that plutonium was fissile when bombarded with fast or slow neutrons. Apparently this information was not passed on to the UK.

In July 1941, the MAUD Committee concluded in its report to the Ministry of Aircraft Production that both an atomic bomb and what was then called a 'boiler' were practicable. The Committee suggested that the 'boiler' project, in view of the load on the British war effort, should be transferred to North America. The report was sent to Lord Cherwell, who recommended to the Prime Minister that action be taken and that the future work should be under the responsibility of the Lord President of the Council, Sir John Anderson, formerly a scientist and now a member of the War Cabinet. The detailed implementation of the work now to be called 'Tube Alloys' was put under the control of Wallace Akers, Research Director of ICI, whose services had been lent to the Government, and he in turn reported to the Secretary of the DSIR, Professor E V Appleton.

As Cockcroft recalled, the MAUD Committee was 'somewhat abruptly dissolved'[6] on the formation of Tube Alloys, and for the next two years, although in touch with the Cavendish team, he was largely unaware of the great scientific and industrial project in the States covered by the code name Manhattan District in the Corps of Engineers set up on 18 June 1942 and headed from 17 September by Brigadier General Leslie Groves. The Corps created the huge establishment at Oak Ridge, Tennessee, where the isotopes of uranium, U_{235} and U_{238} were separated, the enormous reactors (previously called boilers) which were built in Hanford in the State of Washington where the element plutonium was made from uranium, and finally, the complex at Los Alamos, New Mexico, where the atomic bomb was designed. Cockcroft did not even hear, until several months after, about the first self-sustained chain reaction produced in Fermi's reactor in Chicago on 2 December 1942, and then only through 'unofficial channels'. Although almost the only available scientists and engineers capable of working on the British project had to come from industry, Cockcroft, in general, disapproved of the transfer of development to a Government Department headed by an ICI Director with an ICI secretary, believing, correctly in the event, that the Americans would suspect that the British were trying to steal a march on them in the development of industrial applications after the war.

On 2 September 1942, it was agreed that a team under Halban should be sent to Canada to build, in collaboration with the Canadians, a pilot plant for the production of plutonium in a reactor. Halban had visited the States earlier that year as a member of a mission led by Akers, and was responsible for selection of the team which was of a cosmopolitan nature. From the States came Pierre Auger, a physicist and brother-in-law to the distinguished Francis Perrin, Bertrand Goldschmidt, a radiochemist, both of whom had escaped from France and joined the Free French, George Placzek, a brilliant Czech theoretical physicist who became a close friend of Halban, who made him head of the Theoretical Physics Division, H Paneth, a Viennese radiochemist who was appointed head of the Chemistry Division, while from England came F R Jackson and R E Newell, both engineers from ICI. During 1943 they were joined by a contingent from the Cavendish team which had been working under Halban and included Jules Guèron, another French chemist who had escaped from France, Stephen Bauer, a Swiss physicist, Henry Seligman, an experimental physicist used to working on problems of physical chemistry, and Alan Nunn May, another physicist.

A space in the large recently built University of Montreal was converted into a laboratory. According to George Laurence, the leading member of the Canadian team, the project began 'in a mood of enthusiasm and expectation of a great scientific adventure'[7], and, indeed, during that year much information necessary for the design of a reactor and of chemical plants for the extraction of plutonium and uranium 233 produced in the reactor, was acquired. But the need for plutonium and thorium for the reactor made collaboration with the Americans essential.

As might have been expected, from his performance in Cambridge, Halban turned out to be the wrong choice as director of the laboratory. Since 1941, the Americans had suspected that he might be a security risk, while senior Canadian staff, like Laurence, would not accept him as their rightful chief. Halban ran the laboratory in an atmosphere of extreme secrecy and would not tell Mackenzie or other Canadians about decisions regarding the research programme. According to Laurence, he was 'impetuous and vacillating in decisions and unreasonable in his demands of the administrative staff in Ottawa and unfair in criticising them'[8]. Unnecessary squabbles over patent rights on future applications of nuclear energy were also preoccupying the staff. The only way out of the impasse was to remove Halban and appoint a director of the laboratory who would be acceptable both to the Canadians and to the Americans.

In August 1943, after Churchill and Roosevelt had signed the Quebec Agreement establishing collaboration on uranium development between British, Canadians and Americans, some British scientists headed by Chadwick and including Oliphant, Frisch, Peierls and other nuclear physicists and engineers had gone to the States to work on various aspects concerned with the making of the bomb. Chadwick also had an agreement with General Groves and Dr Mackenzie that the heavy water reactor of modest size on which the Montreal Laboratory had been concentrating should be built in Canada with American help, but it had been insisted that the scientist in charge must be British or Canadian. Cockcroft's first intimation that he might be needed in Canada came in October from Oliphant, who had returned briefly to arrange future work of his department at Birmingham. During several meetings with Cockcroft, at one of which Bohr was also present, he suggested that Cockcroft's international reputation and his ability to work with the Americans, made him an obvious choice for Montreal. Hearing that Cockcroft was shortly going to North America on a radar mission, he asked him to discuss the problem with Chadwick in Washington. On 24 October 1943 Cockcroft wrote to Chadwick:

> I told Bohr and Oliphant that I should personally like to work in that field. I would, however, like to be assured that the time scale was short enough to be of use in the war and to justify my leaving the work for the Army which is still pressing[9].

Cockcroft, as already described, met Chadwick in Washington in December, was taken to meet General Groves, and then went on to Montreal to review the work there and to tell Halban, probably confidentially, that Chadwick had asked him to take charge of the Laboratory though no official move had been made.

While the Ministry of Supply was making up its mind about allowing Cockcroft to go, and Cockcroft was still entertaining his own doubts, Halban was becoming desperate. Despite the provisional agreement with the Americans, he appreciated that the laboratory would receive neither information about the heavy water reactor being built at the Argonne Laboratory near Chicago nor the promised raw materials until Cockcroft took over. These uncertainties about the running of the laboratory naturally affected his staff. 'Morale', wrote Halban to Chadwick, 'is running low and temperaments are running high,[10]. He himself was tired and his weak heart was making him draw on his reserve strength.

On 13 April 1944 Chadwick got the final agreement of the Americans to support the Canadian programme and supply the heavy water, and a few days later Sir John Anderson formally asked Cockcroft to fly at once to Montreal to take charge of the laboratory[11]. On 25 April Placzek met him in pouring rain on Montreal Airport, and the next day Halban assembled the staff in the main lecture hall to introduce them to the new Director. In a somewhat fulsome speech he implied that Cockcroft and himself would be running the laboratory together. Cockcroft replied in his usual, slightly diffident manner that Halban was not quite correct in what he had just said, and that Halban would, in fact, henceforward be in charge of the Physics Division (conveniently just vacated by Auger)[12]. Halban left the laboratory later that year when, after the liberation of France, he had visited Joliot, well known as a communist, in Paris, thereby causing the Americans to suspect that he had been passing information to the Russians.

Cockcroft lost no time in reorganising the laboratory with the minimum of fuss. Following his practice begun at Christchurch, he appointed a deputy, E W R Steacie, a Canadian, thus allowing him time to travel around and meet other scientists. He persuaded Kowarski and the rest of the Cavendish team who had not gone to Los Alamos, to come to Montreal. He also decided to increase the number of Canadian professional staff to about 40, roughly equal to the number of scientists and engineers from Britain and the party of New Zealanders under Charles Watson-Munro. His only disappointment was that Rowe of TRE would not allow his old friend, Dee, to be transferred, on the grounds that he was still indispensable for work on radar[13].

Dr Kemmer was one of the latest draft. He was appointed Information Officer because of his experience in explaining fundamental principles of the work to newcomers. He later gave an illuminating insight on Cockcroft's methods of direction.

We had heard [wrote Kemmer] that one of the big grievances about the Halban regime was that by quite absurd 'security' rules of an *informal* kind all information exchange was blocked. All reports bore on top of the official 'Secret' stamp either the mark 'L' for 'Limited', or 'LL', or even 'LLL'. *All* were locked in a filing cabinet in Placzek's office and hardly any were released, even for brief consultation, partly because he was hard to track down most of the time. Evidently Cockcroft was aware of the problem. Anyhow, not only was I summoned to Montreal as Information Officer, but all my anticipated worries as to how to break down the secrecy barrier were unnecessary from the moment of my arrival. I was shown into my new office where, waiting on my desk, was a handwritten 'instruction' from the new Director *ordering* me to collect all classified reports, take charge of them and formulate proposals for their effective circulation. So, all I had to do was to walk into Placzek's office—he was away, but his secretary had the cabinet key—wave the (microscopic) document in front of her and walk away with the reports. This was the clearest proof of how well the 'little notebook' technique worked[14].

Having put in motion the reorganisation of the laboratory to his satisfaction, Cockcroft went to the States. On 4 May he visited A H Compton at the Metallurgical Laboratory in Chicago, and they agreed to exchange information on reactor physics and other problems concerning the building of a heavy water reactor. After talking with Chadwick in Washington, Cockcroft and Newell spent some time at Oak Ridge, Tennessee, looking at the graphite moderated reactor. The Americans agreed to provide uranium metal and heavy water, but refused to provide information about the chemical separation of plutonium. They were prepared, however, to provide Cockcroft with irradiated uranium slugs so that the Montreal Laboratory could work out its own chemical separation process.

Cockcroft's next task was to find a suitable site for an experimental plant containing reactors. He had discussed with A H Compton what were the principal requirements, and they had agreed that the site should be at least 100 miles from large towns and have available a good source of pure water for cooling the reactors. Accompanied by General Groves and Dr C J Mackenzie, he inspected three sites; the first two, Georgian Bay in the Toronto area and a site in the remote forests of the Laurentians north of the Ottawa River, were either unsuitable or too inaccessible. The third site was in the forest, 130 miles north-west of Ottawa on the south bank of the Upper Ottawa River at a point called Chalk River. It fulfilled all the requirements such as rail communications and a plentiful supply of pure water. A small lumber settlement called Deep River could be developed to accommodate the staff. On 19 August 1944 the Canadian Government approved Cockcroft's recommendation. It was decided that while the building was in progress, work should continue at Montreal, and that staff should move to Chalk River as and when accommodation became available. After one of his reconnaissances of the site, Cockcroft wrote enthusiastically to Elizabeth:

> It was very lovely up there and we have a beautiful place. I had a swim in company with eleven others. It was the best swim I've had for years. We'll have a large cottage up there.

Meanwhile, he set about establishing himself in Montreal. He had found a large house—709 Upper Roslyn—in the suburbs to accommodate the

Figure 12   Chalk River, Canada, showing the foundations for the laboratory, winter 1945. (Courtesy: Churchill College, Cambridge)

family. On 18 August, after some vicissitudes in trying to secure a sea passage, Elizabeth arrived in Montreal with the children and a nanny. While they settled in, he used to drive up steep Mount Royal to the Laboratory.

Here designs were being made for the plutonium producing reactor called NRX. It was soon appreciated that with limited technical resources in Canada, construction would take time. Cockcroft therefore agreed that a very simple reactor should be built as a stop-gap. He put Kowarski in charge of the design called Zero Energy Experimental Pile (ZEEP), the engineering work was to be undertaken by the New Zealanders, including A H Allen, G J Fergusson, K D George and W W Young. Cockcroft, who was already on good terms with General Groves, persuaded the latter to provide an additional five tons of heavy water to act as moderator. Incidentally, Cockcroft was most impressed by the great quantities of heavy water now available compared with the tiny amounts used in pre-war days. One day, after the war, he walked into a ground-floor laboratory to find it covered with heavy water which was laboriously being mopped up with cotton wool[15].

The Chemistry Division was greatly strengthened by the arrival of Robert Spence, a chemist from Leeds University, who had recently been helping the RAF on chemical warfare. He joined Goldschmidt to work on the chemical extraction of plutonium from irradiated uranium, and after Goldschmidt returned to France worked out the flow-sheets for the British chemical separation plant. Later, Spence became one of Cockcroft's right-hand men, ultimately being appointed a Director of Harwell.

Cockcroft was particularly concerned about the safety of his staff and the dangers of radiation. He therefore summoned his friend, Joseph Mitchell, the radiologist from Cambridge, and W V Mayneord from the Brompton Cancer Hospital, London, and A J Cipriani and Gordon Butler, both Canadians, to work on these problems. They obtained a 1000 curie polonium–beryllium neutron source from the Americans, enabling them to study the biological effects of neutrons, and for the first time Cockcroft was able to understand fully what was involved in work of this kind. Butler recalled that at one point they urgently required information from the Americans on the toxicity of plutonium.

> When I moved to Chalk River [he wrote] Cockcroft said we must begin to expose some animals, any animals at all, to some radioactive material, uranium should do. We went to the beach at the town site and found a disused bath house, moved it to the plant behind the biology laboratory and installed an exposure chamber for rats, all within a month. I proceeded immediately to expose rats to aerosols of uranyl nitrate and analyse their tissues for residual uranium. Within a week I had the first results of the analyses, and on instructions I told this to Cockcroft and he said we must go and talk with the Americans 'because now we have a need to know'. Within a week he took me to New York, headquarters of the Manhattan Project in the Empire State Building (an unforgettable experience), introduced me to his contact, and left with instructions that I was to get all the information possible about the toxicity of radioactive materials.[16]

Whenever he was in Montreal, Cockcroft used to attend the evening lectures on reactor physics given by G M Volkoff, a 24 year old Russian emigré, who was being groomed to succeed Placzek as head of the theoretical physics division. Cockcroft also learned what was going on in the chemistry, health, physics and engineering divisions in an amazingly short time.

One of the problems with which he had to contend was the suspicion of academic members of the staff about the role played by ICI. Not only was Tube Alloys directed by Wallace Akers, but his deputy M W Perrin was ICI and so were the two engineers R E Newell and D W Ginns, both working at Montreal, whilst at home ICI was engaged on uranium metal production and on the diffusion process for separating uranium isotopes. He had to point out that in the USA several large industrial companies were also very actively involved with uranium technology. In the event, when the war ended ICI was only too anxious to shed the load on its management and scientific resources caused by the Tube Alloys contracts, and extricated itself as quickly as possible.

By the autumn of 1944 Cockcroft's unobtrusive way of dealing with staff problems had made the Laboratory 'a happy and efficient organisation'. Not long after, he wrote to his brother, Eric,

> We have now collected a very good staff, amounting to about 130 graduates. Half of them are Canadian. We have seven New Zealanders, four French, twenty-two Cambridge, six Oxford graduates among the UK contingent. We have physicists, chemists, engineers and biologists, the latter led by our friend Dr Mitchell from St John's College. We have a fine lab in the half-empty University of Montreal, which stands up on the north side of Mount Royal.

Six years later, the French Government bestowed on Cockcroft the order of Chevalier de Légion d'Honneur in acknowledgment of the fruitful relations he had established with the French scientists who had worked with him during the war.

In October 1944, Cockcroft was worried about the progress of construction work at Chalk River and Deep River. He wrote to Appleton that his main concern was to

> get out the drawings required for the contractors to pour their concrete before the winter sets in. They have a large gang at work preparing the site and putting up the service buildings. They will next go on to the laboratory and pile buildings and to the water circulation system. I have got an operating date of 1 May 1945—one that will need hard going to meet. Canadian industry is now our weakest link[17].

Meanwhile, he and his family enjoyed the novelty of a Canadian winter which happened to be an especially severe one. He described in a letter to his mother an expedition from Montreal to the country one Sunday morning before Christmas.

> There was a multitude of skiers out and it was fascinating to watch them shooting over the hill, falling over and climbing up again. There were people on horseback galloping in the snow and sleighs drawn by horses, and boys and girls with toboggans and sleighs. We usually call at the chalet to get a drink—or ice cream—and buy chocolates, these being difficult to find in Montreal but always available up the mountain.

For Christmas presents, the Cockcrofts bought skates and boots and a sledge for the children, and a kind neighbour provided additional clothes against the cold from a store of clothing intended for British evacuees arriving in Canada. 'We shall have to send them a donation', Cockcroft told his mother, 'not being quite destitute'.

During the early months of 1945, he made frequent visits to the States, gathering information under the Quebec Agreement and keeping Chadwick in touch with developments. In March he was host to Bohr who came from Los Alamos to look at the laboratory. In April he flew to England to discuss the setting up of a British atomic energy research laboratory, as will be described in the following chapter.

He was not concerned with the overall operations of the Manhattan project or the test of a bomb at Alamogordo on 16 July 1945. But he was present at an important meeting in Washington, three days before the dropping of the bomb on Hiroshima, also attended by Chadwick and by Richard Tolman, one of Groves's scientific advisers. He was given information which was announced at a press conference in Ottawa the morning after the Japanese surrender, Wednesday 15 August 1945. He, in company with C D Howe, the Canadian Minister of Reconstruction and Supply, Mackenzie, Laurence and Kemmer, answered a barrage of questions which lasted for an hour. They took the opportunity to disclose the Canadian atomic energy project; as he described it afterwards, the press

> wanted to know about the power applications, about what the two kinds of bomb were, about stocks of materials, about Canada's part and so on. A little of what we said found its way into the Press, but a good deal of it was squeezed out by the Jap surrender.

His own views on the dropping of the atomic bomb were described briefly in a letter written to his mother the day after the Nagasaki bomb.

> Many people are very troubled about this new power and most of us working on it have been equally troubled. I have felt, however, that with the advent of rockets and 6000 ton raids, the position of the world, and of England (*sic*) in particular, was approaching a real crisis of civilisation and that the only hope of bringing politicians to their senses was that provided by the new power. I really do believe that we now have the choice between the 'big three' [presumably the USA, UK and USSR] living peacefully together, or of an annihilating conflict. I don't believe we will choose the latter. I think the problems are so difficult that no other nation can come into the picture as potential dangers to the world.

This statement is probably characteristic of what his colleagues and British scientists working on the Manhattan Project were feeling at the time.

He was, in any case, destined to work in the field of atomic energy for the rest of his life. While he had been in London, Sir John Anderson had asked him whether he would consider becoming director of an establishment for research and development similar to that in Canada. The election of a new British Government in August 1945 had temporarily put further discussion in abeyance. As so often happened with Cockcroft, conflicting invitations arrived in pairs: Anderson's approach coincided with an invitation by

Mackenzie for him to become Vice-President of the Canadian National
Research Council—a signal honour for a non-Canadian.

> The salary [wrote Cockcroft] would be upwards of 10 000 dollars so that one
> would be able to live comfortably enough and the work would be interesting.
> I wouldn't mind taking on such a job since I like new places and changes of
> work. But I don't suppose I *will* take it on, for I do feel that there are important
> jobs to be done at home still. So our present plan is to return about Christmas.
> I would like to see our plant in full operation before I go so that it may be
> delayed a little beyond this. If, on the other hand, I were to take on the job of
> starting up work in England I might have to return a little earlier.

For the time being, he had become fascinated with the planning of the Deep
River 'village'. After the Ottawa press conference, he and the family drove
to Deep River, staying in a chalet permeated with the smell of pine trees and
wood smoke. Bulldozers were already cutting out roads through the forest. He
wrote to his mother:

> So far about 70 of the prefabricated wartime houses have been erected. They
> are rather nicely designed little houses. They have a living room, two bedrooms
> and a kitchen and bathroom. Two of our families are living there—the Kowar-
> skis and Gilberts...who enjoy the village very much in spite of being 25 miles
> from a town—Pembroke. They have a shopping bus once a week and the laun-
> dry, eggs, milk and bread are delivered. Later, there will be a village store.

Figure 13   Cockcroft relaxing with members of his staff at Deep
River, Canada, summer 1945. (Courtesy: Dr Henry Seligman)

From the start, Cockcroft made sure that the landscape should be disturbed as little as possible. He brought in a town planner, Professor J Bland from McGill University, for this purpose. Roads and avenues were designed to run in curves rather than straight lines and were named after figures in Canadian history such as Champlain, Wolfe and Montcalm. The houses were built mainly of timber with a large basement holding the coal furnace, laundry room and store room, the furnace providing central heating through the floors during the long winter months.

By the autumn of 1945 quite a number of staff had moved from Montreal to Chalk River. Conditions were, as Goldschmidt recalled, quite primitive at the outset. The houses, for example, had no doors, so blankets were hung in their place until one day all the prefabricated doors arrived. Some of the regulations governing the behaviour of the staff were monastic. Goldschmidt's Gallic spirit rebelled against Rule No 11 which forbade the sharing of staff house rooms by male and female scientists. He raised the matter at a building committee meeting chaired by Cockcroft: it was ridiculous, he argued, to impose such restrictions, not only on adults but on distinguished scientists. Cockcroft, conforming to his customary committee meeting manner, gave no indication of whether he agreed or not. But when the next meeting was due, the rule had been altered to the effect that after 10 PM *no* males were allowed in the female wing of the building, but females were allowed in the male wing (at their own risk!). In this way Goldschmidt claimed to have created an atmosphere more conducive to amorous pursuits![18]

On 10 September 1945 the usual imperturbability of Cockcroft was, as he confessed years later to George Steiner, Fellow of Churchill College and Professor of English and Comparative Literature at the University of Geneva, for once shaken[19]. The previous afternoon several Royal Canadian Mounted Police called at his Montreal home, Upper Roslyn, and requested him to speak on a telephone they had brought with them. On the line was Malcolm MacDonald, the British High Commissioner in Ottawa, who told Cockcroft to drive himself to Ottawa after nightfall, telling no-one of his absence from the Laboratory. On his arrival at about 2 AM MacDonald told him that Alan Nunn May was suspected of having handed over to the Russians microscopic samples of uranium-233 and uranium-235. Cockcroft was flabbergasted. He then told MacDonald that Nunn May had been to Chalk River and had also visited the metallurgical laboratory at Chicago, and was shortly due to return home as Reader in Physics at King's College, London. On account of this, the authorities decided not to arrest him until they had obtained further evidence, not only about him, but about others with whom he might be in contact. Cockcroft had to keep the information of Nunn May's alleged treachery to himself. What proved to be most embarrassing for him was that a farewell party had been arranged at which he had to present Nunn May with a slide rule—a present from the staff[20]. Nunn May was arrested on 4 March 1946, but it was not to be the end of Cockcroft's experience of spies.

The Nunn May affair proved to be embarrassing for Cockcroft in another way. In August 1947, at the conclusion of the trials of the Soviet spy ring in Canada, to which Nunn May had belonged, Kemmer and other scientists

who had worked in the Montreal Laboratory, organised a petition to Chuter
Ede, the Home Secretary, that Nunn May's sentence of ten years penal
servitude should be mitigated, on the grounds that it was out of proportion
to the offence committed. (It was held against Nunn May that the information
he had passed on had shortened the time for the Russians to reach a similar
point in their experiments.) Kemmer insisted that the petition, which was
explicitly non-political in tone, would never get off the ground unless
Cockcroft was prepared to sign it. Signatures were collected from all but one
of the scientists approached, all of whom had worked with Nunn May.
Cockcroft also signed, after writing to Kemmer to suggest a change of word-
ing, which was accepted. The appeal was unsuccessful. After the conviction
of Fuchs three years later, Cockcroft, then Director of Harwell, asked Kemmer, who was back at the Cavendish, to return the letter about Nunn May
which Cockcroft had written to Kemmer. The latter admitted that his admiration for Cockcroft 'slightly wavered'[21], though he conceded that Cockcroft
must have been under considerable strain at the time. When Nunn May was
to be released, Cockcroft suggested that he might work on radioisotopes or
as a hospital physicist.

Cockcroft felt that, although it would be more convenient and comfortable
for the family to remain in Montreal (the children were going to a local school)
while the establishment at Chalk River was being built, he ought to be on the
spot to 'push along the work at the plant more effectively'. Elizabeth wanted
to be with him, so she and the children moved into No 17 Beach Avenue in
the first week of October 1945. Like the other houses, it was built of wood,
but had an additional floor to accommodate the children, and from the living
room they looked out across the mile-wide Ottawa River to the wooded
Quebec hills beyond. As Cockcroft recalled:

> Tables for the house had been made by the plant carpenters; as yet we had no
> curtains and could look into our neighbours' houses—equally unprovided.

At the time, he was on a visit to England (where he was again asked to
become Director of the proposed atomic energy research establishment at
Harwell), and he joined the family a little later in Chalk River. After telling
Elizabeth that he had finally accepted the Directorship, sad news in a way as
he was reluctant to leave Canada where the children had settled so happily,
he went to look at ZEEP which had recently gone into operation—the first
nuclear reactor to be built outside the United States. Apart from a number
of journeys to the States, Cockcroft remained at Chalk River for the next two
and a half months. On 31 December 1945 he wrote to his brother Leo:

> On Christmas Day we had lots of snow with a temperature up to 32°F so that
> it was very pleasant out. On Christmas Eve the children from the school,
> including our two (Dorothea and Jocelyn), went carol singing and as I happened
> to meet them, I joined up with Carmichael and the Roafs and increased the
> volume. We went quite a long way round the village and Dermot Roaf, dressed
> as Father Christmas, collected offerings for the Red Cross.

He went on to describe how he was learning to ski

> down gentle slopes. It is very good fun and gives one needed exercise. The

valleys and river and hills are exceedingly beautiful and we could not wish for a more idyllic place to spend Christmas.

His small daughter Cathie, who had not seen much of her father yet, recalls that

At Deep River he seemed to play a more regular part in my life. I can remember him shouting encouraging remarks from half way across the nursery slopes and across the skating rink. I can remember his exasperation when I, for fear of the bears which came out of the forest, refused to go on a summer trip to the rapids upstream. Our old automobile had punctures with great frequency, a perfect bear-trap to my way of thinking[22].

CHAPTER ELEVEN

'ENGLAND HAS NEED OF YOU'

Cockcroft's colleagues like Chadwick, Oliphant and Peierls had assumed from the time of the Quebec agreement on 25 August 1943 that, if Britain were to become a nuclear power, Cockcroft would take charge of research and development. Cockcroft, however, had mixed feelings about this possibility. He was wearied by the continuation of the war and wanted to return to academic life. At the same time, whenever the subject of a British nuclear research establishment arose, he was ready to offer constructive ideas. In company with other senior British nuclear physicists, he was to become critical of the Government's slowness in coming to a decision about the development of atomic energy. In January 1944 Anderson had stated that it should be given high priority 'as soon as possible at the end of the war'.

In November 1944 Cockcroft, who was now a member of the Tube Alloys Technical Committee because he was head of the Montreal Laboratory, outlined a possible British research establishment which would include a graphite reactor, an electromagnetic separation plant for the separation of uranium and other isotopes, an electronics division and an accelerator for fundamental research. The following month he set up in Montreal a Graphite Group under John Dunworth, the object being to prepare a design for a graphite reactor more powerful than the one at Oak Ridge but with improvements based on experience of the operation of the American reactor[1]. Proposals for a plutonium production reactor and a power reactor using enriched uranium fuel were also considered by the Group; all this theoretical work was later put to good effect in the new British atomic energy project.

The first move to found a research establishment took place in April 1945 —a month before the end of the European war[2]. Cockcroft, who had been summoned from Montreal, and Oliphant, who had recently returned from Berkeley to Birmingham University, looked at airfields in East Anglia and southern England which might provide a suitable site for an establishment. Like Chalk River, the requirements included a fresh water supply, good communications and also a university town within reasonable proximity to satisfy the intellectual needs of the staff.

The most likely site appeared to be the RAF station at Harwell, about 10 miles due south of Oxford, possessing one of the longest runways in the country, situated on the edge of the Berkshire Downs not far from the ancient

Ridgeway in open rolling country containing a few scattered farms and cherry orchards. The Thames meandering from Oxford to Reading would provide a plentiful water supply. Oxford University and London were both within convenient reach, providing intellectual stimulus and contacts with the seat of government. While Cockcroft was in London, Appleton sounded him about being director of the establishment. Cockcroft wrote to Elizabeth: 'I told him I'd have preferred to return to Cambridge for a year or two and that he should try Uncle James [Chadwick] first'. He was even interested in joining 'a Scientific Advisory Council on housing with Bernal as chairman... I'd like to do that and indulge my passion for building'. After Appleton had written to Chadwick, the latter, who was determined to return to Liverpool University, replied on 2 June 1945, supporting Cockcroft's nomination and acutely summing up his character.

> For example [Chadwick wrote] his knowledge is wide but it is not at all profound; his views are of rather a dull everyday hue. On the other hand his temper is so equable and his patience and persistence so inexhaustible that we can put in lively and relatively irresponsible men who have the real feeling for research without fear of upsetting the balance[3].

On returning to Montreal, however, Cockcroft was prepared to accept the offer of the directorship on 13 July. His acceptance was overtaken by the General Election and the return of a Labour Government, unfamiliar with what had been done in the atomic energy field. After the dropping of the atomic bombs on Japan his mood changed again. On 26 August, he wrote to his brother, Eric, from Chalk River.

> Canada's interest is undoubtedly in the peacetime application, so her project will go on. Britain is interested in both war and peace. I think myself that the project reaches outside the greater part of present armaments. Its effect is so stupendous that the world has really got to use it solely as a threat to aggressors. I hope the new British Committee [the Advisory Committee on Atomic Energy to which Attlee reappointed Anderson as chairman] to report on the UK project will get a move on. They, ie the previous [Tube Alloys Advisory] Committee have clearly dithered for 15 months and done nothing. If it had not been for starting a show in Canada, the UK would have been left in a few months time with no-one working on the problem at all.

Oliphant was, typically, more critical. On 14 September, he told Cockcroft that

> if Anderson and the Government had really wished to do anything, we could by now have talked in technical terms with our colleagues in the USA. As it is, we have now to set up this organisation in the ticklish atmosphere of complete American supremacy.

He continued that he had been told that

> Rabi [until recently a member of the wartime Radiation Laboratory at MIT] has stated categorically that only real achievement on our part can ensure full and willing collaboration on the scientific level. Real collaboration will be achieved, as it was in Radar, only when American scientists feel it essential to visit this country to keep in touch with our advances in technique and applica-

tion... If we fall behind now we shall lose the men we really need to get things going and lose time which we can never make up. If the economic use of nuclear energy proves practicable, it is a matter of vital practical importance to this country and the Empire, and our future as a real factor in the world of industry and politics depends on our position in Tube Alloys[4].

Such was the atmosphere in which Cockcroft flew to England on 30 September to learn the intentions of the Advisory Committee. Blackett, who was one of the few nuclear physicist members (though according to Oliphant 'interested only in the political aspects') suggested that research should primarily be directed towards the development of power; secondly, that a separate establishment should conduct experiments with nuclear weapons but not actually manufacture a bomb. The whole research organisation should be controlled by the Ministry of Supply. Cockcroft later wrote that Blackett's 'memorandum was therefore rather decisive in determining that we were to become part of the Civil Service'[5].

There had been considerable speculation among the British scientists at Montreal and Chalk River, in the meantime, about the policy for a Government-run nuclear research laboratory in England. A memorandum addressed to Chadwick, signed by Dunworth, Alan Nunn May and M H L Pryce, insisted that the establishment

> the most important in the British Commonwealth must be given all the encouragement to reach and, if possible, surpass its American rivals in the shortest possible time and regardless of cost. It must therefore be free from all the deadening influences of the Civil Service.

They believed that the staff should, as far as was consistent with security, have the same freedom as if they were in a university laboratory, and be able to publish papers, to lecture, and to attend scientific conferences[6]. Another memorandum signed by 31 scientists addressed to Cockcroft declared it was essential not to neglect fundamental research.

> Nuclear physics is in its infancy and there is no reason to expect that the phenomenon of nuclear fission is the only possible means of obtaining nuclear energy. Hence it is necessary that pure research should be pursued on a broad front. It would be a grave mistake to concentrate too much effort in the field of nuclear fission.

They were unanimous in their feelings, so well expressed by Skinner, then working at Berkeley, probably the most voluble of Cockcroft's colleagues, who stated that 'Cockcroft is the only possible head of the Establishment and his appointment is indispensable... he should be given as free a hand as possible'[7]. Dee, who had recently visited him at Montreal, told him:

> I don't envy you your job one little bit—it is clearly most difficult in all political and administrative aspects. Don't be too self-effacing, though, John. I'm sure most of us would like you as Controller of this work and my only fear is that you may not throw your weight about as much as you have a right to do[8].

Blackett summed up their feelings when, on an earlier occasion, he urged Cockcroft to return from Canada with the words 'England has need of you'.

Heartened by all this support, Cockcroft met Anderson on 2 October 1945.

He insisted that his staff should not be subject to the stringent security restrictions imposed on scientists working in the US atomic energy establishments. Anderson said he would do his best[9]. Cockcroft had to accept control by the Ministry of Supply, but he found a sympathetic ear in its Permanent Secretary, Sir Oliver Franks, who reassured him that his staff would be given as much freedom as possible. Another ally was Sir Alan Barlow, Second Secretary at the Treasury, and ultimately responsible for funding the new establishment. Despite these reassurances, Cockcroft still had reservations about accepting the post; it had been and still was his wish to return to Cambridge and he was, by many, expected to do so; as he wrote to Elizabeth:

> Everyone asks me when I'm returning to Cambridge. All I can say to them is that I wish I were returning to Cambridge now which is the real truth.

As the decision to select Harwell still had to be made, Cockcroft left London to take another look at the site. Afterwards he visited Tizard, then President of Magdalen College, Oxford. 'I talked long and earnestly with Tizard on the location of the Establishment. We favoured the place near Harwell very much'. The next day he looked at an alternative site at South Cerney near Cirencester which the Air Ministry was prepared to offer instead of Harwell, but he considered the site would be unattractive to staff as it was a long way from Oxford. He spent that night at Oxford in a small hotel near the station,

> Tizard being occupied with buildings and being minus family. I had to knock up the proprietress at 11.30 but it was quite comfortable in the end. [He summed up] It seems to be a choice between an easy immediate solution at South Cerney and the difficult way of building on an open site at Harwell.

Harwell it was to be, making use of the airfield buildings to be converted to laboratories and to house the experimental reactors. On 9 October, Cockcroft met Barlow, Franks and Air Marshal Whitworth Jones, representing the Air Staff; although the meeting finally clinched the matter the Air Marshal had first to be convinced and he put up a good fight emphasising the importance of Harwell to the Air Ministry, but in the end surrendered—and in due course, the Air Council agreed to sell Harwell[10]. Already Cockcroft's interest had been stimulated.

> We are [he wrote] to build 150 houses straight away. There is a battle on to get a nice design as the MoW [Ministry of Works] produced a very poor one. There were strong winds blowing across Harwell and altogether its been a tempestuous rainy weekend. We ought to plant more trees—probably beech. We might also put in cherry and plum and apple in our own place.

(The Cockcroft family would be taking over the house of the former Station Commander.)

Cockcroft was offered the directorship of Harwell on 9 November 1945 at the astonishingly low salary of £2000, and although this was increased to £2500 the following year the salary was by no means generous and the conditions of service compared unfavourably with the Jacksonian Professorship, which it now became necessary for him to resign. He was entitled to hold the latter appointment until 65 (he was then 48), whereas the Harwell appointment was only for a period of five years. However, he had learned from experience at ADRDE, and before finally accepting the appointment insisted on the following conditions: firstly, that he should have the right to express views on policy and would not be subordinate to the Controller of Atomic Energy; secondly, that an administrative officer should be responsible for the day-to-day running of the Establishment; thirdly, the freedom of expression won for his staff should not be withdrawn after he had ceased to be Director; and fourthly, that he should be given an adequate allowance for the entertainment of VIPs[11].

On 29 January 1946 Clement Attlee, the Prime Minister, announced the appointments of Lord Portal, wartime Chief of Air Staff, as Controller of Atomic Energy, responsible for the production of uranium metal and fissile materials, and of Cockcroft as Director of the Atomic Energy Research Establishment. The other two members of the project, whose names were not then announced, were Christopher Hinton and William Penney. Hinton, who had been an ICI engineer who had won a reputation for building ordnance factories during the war and was then Deputy Director, Filling Factories, Ministry of Supply, became Executive Head of the Production Group and was responsible for building the uranium metal plant, the plutonium production reactors and the chemical separation plant. His deputy was another ICI engineer, Leonard Owen, and in February 1946 they established their group at Risley near Warrington, mainly because it was an industrial area and was near to the ICI plant at Widnes. Penney, who did not arrive on the scene until 1947, was a mathematician who had done distinguished work on the wartime Mulberry harbours project, and then at Los Alamos, from where he had gone to the Pacific as an observer of the dropping of the atomic bomb on Nagasaki. He was in due course to be appointed, though this was not publicly announced, Superintendent of Armament Research, and responsible for the design of an atomic bomb. In 1952 he became Director of the Atomic Weapons Research Establishment at Aldermaston, Berkshire, not far from Harwell.

The first of Cockcroft's future colleagues to meet him was Hinton. They were introduced to each other by Akers on 28 January 1946 at Crewe Station where Cockcroft, who had just arrived from Canada, had broken his journey from Todmorden to London. The main topic of discussion was the experimental graphite reactor (known as British Experimental Pile O— BEPO) which was to be designed and constructed by the Risley organisation for Harwell. The relationship between scientist and engineer, although at this stage reasonably cordial, proved in the long run to be far from harmonious. The main reason for this was the totally different personalities and methods of working of the two men. Hinton was a tall, imposing man, used to command, moderately eloquent and forceful. He found it difficult to penetrate Cockcroft's impassive exterior, and the latter's inability to have a row with anyone only served to exasperate him. At the same time Hinton was only too well aware of Cockcroft's outstanding scientific reputation; physicists the world over fully expected that the Cockcroft – Walton experiment of 1932 which had given such a great impetus to the development of atomic energy would soon be acknowledged by a Nobel Prize to the two men; there had been no prizes in physics or chemistry for three of the war years.

In their approach to work, Hinton was accustomed to working to clearly defined instructions. The job, like building a filling factory, had to be completed by a certain date. He therefore looked for subordinates who would act as his unquestioning lieutenants and carry out what they were told. But Cockcroft, in choosing his staff, looked among his peers. Not always sure of what he wanted, he regarded them as an intellectual sounding board, and he selected those who might be able to provide an answer to a particular problem. He and his staff, unlike Hinton's team, were ever seeking a better solution to a physical problem—which might take two or three years to complete. Hinton's aim, and indeed his duty, was to bring a reactor into production as quickly as possible. He liked to be given several alternative proposals and told which was the most likely to be working within a given period of time.

Some of the trouble arose from the different training of engineer and scientist. While Cockcroft was respected by his colleagues for having graduated in electrical engineering, having served a full College apprenticeship with one of the best Companies in the country, then having taken the mathematical tripos and a Cambridge PhD in physics, he had never held a responsible post in industry or elsewhere practising as an electrical engineer, whereas Hinton, after spending five years as a school apprentice in the Great Western Railway works at Swindon, followed by taking the Mechanical Engineering Tripos in Cambridge, had then held a very responsible position in ICI as Chief Engineer of one of the Divisions of the Company, and since 1940 had controlled a vast organisation in the Ministry of Supply. Cockcroft was really an 'applied physicist', and when many years later he was asked whether he considered that engineering was 'applied physics', he replied, 'to this question I return a decided negative'. He went on to explain that the design engineer had to 'synthesise' the contributions of a broad spectrum of technologies, some physical, others, the concern of the materials scientist or the chemist'[12].

Apart from the inherent dissimilarities in professions, difficulties were created by the different terms of reference given to Hinton and Cockcroft. The former's instructions were simple, to design and build reactors to provide a specified quantity of plutonium in the shortest possible time. Cockcroft's Harwell, on the other hand, had a much broader remit—to conduct research in all aspects of atomic energy. At the same time Harwell had a specific commitment to provide the Risley group with the basic data and information to enable them to carry out its task.

Mr. F C How, who was then Under Secretary in the Atomic Energy Division of the Ministry of Supply and was well placed to observe Cockcroft and Hinton, wrote years later:

> To the engineers at Risley it seemed that nothing could be more urgent than their production of plutonium; to the scientists at Harwell fascinated (in the jargon of the time) by their work 'on the frontiers of science' the humdrum requirements of Risley were a distracting and tiresome chore. It was this differing view of priorities which caused friction at all levels between the staffs of the two sides of the project. Even if the top men in the two organisations had been

natural 'buddies' (which Cockcroft and Hinton were not), some of the feeling below must have rubbed off on them and affected their relationship[13].

Cockcroft and Penney did not meet until some eight months later in Chalk River. Here, too, there were differences in temperament, although far less marked than in the case of Hinton. Cockcroft's first opinion was that Penney had 'all the right ideas'. After the decision had been taken in January 1947 to make a bomb and later the setting up of the Aldermaston establishment, there were occasional moments of friction. At a time when nuclear physicists were in short supply, Cockcroft assumed that Harwell had first priority, and sometimes he offered posts at Harwell to scientists who would have preferred to work on weapons. Similarly, there were disputes over the supply of new equipment. Penney had difficulty in obtaining a Van de Graaff accelerator which he believed would be more useful at Aldermaston than at Harwell†. When Penney began fusion research, creating quite unnecessary competition with Harwell, there were arguments over the allocation of funds between the two establishments, and rivalries were not eliminated until 1960 when the Culham fusion research laboratory was formed. Penney maintained that none of these relatively minor disagreements diminished his respect for Cockcroft[14], but of course he had achieved his own objectives. The two scientists later worked together harmoniously in the field of international scientific collaboration‡.

Portal, who incidentally had no written terms of reference from the Government, invited Cockcroft to lunch at the Travellers Club for their first meeting on 13 February 1946. The informality of his invitation, which began 'My dear Cockcroft§, As fellow Government servants may we cut the frills of address?' seemed to be a good augury for the future. Cockcroft had favourable reports from Chadwick and Dee about Portal's support of scientists in the air war, and his first reaction was that Portal seemed to be 'very nice and able'. Portal assumed his appointment in March and met Cockcroft soon afterwards at Chalk River in May, when they went fishing (a sport in which Cockcroft only indulged when in Canada) and discussed the system of policy making and the most effective system for controlling research and production.

Cockcroft's insistence that his appointment should rank equal with that of the Controller made it difficult for Portal to coordinate policy on research under Cockcroft and production under Hinton. At the outset they arranged to report directly and independently to Franks, and as Cockcroft wrote later, 'This unconventional organisation might have produced difficulties, but Portal and I worked together harmoniously'[15]. It certainly was a strange set-

---

†In due course, Aldermaston acquired two Van de Graaffs generating 3 million electron-volts (MeV) and 6 MeV respectively; and a 12 million electron-volt (MeV) accelerator similar to the one at Harwell.

‡A very comprehensive analysis of the characteristics of these three men has been printed in Margaret Gowing's *Independence and Deterrence*, vol 2, pp4–9.

§It might be mentioned that at the time the use of surnames alone was the usual informal manner of address between colleagues.

up with the Controller only in parallel with the Research Director. Chadwick was only one of those who had doubts about how the arrangement would work, and told Portal on 8 April 1946 that it was a great pity that the production side had been separated from research and development and that it would only lead to confusion and division of purpose[16].

Portal tried to make the best of an unsatisfactory situation, and before the end of 1946 had devised at least a more workable instrument for coordination. He set up an Atomic Energy Council with himself as chairman, the other members being Michael Perrin, who had served as Deputy to Akers in Tube Alloys, Cockcroft, Hinton, and later Penney, and senior Ministry of Supply officials. He and Cockcroft acted as alternate chairman to an Atomic Energy Technical Committee which included distinguished scientists and engineers, such as Cherwell, Chadwick, Claude Gibb and C F Kearton.

Portal never claimed to have mastered the technicalities of atomic energy, and he had to rely heavily on the advice of Cockcroft, Hinton, Penney and Perrin. He was fortunate to have these good men. At the same time, he was a distinguished figure commanding respect in the non-scientific world, and he proved to be invaluable when the Council had dealings with the Chiefs of Staff.

Both Perrin and How, who also attended Council meetings, believed that it

worked reasonably well. Certainly, there was some underlying tension and there were, quite properly, some strenuous arguments about matters of policy; but I [How] never saw anything in the nature of a personal confrontation—and I was well placed as an observer[17].

How believed that Portal was 'an unobtrusive and very effective "oil can"', accustomed to dealing (though not always very effectively) with strong personalities like Harris, Commander-in-Chief of Bomber Command, or Tedder, Deputy Supreme Commander to Eisenhower in the war, and that he evolved a technique of discussing problems with Cockcroft, Hinton and Penney individually, leaving broad policy decisions to be taken in Council.

Relations between Harwell and the Ministry of Supply were another matter. Cockcroft recalled that he and Franks, who was succeeded by Sir Archibald Rowlands as Permanent Secretary, used to settle difficulties over a whisky in the latter's office. How remembered that 'the aura of glamour and mystery which surrounded the project in those early days' had the effect of making it practically autonomous, controlled neither by the Ministry of Supply nor by the Treasury. Less senior men at Harwell, however, saw the Ministry of Supply as inflexible and overcentralised. Denis Willson, who became head of the Extra-mural Division, responsible for research contracts with industry and the universities, remembered that A B Jones, whom Cockcroft had obtained from TRE as Chief Administrative Officer though his rank was only that of Chief Executive Officer, had great difficulties in obtaining Harwell's requirements. He had, for example, to refer to London in order to recruit staff more senior than typists and workers paid by the hour. It was not until R G Elkington, whose rank was Assistant Secretary, was appointed Secretary to the Establishment (he was succeeded by Willson) that the main administrative responsibilities could be taken off Cockcroft's shoulders.

When Cockcroft was in Canada, Herbert Skinner looked after the Establishment at his request and selected staff; Skinner's impetuous nature led him into brushes with the Ministry officials; in May 1946 he was incensed when they refused his daughter permission to travel to school near Oxford in the Establishment station wagon, the alternative was a journey of one and a half hours by public transport. From Chalk River, Cockcroft had to intervene with Franks over this relatively trivial complaint, although he was personally concerned because he would have to send his four daughters to school when they returned to England! The matter was settled amicably after Cockcroft offered to lend an ancient Austin he had laid up during the war for carrying children of staff to school[18]. The incompatibility of scientists' and civil servants' interpretation of regulations became a major factor in the discussions leading to the setting-up of the Atomic Energy Authority in due course.

Cockcroft had to remain at Chalk River until a suitable successor was found. Unfortunately information of his appointment to Harwell had been 'leaked' to Chapman Pincher, Science Correspondent of the *Daily Express*, two months before the official announcement and before the Canadians themselves had been informed. They deeply resented the manner in which the change had been made, even though at the outset of the project it had been made clear that British scientists would be withdrawn after the war, and they even argued that Cockcroft's departure removed the basis of cooperation between the two countries. Thanks to skilful diplomacy by the High Commissioner, Malcolm MacDonald, by Cockcroft and by Chadwick, and by Portal who visited Canada, the Canadians were mollified[19]. W B Lewis, Cockcroft's long-standing friend, and now Superintendent of TRE, where he had played an important part in developing shortwave radar, was appointed to take over Chalk River. He arrived on 7 September 1946; Cockcroft met him in Ottawa and drove him to the plant, providing him with all the necessary information. The car broke down on the way! But that was to be expected, his aging cars were legendary, one of the authors had to give him a new battery to get him home from the AEI Research Laboratory where he had been for dinner one evening.

Until then Cockcroft had been fully occupied overseeing the construction of the heavy water reactor which did not become active until July 1947. The Reactor Group at Chalk River, meanwhile, was engaged in designing a small experimental reactor for Harwell—GLEEP (Graphite Low Energy Experimental Pile), and Spence and the other chemists were producing the brilliantly novel flow sheets to separate uranium from the plutonium to be produced in the Windscale reactors. The Deep River village had now been built, a pattern of family life was developing and the houses reflected the tastes of their occupants. After work in the hot summer weather the staff and their families bathed in the river, but the Cockcroft family missed all this as Elizabeth and the children had returned to England to set up house in Harwell. Cockcroft wrote to his mother, 'forty children have been born in the village, so romantic is the atmosphere!', and described a regatta to Elizabeth, 'The whole village assembled on the white sandy beach to watch and eat ice cream between while'. He was delighted to find that a music group had been formed, not only to listen to records, but to play woodwind instruments. 'The

UK boys seem to provide all these concerts. I hope the fashion will have spread to the Canadian staff before the UK group is too much diluted'. He had moved into the Staff House and, while recovering from one of his usual heavy colds, speculated on how he would improve the place if he were permanently in residence; essentials were his own room, quiet, and a well furnished library at hand.

While still in Canada, Cockcroft was instrumental in persuading the leading members of the British staff at Montreal and Chalk River to accept appointments at Harwell. A T Sumner, from the Ministry of Supply, and H S Hoff†, from the Civil Service Commission, had gone to Montreal to recruit staff for Harwell, having been empowered to waive normal Civil Service procedures, provided the customary 'establishment fee' was paid on the spot. At several stormy meetings, with Cockcroft in the chair, they met with a hostile reception, one scientist actually blowing a raspberry at them![20] Only when it became known that Cockcroft was definitely going to Harwell did the staff seriously consider the offers, and Cockcroft in some cases actually had to persuade the Board that the salaries being offered were too low. It was the chemist, Colin Amphlett, who later declared that

> it took many months of patient work and persuasion by Cockcroft and Spence to produce a reasonable number of acceptances; in many cases (mine included) the initial, rather derisory, offers were improved after Cockcroft's intervention. His determination to staff Harwell with as many of the experienced UK team in Canada undoubtedly helped Harwell in its early years. He knew, of course, that many of the more senior members such as Pryce, Guggenheim, Kemmer, and others, would wish to return to their university posts, but he was determined to capture as many as possible of the younger men.[21].

He was naturally most concerned to appoint good men to lead the divisions in the British establishment. Skinner was to be in charge of General Physics; Spence returned from Canada in 1947 to look after Chemistry; Seligman, who had been promoted by Cockcroft at Chalk River to entitle him to a better salary, in the first instance too low, was to form an Isotopes Division. Frisch and W G Marley returned from Los Alamos to take charge of Nuclear Physics and Health Physics respectively, and Klaus Fuchs, also from Los Alamos, formed a Theoretical Physics Division. Robert Cockburn from TRE (another reservoir of talent) was deputy to Frisch for a short while, and also from TRE came Denis Taylor to head the Electronics Division. The Metallurgy Division was started by B Chalmers from RAE, Farnborough, later to be taken over by Monty Finniston from Chalk River. In 1950 Frisch left for Cambridge to become the Jacksonian Professor in place of Cockcroft, and Dunworth, then deputy to Bretscher, was made head of the newly formed Reactor Physics Division. Harold Tongue, an engineer, was appointed Chief Engineer and responsible for industrial relations.

Recruiting junior staff, when the Establishment began to expand, proved to be much more difficult, particularly in the chemistry and engineering divisions. Cockcroft decided to institute Harwell Research Fellowships which

†Otherwise 'William Cooper', the author.

enabled young university graduates to work on unclassified subjects and to publish their findings. The fellowships, which were tenable for three years, attracted both British scientists working abroad and those who would not normally have been tempted to join the Scientific Civil Service. Another attraction for these young scientists who had been accepted was that they could defer their period of military service (amounting virtually to exemption), but Cockcroft was glad when National Service ceased, as he did not like to think that young graduates came to Harwell to avoid it.

He left Chalk River on 30 September 1946 and joined his family at No 1 South Drive, Harwell, a short walk from the hangar where GLEEP was to be installed. Before starting to grapple with the problems that awaited him, he and his family went up to Todmorden, where he was to receive the freedom of the Borough. The ceremony was held in the Town Hall and his mother and brothers and their wives and children attended in force. Although he considered his wartime achievement was in the field of radar[22], the citation acclaimed his outstanding services to international research which had 'brought distinction and honour to the town of his birth', and recognised his 'distinguished contribution to the discovery of atomic energy whereby incalculable possibilities have been placed at the disposal of future generations of mankind'. In reply to the Mayor and Corporation, Cockcroft acknowledged with gratitude the excellent education he had received at his two schools—Walsden Church School and Todmorden Secondary School, which had equipped him intellectually for Manchester University. No less important in developing his powers of endurance, he said, were his swims in Cophurst Dam and the long walks over neighbouring moor and dale.

The long and bitter winter of 1946–7 tested Cockcroft's leadership to the utmost. From January to March 1947, snow, followed by floods and gales, interrupted work at Harwell, and there was an acute shortage of skilled labour and materials. The job was comparable in scale to Chalk River and Deep River together, he told Mackenzie, a month after arriving at Harwell. Only a thousand men were at work at a time when twice the number were needed.

> We are plagued by Cabinet directives which give overriding priorities to other things, to the coal industry for steel, to temporary housing for carpenters. So we suddenly find ourselves with three carpenters on the job. It will be late spring rather than January before we begin to do effective experimental work, but our theoretical group is very active in planning for immediate needs and for longer term work. We also have a number of active construction groups working on GLEEP, the electrostatic generator and the cyclotron, and our physicists are pretty busy on the problems of production units. I have been very fully engaged personally and am just beginning to get some measure of the problems.

> We have a comfortable house at Harwell and the family like the countryside very well, though they have frequent feelings of nostalgia for Deep River especially when we show our colour film. We have one specially moving one of the steaks at Byeways![23]

How did Cockcroft cope with such a variety of problems? He not only had to oversee the building of the establishment with its laboratories, accelerators, and experimental reactors, but he had to acquaint himself with the engineering problems of Hinton's group at Risley, over 100 miles away in the north of England. In May 1947 he became a member of the Anglo – US – Canadian Declassification Committee which attempted to lift the ban of secrecy on non-military applications of atomic energy. These meetings, which continued over the next ten years, usually took place in Washington and he was away from Harwell for weeks at a time. However, he used to bring back with him a mass of information which he had gleaned from visits to laboratories, both commercial and state, which was of value to one or other of the Harwell divisions. Chalk River was usually included in his itinerary, and again he obtained information at firsthand which was invaluable to Harwell. Another commitment which took him away from Harwell was his membership of the Defence Research Policy Committee (DRPC) of which he became a member from August 1950 and was appointed part-time chairman in 1952 for two years.

In those early years of Harwell, he declined the Ministry's offer of the appointment of a Deputy Director to help him, and whenever he was abroad either Tongue, or later Spence, took decisions on his behalf. Penney recalled in an obituary after Cockcroft's death that the staff at Harwell were always astonished when he asked

> about the progress of work that he had glimpsed in a laboratory visit months or even years before. The little black book in which he noted everything requiring attention or that he needed to remember, his microscopic handwriting, and the crisp, terse notes, were all regarded affectionately as characteristic of this wise and modest man[24].

Whenever possible, he tried to inspect each Division about twice a year; his usual practice being to enter a laboratory and chat with a junior scientist or assistant about the work in hand.

His method of directing the establishment, based on his experience of running ADRDE, was to give heads of Divisions the freedom to run their own show. As he once described it, the problem was 'to focus the work of scientists from several different disciplines on to the major projects with which the establishment, or its sister establishments, were concerned[25]'. He used to be chairman or member of the Building, Research Reactors, Isotopes Plant Design, Chemical Separation and the Publication and Declassification Committees. Some of them were large, but they all represented groups working on the project and had their say. Cockcroft, of course, carried the final responsibility, though he rarely spoke, but when he did it was to the point.

His personal memoranda give little indication of the amount and variety of work that was in progress, any appraisal of his influence has to be deduced from the recollections of senior staff. Most of them agreed that he had no flair for routine administration, and his economical way of expressing his views was sometimes unhelpful; it was never certain what exactly he had in mind. Finniston declared that when he said 'Yes', it only meant, 'Yes, I heard what you said'. To illustrate this, he recalled one occasion when he consulted Cockcroft about a member of his Division who, he considered, had no further contribution to make and should return to academic life. Cockcroft had said 'Yes' and was then unusually annoyed when Finniston reported at their next meeting that he had arranged for the scientist to be transferred.

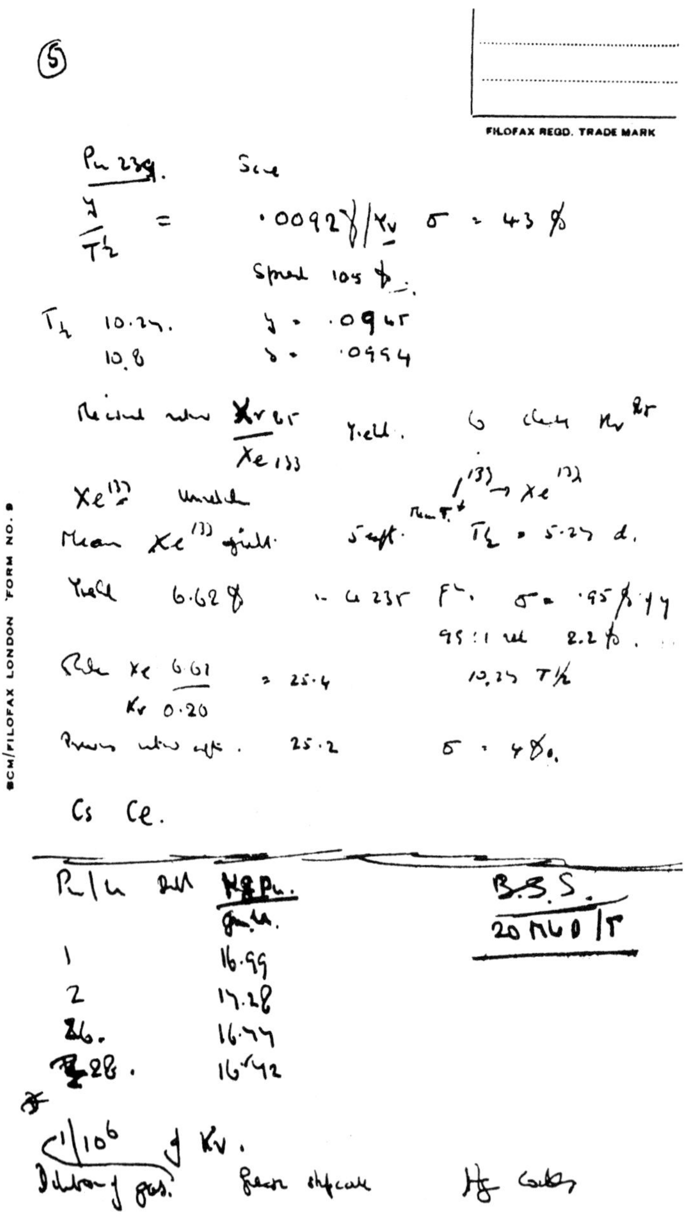

Figure 14   A page taken from Cockcroft's 7 inch by 4 inch pocket book, his 'black book'; he used such books from at least 1926 for the rest of his life. In them he entered thousands of aide-memoires of things he had been told, or had seen, and countless calculations usually made on the spot.

Figure 15 Cockcroft with some of his Divisional heads at Harwell, 1948.
Standing from left to right: K Fuchs, H Tongue, R Spence.
Seated from left to right: H Skinner, B Chalmers, E Bretscher, J D Cockcroft.
(Courtesy: AERE, Harwell)

On another occasion a prospective secretary to the Director had an interview with Cockcroft. Indicating her to a seat in front of his desk, he went on
working at his papers. Eventually, he became aware of her presence and
asked her to remind him of what she had come for. She explained how she
had come to apply for the post. He thanked her and continued writing. In
some confusion, she decided after a while to retire from the room. Only after
investigation by the member of the staff who had proposed her did she learn
that she had been accepted for the job!

Cockcroft's almost illegible memoranda did not help to clarify his infrequent pronouncements. This apparent lack of direction made some of the staff
who had not known him at the Cavendish or at Chalk River 'uncomfortable
or even, in some cases, furious'[26]. Others who knew him better accepted his
mannerisms 'having learned to know and admire him in the rather more
closely knit atmosphere of the Montreal and Chalk River Laboratories'[27]. It
was this reputation that made it possible for problems which had 'surfaced at
Harwell' while he was away to disappear 'without trace on his return'[28].

Impressions of Cockcroft at Harwell tend to contradict each other. It was generally believed that he was an accessible Director. Some of the non-physicists thought, however, that he encouraged an élite among the physicists, and to Alan Cottrell, then a young metallurgist, he was a rather forbidding figure,[29] but both Spence and Amphlett agreed that

> unlike some senior physicists, he always gave credit to the chemists and the metallurgists, and for that matter, the health physicists, for their efforts[30].

Off duty, he was, as Denis Willson remembered, always ready to join in the fun. At one of the New Zealanders' parties, organised by Watson-Munro,

> we had to mime something for others to guess. Cockcroft lay down on the floor and rolled around, hissing and prodding himself in the ribs. He got up, joined in the laughter and announced that he had been 'a sausage frying in the pan'.

Stories about his imperturbability were relished. Edwin McMillan recollected going to Harwell on a visit from Berkeley and finding senior staff concerned, but relieved, after their Director had walked through a glass door without hurting himself, 'I have often walked *into* a door', mused McMillan on recounting this incident, 'but never through one!'[31]

The Director's house was the scene of much hospitality to staff and their wives. Compared with, for example, the Skinners' parties just down the road, the sherry parties at No 1 South Drive were rather more sedate, but both the Cockcrofts kept up the hospitality of the 'Chalk River tea parties and spared no effort in making those who had recently joined the Establishment feel at home, at the same time establishing strong and lasting bonds with the old hands returned from Canada'. Eventually Cockcroft created, as Spence told him some years later, 'a unique environment at Harwell'. Spence also commented that, 'Discoveries cannot be produced either by organisation or by decree. It is essential to create a free and lively intellectual atmosphere and to establish a high standard of criticism'[32]. Seligman corroborated this view; he believed that Harwell became

> a huge and comprehensive research effort on a scale—as far as I know—never tried before in Europe in such a massive way. And here Cockcroft succeeded so well, in fact, better and smoother than did our friends in the USA. The way he picked the right man for the job and once that was done gave him all the support, and let him lead the field was (and still is) unique and that inspired scientists and made them the excellent crew which he had formed. It is no wonder that more scientific leaders like Finniston, Flowers, Dunworth and Taylor came out of Harwell than any other institution.[33]

Cockcroft's main task in 1947 was to push ahead construction, like the specially-designed 'hot', i.e. radioactive laboratory for radiochemical work. Cockcroft chaired the monthly meetings of the Building Committee which kept a check on programmes and cost. On Saturday afternoons, Sir Charles Mole, Director General of the Ministry of Works, responsible for construction, used to come down from London and stroll round the site with Cockcroft discussing problems and future plans.

In January 1947 construction workers living in a nearby housing estate at Kingston Bagpuize complained about inadequate pay, food and accommodation. Cockcroft was asked to speak to the men and a platform was set up in the BEPO hangar. A trade union official took the chair. In his calm matter-of-fact way, Cockcroft told the men how the scientists had helped the Americans to develop atomic energy during the war and, as a result, the Americans were five years ahead of the British. He concluded by telling them:

> We are not behind the Americans in ideas and inventions. But that is not enough. We have to be backed by a powerful and driving labour force. The time at which we shall develop atomic energy in Britain depends now almost entirely on *you*[34].

The press, excluded from the site for security reasons, gave a garbled account of the incident which they had extracted from patrons of the local pub. Far from being interrupted by boos and catcalls, as Cockcroft wrote to Eric, 'the proceedings finished up with three cheers'. A separate issue, not brought up at the meeting, was the question of overtime pay. Cockcroft explained that the 'trade union had instructed their shop stewards to stop working systematic overtime—as a result of pressure from local employers who were losing men to us because we *could* work overtime'. Agreement was reached with all parties concerned and overtime continued, 'the trade unions being keen to help'.

During that spring and early summer the construction of GLEEP went ahead 'thanks to Watson-Munro's New Zealand drive and forceful language'[35]. In typical Harwell fashion, there was a cricket match preceding the opening of the reactor in which the scientists took on the engineers. On 15 August 1947 GLEEP went into operation and immediately began to produce isotopes, several hundred samples being irradiated for isotope production in the following year.

Shortly after this, the first nuclear physics conference on unclassified topics took place at Harwell; some 150 scientists attended the meeting, 100 of them being visitors. It demonstrated that the Establishment was as much concerned with fundamental research as with nuclear technology. Unfortunately the synchrocyclotron had not been completed. T G Pickavance, in charge of the project, told Ernest Lawrence that it was suffering from 'building delays due to shortages of materials'[36].

At Risley, meanwhile, the design and construction of the larger reactor (BEPO) was going ahead, a number of the Harwell reactor team being provided to assist the Risley engineers. Leonard Owen, who got on well with Cockcroft, was chairman of the BEPO design committee coordinating these activities. The reactor was to be housed in one of the hangars, and the roof had to be raised to accommodate the machine—no mean feat. During the winter of 1947 graphite was machined to shape in the workshops, and in March 1948 aluminium-sheathed uranium fuel elements were being delivered from Hinton's factory at Sellafield. BEPO became critical on 3 July 1948. At a special meeting of the Technical Committee, including Cherwell, Chadwick, Dee and Hinton, held at Harwell, as Cockcroft recalled,

> The final fuel elements were inserted one by one by members of the Committee until the pile diverged at 3.55 PM, the safety rods going in with a crash at a power of 35 watts to celebrate the occasion![37]

High power operation was achieved by February 1949.

Radioisotope production had been in the small reactor GLEEP; it was now transferred to the larger BEPO and, under the able direction of Henry Seligman, a strong Isotope Division developed in Harwell and overlapped similar work being done by Thorium Ltd at Amersham, Bucks, under Dr Patrick Grove. After the war the Government had conceived the idea of a national isotope production centre to be based on the small but well established company, Thorium Ltd, which for years had been distributing compounds of the naturally occurring radioisotopes. Grove had spent some time during the war at Chalk River, and realised that his company could handle artificially produced as well as naturally-occurring radioisotopes; a Radiochemical Centre was set up under Thorium Ltd and an arrangement was made whereby isotopes made in GLEEP not requiring further chemical processing were despatched direct to the customer, those needing to be processed being sent to Amersham first. With the much greater output of isotopes from BEPO and the vigorous selling policy pursued by the Harwell Division, prolonged and bitter disagreement arose between Seligman and Grove, and in order to settle the dispute the Ministry of Supply decided to take over Amersham and make it an outstation of Harwell.

Cockcroft told Denis Willson, in charge of the Extra-mural Research Division, to be responsible for the laboratory which would continue to be directed by Grove. Although this seemed to be a contradiction to Willson, he agreed to do it. He then discovered that Cockcroft had instructed Seligman to direct all work on radioisotopes. Grove was naturally upset and asked to see Cockcroft.

> I was present [recalled Willson] when Grove asked Cockcroft for an assurance that he would have access to him. 'Of course you can, if you are in trouble', said Cockcroft, 'all my Divisional heads do that. But your instructions on running the Radiochemical Centre will come from Denis Willson' (a surprisingly firm statement from the Old Man!)[38].

Cockcroft's informal way of introducing the new arrangement was not at first appreciated by his staff. Their grumbles reached the ears of Sir Ralph Glyn, MP for Abingdon, who used to take a fatherly interest in their problems. Cockcroft had to explain to him that 'a reorganisation of isotopery had been decided on to separate trading from research'. Glyn's reply inferred that the unhappiness was at least partly due to a belief that 'higher remuneration' could be obtained outside the Establishment and the staff only remained there because of its unique nature[39]. When Thorium Ltd was eventually absorbed within the Ministry of Supply, it was discovered that there was no significant difference in pay.

Willson, however, considered that the

> whole Amersham/Harwell fracas was an outstanding example of Cockcroft's ability to rise above organisational niceties and personal feuds between his staff in order to do what he believed was right. I thought at the time that I should feel proud of his judgment that I could sort it out.

Twelve years later, when Cockcroft received the 'Atoms for Peace' Prize, special note was taken of his 'liberal and sympathetic attitude' towards the development of radioisotopes.

While all these activities were in progress at Harwell, construction of the plutonium-producing reactors was under way. Cockcroft, as a member of the Atomic Energy Technical Committee, took part in the discussion in the spring of 1946 as to whether the reactors should be built with a graphite moderator and cooled by water; and whether the fuel should be enriched or natural uranium. He supported Hinton's argument that it would take four years to build a diffusion plant to produce slightly enriched uranium (U_{235}) and that, if plutonium was required by the autumn of 1950, the reactor should be built using only natural uranium.

However, in November 1946, largely due to the insistence of Cherwell, the Technical Committee decided that a low-enrichment diffusion plant should also be built as an insurance policy, and after some argument this was added to the responsibilities of Hinton's Production Group. In November 1948 the Government decided to build a high-enrichment section of the diffusion plant at Capenhurst with a target date for completion in 1955. This, noted Cockcroft later, was the first indication that the Government had decided to embark on a nuclear weapons programme, although this had been envisaged from the beginning. Harwell did not have much to do with this project except through membership on the Design Committee. The availability of highly enriched uranium in the future did, however, greatly extend the possibilities open to the Establishment in developing the nuclear power programme.

Cockcroft also took part in the discussions about where the production reactor should be sited and what type of reactor it should be. It was then believed that a water-cooled reactor, similar to that which the Americans had designed at Hanford, would be prone to runaway instability if the coolant water flow failed; the neutron flux would increase rapidly, overheating might ensue particularly if the shutdown mechanism failed, and then the atmosphere would be polluted by radioactive products. Hence the site would have to be located very many miles from a city, as indeed had been the reactors at Hanford, in the remote far corner of the State of Washington. A site in the Scottish Highlands was provisionally selected, but it had serious disadvantages from the aspect of construction. Risley and Harwell therefore concentrated on an air-cooled design, reaching the conclusion that a reactor fuelled by about 100 tons of uranium could produce a reasonable output of plutonium. At a Technical Committee meeting in April 1947 Cockcroft presented the case for changing from a water-cooled to an air-cooled reactor. Hinton agreed, and a suitable site was chosen at Sellafield, later known as Windscale, on the Cumbrian coast. Two reactors were to be built, each producing about 200 MW of heat.

Thus by the summer of 1948 the atomic energy project was well underway. The two experimental reactors were operating at Harwell and much useful work was being done, while at Windscale Hinton's group were constructing the plutonium reactors. Considering the difficulties encountered in postwar Britain, it was a satisfactory beginning.

CHAPTER TWELVE

SUCCESSES AND DISAPPOINTMENTS

Cockcroft had by now become a public figure, familiar to newspaper readers as the 'atom chief'. In that bleak period of power cuts and fuel shortages, the prospect of atomic energy was seen as offering a solution. John Wilmot, the Minister of Supply, had circulated a memorandum to the Cabinet in January 1947 urging the vigorous prosecution of the atomic energy programme on the grounds that it might be a 'necessity for our economic survival'[1]. Only the month before, atomic energy had been discussed in the popular weekly *Picture Post*, the article was illustrated with photographs of the Cockcroft family relaxing at South Drive, while he was shown with back to camera striding along the Ridgeway in overcoat and the broad-brimmed hat that he liked to wear[2]. Later, he featured in a strip cartoon by Ruggles of the *Daily Mirror*, Ruggles representing the enquiring layman wanting to know about reactors and isotopes.

He made a point of explaining the project in simple terms to the general public. In March 1947 he took part in the BBC's series of programmes entitled *The Problem of Nuclear Energy*; he gave an outline of the discovery of fission, and was followed by Oliphant who gave an account of how the atomic bomb was made, while Blackett forecast the peaceful uses of atomic energy[3]. In the final programme there was a discussion on how atomic energy could be controlled in a world overshadowed by the 'cold war'; Cockcroft had the last word when he warned that 'science is in danger but no more than civilisation itself. That is why we *must* solve the problem of control of nuclear energy'. He used to lecture, on an average, once or twice a month to scientific and non-scientific audiences up and down the country. One day it would be to one of the small communities near Harwell anxious to understand what the mysterious establishment was doing; on another day it would be to a branch of the Institute of Physics, or an engineering society, or to a Service audience. At the end of 1947 he complained of being 'over-burdened with outside lectures and have been neglecting my real work somewhat. I shan't be appearing in public again until March'; he had, of course, only himself to blame for accepting invitations from all and sundry to address them.

In later years his lecturing style had improved somewhat, though it was never inspiring; indeed, an eminent engineer who was an undergraduate in the 1930s has written:

> I remember Cockcroft's lectures as dry and precise; they told us just what we
> needed to know about electrodynamics, but the manner in which they were
> delivered gave no hint that he might have any particular interest in the subject.
> I concluded at the time that, as a junior lecturer (even though he was already
> famous) he had been assigned the task of giving a course of lectures that nobody
> else wanted to give. In fairness, I add that I was comparing him with magnifi-
> cent lecturers such as Alex Wood and J A Ratcliffe, plus others such as Ruther-
> ford and J J Thomson whose infectious enthusiasm made up for their shortcom-
> ings as lecturers.

On another level, in company with his friends, he urged how necessary it
was to bring nuclear weapons under international control, a theme that was
to concern him for the rest of his life. He joined an 'atomic energy study
group' which used to meet at the Royal Institute of International Affairs at
Chatham House and which hoped to collaborate with similar bodies in other
countries. Sir Henry Dale, the former President of the Royal Society, was
chairman, and other scientists who took part, besides Cockcroft, were Chadwick, Oliphant and Harrie Massey; Hankey, Sir Arthur Salter and Sir Oliver
Franks represented the diplomats and politicians[4].

Figure 16   The Cockcroft family relaxing at No 1 South Drive, 1948.

In the New Year's Honours for 1948 Cockcroft was made a Knight Bachelor in recognition for establishing Harwell as a centre for fundamental and applied research in nuclear physics. In answer to a letter of congratulation from Cherwell, he wrote, 'We are rather immersed in mud but showing good progress still'[5]. That autumn he resumed some of his prewar scientific activities in Europe by attending the eighth Solvay Physics Conference—15 years after the historic meeting on the 'constitution of matter' which he had attended with his colleague, Walton, in company with Rutherford, Lawrence and other pioneers of nuclear physics. Now the theme was *Elementary Particles* —an entirely new branch of physics just beginning to be investigated. During the early part of the year Cockcroft helped Bragg, chairman of the scientific committee, to make it a truly international occasion. Among the participants were Bohr, Casimir of Philips Company, Teller of the USA, Blackett, Dee and Frisch from England and Homi Bhabha, a former Cavendish colleague, now planning nuclear power programmes in India.

During the early part of 1949, both Tizard, then chairman of committees dealing with military and civil research for the Government, and Rowlands, Permanent Secretary of the Ministry of Supply, invited Cockcroft to succeed Sir Ben Lockspeiser, Chief Scientist at the Ministry of Supply. Although the salary was tempting, he decided to turn it down on the grounds that the research programme at Harwell was reaching an interesting and critical stage; he believed that his 'responsibility for research in atomic energy, together with its associated problems in the field of USA collaboration is a fulltime job and not one that should be shared with other important duties'[6]. Anyway, he preferred to remain at an experimental establishment, and his decision was supported by Dr C J Mackenzie, whose advice he asked when on a visit to Ottawa. Before the year had ended, however, Tizard again invited him to be prepared to leave Harwell for Whitehall, this time to succeed him when he retired in two years' time from being chairman of the Defence Research Policy Committee. As will be seen, he eventually decided to accept this offer.

During these years the Cockcroft family spent spring and summer holidays at a windmill at Burnham Overy which he had begun to use shortly before the war, it being near the scene of his brick-hunting expeditions; it was near the sea where the family could enjoy sailing and walks along the beach. In the spring of 1949 there was a different kind of holiday, the whole family going for a tour of Brittany and the Loire valley. Also he made regular visits to his mother and brothers at Todmorden, keeping in touch with the family business at the same time, and usually these visits were combined with a meeting of the Atomic Energy Council at Risley or an inspection of progress at Windscale.

In August 1949 he had gone to South Africa. Ostensibly this was a lecture tour to universities, but the real purpose was to discuss terms with the South African Government for obtaining supplies of uranium, of which there were large, untapped resources in the country. He stayed with Schonland who, after being President of the South African Council for Scientific and Industrial Research, was about to return to the Bernard Price Institute of Geophysical Research at Pretoria, of which he was the Director. Cockcroft already had him in mind as a possible Deputy Director at Harwell. On 23

August, he gave an important lecture at the University of Witwatersrand in Johannesburg, in which he touched on the military consequences of atomic energy, contrasting the attitudes of British and American politicians towards the subject. While the US Congress, on account of the McMahon Act, was continually preoccupied with the affairs of the Atomic Energy Commission, it was in fact

> Great Britain which has most to fear from atomic bombs. This is a natural con-
> sequence of the high density of population in our country and the great concen-
> tration of industry in a small number of centres[7].

He deplored the failure of the Russians to accept the Acheson–Lilienthal Report which advocated an international authority to operate and develop the nuclear industry on behalf of all nations, and concluded:

> The plan would have removed the very great fear of atomic weapons from the
> world while facilitating a real international effort on the development of nuclear
> power.

Cockcroft's impressions of South Africa were that the people were, on the whole, friendlier than the Canadians, but were rapidly becoming a consumer society based precariously, as he saw it, on gold. His liberal sympathies reacted against apartheid. He wrote to Elizabeth: 'The big curse of the coun-try is politics—that is, race feeling'; and he was shocked to learn that the Colonial Office had squashed a plan for 'a Pan-African scientific conference, seeming to resent scientists getting together on the spot to discuss problems of mutual interest', that is to say, scientists of different race and colour.

In Cape Town he met his old Metro–Vick friend, B L Goodlet, who had had a distinguished career in the South African Navy, had degaussed Cape Town harbour early in the war and had now returned to his chair of electrical engineering in the Cape. Cockcroft invited him to Harwell to come as Deputy Chief Engineer, where a few years later he inspired the concept of the carbon-dioxide gas-cooled reactor, known as PIPPA, the basis of the civil reactors to be described in due course.

Whilst he was away the Russians exploded their first atomic bomb, and sent shock waves through the corridors of power in the American hierarchy; the leading scientists had expected that the making of a bomb would take more than 4 years after Alamogordo, and leakage of information was suspected. A fresh examination of the security which had been in operation at Los Alamos was set in train and led to Klaus Fuchs; he had shared some of the innermost secrets of the weapon development at Los Alamos and had, rather surprisingly, visited Santa Fe, down in the valley below the mesa, a number of times during the war. Since 1948 he had been head of the Theoretical Division at Harwell, and had been given the job of getting an analysis of the radioactive fallout collected by the RAF from the Russian bomb test. A week after returning from South Africa Cockcroft was due to go to a meeting in Washington, and it was just before leaving to board the *Queen Elizabeth* that he learned the dreadful news that Fuchs was suspected of having spied for the Russians, not only during the war but also whilst being employed in Harwell. His first reaction was one of shock: 'Well, thank God,

I'm just off to Southampton. Don't tell me any more of this; I'm going away and can't be got at'[8]; and who can blame him!

Several families at Harwell had befriended Fuchs because he was a bachelor; he was good with children and was frequently used as a babysitter. Cockcroft respected Fuchs's work, and only a few months after Fuchs had been at Harwell recommended that he should be upgraded to a higher salary level, describing him as holding 'a key position in the whole world of atomic energy. He is one of the senior physicists not occupying a university Chair and could be a strong candidate for future Chairs'. During the spring of 1949 he was unwell and his doctor suspected that he had TB. That May when Cockcroft was on a visit to the States, Elizabeth reported that when Fuchs was advised by his doctor to take a complete rest, he 'became rather broody and unsociable altogether, having no interests of any kind to distract him'. He was never popular among the staff, though with one or two exceptions no-one suspected that he was the kind of person who might be a traitor.

Fuchs's treachery was naturally a shock to Cockcroft, though he later declared that it had not affected him as much as had the Nunn May treachery. As with the latter, he had to work with Fuchs until he was arrested, on 3 February 1950. Three days later, Oliphant wrote to Cockcroft from Birmingham:

I'm very sorry indeed about the Fuchs business. It must be a bitter blow to you and to AERE and, of course, to the position of the scientist in general. I don't suppose there is anything I can do to help, but if I can please call on me.

Cockcroft replied on 8 February:

The Fuchs affair has been a great shock to us all and, as you say, will be very bad for the general prestige of science.

After Fuchs had been committed for trial, Cockcroft received a letter from Philip Dee:

I have been rather shocked to find that quite a number of people seem to have been very well aware of the extreme communistic views of Fuchs. [Max] Born [who had been head of the Department of Applied Mathematics at Edinburgh where Fuchs had studied at the outbreak of the war] indeed told Tompsett since the event that Fuchs did not choose to leave Harwell for university life because he said he had a greater task to perform at Harwell. As far as I can gather, Born knowing Fuchs's political views felt this to be a remarkable statement. I greatly fear that there has been a very unfortunate blindness on the part of many people[10].

But Cockcroft must have been specially pleased with a letter from his American friend, Carroll Wilson, who had become General Manager of the US Atomic Energy Commission and who wrote to Cockcroft on 3 March.

We too have been deeply shocked by this affair. The task of providing information, perspective and a belief in the goodness of most human beings for your organisation must place an exceptionally hard burden on you in these trying days. I know that you will give your team the kind of leadership which will carry them through this crisis which may not be of short duration. As you say our mutual hopes for better cooperation will be affected seriously by the events thus far. How this will turn out in the longer term we cannot yet foresee. If you and I were seriously discouraged we would not still be in this business.[11]

Wilson's conjecture that the crisis might not be of short duration was confirmed in August 1950 when Bruno Pontecorvo, who had worked under Cockcroft in Canada and was considered to be an outstanding nuclear physicist and had transferred to Harwell in February 1949 to work on cosmic rays, defected to the Soviet Union. Earlier that year the authorities appreciated that because he had relations who were communists living in Paris, he was a potential risk as he had access to classified information. He was therefore encouraged by Cockcoft to take up a teaching post at Liverpool University, where he would have gone had he returned from the Continental holiday on which he disappeared.

Cockcroft, in the meantime, continued to be absorbed by engagements outside the Establishment. On 2 June 1950 he delivered the much-coveted Romanes Lecture at Oxford on *The Development and Future of Atomic Energy*, in which he gave a concise historical account of his and Walton's transmutation experiments, noting that Rutherford had said in 1932 that the idea of obtaining power from a nucleus was moonshine, confirming that, at that time, scientists conducted experiments for their own sake and that they were not seeking a new source of power. He continued,

I can testify to the truth of this general attitude amongst scientists at the time. Around 1934 the concept of fission as a possible mode of transmutation seemed to occur to none, we thought in terms of transmutation of the, by now, classical type in which alpha particles or hydrogen nuclei or radiations were emitted but never in terms of a splitting into two massive fragments. As Rutherford said on one occasion, 'it is a characteristic of science that discoveries are rarely made except when people's minds are ready for them'.

Cockcroft then described the events leading to the discovery of fission and the developments which led to the arrival of the French scientists in Britain, following the fall of France. Finally, he turned his attention to the possibilities of nuclear power in the future, dwelling in particular on its 'duality', i.e. its potentiality for good or evil. He explained that a duality for good or evil had existed since the first days of *homo sapiens* and warned his audience that they should not expect too much from nuclear energy in the immediate future. He said:

I think it is generally agreed that the development of nuclear energy from uranium is more difficult than had been supposed in the first flush of postwar enthusiasm. We shall not be able to predict its future with any certainty until we have built experimental power producers and obtained experience by their operation for some years. We shall require at least the next decade for this phase.[12]

He had always wanted to hold an international conference on nuclear physics at Harwell. The fourth anniversary of the Establishment in September 1950 was chosen for the event, the subject being 'Reactors and Particle Accelerators and Nuclear Physics Research carried out with their aid', and the participants came from Europe and North America. A garden party was held at Buckland House, an 18th century mansion 'embellished with sunken marble bath tubs, damask-canopied beds and a deer park', recently acquired by Harwell; Cockcroft had seen it advertised in *The Times* as being suitable for either religious or educational purposes. Members of the conference took part in a dinner at Christ Church, Oxford, at which Cherwell was present as host.

Cockcroft did not allow his interest in fundamental research to overshadow the importance of reducing hazards to those working in nuclear plants. He was a member of the panel on radiation tolerances chaired by Sir Ernest Rock Carling, a distinguished surgeon who became closely concerned with all aspects of radiation protection. Two important conferences on radiological protection and biological hazards were also held at Buckland House and in Oxford, in which Cockcroft took part.

He had by this time begun to develop ideas about the role of scientists in society, and one of his early lectures on this theme was given in Oxford on 9 August 1951. It was entitled *Pure Science* and discussed the meaning of scientific freedom and how it was changing under the stress of world events, and whether science 'has, in fact, been responsible for the troubled state of the world, and whether this has any effect on our attitude towards scientific freedom'[13]. After examining the working conditions of the scientist in Britain, he did not think that 'scientific freedom in this country is imperilled by State planning', but he was concerned about the

> American Internal Security Act 1950, carried against the veto of the President. As a result of the Act scientists now experience long delays in obtaining visas for visits to the United States, even for short term conferences, whilst there are similar, though different, restrictions on the visits of United States scientists to some of the countries of the Western world. It is, I think, the future of this freedom within the Western world which gives scientists most concern at the present time. We believe that our country and the Western world is strong because there is freedom of thought, freedom of discussion and political freedom. If we have confidence in our own strength we should see that these restrictions can only reduce our strength.

As to whether scientists were responsible for the 'world's present troubles', he answered by describing the work of the MAUD Committee.

> Thinking back to those dark days of 1940 I am sure that we had no doubts as to where our duty lay. If Hitler had been able to develop the atomic bomb first he would undoubtedly have been able to defeat this country and freedom might well have disappeared from the world. The project therefore went ahead, and within a year our Government had been convinced of its feasibility.

Dealing with the 'cold war', he observed that scientists had to

> make a choice, whether or not to work for the policy of their Government, and most of them have made their choice. If you asked a typical scientist what he thought was likely to be the outcome he would probably reply that he was hopeful that the policy of containment by strength would succeed, that the over-whelming power of the West...will make a world war impossible and the counsels of reason be listened to once again in world affairs.

In the summer of 1951 the development of Harwell as originally conceived was nearly complete, and the Windscale reactors were in operation. Cockcroft was about to agree to leave the Establishment to succeed Tizard as fulltime chairman of the Defence Research Policy Committee, other senior members of his staff were leaving for academic life or industry, and the future of atomic energy, whether or not it should be controlled by a Government department, was under discussion. On 18 May Cockcroft wrote a memorandum headed *Organisation of Atomic Energy Work in Britain* which, after the General Election that autumn in which the Conservatives were returned, was circulated to members of the Administrative Steering Committee of officials considering the feasibility of transferring control of atomic energy to an independent authority. He appeared to be on the defensive: the first part of the memorandum reviewed progress over the past five years, comparing the British project with the Manhattan project which, under pressure of war, took three years to produce plutonium and to separate Uranium-235, and Cockcroft claimed that it would have been impossible to complete the British project six or twelve months earlier[14]. He maintained that Harwell had a first class staff, though, as will be described in chapter 15, the second part of his memorandum set out his proposals for a change in organisation if the best of the scientists were not to find jobs elsewhere. Nevertheless the Risley Group had complained about delays due, partly, to errors of design or calculations of the Harwell physicists; one of these errors was an inadequate allowance for Wigner expansion† in the design of the graphite structure; another, all the fuel cartridges had had to be removed from the first Windscale reactor and a tiny piece of aluminium clipped from each of the aluminium fins by hand, for without this modification it is improbable that the reactor would have gone critical. Finally, after the reactors began to operate, a further error in calculation was found when the energy produced per fission proved to be below expectations. This, as Margaret Gowing, historian of the atomic energy project, wrote, 'was a mistake in the conversion factor and nothing at all could be done about it'[15]. The expected output of plutonium was diminished by the faulty conversion figures, but developments in weapon design ensured that the number of weapons produced was not affected. However, the shortfall in the performance of the first reactor was not repeated by the second reactor which achieved 90 per cent of its designed rating.

Inevitably some people had criticised what they considered to be the slow progress in the completion of the plant at Harwell. But a steady stream of visitors, including Cherwell, Vannevar Bush and Walter Zinn, Cockcroft's American counterpart, were impressed, as Cockcroft once told Mr W Davies, the Ministry of Works site engineer, 'by the remarkable progress... particularly in view of the difficulties of the time'[16]. Help had also been provided by Ernest Lawrence who had obtained permission—necessary because of the McMahon Act—for a small team of British scientists under T G Pickavance to stay at the Radiation Laboratory at Berkeley for several months and study the synchrotron. Lawrence also arranged for drawings of the Harvard

†Changes in the dimensions of graphite under irradiation known as the 'Wigner effect' after the Hungarian physicist, Eugène Wigner.

synchrotron to be sent to Skinner, now in Liverpool University. In July 1951 Lawrence and his wife stayed with the Cockcrofts, and his letter, written after they had left, must have given great pleasure.

> I was tremendously impressed by what I saw. I hope we will be able to keep increasingly in touch with each other and, as time goes on, develop much more extensive and sensible procedures for the exchange of information, for we can get much more done if we can have the benefit of each other's endeavours[17].

Cockcroft's personal contribution to the building of Harwell was well put by Denis Willson after his promotion to Secretary of the Establishment, and which probably reflected the feelings of other senior members of the staff.

> I am not very good at this sort of thing, but the moment does seem appropriate to say how happy I have been in AERE for the last five years and (on the whole!) what fun it has been struggling with the apparently insoluble. Thank you for producing the conditions in which such an outlook can survive[18].

In November 1951 it was announced that Cockcroft and Walton, then Professor of Experimental Physics at Trinity College, Dublin, were to be jointly awarded the Nobel Prize for Physics on account of their experiments in artificially disintegrating the atom in April 1932. Why did the Swedish Academy of Sciences take 20 years to make up their minds? It was certainly right and proper that Chadwick should have been so rewarded in 1935; and the 1939 award to Ernest Lawrence 'for the invention and development of the cyclotron and for results obtained with it, especially with regard to artificial radioactive elements', was most popular among physicists, but a careful analysis of the reasons for the awards in later years leads to the conclusion that there were awards for discoveries and developments which had far less influence on the progress of Mankind than the discovery of artificial disintegration of atoms and all that quickly flowed from that first experiment. It seems unlikely that there will now be a credible explanation. One *theory* is that some time before his death, Rutherford was approached about receiving the Physics Prize for the work done at the Cavendish under his direction (he already had been awarded a Nobel Prize for Chemistry). Rutherford is said to have insisted that the prize should go to one of his young men, and Cockcroft's name was suggested, but Rutherford insisted that if Cockcroft was nominated, Walton's name should also go forward. What was remarkable about the award was that whereas Cockcroft had, in the intervening years, won an international reputation as a scientist, Walton, apart from designing, but never actually building, an accelerator at Dublin, had been content to forsake original research for an uneventful academic life; but the prizes are generally given without waiting half a generation to see if the would-be recipient has lived up to the promise shown by the original discovery! Let it be noted, however, that there are other Laureates who have had to wait a long time before their pioneering work has been rewarded by the Nobel. *'Theirs not to reason why!'*

Before attending the prizegiving at Stockholm, the Cockcrofts went to Oslo for the opening of the Kjeller reactor, built jointly by the Norwegians and the Dutch. The ceremony was performed by King Haakon on 28 November in the presence of leading nuclear physicists, including Bohr, Lawrence, who was visiting Scandinavia to see his colleagues Edwin McMillan and Glenn Seaborg receive the Nobel Prize for Chemistry, Amaldi, Hafstad, Kowarski and Francis Perrin. The occasion provided an opportunity for discussions about the recently proposed European nuclear research laboratory and where it should be located. Cockcroft, accompanied by Denis Willson, spent some time at an official lunch at the British Embassy talking about the peaceful uses of atomic energy with Crown Prince Olaf. It was typical of Cockcroft that, finding their Embassy driver had gone home, they walked down the long drive from the Embassy to the main road and waited patiently in the cold for a tram to take them to their hotel[19].

The Cockcrofts arrived by train in Stockholm on Saturday, 2 December. After being received by members of the Royal Academy of Sciences and the British Embassy, they were taken to their hotel where they were provided with 'a magnificent suite looking across the water to the Royal Palace and the old city of Stockholm with its churches and spires. Below us, the little boats come and go to the islands'. They spent a hectic week before the prizegiving,

Figure 17   Cockcroft receiving the Nobel Prize from the King of Sweden, 1951.

sightseeing and attending the opera and receptions, while Cockcroft gave a lecture to the Swedish Academy of Sciences. On 8 December, they went to Uppsala for the opening of a cyclotron at the new Swedborg Institute. The Swedes had decided to enliven the ceremony by advancing the feast of St Lucia from 13 December. The party 'sat at tables in the deep cyclotron pit with candles and cakes' while a procession of girls dressed in white paced round them singing carols. Finally, Lawrence pressed a button in the control room upstairs to start the cyclotron.

On the afternoon of 10 December the Cockcroft and Walton families assembled with the other Prizewinners in the concert hall of the Palace to receive their awards from the King of Sweden. The citation for Cockcroft and Walton, read by one of the Swedish professors, described their experiment in detail, concluding that

> By its stimulation of new theoretical and experimental advances, the work of Cockcroft and Walton displayed its fundamental importance. Indeed, this work may be said to have produced a totally new epoch in nuclear research[20].

The King then handed to Cockcroft the Book of the Award, a medal and a token for a cheque (collected next day and worth £5800). Cockcroft later told his mother that it was 'most acceptable' and it was mainly to be spent on the education of his children.

> The King then talked rather vivaciously and warmly. He congratulated me and said he hoped our future work would prosper—all the time shaking my hand. It was certainly much more human and pleasant than our formal ceremony at Buckingham Palace.

At the banquet which followed, Cockcroft made a short speech in which he said, according to his account written to his mother:

> Although science was being blamed for the present state of the world, the overwhelming evil and danger came not from science but from political ideas which denied the freedom of the human spirit, and the values and rights of individual human beings. I also said that, in the present difficult situation, science could be one of the greatest shields of western civilisation, and that the honour which had been paid to science that day would strengthen us at a time when we more than ever needed understanding.

The next day Lawrence, Cockcroft and Walton lectured at the Technical University. Cockcroft spoke[21] on *Experiments on the interaction of high speed nucleons with atomic nuclei*, 'partly historical and it was rather fun to go back over our early experiments and to interpose tales of Rutherford at the Cavendish'.

Two months later, on 13 February 1952, Professor E A Bennions, Master of St John's College, died. This provided an opportunity for Cockcroft to stand for election as Master and so enable him to gratify his longfelt wish to return to academic life. Although he had resigned his Fellowship on becoming Director of Harwell in September 1946, he had been elected an Honorary Fellow a month later. While he sometimes visited the College to attend meetings of the Book Club, a select gathering of Fellows, he had been rather out of touch with domestic affairs since 1939, after which a new generation of Fellows had taken charge. All the same, he had left his mark as Junior Bursar, indeed a considerable mark, as he had been responsible for restoring so much of the old and for the planning of the new buildings, quite apart from his international reputation as a scientist, recently enhanced by the Nobel Prize.

Unfortunately Cockcroft's eligibility as a candidate for the Mastership was complicated by uncertainty of what the new Government was proposing to do about control of atomic energy. Lord Cherwell, who, it has been seen, had been a member of Portal's Technical Committee from the start, had recently been pressing that atomic energy should be transferred from the Civil Service to an independent authority. Cockcroft, since the war, had got to know Cherwell quite well as the latter had proposed him as a member of High Table of his college, Christ Church. To some extent he shared Cherwell's views, and the two must have discussed what would happen should the Conservatives return to power. If Cherwell got his way, and he was now a member of the Cabinet, it was not unlikely that Cockcroft would be invited to stay in atomic energy instead of taking the appointment in the Ministry of Defence.

In the Statutes of St John's the qualifications for Master state that he

> shall be a person who is distinguished for his attainments and learning and, in the judgment of the electors, the best qualified by his piety, discretion and knowledge of affairs to secure the good government of the College as a place of education, religion, learning and research[22].

Election of the Master is in the hands of the Fellows, and there are no nominations for candidates beforehand. On the day of the election the Fellows assemble in the Chapel and write down the name of the person each thinks most suitable. The papers are then presented to the President of the College, whose duty it is then to announce the name of the person who has gained the majority. Election of a Master at Cambridge is an important affair, but particularly at St John's where there are responsibilities for the administration of its large estates.

The election had to be held within 30 days of the late Master's death. Although the Statutes were observed and there was no canvassing, naturally some approaches were made to sound out Cockcroft's attitude to the possibility of becoming Master. In his characteristic manner, it seemed that without committing himself either way, he gave the impression that he would not be unhappy to return to Cambridge at that time but—and this was alas *so* characteristic of him—a listener would have been hardpressed to decide just what his wishes were. The other most likely candidate appeared to be J M Wordie, then Senior Tutor and President of St John's, who was at one time Cockcroft's tutor. Although Wordie had never held a university post, he had won something of a reputation as an Arctic explorer and could claim an unbroken relationship with the College for many years, but he was not a figure of the eminence and distinction of Cockcroft, factors to be taken into account if the Statutes were to be strictly observed.

Cockcroft was in Washington visiting the US Atomic Energy Commission at the time of the election. On 6 March he wrote to Elizabeth from aboard the *Queen Mary*:

> I am strongly detached about the St John's issue, feeling now that I don't much
> care either way, though I expect you are more drawn towards Cambridge. It
> would certainly be an easier life for you in many ways with the children away
> at school, save perhaps for Chris. Basil [Schonland] would probably come to
> replace me—at any rate by early 1953—if Churchill is desirous of this.

And a week later he wrote from Deep River:

> I have been wondering what St John's have decided though still with a fairly
> detached feeling about it.

To nearly everyone's surprise, especially those outside the College, Wordie
was elected. Oddly enough, C P Snow's novel 'The Masters', which depicts
the closely contested election of a Master at a Cambridge college, in circumstances not so unlike those at St John's, had recently been published and
Elizabeth wrote to John:

> I am afraid that, like Mrs. Jago, I'm not going to be able to call myself Mistress
> of St John's! I did so want to go back to Cambridge which is 'home' for me in
> a way that no other place is, not even Todmorden.

Close observers of Cockcroft believed that he too was bitterly disappointed,
but he replied philosophically to Elizabeth from Washington that the result
was

> not really unexpected. I am really very sad for you and the children, for it would
> have meant an easier and better life. For myself, I have been very divided. I
> should have loved to return to Cambridge and to have had more time to enjoy
> things. On the other hand, I am more certain to achieve important things where
> I am—to put nuclear power on the map and to get important research projects
> going. I had a letter from Cherwell today, written before the news was out, to
> say he thought that it was of the greatest importance to the National Interest that
> I should stay and he hoped that I would not decide until I discussed with him.
> Harwell was my creation. So there it is. I think we will settle down for three to
> five years and make ourselves comfortable at Harwell. I will certainly take life
> a little more easily and spend a little of the Nobel Prize on holidays together.

Elizabeth, now more reconciled to staying at Harwell, replied,

> I'm glad to know that old Churchill and his henchmen have the sense to realise
> your value. I hope they'll show it properly.

They realised his value to a greater extent than Cockcroft expected, for a
week after his return from the States on 29 March 1952, General Sir Frederick
Morgan, the new Controller of Atomic Energy, confirmed that,

> Since you set sail several things seem to have happened. (1) The wind-up about
> St John's College seems to have blown itself out. (2) You have been shot for the
> DRPC (Defence Research Policy Committee)—which will take up two days a
> week[23];

he had been appointed at a supplementary salary to augment his Harwell
salary.

CHAPTER THIRTEEN

POLICY-MAKING IN WHITEHALL

Committee work of one kind or another made it impossible for Cockcroft to keep his promise to Elizabeth to take life easier. His son, Christopher, then a schoolboy, often accompanied him on journeys from Harwell to London, sitting next to the chauffeur while his father worked at his papers, illuminated by a small desklight at the back. In Whitehall Cockcroft would, as he once wrote, 'flit from office to office', talking to Ministers or officials, lunch with a colleague at the Athenaeum or the Savile Club, attend a meeting of the Royal Society, and end the day by crossing the river 'to eat a sandwich and listen to a concert' at the Royal Festival Hall, completed in time for the 1951 Festival of Britain.

His introduction to Tizard's Defence Research Policy Committee (DRPC), already touched on, began in August 1950 when he became a member of its Atomic Energy Sub-Committee; this was intended to be the first step in appointing him fulltime chairman of the DRPC when Tizard retired some time in 1952 or earlier. The purpose of the DRPC was, as Tizard put it,

> To study war from the scientific aspect and... in relation to the general lines of defence strategy which the Chiefs of Staff have recommended and which the Defence Committee has adopted[1].

In it senior representatives of the three Services and the supply authorities and their scientific advisers met to decide what new equipment should be purchased for the 1950s. Tizard thought that Cockcroft would be a suitable successor, acceptable to both Service chiefs and to Defence scientists. Tizard combined being chairman of the DRPC with that of the Advisory Council for Scientific Policy (ACSP) formed at the same time as the DRPC but answerable to the Lord President of the Council on matters relating to nonmilitary fundamental and applied research, the recruitment of scientific manpower, and some other subjects, and he anticipated that Cockcroft, like himself, would take charge of both committees. As usual when offered an appointment which would take him away from the actual direction of research, Cockcroft hesitated and wondered whether he could fulfil 'such an important and difficult office'. The job would mean living in London, and his family commitments, which now included school fees for all the children, made him ponder whether he could afford to buy a house and continue private education for his five children. As he had to retire at 60, he could only hold the appointment for eight years, so that he needed, as he told Tizard, an academic or similar post which would continue until he was 65—'super-annuation being at its present low effective level'. At the same time, he could not simply turn down an increase of £1750 to his salary, then about £2670 net.

A year and a half passed before the terms and conditions of Cockcroft's future appointment were finally settled, partly due to changes in policy, and partly to changes in the political situation. Tizard's appointment as scientific adviser for both civil and military applications was dropped when the Lord President, Herbert Morrison, decided to have a fulltime adviser on civil scientific policy[3]†. With the job now restricted to only the military side, his proposed salary was readjusted downwards to one which was comparable to that of the Secretary of the DSIR. After a review of senior civil service salaries it was then augmented to £4500—a figure much more in line with his responsibilities. Even so, he doubted whether he could afford to buy a London house, pay school fees and be able to entertain[4]. Meanwhile, he continued to chair the Atomic Energy Sub-Committee of the DRPC which met, on an average, every two months, its function being

> to assemble all available information regarding the possible effects of the use of atomic energy for military purposes on the general strategy of defence, and to prepare a draft report for the information of the Ministry of Defence and the Chiefs of Staff by the DRPC[5],

a report which is still classified.

His appointment as Chairman of the DRPC was again deferred because of the General Election in February 1950 which returned a Labour Government with a majority of only six, and by the replacement of Morrison by Lord Addison, actually a scientist himself. Eventually on 31 July 1951 Cockcroft accepted *fulltime* chairmanship of the DRPC, and suggested that Basil Schonland should be his successor at Harwell[6]. Rumours of his imminent departure circulated in the Press in early August. After investigating the possibilities, the Cockcrofts settled to buy a house in Knightsbridge. But the future of the Labour Government with its small majority was in doubt. Cockcroft evidently had no firm preference for any party and would have accepted the Chairmanship of the DRPC whatever the shade of the Government; indeed there is an amusing insight into his political views given to us at the time of the 1953 Abingdon by-election when he happened to be abroad. Elizabeth wrote to him, 'The voting proxy has come but you never told me who to vote for. Con? Lib? Lab? Which?' When Parliament was dissolved in September 1951 he was in North America as chairman-designate of the DRPC, and on the 20th wrote to Elizabeth: 'I must get them to hold up an announcement about my moves until the new Government decides whether they want me or otherwise!'

Lord Cherwell, as we know, wanted Cockcroft to remain at Harwell, and

---

†Informed opinion felt that this decision was a bad one and that the Government only had a comprehensive and coherent scientific policy while Tizard chaired the two Committees.

on 9 November they met at Fort Halstead, where research on the atomic bomb was in progress, and presumably discussed Cockcroft's future. Shortly afterwards, Cockcroft informed the Ministry of Supply that he would probably be prepared to remain at Harwell and chair the DRPC on a part-time basis[7]. In the meantime he cancelled the contract for the London house. As related, he was in Washington when he was offered the appointment of parttime chairman of the DRPC in March 1952, and he wrote to Elizabeth on the 19th:

> I have said that I would accept and assumed the Minister of Supply [Duncan Sandys] concurs! I shall have the £4500 salary originally proposed which will give us about £280 more net salary which will help to pay for those holidays[8].

While he was in the States he took the opportunity of meeting his American opposite numbers from the Defence Research Board in Washington,

> a small group of people who evidently know a lot about the DRPC. So we compared notes about the most important problems facing us and found a great deal of common ground. It is always easy to talk to the US people—the difficulty always comes when we try to get documents transmitted. They then have to go through a wonderful red tape machine and little comes out at the far end.

He was impressed by the Weapons Systems Evaluation Group,

> a sort of super Operational Research Group for which we have no counterpart, though I think we need one.

Cockcroft presided over his first DRPC meeting on 22 April 1952, and thereafter used to attend meetings twice, and occasionally three times a month. He reported to Elizabeth the day after his birthday on 28 May that he had celebrated it by 'buying a grey top hat, an umbrella and a town hat, not black but navy. So I'm not quite the complete civil servant yet'. He never was, and according to several of his colleagues, his heart was never in the Ministry of Defence work. One observer, Chapman Pincher, who reported on defence and science matters for the *Daily Express*, was later to comment that Cockcroft 'took little interest in the Ministry of Defence, leaving Fred Brundrett to do the work'[9]. Sir Frederick Brundrett was Deputy Scientific Adviser to the Ministry of Defence and had previously been Deputy, and then Chief, of the Royal Naval Scientific Service. He was a good departmental scientific adviser and in the war had played an important part in recruiting scientific manpower and, as chairman of the Coordination of Valve Development Committee had accelerated the introduction of new electronic equipment to the Services. But he did not have the intellectual calibre of Cockcroft and had no standing in the scientific world. This was most unfortunate when important decisions, like the introduction of the V-bombers, guided weapons and advanced radar and radio equipment had to be taken. Robert Cockburn, who had left Harwell to become Scientific Adviser to the Air Ministry, attended DRPC meetings in that capacity and later described its inadequacies.

> The Chiefs of Staff laid down the policy and it was not easy to keep them informed of changes in their original assumptions. Moreover, each Service was responsible for drafting its operational requirements and this led to overlapping

specifications and duplications in projects. Financial control was vested elsewhere, and it was difficult to identify the total cost of a new weapon system and to relate it to the policy decision which had led to its development.[10]

It seems that, at the outset of his appointment, Cockcroft wanted to improve scientific relations within the Commonwealth, which was typical of his way of thinking. Some months before he became chairman of the DRPC he received a letter from Oliphant, now Director of the Research School of Physical Science at the National University of Australia, Canberra, which said that he had heard that Cockcroft was 'seriously concerned about the barriers to proper cooperation with the Dominions on defence matters'—and that he was going to 'take over some of Tizard's duties', continuing, 'You've been carrying a heavy load for some time now. Don't let it crack you as it has H.T.'[11]

In August 1952 Cockcroft had to make an official visit to Australia on behalf of the DRPC, and he also went to deliver the Royal Society Rutherford Memorial Lecture in New Zealand. Oliphant successfully persuaded him to board the children for the autumn term and thus enable Elizabeth to travel with him. They left London by air on 16 August, breaking their journey at Beirut in order to visit the ruins of Baalbek. When they arrived in Sydney the centenary celebrations were in full swing, but first Cockcroft had to visit the rocket range at Woomera where there was to be an atomic weapons test the following year. He went to Canberra to attend a meeting of the Defence Committee, afterwards talking with the Prime Minister, Robert Menzies, one of the topics of discussion being the possibility of Cockcroft becoming Chief Executive of the Commonwealth Council for Scientific and Industrial Research. It had, as he wrote later, an entertainment allowance of £2000 and a salary of around £3500, but when he met Menzies again in London at the end of the year, he told him that 'he didn't want to move from Harwell for three years for various reasons, including family, so we got on to other possibilities such as Basil [Schonland], Oliver Franks and other imponderables'. While in Canberra, Cockcroft addressed the Australian and New Zealand Association for the Advancement of Science, and took part in a recorded discussion with Oliphant and Sir Douglas Copland, Vice-Chancellor of the Australian National University, on the theme *This Technological Age* which was transmitted by the Australian Broadcasting Commission on 10 November. Questioned on future sources of energy, Cockcroft said,

> I think that atomic energy will be developed in a small way at first, and then we'll gradually supplement the power we now get from coal and water power and so on, and this will probably take us on for perhaps a century. But I'm quite sure... that new developments will come along and we'll probably learn in time to use the energy from the light elements which are always inexhaustible. There is far more energy than we can ever need coming down to us from the Sun, and I should imagine that the biological scientist will find a way of turning this solar energy into fuels which we can use, and so on. So I don't really believe that, in the long run, we're going to be short of power.

In regard to the increasingly higher standard of living enjoyed by industrialised countries, he said:

> I do think that it's quite impossible for the world in general to have, say, the
> number of motor cars per human being, the number of refrigerators, and so on,
> that the United States have. That isn't what we should think of in the future.
> We should think of giving them certain improvements in the other factors in
> human existence which make life really worth while, not expecting to get all the
> material comforts of the American civilisation.[12].

Another old Cavendish colleague visited by the Cockcrofts was Leslie
Martin, now Professor of Physics at the University of Melbourne, who was
full of plans for a cyclotron to be used to do fundamental research and to
produce radioactive isotopes for medical purposes.

On 15 September they left for Wellington, New Zealand, where they met
Professor Watson-Munro who had recently completed his work on reactors at
Harwell and returned to his homeland; Cockcroft lectured on the latest
developments in experimental power reactors. A few days later he delivered
the first Rutherford Memorial lecture at Canterbury University College,
Christchurch, where the great man had graduated in 1894. Lady Rutherford
was in the audience. Cockcroft recounted Rutherford's discoveries, emphasising his connections with New Zealand, and referring to the experiments of
Ernest Marsden with alpha-particles which led directly to Rutherford's
concept of the atom as a solar system having a very small massive nucleus
surrounded by electrons, this model, in turn, leading him to the bombardment of the nitrogen nucleus with alpha-particles in 1919 and the start of the
disintegration of the elements. The second part of the lecture was devoted to
an outline of recent work at Harwell, again drawing attention to the New
Zealanders' contribution. On the following evening, Lady Rutherford invited
the Cockcrofts to dinner.

After leaving New Zealand, the Cockcrofts returned home via San Francisco, where they visited friends at Berkeley, going on to stay in Chalk River
and finally reaching London on 12 October.

The following spring, Cockcroft, as chairman of the DRPC, went to India
and Pakistan, this time travelling without Elizabeth who felt unable to cope
with the heat. He left London on 27 February 1953 in a Comet jet airliner
which had just come into service, accompanied by Sir John Carroll, Scientific
Adviser to the Admiralty, Robert Cockburn, Scientific Adviser to the Air
Ministry, and Walter Cawood, Director of Scientific Research at the Ministry
of Supply. Their main purpose was to attend the Commonwealth Defence
Scientists Conference in New Delhi, but they spent the weekend of 28
February in Pakistan and talked to Mr. Khawja Nazimuddin, the Prime
Minister and his Finance Minister, Chaudhuri Mohammed Ali. The latter
told them that

> Pakistan was suffering from the fall in the price of cotton and jute and the
> necessity to import a million tons of wheat at a cost of £50 million per annum.
> So finances are somewhat tight. They never devalued the rupee so that it is not
> surprising that they didn't sell their cotton.

They met Pakistani Service chiefs who gave them the impression that

'Pakistan is running down and that only the emergence of a man of genius and decision... can save her'. This was soon to be achieved by General Ayub.

Cockcroft's party left for New Delhi on Sunday evening, arriving in the early hours of the following morning; they were met by the British Military attaché and representatives from the British High Commissioner's Office and the Indian Ministry of Defence—'pretty good for 4.15 AM'. Cockcroft described his stay in New Delhi in several long letters to Elizabeth. The inaugural session took place later that day at the Indian National Physical Laboratory, the conference being formally opened on Tuesday. Meanwhile Cockcroft had a chance to look at New Delhi, admiring 'its monumental character, the huge Government buildings, Herbert Bakerish and Lutyensish styles, tree lined avenues and large houses of senior civil servants'. On Wednesday evening the British scientists entertained the American representative, Dr Howard Robertson, Director of the US Weapons Systems Evaluation Group, who had been Eisenhower's scientific adviser in North-west Europe. After the end of the session on Thursday, Cockcroft called on the British High Commissioner, Sir Alec Clutterbuck, and 'found him in bed with phlebitis'. They 'talked about India for half an hour and I got the general picture of the situation'. He had to give a lecture on atomic energy developments and was invited to a cocktail party given by the Canadian High Commissioner where he met Bhabha again, now chairman of India's Atomic Energy Commission, and other prominent Indian scientists,

> a Poet and a Lady Professor of Palaeontology from Liège. A beautiful lady running an artistic centre in Madras talked to me about the temples in southern India and how they used to be a centre for village life for plays, music, dancing and sculpture.

On Friday he lunched with Sardar Vallabhbhai Patel, the Deputy Prime Minister, and met defence scientists and staff officers.

> Most of [the latter] had been to the Imperial Defence College for a year. The atmosphere was pretty friendly and that I find is pretty general. I think if India continues to receive help both from ourselves and, in future, from the US, that it has a good chance of settling down and becoming a big influence in Asia for the good. That is the principal justification for our being out here.

He spent the weekend at Agra as the guest of the Brigadier of the local command, 'British-trained and very courteous'. On the way, he saw the Taj Mahal where 'I could have stayed and looked at it indefinitely—the beauty was in the exterior and in the setting'. He visited the Red Fort at Agra and in the evening watched two pipe bonds beating Retreat. 'The British tradition stays on. In fact, we were impressed everywhere by the fine bearing and discipline of the Army'. On Sunday he went to Fatehpur Sikri, an old Mogul city about 50 miles from Agra

> travelling in an Army battle wagon which provided a great opportunity of seeing Indian village life and agriculture. This is humanity at low level in the mass, far removed from the Brahmins of the towns. I think I'll ask Sharti [Sir Sharti Bhatnagar, Secretary of the DSIR of India] just what impact his science has so far had on the villages, though he'll probably say they had to start from scratch

and build fertiliser factories and import new stock and new ideas into agriculture [as will be seen, he was to devote more thought to this subject towards the end of his life]. I imagine that the British Civil Servants confined their activities to canal-making and didn't try to educate the villagers. I should think that a fall in the birth rate is the most important single factor required in India and I believe it's beginning, but may be more than counterbalanced by longer lifespan.

When he returned to New Delhi he met the Prime Minister, Nehru—a 'very impressive person'—who presided over a meeting of the Indian Atomic Energy Commission, though they 'talked mainly about world politics and the chances of future wars and what they might be like'. The remainder of that week was devoted to visiting defence establishments, and before leaving India Homi Bhabha took Cockcroft to Bombay to visit the site of the proposed Trombay Atomic Energy Establishment. He arrived back in London, somewhat exhausted, on 16 March.

While he was in India, Elizabeth wrote to him: 'Your Establishment will be kicking over the traces if you leave it too much. Denis Willson wanted me to join his campaign for preventing you from doing more than one job at once'. Willson recalled that 'I could not reconcile Cockcroft's leadership of the overlarge Establishment with his lengthy and frequent absences abroad and, in particular, with his chairmanship of the DRPC. Nor (as it turned out) could he'[13]. Thus it was with some relief on all sides that he resigned as chairman of the DRPC in April 1954.

As there is still no detailed study of the work of the DRPC, it is necessary to rely on the impressions of his colleagues in assessing his contribution. Sir Robert Cockburn remembered that there was

> rarely any debate on the philosophy of defence research. Cockcroft would listen in almost total silence to the opinions expressed, but decisions would nevertheless materialise. I used to wonder how he managed to achieve this. The normal procedure in Whitehall is to lunch people, to build up lobbies—to build up pressure groups. I don't believe this was Cockcroft's approach at all. He was more like a detective carefully searching his way through the labyrinth of Whitehall, following each clue until he finally discovered where the one man lived who had to face the decision and take it.[14]

On the other hand, Sir William Cook, Chief of the Royal Naval Scientific Service, who had previously served under Penney, confirmed that Brundrett took decisions on policy[15]. He remembered that Cockcroft rarely contributed to the proceedings, though he was always interested to note the progress of new technical devices. Cook thought that Cockcroft had already switched his interest to the international field, in particular to the setting-up of a European nuclear physics laboratory.

Cockcroft's own views on the value of the DRPC were expressed briefly in a review of Ronald Clark's biography of Tizard when he wrote that

> the main difficulty in running the DRPC was that it had no executive powers; it was not loved by the senior members of the Ministry of Supply responsible for weapon production, and the Service representatives were concerned primarily to represent the views of their own departments.[16]

In a lecture he delivered at Leeds University on 8 February 1963, he drew a comparison between the DRPC and the Advisory Council on Scientific Policy.

> In my limited experience of the DRPC I found that it was rather too much dominated by Services' interests and lacked the independent members of the ACSP.

They, on the contrary, were

> more concerned with the *strategy* (author's underlining) of research and not with the day-to-day or month-to-month problems, or with the allocation of research grants[17].

A greater objectivity was later achieved in defence research under the chairmanship of Sir Solly Zuckerman when he nominated *ad hoc* panels of technical advisers to study important problems. Even so, Cockcroft continued,

> the difficulties we and the US experienced with Skybolt [the American-made air-launched missile which President Eisenhower agreed to sell to Britain after the cancellation of the British ballistic missile Blue Streak and which also ran into difficulties leading to its cancellation in November 1962] shows the considerable pressure brought to bear by political, military and industrial interests on a problem which was capable of resolution on technical and operational grounds alone.

Some years after Cockcroft had left the DRPC, new procedures for evaluating weapons requirements were introduced, and the five-year costing system led to more realistic estimating and to a more responsible approach to procurement and to greater stability in expenditure.

The Advisory Council on Scientific Policy, like the DRPC, had a part time chairman, Professor Alexander Todd, a distinguished chemist who was in charge of the Chemical Research Department at Cambridge University. He was supported by 17 Council members, one half of them being official and the other half unofficial members from industry and the universities. Cockcroft attended not only as Director of Harwell and later as Research Member of the Atomic Energy Authority, but also in his own right as a leading physicist, rarely appearing at more than three out of the nine annual meetings, the first being on 7 January 1953 when he succeeded Chadwick, who had kept the Council informed of non-military aspects of atomic energy. He continued to attend meetings until the Council was dissolved by the Labour Government in 1964 and replaced by a Council of Scientific Policy.

According to Professor Todd, Cockcroft was 'almost wholly silent' at Council meetings[18]. But this by no means meant that he was uninterested, as may be seen by his articles and addresses on technological education in the 1950s and the interest he took in Parliamentary debates on science, such as the important debate in the House of Lords in May 1951 on the policy the Conservative Government proposed to adopt to promote the higher education of technologists. Letters exchanged between Cockcroft and Todd also reveal his concern, as in one which he sent to Todd on 12 May 1952 about the need to find out the facts on proposed capital expenditure on university departments of technology and on technical colleges.

I am being told that the real limitation of expansion of technology in universities is solely one of building and accommodation. On the other hand, I was told only this weekend of a project for spending £2 million on a single technical college in a provincial city.[19]

Nevertheless, Cockcroft was probably happier and more effective as a member of the Council's Scientific Manpower Committee chaired by Professor Solly Zuckerman which dealt with 'the technical needs for scientific and technical manpower, for employment both at home and abroad and which had to report to the council from time to time'. Apart from Cockcroft, the other members represented industry and the universities. One of their most important tasks was to carry out three-year forecasts of the requirements for qualified scientific and technical manpower, and Cockcroft later asserted that

the overall forecasts have proved to be reasonably good, overestimates for one industry balancing underestimates for another. These forecasts have had an important effect in determining Government policy in university expansion.

A forecast[20] of the Committee for the decade 1960–70 had

the good effect of stirring up the universities into trying to improve the present inadequate output of graduate mathematicians†.

Zuckerman recalled that, on one occasion, the question of standards for sixth form education was being debated. Some members felt that the specialisation demanded by Oxford and Cambridge helped to raise and maintain standards. Cockcroft did not dissent, but felt that the raising of standards for entry to the older universities caused an intolerable pressure on sixth forms, and argued that the nation lost more through the deterrent effect of high entrance standards and scholarship examinations than it gained. Cockcroft and Zuckerman were then asked when they had last looked at an entrance paper. Neither of them had for many years! A few days after the meeting, Zuckerman received from Cockcroft a batch of entrance and scholarship papers with a covering note in the latter's tiny script: 'I couldn't get in. Could you?'[21]

He was one of a number of leading scientists who kept urging the authorities to improve the supply of scientists and technologists to which the Barlow Report of 1946 had first drawn attention. Not long after the war, in 1948, he addressed a British Thomson Houston summer school for professors of electrical engineering, and reminded them that in 1940 the

margin between defeat and survival was perilously small. I shall remember always the nightly discussions on the war with my scientific friends—the discussion then being always on how we could avoid defeat. We must see to it that never again shall we have so little margin to spare.

He continued,

There is much talk in high places about the need for MITs in this country, but

†According to Zuckerman, the annual output of qualified scientists and engineers grew from about 6000 to 20 000 during this period.

quite inadequate action in improving the funds necessary for effective work. Why don't the electrical engineers ask the DSIR for more help? I have never known them turn down a worth while project.[22]

His opportunities of comparing British and American production engineering methods convinced him that the British were handicapped by deficiencies in technical staff. In 1952 he told a meeting of the Royal Society

In spite of all that has been done to improve the output of technologists since the war, there is still an acute shortage, particularly of first-class design and experimental engineers, of radio engineers and chemical engineers.[23]

There was much discussion in the 1950s over the kind of institution in which technical subjects should be taught. Britain had nothing comparable with the institutions of technology or technical universities on the continent, like the Federal Institute of Technology at Zurich, or the Technical University of Delft. It was believed that the foundation of such an institution in Britain would probably milk the universities of their best teachers of science, while it was said that the older universities had little room in which to expand. Cockcroft, like a number of other scientists, thought that the imbalance between science and the humanities should be corrected, even to the extent of creating a 'new technology university'. Five years later Todd told him about the proposal for Churchill College which was intended to fill this need.

Cockcroft also wanted to improve the quality of university teaching. 'We ought', he said, to include some instruction in economics and administration so that the student becomes at least aware of the importance of this side of industry'[24]. He thought that postgraduate technological education in universities should be increased and improved and that the standards of experimental engineering should be raised. At the same time he never forgot the advantages derived from a broad general education such as that he had received at Manchester. Science students should be taught English literature, history and at least one language before specialising for university entrance— he said. He disapproved of culture being crammed into students at university, and believed they would widen their interests by joining societies devoted to the arts and so continue the initiation which should have begun at school.

These were some of the ideas that influenced him while he was a member of the ACSP. His way of putting them into effect was usually unobtrusive, as illustrated by the following incident. In 1957 his friend, Joseph Mitchell, who had returned to Cambridge after his spell at Montreal and Chalk River, had been appointed Regius Professor of Physics. Shortly after, he applied to the Rockefeller Foundation for help to found a badly needed postgraduate medical research centre in Cambridge. Cockcroft, in the course of a busy tour of the States, found time to lunch with Dr John C Bugher of the Medical Faculty of Cambridge, Massachusetts, who was a member of the Rockefeller Foundation and had been head of the Medical Mission of the US Atomic Energy Commission; he smoothed the way for a visit made by Mitchell the following March, after lecturing at Harvard. 'I shall never forget the meeting with Bugher', recalled Mitchell, 'it was just one example of the way Cockcroft always tried to help other people.'[25]

Cockcroft summed up the achievements of the ACSP in its latter years in a lecture in Leeds in 1963:

> It advised the Minister for Science on the policy for cooperation in space research with European countries and the USA; it took the lead in proposing the foundation of the National Lending Library for Science and Technology at Boston Spa which has recently come into operation; it has studied the gaps in our research programme and advocated more effort on oceanography, geophysics and materials technology: it has discussed and endorsed some of the Royal Society proposals such as the Institute of Theoretical Astronomy†: and the provision of greater support for the Biological Sciences. It has also advised on the policy which should be followed in founding centralised research establishments such as the National Institute for Research in Nuclear Science for the common use of universities and on the criteria for founding new international research organisations. It has also advocated a more vigorous use of development contracts for promoting industrial research.[26]

Zuckerman, however, thought that the ACSP did not fulfil the expectations of those who created it. Despite its access to the Cabinet via the Lord President it could not

> penetrate the fastnesses of individual Government departments. Only very rarely could it see papers dealing with the main stream of Government policy. Thus it proved to be most useful when dealing with matters falling outside the remit of individual departments, like manpower. This view was expressed in the Council's final report in 1964 which noted that the main issue by which it had been exercised during the 17 years of its existence was 'the scale and balance of our national scientific effort'.[27]

The disappointing results being obtained by the DSIR and the Research Councils since the war led the Conservative Government in 1962 to appoint Sir Burke Trend, Secretary to the Cabinet, to 'review the existing organisation for the promotion of civil science of the Government'. Cockcroft was on the Royal Society Physics Committee, chaired by Professor Cecil Powell, which provided evidence. Members of the committee were asked questions about the education of physicists, the financing and promotion of physics, and whether collaboration between universities and industry could not be improved. Cockcroft, then Master of Churchill College, was asked whether he was satisfied with the present multiplicity of authorities involved in the training of physicists. Confining himself to the field of higher education, he said he believed strongly that colleges of advanced technology and universities should be under the same control and that there should be a technological grants committee of the University Grants Committee to deal with them. He believed that there could be 'very much more interchange and direct links between colleges of technology and industry'[28].

---

†Cockcroft apparently set the ball rolling in a casual way asking the astronomer Raymond Lyttleton, why the Astronomer Royal should be an appointment of the Admiralty. Lyttleton believed that Cockcroft played an important part behind the scenes in getting the Wolfson Foundation, for which he was one of the Trustees, to put up money. In July 1966 Cockcroft agreed to be Wolfson Foundation nominee on the Council of Management.

This applies even more to the Government reseach establishments such as the National Physical Laboratory and the National Chemical Laboratory where the links at the present time seem to be very tenuous. For example, I was at the Chemical Research Laboratory a week or so ago and was shown work on the development of a new high temperature plastic with properties suitable for going up to temperatures of 600°C and providing good electrical insulation. I was told that, since Du Ponts had come out with a patent, all work on this would now stop and no arrangements whatever were being made for a follow-up. This is the sort of thing that makes a nonsense.

Trend's proposals, adopted by the Conservative Government and carried still further by the Labour Government in 1964, replaced the *ad hoc*, mutually independent DSIR and Research Councils by a group of interdependent research councils controlled by the Ministry of Education and Science, though this was rather contrary to Cockcroft's wish for a 'greater use of panels which would devote adequate time to important problems'.

During the late 1950s and early 60s there was general concern about British scientists and technologists going abroad after their training to earn higher salaries and to enjoy working in better equipped laboratories—the so-called 'brain drain'. While he was at Harwell, Cockcroft discussed this problem with C P Snow, then head of the Civil Service Commission Scientific Section, and some thought was given as to how to attract people back to work in industry or the universities. Denis Willson and Snow worked out a plan which became known as the Hoff Recruiting Missions and which met with much greater success than the attempts to lure scientists to Harwell in 1945.

On 12 November 1961, Sir Winston Churchill, who had, it will be seen, recently given his name to a college intended primarily for the education of scientists and technologists, wrote to Cockcroft, the Master, about the wastage of scientists and technologists who went abroad after being trained. Sir Winston suggested that there should be an apprentice system whereby young scientists should work in Britain or for a firm for a period[29]. In his answer to Sir Winston on 16 November, Cockcroft drew attention to the value of obtaining experience abroad, the important question being how many scientists returned. He believed the answer was about one quarter, and that 'we may be losing 22 out of 170 PhD scientists every year'. He suggested that it was necessary for counterattractions to be made available, such as a panel in the AEA to offer jobs, that laboratories and other facilities at the universities should be improved so that they equalled the American establishments. He did not believe that overseas research fellowships should be interfered with, but suggested that fellowships might be made conditional on returning to work in the UK for several years[30].

He had already been asked that year to give evidence to the Robbins Committee on Higher Education. Most of the points he raised were drawn from his addresses over the past ten years, such as the collaboration of Government scientists with universities (at Harwell he had made the cyclotron available for academic research), the raising of the standard of mathematics teaching for those going into industry or the teaching profession, while scientists and engineering students should serve an apprenticeship in industry before going to university. He proposed that the output of scientists and engineers should be doubled during the next ten years[31]. He thought more emphasis should be given to character training to enable scientists to lead their own research groups by the time they were 30. More should be done to encourage private charitable institutions like Ford, Nuffield, Rockefeller and Wolfson, to support educational establishments. He wanted science teaching in girls' schools to be improved† and, finally, he deprecated the creation of new departments in universities for subjects already well provided for, such as classics, oriental studies, botany, medicine and agriculture.

Cockcroft's excursions into policy-making in Whitehall may be summarised by stating that, as far as we know, he made little impact on defence policy, but that on the civil side he was one of a small group of senior scientists who regularly made public pronouncements on the need for improving the quality of science and technology and for improving relations between industry and the universities in the postwar years. His most useful contributions, however, were made not in committee rooms but in brief conversations over the dinner table, or in university common rooms, or in the departure lounge of London Airport. In such an informal atmosphere, he was usually able to help those who sought his advice.

†A headmistress said, after he had lectured to her school, that his audience thought 'he really seemed to care about womens' education'.

CHAPTER FOURTEEN

'PUTTING NUCLEAR POWER ON THE MAP'

Our account of Cockcroft's role as Director of Harwell has so far been restricted to the part he played in promoting the research undertaken for the production both of fissile material in the Windscale reactors and of radioisotopes in the two experimental reactors at Harwell. Of greater importance, in the long run, was the research programme for power reactors which would make possible the generation of electricity in the UK by a series of nuclear power stations. This objective had always been in Cockcroft's mind, and towards the end of 1944 he set up the Future Systems Group in Montreal for the purpose of studying possible methods of producing nuclear power. In May 1945 the two leading members of the Group, Stephen Bauer and J Diamond, wrote a report which considered five types of reactor—breeders, converters, power reactors using enriched uranium fuel elements, uranium hydride reactors to be used as pulsed neutron sources, and a high temperature reactor to be used with gas turbines. It was not possible at this time to follow up their study with technological work[1].

These studies were resumed shortly after the foundation of the Establishment at Harwell, but at a low priority compared with the urgent needs of building the experimental reactors—GLEEP and BEPO—and starting work in aid of the Windscale production reactors and the chemical separation plant. There was at this time a good deal of scepticism, even among such distinguished scientists as Chadwick, Blackett, Cherwell and Tizard, about the chances of achieving nuclear power, and Cockcroft later recalled a discussion at the Clarendon Laboratory in Oxford in 1946 at which Cherwell expressed his scepticism and Blackett responded that 'Oxford was the home of lost causes'. Cockcroft's optimism and enthusiasm in those postwar years may aptly be compared to his persistence in developing shortwave radar during the war.

Cockcroft commented:

There was naturally at this time a great lack of knowledge about the technology of nuclear power. The reactors built during the war operated with low fuel element temperatures, water-cooled reactors with exit coolant temperatures of about 80°C and aircooled reactors with temperatures of 200–230°C. No serious effort had been made to study the materials problems involved in increasing these temperatures. There was also a great lack of knowledge about radiation

180

damage to reactor materials although the 'Wigner effect', the distortion of graphite under irradiation, was well known and had given rise to such uneasiness at Hanford that a six-lane highway had been built to evacuate the plant in case of any major reactor accident. We also learnt in 1947 from the experience with the Chalk River reactor that the 10-foot long uranium metal rods could expand or contract under irradiation by as much as six inches. The heat transfer capabilities for gases and liquids were also indifferently known. Little was known about the chemical problems of reactors, the interactions of coolant with moderator and metals under irradiation. All these problems were now to be studied at Harwell.[2]

At the outset, Cockcroft enlisted advice on the solution of these problems by holding a series of Power Committees and Power Conferences to which, in addition to the Harwell staff of physicists, chemists, metallurgists and engineers, a number of consultants were invited from industry, from the British Electrical Authority, from universities and other Government establishments. Hinton was also invited to send a member of his staff, but did not do so at that time as the Risley engineers were fully stretched building the factories and reactors for the production of fissile fuel and the large BEPO for Harwell. The Power Committee met every two months during the early years of the Establishment, the first being held while Cockcroft was still at Chalk River, Blackett taking the chair: Cockcroft was present for the second meeting, held in the early summer of 1946, as he happened to be in the UK. He remembered that he

directed attention to three major problems; the chemical problems of reactors; the disposal of radioactive fission products; and fast neutron reactors. Guggenheim reported on some of the technological problems of power reactors— chemical compatibility problems, the thermal conductivity of water, the effects of radiation on binary compounds and the thermal conductivity of gases at high temperatures.[3]

He had returned to Canada before the third meeting held in August 1946 at which, according to Cockcroft,

Fuchs reported on the properties of fast reactors and told the meeting that US scientists considered using liquid sodium or liquid mercury as the most promising heat transfer media for such reactors. He proposed the following reactor programme in order of priority; (1) a small plutonium-fuelled fast reactor and (2) a medium scale or large scale U-235 fuelled reactor. He considered that eventually all nuclear power stations would use plutonium or U-235—a vision of the 1980s.[4]

About this time there was a talk by Dr Constant, Director of the National Gas Turbine Establishment, on the possible application of gas turbines for nuclear power, though Sir Francis Simon, head of the Clarendon, pointed out that at gas temperatures below 700°C steam turbines were more efficient.

As soon as the Harwell laboratories and reactors became available, work on all of these technological problems started, including those connected with heat transfer, chemistry, graphite, fission product disposal and so on. Towards the end of 1947 work began on the development of a high-temperature reactor based on a scheme of Stephen Bauer's. Known as the 'marble' reactor, it was to have a core consisting of a random array of ceramic spheres containing either plutonium oxide or enriched uranium. However, it was realised that the project was in advance of its time and it got no further than an engineering study, though in due course an improved version was built at Julich in West Germany and, more importantly, a successor took shape in the high-temperature 'Dragon' reactor built at Winfrith in the late 1950s.

Another scheme was for a carbon dioxide cooled graphite moderated natural uranium dual purpose reactor on which a team from Risley worked in collaboration with a group from Harwell. The reactor would contain about 150 tons of uranium and would operate with fuel surface temperatures of about 400°C. The carbon dioxide would leave at 300°C and return at 200°C, steam would be raised at a pressure of about 200 pounds per square inch, giving a net efficiency of the order of 20 per cent and the reactor would develop 200 MW of heat and 35 MW of electricity. The Reyrolle Electricity Company, Babcock and Wilcox and C A Parsons, sponsored by Risley, participated in the scheme from February 1948. But owing to the pressure of work for the military programme, the Risley team was unable to take part in these studies after 1948 and they were continued at Harwell.

Meanwhile the Americans were starting to build experimental power reactors, and at the end of 1947, Cockcroft, as will be explained in a later chapter, was largely instrumental in helping to negotiate a *modus vivendi* whereby information could be exchanged with the Americans on non-military topics, including the design of natural uranium power-producing reactors, and on research experience with low power experimental reactors. No time was lost in sending reactor specialists from Harwell to visit American laboratories. On 3 September 1948 Cockcroft wrote, 'During the last six months we have developed an interchange of information with the Americans in limited fields'[5], including the design and operation of natural graphite reactors. C A Rennie, in particular, went to the Brookhaven Laboratory to learn about its experimental natural uranium power reactor. Cockcroft considered that for the next five years the principal difficulties would have to be dealt with by the chemists and chemical engineers.

Shortly before this, he had presided over the second Power Conference at Harwell in August. Some progress had been reported, as BEPO was in operation and could be used to study the effect of radiation on reactor materials and reactor compatibility problems; the NRX reactor at Chalk River was providing information on the irradiation damage to graphite. In October, while on a visit to North America, he was able to collect valuable information about power reactors from visits to various laboratories. At the end of his tour he reported to Dr F N Woodward, British Scientific Liaison Officer in Washington, that he had been received at Brookhaven 'in a very friendly way and almost killed by hospitality. The information received is of the greatest importance to us'[6] and he wrote to Elizabeth that he had spent a whole day at the Argonne Laboratory 'where they are building something like Harwell'. Unfortunately a year later Fuchs's treachery caused the flow of information to dry up. During the visit he heard that 'at Chalk River they are likely to have three grams of plutonium separated early in the new year', and he told

Michael Perrin that 'we ought to arrange with the Canadians to transmit one gram to Harwell early in 1949'.[7]

During that year Harwell began to examine power-producing reactor schemes which were more orthodox than the high-temperature reactor, especially reactors which would be fuelled by enriched uranium. There were many discussions in the Harwell Power Steering Committee which were, according to Margaret Gowing, the atomic energy historian, 'often "prolonged", "heated", or "inconclusive" ', and Cockcroft had difficulty in pulling a clearly defined programme out of the debates. However, on 22 November 1949 he had, at last, worked out what he called a 'UK Nuclear Power Reactor Programme', which he submitted to the Atomic Energy Technical Committee and which defined work to be done over the next five years, if approved[8]. His objectives were as follows:

(1) Development of a breeder reactor which would produce more secondary fuel (Plutonium or U-233) than primary fuel consumed.

(2) Development of a reactor in which the heat developed in fission could be converted efficiently into electric power while the reactor would have an economical operating life.

(3) Development of methods for processing nuclear fuel which would lead to low overall power costs.

(4) Propulsion for a nuclear submarine.

The nuclear power development programme would take place in two phases:

(a) the technical research and development programme at Harwell to solve the basic physical, chemical and metallurgical problems likely to be met in nuclear power development;

(b) construction of a number of experimental prototype reactors.

The Technical Committee recommended that work should start on a breeder reactor using highly enriched nuclear fuel as it would be of value 'in providing the first practical experience of nuclear power generators and would serve as a prototype for a nuclear power unit for propelling a submarine'. With this remit, Cockcroft formed a group to investigate using enriched uranium in a reactor, which began work in 1950. Their design, however, proved to be too large for a submarine, and the project was shelved until highly enriched uranium became available, making it possible to use a much smaller reactor core. Highly enriched uranium did not become available until 1956, but in the meantime, as Cockcroft wrote,

> an offer of collaboration with the US, sponsored by Admiral Rickover, developed, and so an Admiralty/Rolls Royce/Westinghouse agreement led to the production by Rolls Royce of the US design of nuclear propulsion units. Harwell was able to help by carrying out a zero-energy reactor check on the core design and by testing Rolls Royce produced fuel elements in the DIDO reactor, and also by the training of naval staff.... However the Harwell engineers were never very keen on nuclear propulsion mainly because they could not see any commercial application to maritime propulsion.[9]

The Harwell Reactor Group meanwhile continued studying the possibility of a reactor for generating electricity, and by the autumn of 1950 had made sufficient progress for a conference on natural uranium power reactors to be held. It began on 29 September and many industrial leaders were present. Cockcroft related how the results of the work were presented by R V Moore, and

> estimates of costs of nuclear power for the 90 MW (Electrical) graphite moderated carbon dioxide reactor were given. The capital cost was estimated (or guessed) at £9 million or £100 per kW. Fuel costs were estimated for burn-ups varying between 1000 and 8000 MW day/ton and for fabrication and uranium costs ranging from £5000 to £15 000 per ton of fuel elements, interest on capital was assumed to be 4 per cent (the current rate), the life of the station was assumed to be 25 years and the load factor 60 per cent. On this basis the overall cost of the generation for a 3000 MW day/ton burn-up and uranium fuel element costs of £15 000 per ton was about 0.6 old pence per unit, about equal to the cost of generation from an average steam station. This was considerably lower than previous estimates and provoked a good deal of discussion, especially by the supporters of fast reactors. It was decided, therefore, to form a Harwell Design Group using natural uranium fuel and for the technology to be studied by Harwell Divisions. At the dinner following the conference, Lord Hives of Rolls Royce congratulated us on 'having taken a decision'. The progress of work on the design of a fast reactor was also reported and seemed to be very promising. The breeding prospects were good and the absence of a moderator would eliminate trouble from the Wigner effect. Plutonium was assumed to become available by 1952.[10]

The decision to use natural fuel in a thermal reactor was based on a belief that enriched uranium would not be available in sufficient quantities for a nuclear power programme. This decision ruled out the possibility of using ordinary water as a moderator. Heavy water was not available in adequate quantities but graphite of nuclear purity† could be produced industrially. The principal disadvantage of using graphite was that the reactor had to be large so that comparatively low power densities would be achieved. A study of the possible gases for heat transfer—helium, hydrogen, nitrogen and carbon dioxide—led again to the choice of carbon dioxide as helium, the most suitable gas, was not then available in sufficient quantities. The Chemistry Division checked the compatibility of carbon dioxide with graphite under irradiation by experiments in BEPO, and their small-scale results checked extremely well with later experience in Calder Hall. The most important technological problem, Cockcroft continued,

> was the design of the uranium fuel elements. Metallurgical research showed that the distortion of uranium metal under irradiation could be minimised by heat treatment which would produce a metal having fine grained randomly orientated crystallites. A study was made of a method for sheathing the uranium with some material having better physical properties than aluminium which had been used in all previous gas-cooled reactors. As a result of this work an alloy of magnesium, beryllium and calcium we called magnox was developed which had a melting point of 650°C allowing surface temperatures of the order of 400°C to be used. Studies were also made of the optimum design of the fuel element sheathing surfaces for maximum heat transfer.[11]

---

†i.e. graphite as free as possible from elements which have a high affinity for neutrons.

Studies by the Natural Uranium Group under Brian Goodlet continued throughout 1951. In order to supplement the limited resources of Harwell, Cockcroft asked Sir Claude Gibb for some specialist assistance; Gibb's companies, Parsons and Reyrolles had, as already reported, given serious consideration to the gas-cooled reactor in 1947 – 48 at Hinton's request. Gibb sent several of his engineers to Harwell to help with the studies on heat transfer and the design of the gas circulation system. They were assisted by other engineers from Babcock & Wilcox, Whessoe and the British Electricity Authority. Cockcroft also invited all engineering firms which had an interest in nuclear power to allow some of their promising young men to gain experience at Harwell. A number took advantage of this opportunity, and usually returned to their firms with reluctance. They were impressed not only with the quality of the work at Harwell, but also by the 'grinding clash of powerful personalities'[12] and were astonished that Cockcroft was able to hold the place together.

By the end of 1951 the Harwell Power Conference declared itself in favour of the natural uranium reactor as the only way of making an early beginning with nuclear power, their feelings being voiced by Sir Harold Roxbee Cox, Chief Scientist of the Ministry of Fuel and Power, who said

> We must build a nuclear power station. Nothing can be proved on its economics until we have tried it.[13]

However, early in 1952 Cockcroft submitted a revised reactor programme which, although including PIPPA (Pile for Industrial Production of Plutonium and Power) as the natural uranium project was now called, also contained proposals for a heavy water moderated reactor (HIPPO), similar to the one at Chalk River, and a fast reactor (ZEPHYR). He thought that PIPPA and HIPPO should be handed over to industry for further design and construction[14]. The Technical Committee decided, however, that PIPPA should be placed on a lower priority to the other schemes, mainly on the grounds that it would make no contribution to the long-term power problem because it had a very low burn-up of fissile atoms; even Hinton, in spite of the early work at Risley, was unenthusiastic.

As it happened, PIPPA was saved that summer because, in Cockcroft's words,

> at an important meeting of the Technical Committee on 8 August, I told the Committee that the Chiefs of Staff had asked for a statement of what would be required to double the output of plutonium and that we could either repeat the Windscale production reactors or build one or more PIPPAs. R V Moore reported on the PIPPA design and economics. He said that the cost of production of plutonium would be about 60 per cent of the cost of the plutonium from the Windscale reactors.[15]

By the end of 1952 project PIPPA had become a concept for a nuclear power station capable of producing 150 MW of heat and 35 MW of electricity, and supplying the Chiefs of Staff with military plutonium.

On 8 January 1953 Cockcroft gave the opening address at a symposium on Nuclear Reactor Instrumentation held at the Institution of Electrical

Engineers. Entitled *Nuclear Reactors and their Applications*, it presented some comparative costs for fossil fuelled and nuclear power stations, thereby incurring the displeasure of Duncan Sandys, the Minister of Supply, who 'considered that such important pronouncements should be reserved for Ministers'. Cockcroft concluded:

> It seems to be fairly certain now that large-scale nuclear power stations of the natural uranium type can be built and that they will work with reasonable efficiency and produce power at a cost not much greater than that for existing power stations.[16]

His estimate was further elaborated at a Nuclear Power Conference by Goodlet and Moore later that year. As Cockcroft wrote in 1967:

> The capital costs which were still guessed rather than closely estimated were now assumed to be £227 per kW. Fuel costs were estimated on the basis that heat extraction would be achieved corresponding to 2000 MW day/ton. The reactor was assumed to have a 20-year life—though it was not possible at that time to estimate the life of the graphite. Finally, an 80 per cent load factor and the prevailing interest rates of 4 per cent were taken. The overall result was a prediction of a generating cost of about 1d per unit with no credit taken for plutonium production. Goodlet in a companion note said that the cost was some 50 per cent higher than generating costs from fossil fuelled power stations and that the 20-year life might be optimistic.[17]

In March 1953, the Government at last decided that PIPPA should be built in the form of a two reactor power station at Calder Hall, near Windscale. Final design and construction were to be Hinton's responsibility. Removal of the work to Risley caused some consternation among the PIPPA team at Harwell, and Goodlet in particular was heartbroken; to Cockcroft he wrote:

> PIPPA will give Harwell plutonium, all of which we need. PIPPA for Harwell is therefore a solid proposition even if we never build another.[18]

and he told Denis Willson, then Secretary at Harwell, 'Harwell is *finished* if we cannot build PIPPA'. Willson was unable to convince him that 'Harwell might equally be finished if we tried to build everything'.[19] R V Moore, however, accepted Hinton's offer to take on all the engineers in the Harwell team.

Three and a half years later, on 17 October 1956, Cockcroft was present when the Queen opened Calder Hall, the world's first large nuclear power station. There is no record of his impressions on that occasion, but he was to write later

> Since that time this 'Model T' nuclear power station has played an invaluable role, not only in producing plutonium but in providing full-scale operating experience of nuclear power, serving also as a training school for nuclear power station engineers and as a test bed for fuel elements for the later commercial power stations. Calder Hall was built within the estimated cost of £16.5 million and within the estimated time—a triumph for the Risley Engineering Group.[20]

In 1958, when about to leave the atomic energy project, Hinton gave the James Forrest Lecture on the theme *Nuclear Power Development: Some Experiences of the First Ten Years*. Cockcroft wrote on the Harwell copy, 'Not much credit for Harwell PIPPA work!'. He passed it on to Denis Willson who wrote back:

> The major problem of the early years arose from the fact that we were then a small organisation working against an almost impossible timetable in a field in which we had incomplete knowledge. By 1953 and Calder Hall the organisation was solidly founded.

He felt that there was a

> growing danger that the load of financial responsibility will stifle initiative.[21]

Commenting further on the lecture, Willson felt that there had been

> no credit given for heat transfer work helping on finning problems; no credit (naturally) for basic principles of burst slug detection gained from the USA, nor for ICI help on the plutonium extraction process.†

The fast reactor had always been a close second to PIPPA, and in February 1952, the Technical Committee agreed that a zero energy fast reactor (ZEPHYR) should be built at Harwell and that a full-scale fast reactor design should be carried out at Risley. George Dalton, a New Zealand ex-Rhodes scholar, was put in charge of ZEPHYR to study the physics of fast reactor systems and the fuel element technology. Harwell had already produced the first speck of plutonium in December 1951, and soon sufficient plutonium had been extracted from fuel elements to fabricate small plutonium rods in the plutonium wing of the 'hot' laboratory. Due to the combined efforts of engineers and technologists, ZEPHYR was completed and became critical in February 1954. One of its spectacular achievements was to show that under its idealised conditions the breeding factor was two, i.e. two plutonium nuclei were produced for each plutonium nucleus fissioned. According to Cockcroft, 'a rather casual announcement of this at the 1955 Geneva Conference resulted in a considerable stir'.[22]

At Risley the engineering study was carried through by James Kendall and D J M Kay. Cockcroft related that

> They reported to the Harwell Power Committee of August 1953 on a 100 MW (Heat) reactor with a core size of two feet in diameter and height, pointing out that the heat removal capability would have to be six times that of the most highly rated boiler existing at that time and six times more of a jet engine combustion chamber. The heat flux from the fuel elements would be about 1 kW per square centimetre. Distortion of the fuel elements under irradiation would be a crucial problem. The core would be cooled with liquid sodium or sodium potassium alloy. A meltdown of the core might lead to a nuclear explosion equivalent to about eight tons of TNT so that a safe design of the core with a guaranteed coolant supply would be essential. The designers concluded in their report that: 'At first sight, the Fast Reactor seems unrealistic. On closer examination it appears fantastic. On the other hand, to build a modern coal-fired power station would have appeared ridiculous to James Watt had it been put forward in 1763. We are now in the same position with nuclear power as

†See Gowing *Independence and Deterrence*, Vol.2, pp.171–6.

James Watt was with coal-fired steam power at his time. We cannot claim to have had such a good idea about our power plant as James Watt had about his. The physicists tell us that breeding can only be achieved in a fast reactor. They may change their minds next year but whether they do or not it is left with the engineers to get on with the job.' This report provoked a lively discussion at the Conference at the end of which Leonard Owen got up and declared his faith in Fast Reactors. And so this design work went on and a decision was taken at one of the early meetings of the newly-formed Atomic Energy Authority in late 1954 to proceed with what was to become the 60 MW (Thermal) Dounreay Fast Reactor.[23]

This was built remarkably quickly and operated for the first time in 1959; it has had a wonderful record of operation and experimentation, and thus paved the way for the design and construction of the Prototype Fast Reactor which was started in the year of Cockcroft's death.

The Americans meanwhile had, for their own reasons, gone on to develop pressurised water reactors and boiling water reactors, schemes which required enriched uranium, and in the early 1950s the British had little of this to spare for a power programme. Cockcroft, however, paid close attention to American developments, and looked at the boiling water reactor at the Argonne Laboratory and visited Idaho where water moderated reactors were tested for safety. At Harwell, the Reactor Group made annual comparisons with the American equivalents, the capital costs of the British reactors being, according to Cockcroft, 'generally about £10 per kW higher than the water moderated reactors but the generating costs were the same within the error of estimating'.

As he told Sir Edward Appleton when the latter was preparing the Reith Lectures for 1958 entitled *Science and the Nation*, the British decision to

go their own way in developing the gas-cooled, graphite moderated reactor...has turned out to be a good bet. The US have largely followed the water moderated route because on paper it looked better and they had the necessary enriched material. In practice they've had a lot of difficulties with corrosion and the first model built by Westinghouse will be quite uneconomical. However, I've a great respect for US technology and they will rapidly get over this and be formidably competitive[24]

—a sadly prophetic statement in view of the outcome; at the present time there are roughly 135 000 MW of electricity derived from water-cooled reactors in the world and about 9000 MW from gas-cooled reactors; the Generating Board today wishes to build at least one water-cooled reactor to gain experience.

The last power reactor project with which Cockcroft was associated was an improved version of the high temperature reactor which had been first considered at Montreal in 1945 and then at Harwell in 1947. The principal advantages of such a reactor were believed to be the reduction of capital cost per kW of the reactor and the ability to obtain high thermodynamic efficiencies. This scheme, known as Dragon, was put into effect at Winfrith and therefore falls into a later chapter.

Cockcroft's ambition in 1952 'to put nuclear power on the map' was fulfilled three years later when the Government decided to launch a construction

programme of 2000 MW of electrical generating stations to be built by industry after competitive tender, all to be of the gas-cooled, graphite moderated
form of reactor similar to, but larger than Calder Hall, and fuelled by natural
uranium rods clad in magnox; these to be supplied by the Risley organisation.
After the Suez crisis the programme was revised upwards to 5000 MW. Much
of the original research and later design of the PIPPA reactor was to Harwell's
credit, and was due to Cockcroft's enthusiasm and encouragement of the
team responsible for the studies. Indeed, there are those who would say, like
Sir Nevill Mott at the time of Cockcroft's death, that his real claim to fame
lay not in fundamental research in the 1930s, but in the development of
atomic energy, and that

> with his contacts in business and Government [to which might be added, and
> those in the USA] he was immensely effective in getting things done.[25]

Cockcroft's own estimate of the work on power reactors was expressed in
an answer to one of the questions put to him by the editor of a Russian
journal, *Technology of Youth*, in February 1967:

> What are the most likely projects for the development of that branch of science
> in which you yourself are most involved, and what development may this have
> on the future of mankind? ANSWER. During the last 25 years I have been
> mainly interested in the development of nuclear power for the production of
> electricity. I think this will have a profound effect in ensuring future supplies
> for the next 1000 years.[26]

CHAPTER FIFTEEN

MEMBER OF THE ATOMIC ENERGY AUTHORITY

The narrow majority by which the Labour Government won the General Election of February 1950 made it likely that it could not survive for very long, and this gave additional point to criticism about the slow progress of the atomic energy project that had been growing since the explosion of the Russian atomic bomb in the autumn of 1949. Cockcroft had always felt that his demand for autonomy for the Establishment had never properly been met and that there was a lack of elasticity in the Civil Service procedure and salary scales, feelings which were echoed by other scientists working there. The Government, however, refused to entertain the possibility of a need for change until it was conclusively proved firstly, that the present arrangement was hampering progress and secondly, that an independent body under broad Government control would be more efficient.

Early in 1951, Cockcroft had been considering whether to leave Harwell for Whitehall to become chairman of the Defence Research Policy Committee and whether to ask Schonland to take his place. He evidently told Herbert Skinner at Liverpool University, that he had named Schonland to succeed him at Harwell. On 4 March 1951 Skinner wrote to Cockcroft:

> I was upset by what you told me last week and perhaps should not have mentioned my own impressions as these were admittedly based on only slight knowledge. The main point, however, remains: Schonland does not know the job. General fears for the whole project were increased when Perrin told me he was going to leave. How can the Atomic Energy Council function in, say, two years from now, with no-one remaining on it who has a comprehensive knowledge of atomic energy matters (especially if Penney should also leave)? The prospect is alarming, and I should think that if further large expenditures are to be made, some other sort of authorisation will be necessary. I believe we should either go full steam ahead, or else be satisfied with the present situation and merely operate existing plants. To drift on with research and development under increasingly Civil Service conditions will not get anywhere worthwhile. And to get the organisation out of the Civil Service without having suitably experienced people in control would be merely foolish. Perrin's decision is bound to make the future much more difficult, and is serious also from another point of view—namely that he, who is probably in the best position to know, has lost faith in the job. I hope that I am being unduly pessimistic, but I think you will agree that the future will require careful planning.[1]

Cockcroft's memorandum on the *Organisation of Atomic Energy in Britain* of May 1951, already quoted[2], shows that, while he believed that Harwell and the plutonium reactors could not have been completed more quickly than they were, change was necessary in the long run. He wanted to maintain a core of around 30 outstanding scientists, and was concerned that some of the best were leaving for industry or the universities; he noted that with the exception of those joining the Establishment on Harwell Research Fellowships, current intake was disappointing in quality, and he thought that this was due to the fact that universities could offer better salaries and he concluded that, 'it would be impossible to get good staff so long as salaries and conditions are tied to an absolute parity with the rest of the Scientific Civil Service'.

Public expression was given to this dissatisfaction by Lord Cherwell, who introduced a motion in the House of Lords on 7 July 1951 criticising the slow progress in developing atomic energy and proposing that it should be removed from the Ministry of Supply to a separate organisation under the direction of the Head of Government. The motion was carried, and this encouraged Chapman Pincher of the *Daily Express* to write an article two days later headed WHY BRITAIN HAS NO ATOM (*sic*), and he gave as reasons, 'poor pay, departmental jealousy and sheer inefficiency'[3], and the inability of the Government to prosecute the scheme. He wrote that construction of laboratories at Harwell had been held up because of lack of steel, and quoted Cockcroft as telling a Parliamentary Select Committee on Estimates in February 1947 that his staff were having to 'work in holes and corners', though omitting to add that Cockcroft continued, 'they are doing effective work under difficulties' and that, although they were about six months behind schedule, he thought it likely that the schedule had been over-optimistic[4]. In any case, the laboratories and the experimental reactors had been completed over a year earlier. Chapman Pincher echoed Cherwell, urging that the project be handed over to 'high-powered executives with freedom to engage good men and sack bad men'.

However, there were scientists at Harwell who did not relish the idea of leaving the Civil Service, and shortly after the new Government had taken office in October 1951, Cockcroft called a meeting of Divisional heads to discover their views about a possible transfer of control. Seligman was the only member in favour of leaving the Civil Service, the others being either neutral or opposed to the idea. Cockcroft noted the weight of opinion and advised Cherwell, who was now Paymaster General and in the Cabinet, that the Establishment should be removed from control of the Civil Service at once. Despite what Denis Willson described as Cockcroft's 'apparent breach of faith with his staff'[5], only a tiny fraction opted, when the time came, to leave Harwell, among them the Secretary of the Establishment, R G Elkington, who was replaced by Denis Willson—a much smaller number left than the number of scientists who left Risley and Aldermaston. Willson believed that their final choice to stay was due as much to Cockcroft's influence as to any other consideration.

This was still in the future; Cherwell had first to contend with the new Minister of Supply, Duncan Sandys, one of his antagonists of wartime days, and all that happened in early 1952 was the setting up of an Atomic Energy

Board, Lord Cherwell being made responsible for policy at Cabinet level and Sandys answering questions on atomic energy in the House of Commons. Cockcroft, Hinton and Penney became members of the Board, while the Controller of Atomic Energy was now General Sir Frederick Morgan, who took over from Lord Portal when he resigned with Perrin from the Atomic Energy Council. It was said that the Prime Minister had really wanted General Sir William Morgan, an officer he had met and been impressed by on a visit to Washington during the war. Cockcroft, however, liked Sir Frederick Morgan, who had been an able soldier and had been responsible for planning the Normandy landings; but he was perhaps rather too old for the job and, like Portal, was devoid of knowledge about atomic energy matters.

Although various investigations were held by Civil Servants, the Government took no action to try to change the atomic energy organisation until the autumn of 1952. In May of that year Cockcroft appeared before a Parliamentary Select Committee on Estimates, but gave no indication that anything was amiss; he quoted a figure of £40 000 earned by the sale of radioisotopes at Amersham, and said that although the salaries of his staff had to conform to the scales of the Scientific Civil Service, and that the wastage rate was a little high, 'some turnover of staff is a good thing as they make way for younger people. So I do not take a serious view of that matter'[6]. But by October 1952 Cherwell had persuaded the Prime Minister to set up a small Cabinet committee to examine the administration of atomic energy. After their findings were reported, the Government agreed that a Committee under Lord Waverley, as Sir John Anderson had now become, would decide how atomic energy could be transferred from the Ministry of Supply to an independent authority. An indiscreet disclosure of the existence of this Committee by Chapman Pincher forced the Prime Minister to tell the House of Commons on 28 April 1953 that a plan was actually being worked out by the Committee, but as Lord Cherwell's biographer wrote, 'No Government decision was stated and no reasons were put forward'.[7]

During this period, the members of the Atomic Energy Board were examined by the Waverley Committee, consisting of Sir Wallace Akers who, since the war, had returned to ICI, and Sir John Woods, Director of the English Electric Company. Their recommendations for an independent atomic energy authority were accepted by the Government and published as a White Paper (Cmd 8986) on 10 November 1953. On 24 November Cockcroft met the chairman-designate of the new Authority, Sir Edwin Plowden, who, though unfamiliar with the technical aspects of atomic energy, was an able administrator who had recently resigned as Chief Government Planning Officer and chairman of the Economic Planning Board. Plowden appointed Sir Donald Perrott, recently in the Ministry of Supply and who also had been in charge of the Labour Government's ill-fated groundnuts venture in East Africa, to be responsible for administration and finance. Perrott suggested, and Plowden approved, the idea that the Authority should be divided into three groups—Research, Production and Weapons, under Cockcroft, Hinton and Penney respectively, an arrangement which provided Harwell with the autonomy Cockcroft had demanded in 1945. The vexatious question of salary scales was also solved, as the Authority was enabled to compete with industry for all its top level posts, though for the lower appointments they were not to diverge widely from Civil Service standards.

In the spring of 1953 Cockcroft was in bed with pneumonia, but had fully recovered by the end of May when he learned that he was to be appointed Knight Commander of the Bath in the Coronation and Birthday Honours List. Among the letters of congratulation was one from Lady Rutherford in New Zealand. She wrote that she had always

> felt that the Order, since the days of William Ramsay and J J Thomson, had been reserved for members of the Services, scientists being put off with a plain Knight and no order to wear. My husband's came soon after that. Anyhow, I am glad that one of his 'boys' has now got it.[8]

Figure 18   Cockcroft after receiving the KCB, with his daughters, Catherine and Elizabeth.

Another letter came from Michael Perrin who

> wondered how Cockcroft managed to keep so much and so many varied activities under control,[9]

referring to the DRPC and his frequent journeys overseas.

Christopher Hinton had been knighted in 1951, and when in the States on 31 October 1953 gave a lecture to the American Atomic Energy Forum in New York on *Atomic Energy Developments in Great Britain*. He naturally dwelt on the work of the Production Division and the development of the chemical separation plants, in relation to which he paid handsome tribute to the

> research work which had been carried out at the Chalk River Laboratories by Dr Spence, this work was done on only 20 milligrams of plutonium and as there was no time for building pilot or semi-technical plant before construction work started, we went into the full-scale construction of the primary separation plant which was very large and quite costly on the basis only of Dr Spence's research carried out on so small a quantity of plutonium... In this case we were scaling up from laboratory bench work to a continuous process and the results of chemical engineering research on the more difficult sections of the plant became available to the designers only after construction was well under way. In spite of this, the plant went into action on the programmed date, virtually without trouble.

In conclusion, Hinton discussed the evolution of advanced types of reactors, stating that

> Accidents almost invariably happen to all plants and machines which break into pioneering fields. Our trouble in the design of reactors lies primarily in the fact that engineers learn from their mistakes rather than from their successes, and in the case of a nuclear reactor the penalty for failure is so great that the responsible engineer dare not risk incurring it.

He suggested that the Americans might find it worthwhile

> to build a reactor, or reactors in a remote district, purely with the intention of making it become super-critical and of finding out what happens under these conditions[10].

The speech attracted quite a lot of attention in the Press, and for the first time Hinton was brought into the limelight. From henceforward he and his Production Division were given as much prominence as the research work being done by Cockcroft and Penney, especially as the likelihood of the construction of nuclear power stations was publicly being discussed. The dissimilarity in character between Cockcroft and Hinton has already been described, and from 1952 considerable friction arose between them from time to time and the attention which Hinton now received did nothing to improve matters.

In any case, Cockcroft could hardly have taken exception to Hinton's address for, indeed, with all the care with which a good engineer bestows on a project, faults of engineering design do arise; think of the faults of the box-section bridges, of the Comet with its square windows (when square holes are notorious for the stress-concentration at their corners), of Concordski, the Russian copy of Concorde, and indeed, of Windscale itself. Another cause for irritation was that after the opening of Calder Hall, Hinton received as much recognition, if not more, than Cockcroft for the development of the nuclear power programme; but bearing in mind the speed with which Calder had been built, that credit was fully deserved.

Cockcroft was present at the first meeting of the Executive Committee of the Authority held at Risley on 18 January 1954, and for the next five years attended assiduously meetings both of the Executive Committee and of the Board of the Authority, usually held three times a month. Plowden

remembered the mutual dislike between Cockcroft and Hinton which occasionally came to the surface at these meetings, though never flaring into a
row[11]. Perrott also remembered a tense atmosphere overhanging the committee at times, but Plowden thought that Cockcroft, despite his reputation for
silence, could be 'quite forthcoming at meetings'. Penney who, unlike
Cockcroft, was concerned both with research *and* production, was able to
assess Cockcroft more dispassionately, and recollected that while he was
usually able to anticipate the next move of Plowden or of Hinton, he found
Cockcroft 'something of an enigma'[12].

The appointment of a Deputy Director of Harwell had been in the air for
some time, and after the new administration had been settled further thought
was given to it. Cockcroft had long had it in mind—ever since his visit to
South Africa in 1949—that his old friend Basil Schonland should fill the job
even though he was not a nuclear physicist, and it will be recalled that when
Cockcroft had agreed to go to the Ministry of Defence in 1951 he had
suggested Schonland should become the Director in his place; Schonland was
uncertain whether to accept the post, being doubtful about salary and conditions of service, and the matter was dropped when Cockcroft's departure was
delayed by the change in Government. Late in 1951 he suggested to General
Morgan that George Raby, who had served him so well at ADRDE and had
later held a senior appointment in the Ministry of Supply, should be asked
to be his Deputy; he was, wrote Cockcroft, 'a terrific driver and would see
that the goods are produced—by fair means or foul'[13]. Raby, however, had
just accepted a post in the Sudan. Schonland was approached again in 1954
with the offer of Deputy Director; this time he accepted, and arrived from
South Africa to take up his appointment in October 1954. Meanwhile, also
in 1954, Cockcroft had persuaded Raby to lead the Establishment's Engineering Division, though omitting to tell him that Schonland was going to be
Deputy Director. Raby accepted, but found he was to be called Chief
Engineer, which to his mind implied a lower status than he was prepared to
accept. As they both knew Cockcroft well, Schonland and Raby went to see
Willson and asked him to sort things out; the latter introduced the title Deputy Director (Engineering) and a suitable organisation diagram which satisfied
everyone[14].

Shortly before Parliament dispersed for the summer recess of 1954 there
had been a debate on whether the UK should develop a hydrogen bomb, and
on Friday 4 September Plowden, Penney and Cockcroft were summoned by
the Prime Minister to lunch with him at Chartwell and brief him on the
military aspects of atomic energy. It happened to be the week of the British
Association meeting at Oxford, and Cockcroft had been presiding over the
Mathematics and Physics Section; he described his afternoon with Churchill
in a letter to his mother. He found the Prime Minister in the library arrayed
in a blue-striped boiler suit and open collar, consuming a modest amount of
whisky with Plowden and Penney who had arrived ahead of time. When they
explained that 'the PM might have to stay below for a week or so if buttons
were pressed', Churchill soliloquised on the defence policy of the future for
over an hour, occasionally asking his guests a question. After a lively lunch
with members of the Churchill family, 'the ladies left and the Prime Minister

held forth on world politics till 4 o'clock—most entrancing'. After this they walked round the garden, pausing to feed the goldfish, and were introduced to two of Churchill's grandchildren. Then the Prime Minister went to have his portrait painted by Graham Sutherland, who had just begun making studies for the portrait to be presented that November by both Houses of Parliament for Churchill's 80th birthday—a painting which Cockcroft later hoped would hang in Churchill College, a vain hope, alas, as the portrait was destroyed by Lady Churchill.

It would have been at the end of this visit that Cockcroft invited Churchill to come over to Harwell. He did so on 17 December, causing, as Seligman recalled, a ripple of amusement by demanding to be shown 'the neutron'. No more than four months later he had been replaced by Sir Anthony Eden,

Figure 19   Sir Winston Churchill's visit to Harwell, December 1954, with Dr B F J Schonland beside him and Cockcroft behind. (Courtesy: Public Record Office)

though he approved the decision in February 1955 to develop a hydrogen bomb.

Since the setting up of the Authority, Plowden had been preparing a plan for the Government's nuclear power programme, and Cockcroft had to advise him on research and development. During Christmas 1954 he received a letter from Plowden thanking him for help during Plowden's first year of office.

> It will [wrote Plowden] have been apparent to you that I lean more heavily on you than on the rest of my colleagues. I shall continue to do so if you will bear it. I feel that we have a long way to go and many mistakes to make before we find the ideal organisation for the AEA, but I think and hope we are going in the right direction... [The preliminary draft of the White Paper *A Programme of Nuclear Power* to be published in February 1955] seems to me to be an important event in the technological history of this country and one that reflects great credit on all those that have taken part in these developments and on you in particular.[15]

The White Paper stated that

> During the next ten years two types of reactors are likely to be brought into use on a commercial scale. The first type will be similar to those now being constructed at Calder Hall, but improvements in design during the period should enable the later models to show a great advance in efficiency compared with the earlier ones. They will be gas-cooled graphite moderated 'thermal' reactors using as fuel natural uranium or slightly 'enriched' uranium, i.e. having a slightly higher fissile content than natural uranium. The first improved models could be designed and built so as to come into operation in about six years time.[16]

The programme called for the construction of stations having a net output of 2000 MW of electricity, that is to say, about five or six stations each generating some 300 to 500 MW. The second type of reactor was to be a liquid-cooled thermal reactor requiring more complicated techniques, but with further development 'might eventually prove more economic than the gas-cooled reactors although the comparison will depend on how much the gas-cooled type can be improved'. It was estimated that the cost of electricity from the first nuclear power stations would be about 0.6 old pence per unit. Oliphant was one of those who were critical of the Government's plan, and during one of his visits from Australia, wrote to Cockcroft that he had been informed that industrialists needed atomic energy within *five* years rather than ten years and that they were quite prepared to pay two or three old pence a unit so long as the supply was reliable and fuel was guaranteed[17]. The answer to his criticism would doubtless have been that there was no comprehensive experience of nuclear technology available in private industry for building nuclear power stations. When asked to comment on the part Cockcroft had played in introducing the programme, Oliphant wrote

> In my view, he was indeed over-optimistic about the gas-cooled Magnox reactor. I questioned this several times after visiting nuclear power stations in the UK, but he always replied vigorously, refuting with statistics the doubts which I had.[18]

Cockcroft appreciated that with the expansion of the power programme design engineers would have to be trained to operate reactors, and he formed a reactor school at Harwell which opened in September 1954. Courses lasting three months were held to instruct both new Harwell staff and engineers from industry, and when possible Cockcroft gave an opening address. At about the same time members of the Institution of Mechanical Engineers and the Institution of Electrical Engineers interested in atomic energy were discussing the possibility of a forum for those interested in this field and enlisted Cockcroft's support. They proposed to hold regular British Nuclear Engineers' Conferences, emphasis being placed on the education of engineers in nuclear engineering and technology. Cockcroft was very much in favour and became a regular chairman of the conference, the first being held on 15 December 1955.

Similar encouragement for industry to participate in atomic energy came from Hinton at Risley, especially after the opening of Calder Hall, which gave the impression that a bonanza was ready to be exploited and which, of course, had the additional support of Cockcroft, but as Lord Plowden explained in retrospect, the danger arose that the whole effort would be dissipated as the economy could not support such an extensive expansion as well as meet the other demands being made upon it[19]. Industrial companies immediately prepared to meet the challenge, and organised themselves into four groups, each comprising one of the large electrical companies AEI, EE, GEC and Parsons/Reyrolles, associated with one of the boiler-making companies so that each of the four groups could quote for a complete nuclear power station comprising reactor, turbine and generator. The first order for a complete station had hardly been placed—December 1956—when the Suez crisis was upon us, and in April 1957 it was decided to increase the number of stations to be ordered, a new White Paper (Cmnd 132) trebled the 1955 programme, calling for 5000 to 6000 megawatts of electrical generating capacity to be built by the end of 1965.

A step towards that objective had already been taken in June 1955 when the Government decided that another six reactors of the Calder Hall type should be built to meet increasing needs for military plutonium. This raised the question of Harwell's future and what role the Establishment was to play within the Authority, and in particular how would Cockcroft react towards a rationalisation of the Establishment's activities, bearing in mind his opinion, quoted earlier, that an establishment should spend 30 per cent of its time on projects thrown up internally and on fundamental research. Before the Authority was set up, Cockcroft had enjoyed direct access to the Minister of Supply and his Permanent Secretary, and he had made use of this privilege whenever he wanted to solve a difficult problem. In recent years, moreover, his own prestige had been greatly increased; honours and awards bestowed on him included the Gold Palm of the Medal of Freedom from the USA for his wartime collaboration with American scientists, the Military Order of Christ from the Portuguese, and at home he had received a Royal Medal from the Royal Society and numerous honorary degrees and fellowships from universities and learned bodies. Despite his diffidence, such a showering of honours had caused some jealousy and had also made him virtually unassailable from criticism, and confident of the causes he espoused.

However, he found Sir Edwin Plowden, with his deep knowledge of economics and experience of planning the economy, to be much more implacable than previous high-ranking officials. As Chairman of the Authority, Plowden had to take into account three factors: first, a Treasury demand for cutting funds for Government supported research programmes unlikely to be financially productive in a reasonably short period of time, say a few years; secondly, competition between scientists and engineers in the Authority over the funds allocated to their pet projects; and thirdly, grumbling by the nuclear physics departments of universities that they were getting less than their fair share of money for really long-term basic research work which had always been their prerogative and which was now being pursued in Harwell at tremendous expense.

Dr E Glueckauf, in his Royal Society memoir of Robert Spence, has described how Harwell was pulled in three directions from the mid-1950s onwards:

(1) by the need to support the UK nuclear power programme,

(2) by opposing groups within Harwell which wanted diversification outside the nuclear field,

(3) the concept that had existed from the start of Harwell that it was a kind of university where the staff, having obtained knowledge and information, were free to go 'to other universities and instruct people in the ethics of atomic energy'.

Plowden soon became aware of Cockcroft's indulgence towards long-term research, later describing him as a 'soft touch to his younger colleagues', and certainly Cockcroft wanted to continue to initiate

> basic research and early development work on all aspects of atomic energy and, in particular, to provide new ideas and basic designs for power generation.[20]

Since the completion of PIPPA in 1953, Harwell had been planning a variety of schemes which were alternatives to the gas-cooled reactor, such as HIPPO, a more powerful version of the Canadian NRX reactor, which had to be abandoned because a suitable site could not be found for it at Harwell, and design work had begun on LIDO, the so-called 'swimming pool' reactor and DIDO, the first British reactor to be moderated with heavy water. DIDO, like another reactor, PLUTO, was modelled on the American CP5 reactor at the Argonne National Laboratory, becoming critical in November 1956 and October 1957 respectively. Although more expensive to use than BEPO, DIDO proved to be most useful for testing materials and for carrying out experiments in solid state physics and crystallography, one of its successes being, as Cockcroft recalled, 'the study of the structure of Vitamin B12 by Dr Dorothy Hodgkin'[21]. In due course, its power was increased from 10 MW to 15 MW. The Reactor Division was about to start investigating a number of other systems at this time.

The problem facing Plowden, therefore, was, as Spence later described it, 'to select a sensible reactor research and development programme from the almost bewildering number of alternatives which were appearing'[22]. Plowden appointed Mr William Strath, who had been a member of the Economic Planning Board and who now became Member for External Relations and Commercial Policy in the Authority, to draw up a plan which would concentrate these projects in a way most beneficial to the Authority. He was told to review the

> Programme of major reactor schemes in the Authority requiring substantial expenditure on research, development and design effort and to make recommendations for varying the programme and to give an indication of priorities.

He met Cockcroft to discuss the problem on 11 November 1955, the latter continuing to maintain that Harwell should continue to work on new designs and that a reorganised research group should study 'advanced reactor concepts... and the most promising ideas in small experimental reactors'[23]. They agreed that this should be done on a new site outside Harwell. At the time, and certainly in retrospect, this appeared to industry to have been a tragic extravaganza; the country could not support many new reactor concepts coming along in parallel, three were at that moment being pursued, yet Harwell was wanting to add another two or three designs to be taken up to the prototype stage. History has shown none were wanted, and much of the money has been unproductive.

Cockcroft, accompanied by senior members of his staff, now began to look at possible sites in Dorset. The eventual selection of Winfrith Heath inevitably caused a storm of protest from the public, and approval to develop the site and begin construction work was not gained until February 1957. Cockcroft, anxious not to disturb the peace and character of the Dorset landscape, was impressed by the 'desolation and beauty' of Winfrith Heath, though, as he told a school audience at Weymouth,

> it did not appear to me to correspond to Hardy's Egdon Heath, so I thought that we would be unlikely to be troubled by his ghost if the Atomic Energy Establishment were to be founded there, provided we did our utmost to preserve the beauty of the Dorset landscape by good design and layout in planting of trees and shrubs to soften the harshness of industrial buildings.

In planning the services for Winfrith the site of the old radar station at Worth Matravers was considered as a possible location. Denis Willson remembered looking at it with Cockcroft, Schonland, Raby and Dr D W Fry, head of the General Physics Division, who was to become first director of the new establishment.

> I suddenly realised what memories it held for the others. Raby was delighted to find his old wooden masts still standing and for some minutes they all slipped back into the wartime days. The place, however, was too far from Winfrith to be of much use.[25]

Within a year Fry had established a team of physicists and engineers at Winfrith, the main project being the construction of a prototype steam-generating heavy water reactor which was intended to be an alternative to the American pressurised water reactor. Secondly, the team of R L Fortesque,

L R Shepherd and P D Hall working on the high-temperature reactor called Dragon, previously mentioned, was transferred to Winfrith, but as the Authority did not have sufficient money to support it, Cockcroft, making use of his contacts abroad, obtained the support of a number of influential leaders of nuclear projects in Europe, and during 1959 Dragon became a project of the European Nuclear Energy Agency. To reciprocate, Cockcroft agreed to help the Norwegians with their new reactor at Halden; in September 1958 an international design team began work on designing the reactor, and in April 1960 Cockcroft and Francis Perrin, the High Commissioner of the French Atomic Energy Commission, set the reactor in operation, and in due course, it achieved its designed power of 20 MW (Thermal) and planned output of 750°C. It was finally closed down in 1976. A third experimental reactor called ZEBRA was built to test fast reactor cores. These projects fulfilled Cockcroft's aim of establishing an additional experimental reactor centre to Harwell.

Since 1951 a handful of scientists at Harwell had been working on a far more revolutionary project than those described above, namely on 'controlled thermonuclear fusion', a project aimed at producing energy from the fusion of nuclei of deuterium (heavy hydrogen, mass = 2) with one another, or of deuterium with nuclei of tritium (an extra heavy form of hydrogen, mass = 3). In 1934 Rutherford and Oliphant had bombarded deuterium with deuterium ions accelerated in their very small generator, and had shown that helium is produced by the fusion of two deuterons with the evolution of seven times more energy than is released when an equal weight of uranium undergoes fission. This is the reaction which occurs in the hydrogen bomb— so to speak an 'uncontrolled thermonuclear' fusion—and is the main source of energy given out by the sun, the conversion of hydrogen into helium.

It offered an exciting prospect, for the fuel, heavy hydrogen, is found in the ocean and can be recovered cheaply, and in a 'fusion reactor' no dangerous, long-lived radioactive isotopes would be formed so no serious disposal problems would arise; the reactor itself would become radioactive in time so a decommissioning process for the reactor and its shield would arise, but no worse than that for a fission reactor. Expressed briefly, all that was necessary was to heat the gas, deuterium, or the mixture of deuterium and tritium to a temperature comparable to that prevailing inside the sun, and then helium and energy would be produced. Scientists could visualise what had to be done; how to do it was the essence of the matter. By the late 1950s Cockcroft seemed to think the 'how' was not far away; today the practical application of fusion apparently lies many years ahead.

Thermonuclear research in Britain took two forms. In 1946 Sir George Thomson, then Professor of Physics at Imperial College, who knew about the early work of the Americans on a thermonuclear weapon, and M Blackman, a member of his staff, calculated that a sufficiently high temperature might be reached by passing a large current through deuterium contained at low pressure in a toroidal vessel, provided that the electrodeless discharge, pinched in a narrow core by its own self-magnetic field, remained in a stable orbit in the centre of the torus. During the next three years Thomson formed a small group at Imperial College to develop the torus concept, using vessels made first of glass, then of quartz, and then of porcelain. At the same time

Peter Thonemann, a young Australian physicist, with another small group had begun to work quite independently on the same problem at the Clarendon Laboratory in Oxford, though unlike Thomson's group, they were working with straight glass tubes each fitted with a pair of electrodes between which they passed very large currents. Cockcroft took a great interest in the work of the two groups, giving some financial help to Imperial College and in 1951 willingly accepting Thonemann to continue his work in Harwell.

Neutrons are one of the products of the fusion reaction, and it was realised that if fusion experiments were successful a source of neutrons would become available and might be used to produce plutonium for a weapon. So the Authority decided that all the work must remain secret. Thomson disliked the idea of secret work being carried out in a university laboratory, and he did not want it to go to Harwell where it would have played second fiddle to Thonemann's work. He therefore asked Allibone to take charge of fusion research which would be transferred from London to the Associated Electrical Industries Laboratory at Aldermaston Court. The AEI Board accepted the responsibility and offered to pay for the whole of the work to be done, but Cockcroft decided that the Authority must accept financial responsibility as the work must remain secret and therefore must be under the absolute control of the Authority. So the Imperial College team moved to Aldermaston and the Harwell and AEI teams worked closely together for the next 16 years. Allibone's important contribution was a design for a steel torus built up in segments. Incidentally, Cockcroft had asked him to discuss Sir George Thomson's secret patent with Fuchs, which he did in 1949, so presumably the Russians were given a nice headstart.

By 1955 the two teams had discovered a good deal about the properties of the plasma state of matter and something about the mechanism of plasma instabilities. On the basis of this knowledge Cockcroft approved the construction of a large metal toroidal apparatus having a mean diameter of 1 metre, later called ZETA (Zero Energy Thermonuclear Assembly) by the Harwell team under Thonemann, whilst the AEI team received permission to build a far smaller torus of different design, called SCEPTRE, likewise to study instabilities; the teams considered that with tubes of these designs it might be possible to give a practical demonstration of thermonuclear fusion.

Secrecy surrounding thermonuclear research began to be lifted from August 1955 after the Indian nuclear physicist, Homi Bhabha, President of the First International Conference on the Peaceful Uses of Atomic Energy at Geneva, referred to the possibility of fusion. Due both to his remarks and the atmosphere of euphoria generated by the conference, which revealed the considerable progress made by the Russians and the Americans in reactor technology, proposals were put forward that thermonuclear research should be declassified. They coincided with the Russian desire to improve international relations with the West, particularly in the scientific and technological field. Igor Kurchatov, 'father of the Russian atomic bomb', who was very concerned about physics having become associated with the bomb, strongly approved, and at the historic 20th Congress of the Russian Communist Party in February 1956, at which Khruschev made his denunciation of Stalin, Kurchatov made a plea for international scientific cooperation. Earlier, in describing plans for Russian nuclear power, he had referred briefly to controlled thermonuclear reactions and claimed that 'the solution of this most difficult and vast problem would for ever rid mankind of the worry about the power supplies necessary for its existence on earth'[26].

Two months later, on 18 April, Khruschev and Bulganin, accompanied by Kurchatov, arrived in Britain on an official visit. Cockcroft had never met Kurchatov before, and invited him to lunch at the Athenaeum. He was

> greatly impressed by his intelligence and by his eagerness to talk about collaboration in atomic energy work. We had a very animated discussion at the top of the Athenaeum staircase [about the Russian reactor programme] where he was able to go much further than I could reciprocate, having no idea of how the discussion would go. He suggested that he should deliver a lecture at Harwell and I agreed to arrange this.[27]

Cockcroft had already planned to attend the regular declassification meeting between the British, Americans and Canadians held in Washington (see chapter 14) that week and when he met Kurchatov again on Friday 20 April, at a luncheon given by the Lord Mayor of London at the Mansion House, he told him he was going next day to discuss the removal of secrecy on thermonuclear research.

On that Saturday morning Cockcroft received the Russian leaders, with Kurchatov in attendance, at Harwell, where they were shown round the laboratories. Elizabeth always maintained that the arrival of Cherwell abruptly terminated the discussions between Cockcroft and Kurchatov which had already gone a long way to improving friendly scientific relations between the British and Russians. That afternoon Cockcroft had to fly to Washington, and on the 24th the declassification meeting held by the US Atomic Energy Commission agreed that thermonuclear research should be declassified simultaneously by the British and Americans; the chairman, Lewis Strauss, however, refused to allow it to take place straight away.

Kurchatov, who had prepared a paper before leaving Moscow, returned to Harwell on Wednesday, 25 April. His discourse was attended by the Harwell physicists, the Aldermaston team and Sir George Thomson, then Master of Corpus Christi College, Cambridge, was also in the audience. To many of them, as one of Penney's scientists later said, 'the most significant thing seemed to be that the Russians were at Harwell at all', but equally significant from the Russian point of view was that *inside* the security fence of Harwell Kurchatov was accompanied by a huge Russian security man with a pocket bulging with a revolver. Kurchatov astonished everyone with an account of work very similar to the Harwell and Aldermaston efforts, though as Allibone later explained

> he had gone further and could report the detection of neutrons, the characteristics of the instabilities—including a sausage-shaped pinched discharge—and temperature measurements. It was an account of extremely good work....

It should here be explained that the hydrogen/helium reaction could occur very locally, so to speak in 'hot spots' in the gas discharge where local electric fields are greater than the mean values of fields, and it was at these spots that

Figure 20 The visit of Bulganin and Khruschev with Academician Kurchatov to Harwell, 1956. Kurchatov (with the large beard) stands in fornt of Khruschev. (Courtesy: AERE, Harwell)

reactions had occurred which yielded Kurchatov's neutrons; what is ultimately required is a discharge at a *uniformly* high temperature. The Russian work had been done with straight tubes; they had not, by then, worked with toroidal tubes.

On 12 August 1957 ZETA was completed and testing started. On 30 August the machine was run at full power, and early that autumn attempts were made to produce thermonuclear reactions by introducing heavy hydrogen into the torus in place of ordinary hydrogen, and neutrons were detected. In mid-October Cockcroft attended a meeting at Princeton where he exchanged information with the Americans, whose work on fusion, although not officially announced by Strauss until the autumn of 1955, had begun before the end of the war. Cockcroft confirmed with Willard Libby, one of the scientific members of the US Atomic Energy Commission, that results of the two countries' fusion experiments should be published simultaneously when sufficient progress had been made. On 17 December 1957 physicists at Los Alamos under the direction of James Tuck (one of the British scientists who had worked on the Manhattan project) obtained a substantial neutron yield from a similar machine to ZETA called SCYLLA but nicknamed 'Perhapsatron'. It was far smaller than the Aldermaston SCEPTRE, which in turn was far smaller than ZETA, and the fact that three toruses of quite different size were yielding neutrons enabled some scaling laws to be worked out.

Before the end of the year the Harwell and Aldermaston groups had produced pinched discharges with currents of 200 000 amperes circulating for a few milliseconds under reasonably stable conditions. Both ZETA and SCEPTRE III were reported to be producing neutrons, and many experiments were made to check their validity. On 1 January 1958 Cockcroft and Schonland went over to Aldermaston Court to see the AEI torus in operation delivering neutrons; Schonland was full of praise for the work done almost on a shoestring, but as usual Cockcroft was substantially speechless, never uttering a word of commendation, and Sir George Thomson had to insist that the AEI work should be published at the same time as the Harwell work. Later in January the moment had come to make a public announcement on fusion. The British Government appreciated (and Macmillan who had succeeded Eden as Prime Minister after the Suez fiasco just over a year before, had a special interest in science policy and had recently visited Harwell twice) that there were political advantages to be gained by the news of a scientific breakthrough as ZETA promised to be. An event of this kind was needed to smother the feelings of disillusion (such as there were) caused by the Windscale accident (shortly to be described), and it would be valuable commercially in giving a fillip to export of British reactors overseas. The Americans, perhaps even more than the British, needed a boost to their morale since the Russian Sputnik had stolen a march on their own space programme and a small American satellite had just blown up on its launching pad.

Such was the background to the well advertised ZETA press conference held at Harwell on 23 January 1958. Sometime earlier Cockcroft himself had requested that the Editor of *Nature* should leave space for a number of papers on fusion. Then, just before the start of the conference, he took Thonemann on one side and asked him whether he was really sure that the neutrons were thermonuclear. Thonemann was *not* sure, as he was worried about the fact that the neutron output did not fluctuate with the temperature as it should have done[28]. After a cautiously optimistic address to some 300 journalists, Cockcroft asked for questions from the floor. For once his usual barrier of reserve was penetrated. After being nettled by one persistent journalist he rashly declared that he was '90 per cent certain that the neutrons were of thermonuclear origin'.

On the following day the British and American atomic energy authorities officially released details about the fusion experiments. It was the news story of the day. Banner headlines proclaimed that the 'source of energy for all time' had been discovered, just as 26 years before the popular press had hailed the Cockcroft – Walton accelerator experiments as making possible 'a new era of prosperity for all'. They overshadowed quieter, more authoritative statements like Cockcroft's in *The New Scientist* the following week that

> in no case have the neutrons been definitely proved to be due to the random motion of deuterium associated with a temperature in the order of five million degrees. Their origin will, however, become clear as soon as the number of neutrons produced can be increased by increasing currents and temperatures.[29]

Not long after, stringent tests were made with apparatus from the Nuclear Physics Division at Harwell (curiously, they had not been consulted earlier), and it became clear that the neutrons were *not* of true thermonuclear origin; like those reported by Kurchatov, they arose from localised 'hot spots' of instability. On 16 May 1958 Schonland, Director-designate of Harwell, speaking in the absence of Cockcroft, who was attending a conference in Brussels and visiting the International Exhibition at which a model of ZETA was one of the features of the British Hall of Technology, told the Press, at a second and much smaller meeting held at the Authority's headquarters in London, about the revised opinion, though he insisted that it did not make the ZETA results less significant. On the contrary, 'higher temperatures and longer times can be achieved', and he concluded by saying that the machine was being modified to improve its performance and that a more powerful successor was being planned. A similar statement was made by Cockcroft when interviewed by the Press at London Airport on 15 June before flying to Italy for a lecture tour. He retained his optimism about the possibilities of obtaining fusion in the not too distant future, and one of his last actions as Director was to approve the proposal for a scaled-up version of ZETA,

> the purpose of this being to 'breakeven', that is to produce as much energy as is needed to run the machine. After that there will be formidable problems of extracting the energy and making the machine an industrial proposition; this will probably call for a third ZETA, a true industrial prototype and if all goes well such a prototype may be on the drawing-boards in 15 years time.[30]

Unhappily, 25 years later a meaningful drawing of a prototype cannot yet be made.

Now that the subject was declassified, the fusion experiments were transferred from the security of Harwell to Culham, a nearby disused naval air-station which had previously been on lease to Harwell for use as an additional laboratory, where research into cosmic ray phenomena—part of the original fundamental research programme—could take place. Here foreign scientists would be able to participate in the British programme. At the second Geneva Conference in August 1958 there were a number of papers on fusion, but while a good deal of information was disseminated, there were few answers to the problems. Scientists had already begun to work on other techniques for obtaining fusion.

Cockcroft was widely criticised for his optimistic views on ZETA's capabilities, even, probably, against the advice of the fusion team. It was another case of his willingness to give as much rein as possible to Harwell projects, though there was also the likelihood that he was under considerable political pressure to promote ZETA as a British achievement. There can be no doubt that he believed in ZETA. Lord Plowden recalled how Cockcroft told him that he sometimes used to go, when work was over, and sit in front of ZETA, contemplating by himself the prospect of unlimited power that it promised to offer. His friend, Ernest Lawrence, had taken a more cautious view, and on 4 November 1955 told Cockcroft that he thought a 'positive return' was unlikely within the next 20 years and that a 'practical device' would take longer to develop, though when he saw the ZETA experiments in October 1957 he seemed to share Cockcroft's enthusiasm[31].

In August 1961, three years after the ZETA announcement, there was another stocktaking at a conference in Salzburg†. Cockcroft then declared that the 'first lifting of the veil had aroused tremendous interest in the Press' and had 'led to undue optimism about prospects of fusion power in the near future'.

> But [he continued] we emphasised time and time again that many years of in-tensive work would be required to obtain a laboratory thermonuclear device which would produce more energy than it consumed and that, after this, it would take many more years to develop a full-scale power producing plant. We were not believed.[32]

Cockcroft had always wanted Harwell to be a centre for fundamental research because of his pioneering work on accelerators and the construction of the Cavendish cyclotron before the war. In 1949 Harwell's 164 MeV synchrocyclotron began to operate, but after Cockcroft had seen Ernest Lawrence's 184 inch synchrocyclotron and a quarter-sized model of a 6 giga‡ electron volt (GeV) betatron on one of his American tours, he wanted Harwell to emulate them. In November 1953 he persuaded the Atomic Energy Board to give him over one and a quarter million pounds to build a powerful proton linear accelerator (PLA) similar to Lawrence's PLA at Berkeley[33].

This acquisition aroused the envy of universities like Liverpool and Bir-mingham which were not wealthy enough to build such large machines, although Cockcroft had been very helpful in making the first Harwell

---

†ZETA continued in operation for several more years and provided information on which much later work was based.

‡Gigavolt is 1 000 000 000 volts, called a billion volts in the USA.

accelerator available for academic research; for example, Professor Harrie Massey, in charge of the Physics Department of University College, London, had taken advantage of the offer for his students. In 1954 the team working on the Liverpool cyclotron discovered a new method of extracting the beam which was much more economical than that likely to be used in the PLA. Harwell therefore decided to cancel the costly 600 MeV PLA, though it was too late to stop the construction of the first stage of the machine operating at 50 MeV.

Cockcroft and his colleagues now believed that they had an opportunity to exploit the cancellation of the large PLA by proposing to the Authority that, instead, a high intensity machine could be built for the use of universities. In conjunction with this idea support was being canvassed for a national laboratory for high energy or high intensity machines. Dr Brian Flowers, the head of the Theoretical Physics Division at Harwell, argued for a high energy centre resembling Harwell, but without a security fence and without some of the technology groups, which could be moved to Winfrith. Cockcroft supported his proposal and suggested that the first accelerator should be built adjacent to Harwell, and he obtained the approval of the Authority on 26 July 1956.

In the latter part of that year he was instrumental in preparing a plan for the administration of a centre which would be called the National Institute for Research in Advanced Nuclear Science and which would satisfy both the Authority and the universities. His proposal for a proton synchrotron with an energy of 7.5 GeV was not circulated to the universities. But Dr Denys Wilkinson, then Reader in Nuclear Physics at the Cavendish, believed that Cockcroft's way of dealing with the problem

> was the only way in which it could, in practice, have been done and that had the universities as such got involved they would have made a muck of it. That John Cockcroft's benevolent paternalism, knowing best, was the only way is not a popular line to take in these days of open democratic everything, but that does not affect the truth.[34]

Government approval of the National Institute was announced on 17 February 1957, and Cockcroft was appointed a member of the Governing Board and became Chairman of the Physics Committee. In the latter capacity he was responsible for preventing a dispute between the Governing Board and the universities which arose out of an offer made by the Authority to transfer the Harwell 50 MeV PLA and 160 MeV synchrocyclotron to the National Institute. Professors Dee and Skinner, on behalf of the universities, vehemently argued that this would set a precedent and that in the future they might lose out when new equipment was being allocated. No doubt it was Cockcroft's moderating influence that led to the Physics Committee to order the transfer of the PLA to the Institute but to leave the synchrocyclotron at Harwell where it would still be available to the universities. Cockcroft's feelings were illustrated by a letter he wrote on 7 September 1957 to Denys Wilkinson, who had become Professor of Nuclear Physics at the Clarendon Laboratory.

> I too have been very disappointed by the attitude of many of the university

physics professors towards the Institute. I feel that we can only overcome this by patience and going stepwise. I hope that we can at least agree to transfer the PLA... at the next meeting. After thinking things over, it may be best to appoint only the 'Director' of the Bevatron as a starter and leave our further appointment until the PLA has been handed over *and the emotion has cooled off a bit.*[35]

Wilkinson commented on this letter,

I do not think I could possibly indicate more powerfully the strength of university feeling, at least for those who knew John Cockcroft... than by drawing attention to his explicit reference to emotion at the end of his last sentence (my underlining).

On 10 July 1957 Cockcroft cut the first turf at the site chosen for the laboratory to house NIMROD, as the accelerator was called; the name given to the laboratory was Rutherford, appropriately after one of the founding fathers of modern nuclear physics. Its first director was T G Pickavance, who had led the Harwell synchrocyclotron team from the start. On 27 August 1963

it was recorded that 'there was a ripple of a cheer as NIMROD graduated from being the highest energy accelerator in Berkshire to the highest in Britain. The long reign of the Birmingham synchrocyclotron was over.†[36]

Cockcroft served on the Governing Board of the National Institute until it was absorbed into the Science Research Council in the reorganisation of civil science in 1965, but continued to chair the Physics Committee whose main function was to encourage research in the field of elementary particle physics in the UK. Towards the end of the 1950s the Cavendish Laboratory wanted to build a new low-energy accelerator on the site of the new Cavendish Laboratory off the Madingley Road. Naturally Cockcroft was keen to help, and devoted a lot of time trying to persuade the authorities to put up the money for the scheme, and he hoped that Denys Wilkinson would take charge of the team. Unfortunately the scheme met with opposition from the University, Wilkinson withdrew his name from the proposal, and finally nothing was done.

Elsewhere Cockcroft met with greater success. At an important meeting of the Physics Committee which he chaired in Liverpool on 28 March 1960, a working party was formed to consider future accelerator policy in the UK, and they decided in 1962 that a second high-energy physics laboratory should be founded at Daresbury in Cheshire which would better serve the northern universities. Cockcroft maintained an interest in both laboratories until his death, by chairing consultative meetings of senior physicists and by frequent visits.

However much Cockcroft might be concerned with research reactors and high-energy accelerators, he maintained a keen interest in the efforts being made to reduce the hazards inherent in the production of nuclear power. The radiobiological research unit which he had arranged to be set up at Harwell under J F Loutit had by then received international acclaim. Cockcroft was a member of the Medical Research Council committee on medical and

†NIMROD continued to operate until 6 June 1978.

biological applications of nuclear physics. He was usually supported at these meetings on nuclear hazards by Dr Katharine Williams, Chief Medical Officer and Head of the Medical Division, and by W G Marley, Head of the Health Physics Division at Harwell. On 20 April 1955, in an address to the Parliamentary and Scientific Committee which was widely circulated, Cockcroft sought to allay public anxiety about the biological effects of nuclear explosions and the hazards likely to be encountered from the large-scale development of nuclear power. A more detailed assessment, including long-term genetic effects, was made by Sir Harold Himsworth's committee of which Cockcroft was a member, on the hazards to man of nuclear and allied radiation. Their report, published in 1956, was the first attempt to assess rationally what actually were the hazards to the population from the increasing uses of ionising radiation and from radioactive contamination of the environment from nuclear test explosions in the atmosphere. He attended a Cabinet meeting on the report which afterwards evoked, in a letter to his brother Leo, one of his few unguarded comments on politicians. Present, he reported, were 'the PM [Eden], Butler, Salisbury, Macmillan, Walter Monckton, Selwyn Lloyd. I wasn't terribly impressed!' As it happened, the Government, as a result of the report, made an attempt to stop testing, which although unsuccessful was revived three years later at the series of Geneva conferences on a test ban in which Cockcroft took part.

Cockcroft devoted several lectures to hazards to health from radiation. On 11 October 1956 he spoke to postgraduates of the Medical Federation at London University and reviewed the progress made in understanding the implications of nuclear energy over the past decade. He explained that the two principal dangers that had to be guarded against were the release of large quantities of radioactive effluent from the chemical separation plants and the possibility of reactors getting out of control, leading to melting of the fuel elements and thus releasing radioactive products. He believed that an 'established code of practice' and the concentration of radioactive wastes 'into a relatively small volume' took care of the first problem while good design and shielding would ensure the safety of reactors.[37]

On Thursday, 10 October 1957, a year later almost to the day, overheating of one of the Windscale reactors occurred and caused the first involuntary release of radioactivity from a British reactor. Cockcroft first learned about the accident from *The Ocean News* published on board the *Queen Mary*. He was travelling to New York to attend the meeting at Princeton on fusion already described, and to discover, as he told Lawrence in a letter congratulating him on winning the Fermi award, 'some of the new plans on thermonuclear research hatching out'[38], then going on to Harvard to give a lecture and to raise funds for Churchill College. He had been given instructions to take the sea voyage instead of travelling by air to give him a break from the wearying round of meetings and administrative chores. On landing at New York he was met by John Gaunt, British Scientific Liaison Officer in Washington, and he remarked that it looked as if his stay was going to be a brief one. News of the accident in the States was completely overshadowed by the launching of the first Sputnik, and Ken Bainbridge, who was Cockcroft's host at Harvard, rose regularly at 6 AM 'to observe its transit looking like a moving Sirius'.

Without accurate information as to exactly what had happened to the Windscale reactor, Cockcroft could not imagine 'why the things got red hot at all'. Schoniand, who was in charge at Harwell, could cope with the incident from that end, but as Cockcroft was the Member for Scientific Research for the Authority he anticipated he might be needed, so he cancelled a visit to Chalk River and flew home, going at once to Risley to talk to Leonard Owen who had recently become Managing Director of the Industrial Group in place of Hinton.

The trouble began after one of the routine releases of Wigner energy in a reactor. Instead of the expected decrease in temperature, there was a steady increase and fires broke out in the reactor. Remedial action was taken at once and the fires were brought under control through the efforts of the hard-pressed staff, though fires continued for five days and inevitably there was some release, fortunately mild, of radioactivity and this was the reason for the imposition of a ban on milk production in the vicinity until late November.

Cockcroft had indirectly contributed to the original safety precautions by his insistence at a late stage in the building of the reactors, strongly prompted by the senior staff of the Health Physics Division at Harwell, and by Mayneord and Mitchell, that the air which cooled the reactors should be filtered before release. When he visited Brookhaven in November 1948 he had been told that some alarm had been caused when uranium oxide particles were discovered on the ground near the graphite moderated reactor at Oak Ridge. Like Windscale, straight-through air cooling was used, and the Americans decided to instal filters in the air exits from the reactor. (There had been some argument over the design of the Windscale reactors. Oliphant had proposed a closed-circuit air-cooling system, but Hinton believed that plutonium was likely to be produced much more quickly if the reactor was cooled by straight-through air under atmospheric pressure.) As it was too late to insert filters at the base, large filter galleries were built at the top of the 410 feet high Windscale stacks; they were a conspicuous landmark and were known locally (and unkindly!) as 'Cockcroft's Folly'. Early in 1949 Dunworth and Tongue discovered that the uranium oxide particles at Oak Ridge came from the chemical plant stack, about 30 feet high, and not from the reactor stack. As Cockcroft told Hinton on 5 April 1949, 'this does not affect our views about the need for the filters'[39]. In the event the raised stacks served their purpose and caught most of the radioactive particles released from the Windscale reactor. Ironically, only a few weeks before the accident, Owen had declared that engineers learned most from the mistakes they made. This observation without any doubt applied to Windscale. As Cockcroft wrote to Lawrence:

> We are very fortunate in having hurt no-one. We have certainly learned a great lesson about organisation to promote safety and I hope our experience will help everyone.[40]

The accident was, as Mrs Lorna Arnold, the present historian of the Authority, wrote in 1979,

> essentially the result of overloading, for years, an organisation which was seriously undermanned especially in some key positions. Its causes were political

and administrative quite as much as technical, and responsibility was widely diffused. No disciplinary action would have been appropriate and none was taken.[41]

Fortunately, the much more modern and efficient Calder Hall reactors had been in operation for a year producing electric power as a by-product, and the Authority was justified in arguing that a Windscale accident could not occur in one of the civil reactors which operated at higher temperatures. In these, the strains set up in the graphite by neutron bombardment were being continuously 'annealed out' at an adequate rate due to the high temperature of operation.

The lessons of the accident were driven home in the reports of the three committees under Sir Alexander Fleck, chairman of ICI, who was appointed by the Prime Minister, Harold Macmillan, to make an independent enquiry. Cockcroft was a member of the Technical Evaluation Committee which studied the information relating to the design and operation of the Windscale reactors emerging from the accident. When it was all over, it was true, as Mrs Arnold wrote, that

> indirectly the Windscale accident and the Fleck Reports influenced not only the Authority but everyone working in the field of atomic energy and by hindsight the results were almost wholly beneficial.[42]

Cockcroft, who had just entered his sixties, now a stocky figure with thinning hair, looking benignly through horn-rimmed spectacles, was unperturbed by crises such as these as he moved from Harwell to Authority meetings in Charles II Street (he attended some 90 meetings between 1954 and 1961); or travelling north to visit the Industrial Group at Risley; sometimes calling on his neighbour, Penney, at the Atomic Weapons Research Establishment a few miles away; and tirelessly lecturing to learned societies and institutions or attending conferences, giving an address at school speech days; proposing or replying to toasts at dinners; or hurrying off to London Airport for one of his overseas tours. When working at Harwell Cockcroft sat in a spacious office a few hundred yards from his house. He could see from his desk a line of young beech trees which he had planted himself. A B Jones, Head of the Administration Division, said when Cockcroft was leaving Harwell,

> I do not recall any meeting with him over the past twelve years at which his thick black book did not make at least one appearance. To see it drawn out of his jacket side pockets was a certain sign that he had some questions to ask.[42]

He delegated responsibility as far as possible and got his Divisional heads to do likewise, so that instead of

> having the most able people in positions of responsibility where they were loaded down with administration and out of contact with the scientific work in the laboratory,[44]

each Division had its own administrative officer. He also introduced the personal merit post whereby outstanding scientists were appointed to a senior rank without any measure of responsibility. Further flexibility was given by allowing senior staff to change from a post with responsibility to one without.

He expected his staff to work hard, and as at the Cavendish or at ADRDE, it was unusual for him to give praise. The selection of names of staff for the Honours Lists was something he shared with the Secretary of the Establishment, and he was delighted whenever one of his colleagues was recognised. He himself, surprisingly for such a modest man, derived great satisfaction from his many honours and awards and displayed all his medals and ribbons at his home.

However, the improvement of human relationships exercised his mind as much as future scientific policy.

> Problems of organisation in industry, especially labour relations are getting even more complicated. By the time a young scientist reaches the age of thirty he may well be in charge of a group of younger scientists and technicians, and the quality of their work will depend not only on his scientific ability but on his powers of leadership,[45]

he told a schoolboy audience (which included Christopher) at Gresham's School, Holt. What he had in mind was elaborated in a paper entitled *Human Relations in Research Establishments*, which he delivered in 1951 at a conference on management and organisation in research establishments[46]. In it, he showed how important it was for the director of a research establishment to look after his staff, providing houses for married members and hostels for the single; good paintings and prints should be hung on the walls of offices and recreation rooms decorated attractively. Sport and cultural activities must be encouraged and families of staff should be invited to 'open days' to see work in progress.

He always followed these precepts closely. When he was abroad he was always on the lookout for ideas to improve the establishment. On a visit to Dahl's institute at Bergen, he noticed the laboratory was

> simple but elegant. I especially admired the tea and sandwich room—rather different from the somewhat scruffy atmosphere of British canteens. I'll have to keep pushing away at improving ours.

Sometimes at Harwell, after enquiring into the mundane details of typing pools, housing plans and bus schedules for the employees, he would stroll round the grounds and inspect the plantations of young trees or admire the display of roses. On seeing an unsightly heap of scrap metal he would have a quiet word with the appropriate person to have it removed. He encouraged sport, cricket especially, and he even became President of the Harwell Angling Club, although confessing that his knowledge of fishing did not extend beyond the hours he spent on the banks of Chalk River.

He took much trouble in supervising the design of a hall to be used for Divisional colloquia, lectures and concerts. It held 300 people and was also used for international conferences. Celebrated scientists like Victor Weisskopf, Hans Bethe and Edward Teller were invited to lecture, and the staff gathered to hear Cockcroft recount enthusiastically what he had seen in laboratories during his American tours. When Harwell was being built, he had given instructions that roads should be named after deceased rather than living scientists, and when it was suggested that an exception be made to the rule and the new hall named after him, he returned the note with the laconic comment, 'Not until ten years dead'. But in the end he gave in, and Cockcroft Hall was opened in June 1955 with a concert performed by an orchestra composed entirely of Harwell staff. The finale was Haydn's *Toy Symphony*, in which senior members of the staff 'reached for bird whistles, toy trumpets and drums and blew and rattled their heads off'. Sir John, according to his secretary, Miss Joan Pye, played the Nightingale and Elizabeth blew lustily on a trumpet.

Elizabeth ably assisted him at social functions like the garden parties held at the Establishment or at Buckland House. She took a keen interest in the running of the Establishment and made a point of knowing as many of the staff as possible, and more remarkably, keeping their names in her head. 'We could not have wished', said A B Jones, 'for anyone more devoted to a cause in which the guiding hand was that of her illustrious husband'. In this way the Cockcrofts built up a spirit far removed from that usually associated with government establishments.

> One gets so depressed [wrote Sir Lawrence Bragg to Cockcroft after visiting Harwell in 1951] by the rather dreary atmosphere of such places that it came as an encouraging surprise to see a place in which the research people were so much on their toes and obviously enjoying their work. I felt I got a better appreciation of your decision to build up research at Harwell more than in the universities. I do so much believe that keeping people's noses to the grindstone of immediate applied research and development is not wise, that a better sense of what is really important shows that it is far better in the long run for the quality of work to have keen men who are enjoying themselves.[47]

Nor did Cockcroft fail to keep on good terms with the world beyond the perimeter fence and for which the Establishment had early become 'shrouded in an air of mystery and glamour'[48]. His political 'masters' must see the use to which public funds were being put. There was a constant procession of VIPs, including the Queen and the Duke of Edinburgh, Princess Margaret, the Duke of Gloucester, prime ministers from Churchill to Eden and Macmillan, Commonwealth leaders and foreign heads of state. Open days for Members of Parliament were held and Cockcroft would move unobtrusively among the throng. It might have been on such an occasion that a self-important notable engaged him in conversation unaware who he was: after a lengthy monologue, uninterrupted by Cockcroft, he turned to him and asked what was his line of country. 'Scientist', replied the Nobel Prizewinner as the questioner passed on to find another victim. To a journalist from *The Observer*, he was

> a charming and courteous man whose field of scholarship might have been Greek literature or Chinese art, and whose field of inevitably competent administration might have been a college or a government department. Even the alarmingly complex skyline of the atomic research plants fails to make a mystery of the headkeeper who tames, feeds and understands them.[49]

Probably more to his taste was his cultivation of the inhabitants of the small downland villages surrounding the Establishment, which after barely changing for centuries suddenly had to assimilate the influx of scientists and technologists unused to rural ways of life. Their MP, Sir Ralph Glyn, who as chairman of the Parliamentary Select Committee on Estimates had had to cross-examine Cockcroft and who became his friend, had to face most of the resentment and suspicion in the early days. When, in November 1951, it was rumoured that Cockcroft might be leaving to become the chairman of the DRPC, he wrote to him,

> I hope very much that you will not leave...when you have done so much to bring all your scientific folk into neighbourly contact with all the rest of us established in the district.[50]

And when Cockcroft finally left for Cambridge in 1959, Lord Glyn wrote an appreciative letter:

> Looking back, I think we can feel content that most of the difficulties were successfully ironed out and this could never have happened had it not been for the way in which you and your people recognised the importance of integrating the interests of AERE with the local conditions of what was once a very rural area.[51]

While Glyn, who was succeeded by Mr Airey Neave as MP for Abingdon, watched the interests of the local communities, another neighbour, John Betjeman, poet and ardent preservationist of the countryside and buildings of merit, crossed swords with Cockcroft over the prefabricated houses that marred the downland. Cockcroft, no less enchanted by the landscape, explained that a

> start had to be made quickly and the only solution was to provide prefabs and to erect them on our site where services and sewers were available and where the minimum of consents had to be obtained.[52]

Some thirty years later the uncompromising silhouette of chimneys and laboratories and even the prefabs have been softened by the growth of trees which Cockcroft was so keen on planting. The more recent construction of the Didcot power station with its huge condensers dominating the skyline has become a far more conspicuous and offensive landmark.

Poet and scientist became friends, and the former, congratulating Cockcroft on his OM, remarked, 'I'd like to be a Duke, but I'd sooner be an OM than anything'.[53]

Integration, mentioned by Glyn, often took an imaginative form, like the planting of trees for the nearby village of Chilton, or the interest with which Cockcroft followed the progress of the new Chilton school which he opened in 1950. Its headmaster, Mr F J Denzey, persuaded him to establish a link with the school at Deep River, founded by and named after Cockcroft; and where his children had resumed their education after leaving Montreal.

Such preoccupations still left him time to enjoy family life, though his continual absences abroad prompted on one occasion an agreement which read: 'I promise that next time I go on a trip I will take my wife and children'. It was signed 'John Cockcroft. Witnesses, Dorothea, Jocelyn, Elizabeth, Catherine, Christopher', But it was not until after leaving Harwell that members of his family began to accompany him regularly. Even as a father, he was a man of few words and his daughters used to stipulate that 'Daddy must say at least three complete sentences during a meal before he leaves the table'. No doubt they found it easier to rekindle his love of tennis and, after playing with them, he rose, as he modestly said, 'to the standard of the first couple of the second team of Headington School'. Jocelyn, who went to Cambridge to read science, followed her father's interest in cricket, inspiring him to 'bowl again on our bumpy lawn to demonstrate leg-breaks and off-breaks' which reminded him of the cricket he used to play 'on the bumpy hill tops of the Pennines'. She always thinks of him

> as a person whose tremendous energy was always constructively directed. He never wasted time. Most of the time he worked, but when he relaxed, the relaxation was complete; gardening and listening to music were his chief sources of renewal but he read widely too.

There were walks on the Ridgeway and he was interested enough in local antiquities to join the Berkshire Archaeological Society. His daughter Catherine, 'Cathie', recalls how, when she was wanting help from father in Harwell to learn the art of cycling she

> finally acknowledged that he had his head screwed on straight when he decided that a concentrated hour of tuition would, in the long run, give him more time, and we went stopping and starting round the block! He was right! [She goes on to record] One standard walk was around the fence behind which everything mysteriously happened. It was only years later that I realised the full tragedy of 'the fence', that my Father and his colleagues who, before 1939, had believed so passionately in the international brotherhood of university scientists, should have found this disintegrating round about them during the war and on into the 'cold war'.

Tragedy it was, but his faith and convictions were firm: asked by a scientist if he thought it was right to pursue work on atomic weapons, he replied that he considered that the overwhelming danger and evil of the time came not from the atomic bomb but from the policy pursued by Russia

> which has taken over the practices of the Nazi regime—the concentration camps, slave labour, the watcher in every street and everything which goes with that; until there is a settlement I believe we are justified in arming ourselves as strongly as the Russians.

'Cathie' recalls for us also how her Father emerged as a 'person' on holiday, how, from him, she learned the love of poking around old buildings, stately homes, churches and cathedrals. 'It must have been for him the side that emerged during his Junior Bursarship of St John's, but to him I owe my delight in such explorations'. In those years, for her

> Harwell was a strange place to live in, the house was constantly filled with people talking, though it was difficult to understand what it was about. Much of what they were talking about seemed to go on behind that mysterious fence. My father was not naturally very helpful with some of my attempts to clear the air. I think he knew too much to be able to grasp what it was that people did not know. I remember watching a beautiful rainbow from the sitting room of 1 South Drive and asking him why there were seven colours in it; he simply said

there weren't. Perhaps I should have removed the book in which he was immersed, but for a seven-year-old that was quite hard, he wasn't the kind of
person you did that to.

But he wasn't quite infallible; when she asked for some help with algebra, 'I
can remember the day when he took an hour and a half which he could ill
afford, and he kept tearing up his workings in frustration. I was very
impressed'.

They did not own a television, and instead in the evenings there was a flow
of classical music from the record player while he worked at his papers. Music
was indeed one of his great solaces, and as long as he could get home after
a long and tiring day and listen to a Mozart symphony things seemed better.
Other composers to be found in his large collection of records included
Sibelius, Mahler, Berlioz, Verdi, Nielsen, Vaughan Williams, Britten,
Bruckner, Bach and Beethoven. Of the other girls, Dorothea had gone in for
nursing, Elizabeth was to become a social worker with an interest in children,
and Catherine began to study history for Oxford; she realised that if she gave
her Father anything clear cut and decisive he would respond immediately but
'he did not, could not, respond to uncertainty and anxiety', so when the decision had to be taken 'about what I should do at university, we set out to walk
the fence, then extended to circumnavigate DIDO, we neither of us spoke a
word the whole way round! When I finally staggered into Oxford he was as
much amazed as pleased'. Christopher, who had grown up in a succession of
research establishments, went to read engineering at his father's old college,
St John's, after leaving Gresham's School in Norfolk.

Because of his unremitting responsibilities outside Harwell, which will be
described in the following two chapters, Cockcroft let Schonland take over the
running of the Establishment, while retaining, of course, his appointment as
Member for Research in the Authority. He formally handed over the Directorship to Schonland in September 1958, though continuing to live at South
Drive until they moved to Cambridge. During that time Schonland was in the
unenviable position of trying to run the Establishment while his former chief
looked, as it were, over his shoulder. Cockcroft never *quite* relinquished his
authority as Director and he was probably oblivious to some of the consequences. Hanni Bretscher remembered how she and her husband, then head
of the Nuclear Physics Division, were both unexpectedly urged to come to
dinner at the Schonlands after they had already finished supper with their
children[56]. They were wanted to help entertain Dr F A Vick, whom Cockcroft
had just appointed as Deputy to Schonland without previous consultation,
and as Ismay, Schonland's wife, explained afterwards, their presence was
needed to make it impossible to discuss that appointment. Moreover, the need
for continuing retrenchment in government expenditure compelled
Schonland to prune severely some of the more optimistic schemes authorised
by Cockcroft. Aware of this, senior members of staff would head for
Cockcroft's office in the hope of receiving more favourable treatment than at
the hands of the Director. Schonland's loyalty to his friend and colleague must
have been severely tested on these occasions.

CHAPTER SIXTEEN

SCIENTIST/DIPLOMAT

Cockcroft's numerous transatlantic journeys in the cause of Anglo–American scientific collaboration have been briefly mentioned in the past chapters, but due to their politico-scientific nature they have been left to be described as a whole. Despite the collaboration on atomic energy formally established by the Quebec Agreement of 1943, it was not long after the war that the Americans changed their attitude and this was due, firstly, to the fact that they wanted to remain the only nuclear power, secondly they suspected the intentions of the USSR and possibly suspected the British security services, especially after it had been shown that Nunn May, then Fuchs and Pontecorvo had given so much away and this made a number of prominent American politicians reluctant to pass information to a socialist British Government. Even so, it was impossible for them to ignore the advantages that might be gained from continuing to collaborate with the British.

In the postwar years Cockcroft played a major part in trying to restore satisfactory relations with the Americans. He happened to be well suited for the task. Not only did he have a reputation for integrity, and as Sir Archibald Rowlands said, 'knew more about the subject of atomic energy than anybody alive',[1] he also had the advantage of knowing the American scene because of his prewar and wartime visits. All this made him extremely acceptable to the body of administrators and scientists forming the United States Atomic Energy Commission (USAEC) which took over control of atomic energy from the US Army on 1 January 1947.

Cockcroft's introduction to high-level diplomacy came somewhat unexpectedly, when President Truman of the USA and Prime Ministers Attlee of Great Britain and Mackenzie King of Canada met in Washington to discuss firstly, the need for international control of atomic energy, and secondly, what form of technical collaboration should succeed the Quebec agreement. The evening before the arrival of the British delegation on Sunday, 11 November 1945, Cockcroft, while dining at Toronto University after receiving an honorary degree, was given an urgent message to go at once to Washington as scientific adviser. He took the 1.30 AM plane to New York on Sunday and caught the 7.00 AM plane to Washington, arriving half an hour before the Prime Minister's plane touched down. After a sound sleep, he met Attlee for the first time and learned about the British Government's intentions.

Cockcroft's first impression of Attlee, who was just as undemonstrative as himself, was that he 'seemed to know his own mind pretty well and was obviously very moved about the whole problem'.

Over the course of most of the following week, Cockcroft was at hand to give advice on the concerted plan, which was the setting-up of a Commission for the exchange of scientific information for peaceful ends, the elimination of nuclear weapons, and the provision of safeguards against the unlawful manufacture of weapons. On Monday afternoon, while the heads of state cruised down the Potomac on the yacht of James Forrestal, Secretary of the Navy, Cockcroft hurried to discussions at the White House, a building which he described as 'very interesting architecturally and politically', and at the British Embassy with the teams of military and economic advisers in the Prime Minister's party. Meanwhile Sir John Anderson, assisted by Roger Makins, Economic Minister at the British Embassy and responsible for atomic energy matters, and with whom Cockcroft had already become friends (their children were of about the same age) sought with the Americans ways of achieving technical collaboration in the postwar era.

On the morning of 13 November Cockcroft breakfasted with nine American scientists, including Robert Oppenheimer, who, on retiring as Director of the Los Alamos Laboratory, had just made a moving address to his staff about international control of atomic energy[2]. Their purpose was to make specific proposals for the control of atomic energy which were later formulated in the report by Dean Acheson, then Under Secretary of State, and David Lilienthal, shortly to become the chairman of the USAEC. Recalling this meeting Cockcroft wrote that, 'we discussed the problems of the Plan and the Americans were reasonably optimistic about the possibility of their solution. We did not know our brave New World'[3]. In June 1946 this report was presented by the Americans at the inaugural session of the United Nations Atomic Energy Commission, but from the start, was vigorously opposed by the USSR, and an international authority with such powers still remains to be established. A party of British scientists was in Washington at the time of the conference, including Peierls, Skinner and Fuchs, with whom, as Cockcroft wrote, he was 'having talks all the time', presumably about the British atomic energy research establishment, but just how much information about the high-level meetings with the Americans Fuchs passed back to his masters may never be known.

The declaration on international control was signed by the heads of state on 15 November. Cockcroft wrote to his mother, describing the three meetings he had taken part in with the Prime Minister.

> [Attlee] struck me as being quite an efficient chairman of a meeting, with sensible views about international politics. You will have seen that a joint statement was agreed on after much midnight consultation and drafting and redrafting. I don't think it is a bad statement and it now remains to be seen how we get on when we open up UNO negotiations. I am not anxious to spend any time on that side of atomic energy.

An interesting statement in view of the large amount of time he spent later on the promotion of many international conferences and on an international atomic energy agency. Unhappily, the possibilities of international control of atomic energy foundered within a year of the Washington meeting, while technical collaboration between the western powers became virtually non-existent.

The latter was due to the passing of the McMahon Bill in the USA in August 1946 forbidding the exchange of technical information with foreigners until it had been declassified, and, as just stated, the American atomic energy project remained under military control until the end of the year. In spite of the strict rules Cockcroft had been given permission that June to visit Berkeley to look at Lawrence's 184 inch cyclotron and Lawrence had accepted an invitation to attend a physics conference at McGill University in Canada which he intended to combine with a visit to Chalk River on Cockcroft's invitation before the latter returned to England in September[4]. But on 17 August, Lawrence's secretary wrote to Cockcroft that Lawrence had decided that he could not come to Canada, giving the excuse that he 'has to be away from the laboratory so much during the coming month'.[5] A week later Cockcroft wrote to Lawrence:

> I expect you have been told that Manhattan District has vetoed my visit to your lab because of the McMahon Bill. [ending his letter] The McGill Physics Conference will be most disappointed in not having you there.[6]

There is no doubt that he was upset by the ban, for some days earlier he had written to Elizabeth, then at Harwell, that

> The McMahon Bill has temporarily stopped all interchange of visits to the US projects and apparently Berkeley counts since they are run on Army money. So Lawrence won't even come to the Physics Conference on 2 September. I do think the US scientists on the top are short of guts. He [Lawrence] ought to go and tackle any conspiracy (?). In fact, no-one would dare to touch him.

Lawrence had also agreed to receive a team from Harwell to get experience for the Harwell cyclotron but this visit, too, was cancelled until March 1947. On 30 August Lawrence wrote apologetically to Cockcroft:

> Sorry you will not be able to come out as planned. General Groves feels no reason why you should not come [provided that you deferred your visit] until the AEC is set up and they formulate the rules of the game. I am sorry I can't come to Chalk River because of other commitments.[7]

Despite the setting up of the AEC, collaboration was not improved by the spring of 1947 and in May Cockcroft, now permanently based at Harwell, was sent by the Ministry of Supply to Washington to try to find a working relationship which would circumvent the conditions of the McMahon Bill and enable the British and Canadians to obtain information for their respective atomic energy projects. It was strictly an unofficial visit, though he had to shake off inquisitive reporters before he left Southampton and on arriving in New York. In Washington, apart from meeting Lord Inverchapel, the British Ambassador, Cockcroft had useful talks with Carroll Wilson, whom he had not met since the war, and who was now General Manager of the USAEC. Using either Cockcroft's hotel in Washington (the Gralyn) or the Cosmos Club as a rendezvous for discussions, they agreed on the need for collaboration on unclassified subjects like medical research, extraction chemistry and isotopes[8].

Cockcroft then went on to Ottawa to restore relations with the Canadian Government which had reached a low ebb because the latter still believed that the British decision to build atomic energy plants in the UK was a flagrant breach of faith, and a visit by Sir John Anderson and even the appointment of W B Lewis to succeed Cockcroft at Chalk River had done little to mollify the Canadians. Cockcroft wrote to Elizabeth while crossing the Atlantic,

> Our friend Sir John Anderson apparently did a good deal of harm on his last trip by ponderous and tactless blunders. This added to Mackenzie's continually worrying about the future which has produced an unsettled state in our relations which I hope to be able to clear up.

As already described, the research work at Chalk River was essential to the British programme and Cockcroft now proposed that the two countries should collaborate in a power development programme. The Canadians, wrote Cockcroft, 'were pretty well in agreement with what I had to say' and this had the effect of improving relations, though in the end, the Canadians decided to go ahead with their own nuclear programme without British participation.

Before returning home, Cockcroft was allowed to visit the Brookhaven National Laboratory—an American equivalent of Harwell—for discussions on unclassified subjects such as accelerators and power reactors. He discussed the hazards from radiation with Dr Austin Brues 'from Chicago, an expert on our troubles' and Gordon Butler from Chalk River and went on to visit the Bell Laboratories at Schenectady and Columbia University.

Improved political relations between Britain and the USA during 1947, combined with urgent American requirements for uranium and the need for a more liberal construction of the McMahon Act for America's partners because of the Cold War, led to the resumption of talks that autumn. Cockcroft was again the leading negotiator and went twice to Washington before the end of the year. On the first occasion, accompanied by Rudolf Peierls, he enjoyed the comfort and relaxation offered by the *Queen Mary*. He met the other members of the USAEC for the first time and found them only too willing to help. He wrote to Elizabeth that the Chairman, David Lilienthal, was 'a very attractive looking person and obviously very capable' and Robert Bacher, the scientist commissioner, and James Fisk, Director of Research, were 'rather our style' and the 'Harwell type'. At a supper party to which Cockcroft and Peierls were invited, good relations were strengthened as they sat in front of a log fire and 'ate cold chicken and rice'.

The Tripartite Declassification Committee, of which all the members were scientists, agreed to lift restrictions on the exchange of information about experimental power reactors and they produced a joint declassification guide which recorded their conclusions. In return the British promised to hand over to the Americans the total 1948 supply of Congo uranium ore plus a further 700 tons in course of shipment which the Americans badly needed for their weapons programme. Cockcroft remembered that it was 'not exactly an exciting result, but at least it was a beginning'[9].

He then flew to Ottawa to cement British–Canadian collaboration and spent several days at Chalk River where he watched the NRX reactor in operation. He had intended returning home by the *Mauretania* on 26 November, after visiting Princeton to talk with Oppenheimer, then a member of the General Advisory Committee to the Atomic Energy Commission, and to discuss computers with John von Neumann, but Carroll Wilson asked him to return to Washington for discussions with the Combined Policy Committee which met to agree on Anglo–US nuclear programmes. He attended the meetings with Donald Maclean, the British Embassy official who had replaced Makins, and who later defected to the Soviet Union. Maclean was, on first acquaintance, 'a pleasant soft-spoken, most intelligent person, fond of books and paintings and mountains', and they discovered they had friends in common in Norfolk: the Russians certainly placed those spies advantageously! At last he flew home on 5 December.

Five days later he had flown back to Washington, accompanied by David Peirson from the Ministry of Supply, to discuss raw materials. Roger Makins, now Under-Secretary at the Foreign Office in charge of the Economic and North American Departments, followed them to take part in high level political talks and on Saturday 15 and Monday 17 December 1947 Cockcroft took part in meetings at the British Embassy and at the State Department at which the principal members were Lovett, Secretary of State, George Kennan, from the State Department, Forrestal, the Defence Secretary, Lord Inverchapel, Lilienthal and Dr C J Mackenzie from Canada. It was agreed that, in return for a greater allocation of uranium, the British should have access to technical information in the following nine specific areas:

1. Topics declassified under the 1947 declassification guide (the fruits of Cockcroft's previous visit).
2. The entire field of health and safety.
3. Research uses of radioisotopes.
4. Fundamental nuclear and extra-nuclear properties of all developments.
5. Detection of distant nuclear explosions (an intelligence project).
6. Fundamental problems of reactor materials.
7. Extraction chemistry.
8. The design of natural uranium reactors in which power was not wasted.
9. General research experience with low power reactors.

The first four of these areas and the ninth were essentially unclassified and already free for all. Areas 6, 7, and 8 were the only areas of technical importance and presumably were conceded because British work in these areas was just as advanced as in the United States, and in some cases, even more so[10]

This arrangement became known as the *Modus Vivendi* and was announced on 7 January 1948. As it had not been signed, it did not have to be referred to Congress by the President, and it did not fall within Article 102 of the United Nations Charter, which required every treaty and international agreement to be registered with, and published by, the United Nations.

Unhappily, the promise of fresh collaboration offered by the *Modus Vivendi* proved to be short-lived. In the spring of 1948 Cockcroft sent members of his Harwell staff to exchange information on health and safety, chemistry and experimental reactors with the Americans; likewise, American scientists visited Harwell and Windscale, but when they returned home, they reported that the British were not only developing power reactors but were building large-scale facilities for the production of plutonium thousands of miles nearer to the Russians than similar American establishments. Details of the production of plutonium had not been included in the *Modus Vivendi* but Lewis Strauss, one of the Atomic Energy Commissioners who was a right-wing Congressman and Senator Hickenlooper, who had been chairman of the Joint Congressional Committee on Atomic Energy, believed that Britain was 'far to our left and therefore may give away the secrets to the communists, some of whom already sat in Parliament'[11]. (It may be recalled that at the Alan Nunn May trial it was disclosed that communist cells had been set up and certain members were told specifically to behave as noncommunists taking care never to associate openly with other members of the cells; the Americans probably suspected some MP's on this score.) Strauss, Hickenlooper and McMahon henceforward opposed any move by Lilienthal and the pro-British Atomic Energy Commissioners to improve collaboration between the two countries over the next three years. Cooperation in Area 8 (the design of natural uranium reactors in which power was not wasted) was now stopped. However, this veto did not affect the British programme as the Americans had not yet begun to work on nuclear power.

In order to try and repair the damage that had been done, Cockcroft visited North America in October 1948. As usual, he travelled by sea and wrote to Elizabeth while on board:

> I have dutifully paced the upper deck in true British style and have slumbered over Churchill's memoirs for two hours after lunch. I have also dutifully written for four hours a day to keep Rosemary [his secretary] out of mischief. At meals I have the honour of sitting at the Captain's table—a red Devon sea dog brought up in windjammers—a member of a dying race. I have swum twice in a nice pool with a shiny metal shoot down which I went and there was quite a big swell so it was fun. The children would have loved it! [Referring to his recent knighthood, he wrote] I always find myself writing Mrs J D Cockcroft on the envelope—how hard it is to get used to the idea of being amongst the gentry! However, it does seem to help in getting a few privileges on board ship!

This time his programme began in Ottawa and he agreed with Mackenzie on a number of matters in which it would be possible to collaborate with the Canadians. He stayed in Deep River noting that the school, named after him, had been enlarged. Three days later, he was in Washington and found the Commissioners extremely friendly despite the strains caused by the banning of Area 8. Like them, he agreed that the Declassification Committee should try to get the best out of the remaining areas of collaboration, and he wrote a report for the British Ambassador, Sir Oliver Franks, elaborating how mutually advantageous collaboration could be. He soon discovered how anomalies could arise, when visiting Brookhaven before returning home; he was forbidden to look at the graphite research reactor because the heat was used to warm the building and therefore within Area 8. At the same time he was unable to tell the staff (officially) about the experience gained by the

British and Canadians from gas-cooled reactors and the possibility of excess
Wigner energy making them dangerous![12]   '*à bon chat, bon rat*'

In 1949 Lilienthal and his fellow Commissioners and pro-British
Congressmen appreciated that there must be a new approach to the problem
of collaboration. The *Modus Vivendi* was no longer appropriate with Marshall
Aid and American participation in NATO taking shape. At the same time the
vendetta against the Commissioners by Hickenlooper and like-minded politicians continued unabated.

This was the background to Cockcroft's visit to North America in May
1949. His purpose was to discuss arrangements about the exchange of information on power reactors with the Commission and the future of the *Modus
Vivendi* with Dean Acheson of the State Department and W Webster, who had
recently taken responsibility for atomic energy in the Defence Department.
Hickenlooper had just launched a vicious attack on the Commission, accusing
it of giving away too much information to the British. When Cockcroft first
heard about it, he thought it was 'a bigger storm in a tea cup' than he had
ever seen, but he found some Los Alamos scientists 'all het up about the
futilities of the Senate and some vigorous protesting is going on'. Wilson told
him how 'Hickenlooper [in his capacity as chairman of the Joint Congressional Committee on Atomic Energy] had employed two low grade sleuths
—ex-Manhattan District—to dig up these ridiculous charges against the
Commission'. One of them concerned the 'loss' of a bottle of uranium oxide
from the Argonne Laboratory, later found to have been emptied down a
disposal bin.

The remainder of his visit was devoted to obtaining information for
Harwell. In New York he was interested in the chemical separation work at
the Knolls Atomic Power Laboratories of the General Electric Company, no
doubt comparing it with Robert Spence's chemical separation by
counterflow, and he discussed radiation hazards with the Medical Division of
the Atomic Energy Commission. At MIT he exchanged notes on high energy
accelerators. Travelling to the west coast, he spent two useful days at the
Radiation Laboratory in Berkeley. Lawrence was away, but his colleagues
took Cockcroft round. Robert Brode, with whom he stayed, later sent a report
to Lawrence.

> Cockcroft saw the 184 inch cyclotron and linear accelerator and bevatron. He
> took notes. He talked with Seaborg about chemical work and with Ed Lofgren
> about the bevatron. Cooksey showed Cockcroft the facilities for the 'hot' lab
> work and showed him the glove boxes without any discussion of the particular
> problems for which they are used, but only of the principles involved in their
> use as protection against radioactivity. He was also shown the mass
> spectrograph[13].

Afterwards Cockcroft wrote to Elizabeth, 'The Californian physicists always
impress me with their terrific energy and boldness'. At Chalk River he saw
the first specks of plutonium that had just been produced in the NRX reactor
and inspected the chemical engineering work in progress.

Further impetus was given to British hopes for a new approach to collaboration with the Americans in the autumn of 1949 by the expansion of the

former's nuclear power programme and by the development of a British atomic bomb due to be tested in two years' time. The discussions planned for September were overshadowed by the explosion of a Russian atomic bomb on 29 August. The Americans had alerted the British on 9 September that a radioactive cloud was moving eastwards across the Atlantic and this was soon confirmed by the British long-range detection devices. Cockcroft had been informed before leaving for New York in the *Queen Elizabeth* on 14 September and a British intelligence officer provided confirmation when he arrived in America five days later. As the information was officially classified for the British, he was unable to discuss it with Isidor Rabi, a wartime friend and now a senior adviser to the Commission, as they travelled together to Washington for the meetings.

On 21 September he interrupted his discussions in Washington to fly to New York with Makins, leader of the British Atomic energy team, to convince Bevin and Lester Pearson, the British and Canadian Foreign Secretaries, then attending a United Nations meeting, that the Russian test had been verified. (Bevin had been especially sceptical and Cockcroft had to explain the technicalities of detection to him in simple language.) A public announcement was made by Truman on the evening of 22 September.

In Washington, while the Americans were prepared to accept the British proposal of foregoing a third plutonium-producing reactor as well as the construction of a high separation diffusion plant in order to release sufficient uranium to meet the requirements of the Commission, the Americans were not yet prepared to commit themselves to a renewal of collaboration for the next six years. Cockcroft, who had been suffering from a severe cold throughout the proceedings, wrote, 'The Americans have been going through one of their periods of doubts and hesitations'. He had missed the sailing of the *Queen Elizabeth*, on which he had booked a berth, and instead flew home on Sunday, 2 October.

He and Makins returned to Washington at the beginning of December, this time with Portal himself leading the team. Again, agreement could not be reached. Worse was to come. After Fuchs had been arrested for spying in February 1950, the Commission decided that no new areas should be added to the programme with the British.

Cockcroft did not visit North America again until September 1951. Despite unpromising incidents like the defection of Pontecorvo in 1950 and Burgess and Maclean in June 1951, the Americans were prepared to reconsider the McMahon Act that autumn in order to take advantage of experience gained with the NRX reactor and to obtain information about its design. They wanted to collaborate with the British in atomic energy intelligence, hitherto prohibited by the McMahon Act, and in uranium manufacture and in weapon tests.

Before going to Washington, Cockcroft had a heavy programme to fulfil. He visited the Bell Laboratories in New York where the first transistor units were being developed and took back some samples with him for the Electronics Group at Harwell to work on 'at a time when there was a great deal of scepticism as to their future'[14]. He looked at the 'giant cosmotron' (high energy accelerator) at Brookhaven and then went on to Chicago to join a delegation of other eminent British scientists, headed by Cherwell, which was attending an international physics conference. In Canada, after taking part in defence research talks (it will be recalled he had now become chairman-designate of the DRPC), he had two days rest in the 'peace of Deep River which is appealing as ever', before flying to Washington.

The Board of the Commission had changed since his last visit. Gordon Dean, described by Cockcroft as 'an intelligent and sensible person' had replaced Lilienthal as chairman. Marion Boyer had succeeded Carroll Wilson as General Manager, Harold Smyth, well known for his report on wartime atomic energy developments, and a friend of Cockcroft's (described by the latter as 'quietish like me'), became scientific adviser; Keith Glennan was another scientific consultant. The State Department representative was Gordon Arneson and Robert Le Baron represented the War Department.

Although the discussions were overshadowed by the prospect of a British General Election, they proved, as Cockcroft recorded, 'to be very valuable to our programme'. He told the Commission about the British nuclear power programme and warned them that the construction of a high separation diffusion plant would increase the British uranium requirements. The Americans, however, gave no indication of cooperating on nuclear power. As for help on the military side, Le Baron told him that the Americans were prepared to discuss the effects and applications of nuclear weapons, but not to provide information about actual development. Cockcroft rounded off this exhausting tour, during which he had again suffered from a heavy cold, by attending a colloquium on accelerators at MIT. On 6 October 1951 he returned home thankfully on the *Queen Mary*.

In 1952 the presence of a Conservative Government promised a new era in collaboration with the Americans. It was arranged that Cockcroft and Penney should meet the Atomic Energy Commission in March. On the way out Cockcroft was beguiled by conversations with Viscount Samuel, the venerable savant and politician. They discussed the 'aether which went out of fashion 50 years ago. However, Dirac wants to have it back†. So it may become fashionable again'. More relevant to the present day were Cockcroft's arguments on the need for more science graduates and for expanding research in nuclear physics; this provided ammunition for Samuel's speech in the debate on science and industry in the House of Lords on 11 June 1952.

As on previous occasions, he spent the first week of his visit in Ottawa and Chalk River discussing policy and seeing progress in the laboratories. He arrived in Washington on Monday, 17 March and in the course of the following days met Le Baron who was 'cheering and uninhibited' over civil defence and he had a very useful talk with Bedell-Smith, Director of the Central Intelligence Agency (CIA). His meeting with Gordon Dean had to be postponed until Thursday because of the latter's absence from Washington: the purpose of the meeting with the Commissioners was to discover areas in

†*Nature* had recently published a letter by Dirac in which he suggested that it might be necessary to have an aether 'subject to quantum mechanics and relativity, provided we are willing to consider the perfect vacuum as an idealised state, not attainable in practice'.[15]

which collaboration with the Americans could be improved, such as reactor materials, uranium processing losses and reactor development. This evidently required corroboration from Hinton, and Cockcroft wrote to Elizabeth that he had got up that morning

> at 7 AM after telephoning Hinton from my bed. We just don't understand one another! Suddenly I realised that I was supposed to be breakfasting with Jo and Emily Boyce at the Hay-Adams Hotel.

Hinton was worried, according to Gowing, that the topics on which Cockcroft wanted an exchange of information would help the Americans more than the British,

> partly because the British would not be shown the current development work being done in the laboratories and factories of the big American firms which carried out most of the industrial-scale work as agents of the USAEC.[16]

At the meeting held that day and at a subsequent one held before Cockcroft left Washington on 25 March, the Americans expressed interest in the British natural uranium reactors but made it clear that they were not prepared to collaborate on breeder reactors. In the event, no progress was made in improving collaboration and the only solid achievement of Cockcroft's was the gaining of some useful atomic intelligence. Before leaving New York on 29 March he went to Brookhaven to look again at the 'giant cosmotron which is almost working and I saw the beam going round and round 200 times'.

The British hoped that the election of Eisenhower as President in November 1952 would make collaboration revert to what it was in the pre-McMahon Act days. After Churchill's talks with the new President in January 1953, Makins, the new British Ambassador in Washington, wrote to Cockcroft.

> The Prime Minister has come and gone without mishap. I think all went well in regard to atomic energy. The PM told me on the boat that he had been convinced by Cherwell's minutes [probably referring to the need for an independent atomic energy authority described on page 192] and Ike rather encouraged him to go on with our programme, so I hope all is well—so far.[17]

Cockcroft made two visits to the States that year. During the first, made a week after attending the Coronation in June 1953, he took part in meetings with Arneson from the State Department, with Gordon Dean and the Commissioners, and with Allen Dulles, the new Director of the CIA, discussing intelligence matters; at this time numerous nuclear weapon tests were being made by the Russians as well as by the Americans. He stayed in the Embassy at Makins's invitation and, in addition to his official business, dutifully handed over a 'top secret' letter from his daughter Catherine to Virginia Makins. Unfortunately the latter had forgotten how to decode it and in his next letter home, Cockcroft wrote that 'Cathie had better send [the key to the code]'. In Canada there was business to be transacted in connection with the DRPC and before returning home, a routine visit to Brookhaven and the Bell Laboratories.

His second visit in October 1953 began at Chalk River where he attended an international conference on radiation hazards accompanied by Hinton, and they shared a log cabin. The beauty of the Fall must have had a beneficent effect, Cockcroft writing to Elizabeth that he had

> just made an early morning coffee for Christopher Hinton and myself;

the night before they had both dined with W B Lewis and his mother. He went on to Washington for meetings with the American Commissioners now led by the wily Lewis Strauss. The Russians had recently exploded their first hydrogen bomb and it was necessary to analyse the effects by examination of the airborne debris. Cherwell, who led the British team, personally requested Eisenhower to allow information to be passed on to Cockcroft and Penney. Strauss was also in favour and ways and means of legitimising the disclosure of this information were then investigated. Makins had heard, unofficially, that the Joint Congressional Committee was proposing to lift further restrictions from the McMahon Act, and that the latter would include an agreement to exchange information on industrial applications of atomic energy to uranium-producing countries, particularly Belgium which had provided the British and the Americans with all their supplies for a ten year period. (On the following Sunday *The Sunday Times* carried a similar report.) But Strauss showed no signs of relaxation in this respect and, even before arriving at the conference table Cockcroft wrote to Elizabeth

> the US have got cold feet and are withdrawing a lot of their papers. Very typical.
> I expect someone like Le Baron is objecting.

The spread of information on reactor technology, however, had begun to make such an attitude out of date. Eisenhower's proposal for an international atomic energy agency in December 1953, the Anglo – US bilateral agreements for cooperation regarding atomic information for mutual defence purposes and the civil atomic energy agreement in June 1955, followed eventually by an Anglo – US agreement for a wide-ranging exchange of military information on nuclear matters in July 1958, finally opened the way to a more satisfactory relationship. Until that date Cockcroft continued to attend declassification committee meetings.

He had made an enormous contribution over the past eight years to Anglo – American cooperation; as Sir Mark Oliphant wrote in the Royal Society's Biographical Memoir on the life of Cockcroft,

> There is no doubt that the re-establishing of the flow of information between Britain and the United States had been helped appreciably by Cockcroft's determination to achieve a continuous exchange of scientific information in non-sensitive areas, and by his fostering of permissible working relationships with scientists at the Atomic Energy Commission's laboratories[18]

and he might also have written 'and by the extremely high regard in which Cockcroft was held as a scientist by all with whom he came in contact'[19].

During the delicate negotiations leading to the *Modus Vivendi* he was, as his colleague David Peirson wrote, 'an essential link' between London and Washington. While it is true that, as Leonard Owen wrote, 'the McMahon Act made us work and think for ourselves along independent lines',

Cockcroft's reports to Harwell staff after his visits to Brookhaven, Berkeley and Harvard, in addition to a number of commercial laboratories, were extremely valuable. He himself concluded that the most useful areas of collaboration had been in subjects like chemistry, chemical engineering and metallurgy. Information on reactor physics was poor until 1955 when the decision was taken to abandon secrecy at the Geneva Conference of that year.

In a review of an American book describing the negotiations, he challenged the author's statement that the Americans had played a predominant role in the meetings, or that decisions were largely an implementation of the US Security Council's decisions. What usually happened, he wrote, was that the British were ahead of the Americans

> in suggesting the next step in the declassification process. This was because the US delegation were conscious of the need to obtain the agreement of Congress and other US agencies—a process which usually took about six months— whereas UK Government concurrence was rapidly obtained. ... In general there was an excessive US caution about declassification of civil information. Thus in 1950 the USAEC laid down the principle that until international control was obtained there should be no information exchanged with other nations on the use of atomic energy for industrial purposes[20].

Carroll Wilson, who sat at the same committee table with Cockcroft for a number of those trying years, summed up:

> I think that he was the most important single link over a long period of time in the relations scientifically between the US and the UK. That he did not succeed in the postwar era in getting things back operating again is in no sense due to his failure but rather is due to the American distrust of any information going anywhere and the setbacks which Fuchs's and Maclean's defections and treachery gave to all of it[21].

Makins, described by Cockcroft as 'an old comrade-in-arms', when asked to assess Cockcroft's contributions to international understanding, wrote,

> In the many arrangements for scientific cooperation with Allied countries during and after World War II, Sir John Cockcroft was a leading and possibly the most effective figure. He was a quiet man and did not say much, but he was both persuasive and persistent, and he had a sanguine and robust approach to men and matters which inspired confidence and trust. In Ottawa, in Washington, in Europe and indeed wherever he went he was respected and popular, and, in negotiations he usually attained his objectives.[22]

CHAPTER SEVENTEEN

INTERNATIONAL SCIENTIST

Cockcroft's interest in experimental power reactors in the early 1950s was shared by a number of European nuclear physicists and engineers who were actively engaged in research and development, the French even following Britain's example and designing an atomic bomb, much to Cockcroft's disapproval. He wanted scientific knowledge to be shared freely and used for the good of mankind. Such activity in Europe convinced the Americans at last that their policy of secrecy had been overtaken by events and led to their support of the first international conference on the peaceful uses of atomic energy, in the planning of which Cockcroft was able to use his wide knowledge of the subject and the scientific personalities likely to make valuable contributions.

The first intimation of an American change of attitude was the famous 'atoms for peace' speech of President Eisenhower to the United Nations General Assembly on 8 December 1953 in which he envisaged an international atomic energy agency, a stockpile of fissionable material and a start to be made on the building of power reactors which would satisfy the demands of developing countries. Bertrand Goldschmidt, now a Commissioner of the French Atomic Energy Commission, later wrote that this proposal for nuclear détente was at least

> not characterised by the opposing demands of the two major nuclear powers—
> the American demand that the Soviet Union [and, of course, the USA] throw
> [themselves] open to international inspections, and the Soviet demand for the
> prohibition and destruction of nuclear weapons.[1]

The more relaxed attitude of the USSR towards the West after Stalin's death in March 1952 and the numerous atomic and thermonuclear tests being made by the superpowers were other indications of the difficulty of keeping information about nuclear technology restricted.

Eisenhower's political initiative encouraged nuclear scientists in Europe and America to look for more positive means of exchanging information. On 26 March 1954, Gunnar Randers, a Norwegian physicist, who, during the war had been a member of the proximity-fuse group at Malvern, invited Cockcroft and a number of other leading European scientists to discuss the possibilities of collaboration. His idea found general acceptance and an organisation called the European Atomic Energy Society was planned by Randers, J V Dunworth from Harwell and Giulio Milazo, an Italian physical chemist, to hold meetings, circulate reports and institute standards of safety measures. In due course, representatives from Belgium, France, Italy, the Netherlands, Norway, Sweden and the United Kingdom became members of the Society, but neither Americans nor Russians were invited to join as it was felt that the organisation should be politically neutral. Cockcroft was elected first President of the Council, Randers a Vice-President and Bertrand Goldschmidt a Vice-President responsible for arranging the meetings[2].

Year after year, Cockcroft 'was pressed to stay on as President with Goldschmidt as Executive Vice-President', the latter recalling how this happened. True to form as a man of few words, Cockcroft used to tell the Council that they must elect a new President; he would then get up and walk towards the door, to allow them to talk in private. But this was the signal for prolonged clapping and Cockcroft, assuming that it signified re-election, returned to his place at the head of the table. After several years, Goldschmidt tactfully suggested to him that he ought voluntarily to stand down so that someone from another country should have the chair!

Council meetings were usually held in agreeable locations such as Monte Faito near Naples, on board a ship bound for Capri, or they were followed by an excursion, like a tour of the Lake District during which a visit was made to Windscale. The atmosphere was convivial and attempts to turn the Society into a political pressure group were not encouraged. Goldschmidt, for example, opposed a proposal to affiliate the Society to the politically motivated International Union of Nuclear Scientists and told Cockcroft 'we must continue to be a club rather than an efficient scientific organisation'.[3]

In the spring of 1954, at the same time as the European Atomic Energy Society was getting under way, Isidor Rabi, Professor of Physics at Columbia University, who had succeeded Robert Oppenheimer as chairman of the General Advisory Committee to the US Atomic Energy Commission, proposed an international conference on the peaceful uses of atomic energy. He knew Eisenhower quite well because the latter had recently been President of Columbia University, but he had to get Lewis Strauss, Chairman of the Commission,

> to persuade Eisenhower to have such a Conference. We then had to get the State Department to put it forth as a proposal at the United Nations. My whole purpose was not just to get *people* together but to get the governments together.[4]

While Rabi and his fellow scientists were primarily concerned about the exchange of information, Strauss and the politicians realised that they could use the event to promote American nuclear technology, such as the pressurised water reactor and the boiling water reactor.

When he heard about Rabi's proposal, Dag Hammerskjöld, Secretary General of the United Nations, thought such a Conference could be the most important diplomatic event of the 1950s. The US Atomic Energy Commission then decided that Rabi should go to England and prepare an agenda for the proposed conference with Cockcroft. At that time, the British were, after the Americans, the foremost Western power and still had great political prestige.

Cockcroft and his colleagues at Harwell, and, no doubt, the Risley Group wholeheartedly approved of Rabi's idea, but Cockcroft wanted the meeting to be strictly scientific and be limited to about 100 delegates, and not just be 'a jamboree for the world'.[5] Robert Spence thought it would be a splendid opportunity for nations developing nuclear power to show their hands. Rabi was met at London Airport by John Dunworth on 24 August 1954 and they drove to Cambridge where, over lunch at St John's College, he met Lord Adrian, Chadwick, Cockcroft, Nevill Mott, Spence and A K Longair, the British scientific liaison officer in Washington. They agreed that the Russians should be invited to attend as their presence would help to reduce tension between east and west, and, provided current declassification proposals were approved in October, it would be possible to release a lot of information about power reactors. Cockcroft produced a preliminary list of topics for the agenda including medical and biological applications of atomic energy, nuclear power and the type of agency best suited to promote applications of nuclear energy, and fundamental physics. He emphasised the importance of launching a discussion on different types of power reactors which might be supplied with fuel from the 'bank' of the agency proposed by Eisenhower. They agreed that the discussions should be full and frank and that there should be exhibitions of models of projects like PIPPA and DIDO (the experimental Harwell heavy water reactor) and similar designs in other countries[6].

Figure 21   The Cockcroft family at Cley, Norfolk, 1954.

After this meeting, Rabi went to stay with the Cockcrofts for the rest of the week at their recently acquired house *The Gables* at Cley on the Norfolk coast. As they walked along the beach, Cockcroft and Rabi continued to discuss the proposed agenda and suggest possible speakers for the conference.

The United Nations was selected as the sponsoring body and at the beginning of 1955 Hammerskjöld set up a United Nations Scientific Advisory Committee (UNSAC) to coordinate the planning of international conferences on nuclear energy. Leading nuclear physicists from seven countries, either actively developing nuclear power or likely to benefit from it, were then selected. The UK was represented by Cockcroft, France by Goldschmidt, Canada by W B Lewis, now Vice-President of Atomic Energy of Canada Ltd, the USA by Rabi, India by Homi Bhabha, head of the Indian Atomic Energy Commission, the USSR by D V Skobeltzin, Chief of the Central Board of Atomic Energy, and Brazil by Professor L C Prado. They were nearly all acquainted with one another. Bhabha, a member of the wealthy family of Tata, who had earned a reputation for behaving like a 'little rajah', had been at the Cavendish in the 1930s as had also Skobeltzin who according to Rabi, was outstanding among the Russian physicists who attended international meetings in the West; Goldschmidt, since leaving Chalk River, had been a member of the French Atomic Energy Commission working on chemistry problems connected with the first French experimental reactor.

Once the procedure had been settled, the Committee worked fast, meetings rarely stretching beyond half an hour. Hammerskjöld was an admirable chairman, 'very good,' Cockcroft recalled, 'at picking out the essential points in a discussion and at summing up to reach an agreed decision'.[7] He continued to chair meetings until his untimely death in an aircraft acccident in Africa in September 1961. At a meeting of the Committee on 20 May 1955 Bhabha was unanimously elected President of the Conference on the grounds that India not only stood between the two superpowers but was the leading nation of the Third World. It was already anticipated that there would be over 1300 papers and 2800 delegates and observers. Alan Copisarow, Scientific Counsellor at the British Embassy in Paris, who had worked on shortwave radar in the war, remembered how surprised Cockcroft was when he told him that the French and others were going to attend in large numbers. In the event, some 3000 to 4000 people came to the conference, a figure far beyond Cockcroft's original intention.

The conference was held in the Palais des Nations in Geneva during the first two weeks of August 1955. Cockcroft took his family out and they stayed in a house overlooking the lake. He described the proceedings in a letter to his mother, now nearing the end of her life.

There is a strong Russian delegation with the Ukranians and Byelorussians as well. The Americans are here in force [among them was Ernest Lawrence] and have taken half a hotel and set up a full-scale oganisation including security and dozens of typists. We have a small office of about five staff at the Beau Rivage Hotel [the traditional base of British delegations at international meetings] and my secretary and I share an office at the Palais des Nations. When not listening to papers we walk and talk in the corridors where we can get coffee. There we meet innumerable people of interest—Poles we have not seen for 15 years,

Russians, journalists. In the Palais there are exhibitions of models and components of nuclear power stations, provided by the US, UK, USSR, French,
Canadians, Norwegians, etc. There are also scientific films of atomic energy
running continuously and there is a 'music rest room'!

The Exhibition was very comprehensive, showing examples of details of
power reactors, fuel rod designs, health and safety aspects of large-scale use
of nuclear energy, and numerous new instruments designed for a budding
industry. The British were surprised and impressed with the details of the
American water reactors disclosed for the first time and the Russians disclosed
that a 5 MW graphite moderated, water-cooled reactor using 2.5 per cent
enriched fuel had been operating since 1954 and they claimed they had
superheated steam in one of their reactors. One of the authors (Allibone)
recalls that he went round the Exhibition with Brian Goodlet, the designer of
PIPPA, the latter being extremely impressed with the details of the American
high-pressure water reactors and considered them to have great potential
merit as they were essentially 'factory-made' whereas the British designs
needed much more work to be done on them on site. The steel vessels of the
American reactors could be forged, welded, x-ray tested and filled with
nitrogen before being shipped complete to site by road, canal or sea, and the
core made with the new 'zircon' alloy disclosed at the Conference, could be
lifted out of the reactor and be replaced, it was claimed, in a few days.

About 50 atomic energy commissions were formed afterwards, a number
of them being not only supplied with American research reactors but with
grants for future development. Cockcroft was one of the first to admit later
that 'many of these countries were not in a position technically to make use
of their reactors'. But, despite these reservations, he believed that the
conference celebrated 'the founding of a new worldwide industry based on the
scientific work of two generations of physicists and chemists'[8].

He was much sought after during the conference and one of the throng
noted his 'infinite patience and the trouble he took to explain technical details
to the uninitiated'[9]. He described the British atomic energy scene in a paper
and presided over a session on power programmes, leaving Hinton to describe
Calder Hall, then about three-quarters built. Cockcroft gave a summary of
the whole proceedings on the last evening. He considered that

the consensus of opinion was that capital costs of nuclear power stations would
be 50–100 per cent higher than the capital cost of coal-fuelled stations but that
fuel costs would be less than half that of coal. I went on to say that the whole
history of engineering development showed how rapidly costs fall in the early
stages of important new developments and there was good reason to believe that
in the second decade, i.e. in 1966–76, the cost of nuclear power would fall below
that of power from coal and oil.[10]

The technical problems in the construction and operation of nuclear power
stations were not as easily overcome as Cockcroft anticipated. Nevertheless,
the real significance of the conference lay, as he pointed out, in 'strengthening
the hands of those scientists responsible for recommending declassification
and achieving a virtually complete removal of secrecy from the civil nuclear

power programme'. Many of these comments might have come better from Hinton who carried the main responsibility for power production.

Perhaps more important than the contents of the papers was the fact that, for the first time since before the war scientists and engineers from east and west were able to talk and exchange ideas. There was a continuous round of receptions of every kind, including a party, organised by the French, on board a ship which circled the lake while the guests ate, drank and talked. There was little attempt to make political propaganda and exchanges of views were full and frank. Cockcroft was allowed to fly a party of east European scientists to Harwell for the day and show them round the laboratories. This friendly gesture drew from the *Daily Worker* the following tribute:

> Whatever magnificent developments are seen in the next ten years, whatever contribution Britain and her scientists are able to make to the world pool of knowledge and skill, a large share of the credit must go to this calm and unassuming man. On or off duty, Cockcroft is far from the popular idea of a scientist. He is neither the dome headed 'mad scientist' of Edwardian fiction, nor the power obsessed 'new man' of recent fiction.[11]

Both British and Americans discovered that the Russians, who had given priority to the development of nuclear weapons were lagging behind the western power programmes but, it should be noted, the coal reserves in Russia were so huge that there was no urgent need to develop civil reactors, better to concentrate on weapon grade plutonium producing reactors based in Siberia and on development of hydrogen bombs of immense size. They had begun to develop power producing reactors and a graphite moderated, enriched reactor had delivered 5000 kW of electricity for a year, two years before Calder Hall operated.

At the end of the conference, Rabi, Cockcroft, Schonland and others were persuaded by their political masters to sound out Skobeltzin and his colleagues on the proposals for international control of fissile materials. Not surprisingly they met with little response, considering that at the time the Russian stocks were probably only a fraction of the American stock pile, and so the idea of a 'world bank' for fissile materials had to be abandoned.

During the three years that elapsed before the Second Geneva International Conference held in 1958 great advances were made in civil applications of nuclear power. Four large nuclear power stations—Calder Hall, Shippingport in the USA, a Russian reactor in Siberia, a French reactor at Marcoule —had gone, or were about to go into operation. The declassification of fusion experiments opened a new area for investigation. All aspects of power from fission and the latest experiments in fusion and plasma physics were therefore on the agenda. At the same time commercial interests in nuclear power applications were gaining ground over purely scientific interests.

Cockcroft was less concerned with the second conference than he had been with the first, but being President of the European Atomic Energy Society, which was responsible for much of the preliminary planning, and being a member of the United Nations Scientific Advisory Committee, made it inevitable that his advice should be sought. He had to make several visits to Paris in the spring of 1957 where he also took part in the discussions leading to the formation of Euratom†. In May 1957 he visited Marcoule, with other members of the European Atomic Energy Society, to inspect the first plutonium producing reactor in France. He wrote home, 'The second and third power stations are still in construction, though rather inferior versions of Calder Hall in some ways'.

He attended the second international conference on 26 August 1958, shortly after he had taken part in the nuclear test ban meetings in Geneva between Americans, British and Russians. He again summed up the proceedings and 'looking into the crystal ball', attempted to forecast future developments. His statement that 'by 1975 most power stations will be nuclear' appears in retrospect to have been over-optimistic but even at that date was manifestly totally unrealistic[12]. He could have found that the Generating Board had 25 000 MW of installed capacity and 12 000 MW of coal and oil stations on order, producing power by about 1968; by 1968 the nuclear stations of 6000 MW would be operating but by no stretch of imagination could there have been around 30 000 MW of new nuclear stations on load by 1975. His other statement 'We are likely to have developed fusion power long before we run out of uranium' was more realistic, especially as we are not likely to run out of uranium, if the fast reactor goes well, till well after the 21st Century! On the other hand, he agreed with Francis Perrin, who presided over the conference, that 'nuclear power will not perform miracles in undeveloped countries', and that 'fast reactors are unlikely to contribute much to world power before the 1970s': he could have added at least two or three decades to that date. At the same time he was amused by the premature reactions of the business world which felt it could make a quick fortune out of atomic energy developments. More than once he disconcerted his hosts, at receptions given by industrial firms, by his modest appraisal of future trends.

But the fact remains that he, at least, had been instrumental in 'overselling' nuclear power in such a phrase as that quoted above on a number of occasions. Again, one of the authors (Allibone) recalls that on 1 January 1958 he was enjoying a New Year's party at the Cockcrofts' with Basil Schonland and the ladies; there had been much talk of 'research reactors', low-powered reactors specially useful for small experiments and for instructing scientists and engineers, the sort of reactors which the Americans were selling, accompanied by Eisenhower's 'gift' of Uranium-235. Britain had no research reactor to offer. Schonland and Cockcroft both suggested that the author's company 'should develop them and sell them to heathens and Hottentots', but when pressed to say whether Britain would likewise 'give' Uranium-235, both scientists declined to make such an offer. In the event, Britain never sold such a reactor to a foreign country.

As at the first Geneva conference, Cockcroft was pleased to see that 'innumerable discussions in small groups to amplify the knowledge gained in our formal sessions' took place. As he never failed to point out, this was the classical method of cooperation in the scientific world. Again, his main

†The European Atomic Energy Commission set up by the Rome Treaty of 1957 and represented Belgium, France, West Germany, Italy, Luxembourg and The Netherlands. On 1 January 1973 the UK and Denmark also joined the Community.

criticism, as at the end of the first conference, was that there had been too many participants and too many papers and he hoped that it would not be necessary to hold a third conference too soon.

The long projected International Atomic Energy Agency was set up in Vienna in October 1958 and Cockcroft accepted an invitation by the Board of Governors to join its Scientific Advisory Committee,[13] the other members being Rabi, Goldschmidt, Vassily S Emelyanov, an eminent Russian metallurgist, and Bernhard Gross, a German expatriate scientist from Brazil working on cosmic rays and radiation. Henry Seligman, who had been appointed Deputy Director General, Research and Isotopes in the Agency, was appointed to be the Secretary.

Plowden, who had for some time been concerned about Cockcroft's many journeys abroad, warned the Agency that Cockcroft already had a heavy workload and that it might become necessary to appoint another British representative. In the event, Spence usually attended meetings in his place. But Cockcroft served long enough for his advice to be appreciated. He had become a living symbol of international scientific cooperation by his familiarity with so many scientists in east and west.

In June 1959 he attended the Scientific Advisory Committee meeting in Vienna which agreed that the Agency should become a focal point for exchange of information of controlled thermonuclear research and plasma physics, and he took part in suggesting subjects for a number of the Agency's symposia, including an important meeting in 1961 on tritium, discovered at the Cavendish 27 years earlier, and in the preliminary discussions on the third Geneva conference (to be held mainly because of pressure from the Americans) in which reactors were again to be the principal theme. But by 1961 Churchill College, of which he had recently been appointed Master, and which had begun to take in students, claimed him, and that March he sent his resignation to the Director General, Sterling Cole.[14] Seligman, like Cole, was sorry to see him go. 'I have' he wrote, 'two special affections, one for you personally, and one quite honestly for your scientific advice though I may perhaps not always have heeded it in the past!'[15] Penney took his place on the Committee.

His resignation by no means ended his connections with the IAEA, whenever he could he attended the annual general conference. On 22 September 1966, at the invitation of the second Director General, Sigvard Eklund, he gave a notable lecture on *The Impact of Atomic Energy on Society* to celebrate the tenth General Conference. He reviewed the progress made in the development of nuclear energy since 1955; not only had the number of nuclear power stations increased, but the safety standards of reactors had been raised by improved designs; great progress had been made in the application of atomic energy to chemical science and technology and to biology, and it had provided tools for the physical sciences, notably crystallography and solid state physics. He now recognised that the possibilities of obtaining power by fusion were just as far away as ever. Finally, he warned against the dangers of the wide dissemination of nuclear fuels, regarding which the Agency had to display a constant vigilance through its system of safeguards[16].

For the past six years he had been concerned with the spoiling of the environment and the need to conserve resources and had suggested that there should be an international conference dealing with food, energy and population. Three months before his death, he wrote to Rabi[17] on 23 June 1967 suggesting that such a meeting would need to discuss 'measures to prevent the deterioration of the environment' and related topics†. No doubt, in response to the anxiety of Cockcroft and many others a Pollution Committee of the United Nations was set up.

In the late 1950s Cockcroft undertook a number of journeys on behalf of the Authority to visit atomic energy establishments in Russia and eastern Europe, but he also wanted to establish the international scientific contacts which had been suspended during the cold war. Four years before the visit of the Russians to Harwell in 1957, he had accepted an invitation from the Polish Academy of Sciences to visit Warsaw and he lectured at the Institute of Physics where he had spoken as a young man in 1933. But to return to Moscow and see his old friend Kapitza, about whose activities he had had the barest information, was something he had looked forward to for many years. A visit was arranged for November 1958, after which he was to go on to Japan.

He left London on the 8th changing to a Russian jet at Brussels; he arrived half an hour ahead of schedule, taking the reception party of distinguished scientists, including Kurchatov, by surprise. The Kapitzas were returning from holiday and delegated their younger son, Andrew, a geographer and Antarctic explorer and, like his brother, Peter, born in England, to look after Cockcroft and act as interpreter. Cockcroft stayed, as he wrote home, at

> the Sovietskaya Hotel where I was given a suite with office, dining room, TV, radio, bedroom, bathroom and hall! Maids in frilly aprons and collars provided pre-Revolution service, shirts being washed and ironed in a few hours. The list of dishes available seem to run to a hundred or so and was available even for breakfast though I didn't take advantage of the variety.

The next day Kurchatov showed Cockcroft over the Institute of Atomic Energy where he saw the fusion experiments in the OGRA reactor, described at the Geneva Conference. Afterwards he sat over an enormous meal with senior staff in the canteen, 'much like a Harwell crowd but more boisterous' and many toasts were drunk and he was then invited by Kurchatov for a long talk at the latter's house. In the evening he went to the ballet with the Kapitzas who met him at his hotel. 'They are both very well and little changed and very lively. They had been bathing in the Caucasus where the weather was magnificent.' The following day Kapitza acted as host at his Institute which had a staff of about 40,

> and the usual collection of storekeepers and an old lady who looks after coats and makes tea, so it's a small institute. I recognised a lot of the equipment we sent over in 1935, most of it still working.

†Rabi replied that it was unnecessary to choose either environmental or atomic topics, but that the latter should be 'weighted in the direction of discussing problems associated with proliferation'.

He admired the Kapitzas' lifestyle, his 'salary appeared to be £5000 a year with only about 10 per cent tax', though their house was only about half the size of the Cockcrofts' house at Harwell.

The highlight of his visit, however, was an interview on Wednesday with Khruschev in the Kremlin. Accompanied by three members of the Academy of Sciences,

> we were preceded through the Kremlin gates by a police car, but otherwise there was no formality, no books to be signed or passes and no sign of guards along the corridor in the Kremlin Palace where he worked... We had quite a long frank discussion. Kapitza advised me to speak plainly and with no finesse. I said I hoped he'd let Kapitza come to England and that he'd be quite safe and we would return him safely to Russia. This was received quite well—rather jokingly. We talked about nuclear tests and the next steps in nuclear disarmament. He appeared to be anxious to end the cold war and would like to see our PM to discuss all these questions†. We agreed that it was a good thing to try to organise visits at all levels. After 40 minutes we departed. He impressed me as a very quickwitted man, much more so than I'd thought after seeing him before on the official visit [to England]. Kapitza says he's original and constructive in his approach to problems. Both Kapitza and Kurchatov have a Government telephone and they can ring up Khruschev.

Before leaving the USSR he visited the Nuclear Physics Research Laboratory at Dubna outside Moscow where fundamental research was done. He was taken to Moscow University and admired its 'fantastic tower design', though Khruschev had disapproved of it for its extravagance. Since Cockcroft's last visit 22 years before, the city had 'grown enormously—very wide principal streets able to take five cars abreast in all directions'.

The Kapitzas bade him farewell at Moscow airport on Friday 14 November and he flew via Tashkent and New Delhi to Japan where he spent a week in Tokyo, visiting, as he told his brother Eric,

> their Harwell—a quite nice place in the woods by the sea. I have had two oriental meals, Geisha girls brought the food to the low table and knelt in front and served the wine with bows and made conversation in which they are well trained. They also put on a Lion Dance and if we'd been able to stay longer would no doubt have put on Geisha games.

For once, he had delivered no lectures on this tour; he seldom wrote out his own lectures and the staff at Harwell had recently complained mildly about the amount of extra work that was required of them for their preparation of his lectures over and above their normal duties. (His practice was to send them a typescript with spaces left for numbers or tables to be filled in; later he corrected the script heavily.) 'I should be happier', Thonemann, leader of the fusion team, told him 'to arrange sessions in which we can have informal discussions'.[18] He returned home, flying over Alaska, Canada and Iceland, reaching Heathrow on 24 November.

†Harold Macmillan, then Prime Minister, visited Moscow from 21 February to 3 March 1959.

Figure 22   Cockcroft with Geisha girls, Japan, 1957.

No sooner had he returned home than he dashed off to take part in a debate at the Cambridge Union at the invitation of his nephew, John H Cockcroft. The motion was 'That this House believes that the world has been the loser from the splitting of the atom'. Although Cockcroft reported to his brother, Eric, that he 'fell half asleep and hard put to cope', according to the record he supported 'F H Hinsley, also a fellow of St John's, and made a spirited defence against the supporters of the motion led by Victor Gollancz, dealing with the Windscale accident and referring to the 'almost pathological interest of the Press in atomic radiation'; he illustrated this by a recent incident at Harwell when 'a cleaner in one of our labs put a rag on the top of a stove where it caught alight. An assistant pressed the button for the Fire Brigade and the Director heard about it on the 1 o'clock news'. The motion was defeated by one vote.

In June 1959 he toured Czechoslovakia with Elizabeth and their youngest daughter, Catherine. There was a round of sightseeing in Prague where their host was Professor Petvzykla, an ex-Cavendish student (he met them all over the world!). He lectured and, during a drive through the impressive limestone valleys of the Tatras, ascended a mountain on a cable railway to inspect the Cosmic Physics Laboratory. The Skoda Works reminded him of Metro – Vick and prompted the observation that while the Czechs were highly industrialised, scientifically, they were behind the West due to the German occupation, their need to rebuild after the war, and the 'missing' wartime generation.

The autumn of 1960 found him and Elizabeth in Hungary after attending an IAEA conference in Vienna; they were lavishly entertained in Budapest, his official duties being to lecture, look at nuclear research and a steelworks. In the spring of 1961, accompanied by their daughter, Elizabeth, they went to Yugoslavia; at Belgrade they stayed with Elizabeth's cousin from Todmorden, Mary Stansfield Popović, who had married a Yugoslav professor (imprisoned by the Italians throughout the war) while she herself had become head of the English department at the University. Years later she remembered driving the Cockcrofts along a mountain road and, taking the bends rather rapidly, saw out of the corner of her eye the couple seated at the back reassuringly holding hands![19]

He was taken round the nuclear research institutes and materials laboratory and, as always, made perceptive comments, later to be written up as confidential reports for the AEA. Apart from these official observations he had an eye for the passing landscape, often graphically described in letters to his brother, Eric, who had taken his mother's place as chief recipient of letters home. A typical one was about Cetinje, the old capital

> set in a bowl in bare stony mountains with little plots of land not much bigger than Birks [the old family home] garden where the peasants manage to grow a little grain.

Or the one-time Royal Palace, a 'Victorian house with brass bedsteads and all the trimmings of the last century. Surprisingly enough, there was a very good library.'

In September 1961 he and Elizabeth spent a week in Poland as guests of the Polish Atomic Energy Commission and visited three research establishments, while he delivered a lecture in Warsaw. As they travelled from Warsaw to Cracow they saw the

> road packed with narrow wagons in which the peasants were bringing in potatoes, or carrying timber, coal and old ladies. There are one and a half million horses in Poland and few tractors.

Cockcroft's association with two politico-military organisations in the late 1950s should briefly be mentioned. The first was his chairmanship of the Scientific Council of the Central Treaty Organisation (CENTO) or the Baghdad Pact, as it was originally known[20]. Essentially, this was a military organisation modelled on the lines of NATO, but with a small scientific appendage in the form of a regional nuclear research and training centre equipped and temporarily staffed by Harwell to be used to assist health and agriculture. It was first located in Baghdad and then in Teheran after the overthrow of the monarchy in Iraq. Cockcroft was keen on enhancing the role of CENTO and made several visits to the Near East in 1957 and 1958, usually lecturing in addition to his committee work and he always found time to look at places of interest. He was unimpressed with the Royal Palace in Baghdad because it was 'not strewn with Persian rugs' but in Teheran he enjoyed going with Lady Wright, wife of the British Ambassador in Iran, to a meeting of the Muslim Friends of Gertrude Bell whose letters he had read and appreciated during the war.

After the withdrawal of Iraq from the Treaty, he remarked that the main value of the research centre lay in 'disbursing small sums to help overcome bottlenecks [by the purchase of spare parts of supplies] for scientific research'. He resigned from the Scientific Council in the summer of 1961 because of his preoccupation with Churchill College.

Until then the international movement in Europe had also continued to claim his attention. He attended meetings in Paris in connection with the Organisation for European Economic Cooperation (OEEC) in which the Norwegian and Swedish Atomic Energy Authorities took part. He was a member of a NATO study group with H B G Casimir, Rabi, and Solly Zuckerman set up to consider how the quality of scientific manpower could be improved. Meetings were held over the period 1959–60 but did not lead to any important changes in policy[21].

Cockcroft's concern about the need for a national centre for high-energy physics at home was paralleled by his efforts to establish, in company with other leading European scientists, a European laboratory for nuclear physics in which particle accelerators with energies of 20–30 GeV, such as those already operating in the States, would be built. The object was to develop research with mesons and to explore new particles which would probably be produced at very high energies. It was fortunate for the physicists that their need for large machines, which most countries found too expensive to build, coincided with the political and economic movement towards European unity.

Isidor Rabi, as already mentioned, a scientific adviser to the US Atomic Energy Commission, was the first to suggest such an idea at the General UNESCO conference at Florence in June 1950. His proposal was afterwards taken up by Pierre Auger, Director of Natural Science at the headquarters of UNESCO in Paris, and it also had the strongest support from Niels Bohr. In the summer of 1951 Auger asked Cockcroft and Chadwick what they thought about the idea of a European high-energy physics laboratory. Auger accepted Cockcroft's suggestion that a small 500–600 MeV synchrocyclotron could be built quite quickly and it could be accompanied by the construction of a more powerful 10–20 GeV proton synchrotron which would take longer to complete[22]. Just at this time a new invention had been made to focus the ions from time to time as they travelled round the cyclotron orbits; it was called a 'strong focusing' system and it effectively prevented – or at least reduced – losses of ions from this orbit; it came in the nick of time and at the end of 1953 the decision was taken to build a 26–30 GeV machine embodying this principle.

Discussions on the organisation of the laboratory began, it has been seen, at the opening of the Norwegian reactor in October 1951 at which Cockcroft was present. On 15 February 1952, eleven European states formed a provisional organisation for nuclear research called 'Provisional CERN'. Although the UK was not a signatory, she was represented at all subsequent meetings as a very active observer. Cockcroft was among those British scientists who sought to persuade the Government to contribute towards the European laboratory in money and in kind. He was a member of the Royal Society Advisory Committee[23] which offered advice on the project to the DSIR and the universities, and maintained contact with Provisional CERN; his influence among the senior members of the DSIR persuaded the latter to approach the Treasury about the possibility of a financial contribution which would enable Britain to be represented at CERN. The discussions were successful and, on 25 November 1952, R A Butler, Chancellor of the Exchequer, agreed that the UK should become a party to the Convention 'in view of the closely expressed wish...that our physicists should have access to the more powerful machines'.[24]

Cockcroft was also instrumental in convincing the universities, ever suspicious that Government-supported schemes would leave them with less money for their work, that the project was worthwhile and he convened a conference on high-energy accelerators at Buckland House for this purpose, to which he invited a number of physicists interested in other fields, like cosmic ray research. As Dr D W Fry, who was closely associated with the proposals, wrote,

> In the 1950s Cockcroft saw more clearly than the heads of many physics departments of universities that a new pattern for working in the field of high-energy physics would have to evolve. He had the interests of the universities very much at heart and so I believe led and coordinated the advice by the DSIR that the UK should take a major part in the setting up of the international scheme. I think there were reservations about the scheme from some of the university physics departments for possibly a number of different reasons, but Cockcroft and Blackett between them, seemed to steer the thing along.[25]

No British university ever had the power or expertise of Berkeley, California, where the very big machines were first developed and the United States was now concentrating its money on Berkeley on the Pacific and on Brookhaven on the Atlantic coasts; it was entirely proper that European money should be concentrated on one centre to the benefit of all European laboratories.

Cockcroft set a good example himself by lending three leading members of the synchrocyclotron group at Harwell—John Adams, Mervyn Hine and F K Goward to the CERN theoretical group under O Dahl and C J Bakker then forming at Geneva, the site of the proposed laboratory. Goward eventually became Dahl's deputy, and, in due course, Adams became the Director.

In January 1953 Cockcroft and Sir Ben Lockspeiser, head of the DSIR, attended the CERN Council meeting in Brussels and announced that Britain intended becoming a member[26]. At the same time Cockcroft was helping to draft the Convention of the Permanent Organisation, a task for which his knowledge of the European scene made him well qualified. Its objective, as announced, was to provide collaboration between European states in nuclear research of a fundamental and purely scientific character, entirely non-military and all the results would be published. By September 1953 sufficient

Figure 23   Niels Bohr and Cockcroft.

ratifications of the Convention had been received for CERN to be permanently established, the UK's instrument of ratification being deposited that
December.

Cockcroft now turned his attention to advising on how the work was to be
done, suggesting priorities and ensuring that the financial limits were being
observed. Over a period of four years from October 1954 he made many
journeys to Geneva both as a member of the Nominations Committee which
included Niels Bohr, Werner Heisenberg and Francis Perrin, and of the
Scientific Policy Committee, responsible for research programmes, chaired by
Heisenberg. Cockcroft served on the latter committee until 1960 even though
by then he had been appointed Master of Churchill College but C J Bakker,
the first Director General of CERN, wrote to tell him that 'there is certainly
no time at which CERN has needed more wise guidance'.[27]

The Theoretical Study Group had, of course, to wait until the new
machines had been completed at Geneva, but in the meantime it was able to
carry out theoretical work and train research personnel by using existing
laboratories at Liverpool and Uppsala. Construction of the synchrocyclotron
was completed in 1957 and on 6 February Lord Hailsham, Lord President of
the Council and Minister for Science and Technology, formally inaugurated

the protonsynchrotron by cutting a ribbon, while Cockcroft stood modestly hidden among the spectators. He was then called upon to make a speech and it must have given him great satisfaction to observe that the machine had 50 000 times the energy of the accelerator that he and Walton had built 30 years previously. The new accelerator, as John Adams pointed out, meant that

> by 1960 Europe, which had started from practically nothing, had one of two highest energy machines in the world. The other one was constructed at Brookhaven. The European physicists then had available in Europe the same facilities for their research as their American colleagues and no longer had to go to the US to seek them.[28]

On 1 July 1963, Dr Jean Willems, the President of CERN, and members of the Council sent Cockcroft the following telegram.

> On this anniversary of the signing of the CERN Convention the Council would like you to know that it is very much aware of the outstanding service which you have rendered to the institution and wishes once again to express its deepest gratitude.[29]

This 'outstanding service' was, in fact, not merely being present at committee meetings during which he rarely uttered a word, it was, as Adams explained, because Cockcroft

> belonged to two 'Invisible Colleges'[†] as they are sometimes called. He was a member of the small group of prewar nuclear physicists—an international group that included such famous people as Rutherford, Bohr, Heisenberg, Joliot-Curie, etc—and he belonged to the even more exclusive club of Nobel Prize winners. On top of this, he was a powerful figure in nuclear energy developments during and after the war and had great influence with the British Government. All this put him in a unique position in his relationship with CERN. His membership of the 'Invisible Colleges' ensured that his views were listened to with great respect by the other founding scientists of CERN, most of whom were his friends and colleagues, and his influence with the British Government ensured that their views and those of their governments were correctly represented at that level. It should be remembered that in those days Britain was the most powerful and respected country in Europe and it paid the biggest contribution to CERN. Furthermore, he was considered a very wise man and had much more experience than the others in setting up and managing large laboratories. His contributions during the early period of CERN had therefore a unique value. His was the voice of wisdom and experience and the fact that Cockcroft supported CERN not only gave it respectability in the eyes of Governments but also reassured his scientific friends and colleagues throughout Europe.[30]

Cockcroft's work in promoting applications of nuclear energy and fundamental research was rewarded when, towards the end of 1956, he re-

---

†The 'Invisible College' was the name given to a London-based society of natural philosophers' during the English Civil War, and possibly a forerunner of the Royal Society, who they declared, wanted to 'take the whole body of mankind for their care'.

ceived a letter from Sir Michael Adeane, Secretary to Her Majesty the Queen. 'It will give the Queen much pleasure to confer the Order of Merit on you in the New Year... As I expect you know, this award is wholly in the gift of the Sovereign and is not given on Ministerial advice.'[31] Quite unaware that Cockcroft was going to receive this distinction, Sir Edwin Plowden had recommended that Sir Christopher Hinton should be awarded a KBE, in the circumstances nothing could have been more unfortunate! All in good time Hinton likewise was honoured with the award of the OM. The Suez crisis was still causing reverberations and, as already noted, the nuclear power programme was soon to be expanded. Cockcroft's feelings about the Suez affair may be guessed from his reply to Homi Bhabha's letter of congratulation in which he hoped that 'we shall now start to recover from that disastrous episode!'[32] Another letter he received was from a holder of the Order, Sir George Trevelyan, the celebrated historian, who considered himself to be the

> doyen of the OMs, being made one as long ago as 1930. I therefore feel entitled to welcome you as a newcomer. May I say that I have always watched the list with some anxiety lest some second-rate person in the vogue should lower the standard, but it does not happen, and I am particularly delighted that a high-flyer like you should raise the prestige of the Order.[33]

Equally apposite was Tizard's confession that it was

> the one honour I should have coveted had I felt anywhere near up to the standard. You need have no misgivings on that score.[34]

A letter of congratulation from quite a different source, from a member of the Council for the Preservation of Rural England, Mrs E Atherton, illuminates both his courtesy and his concern to safeguard the countryside.

> When you came down to the Forest of Dean Enquiry [relating to a proposal for the burial of radioactive waste in a disused mine shaft†] you were kind enough to answer two of what must have appeared to you, very unintelligent questions. At that time we of the Gloucestershire CPRE were anxious and fearful for the natural beauties of our countryside, but I think today I am right in saying that with due care the majority of us feel in the long run we shall reap the benefits of arduous work and we are grateful.[35]

In October 1958 the Cockcrofts went to Copenhagen to receive the Niels Bohr Gold Medal. This was first awarded in 1953 to Bohr on his 70th birthday by the Danish Institution of Civil Engineers and presented every third year by the King of Denmark to scientists and engineers who had made important contributions to peaceful uses of atomic energy. Cockcroft was particularly gratified, not only because Bohr was one of the founders of nuclear physics, but was also 'a very great personal friend of my wife and myself'. Bohr, now advanced in years, was still 'mentally extremely alert' and was present at a lecture given by Cockcroft which made 'a great impression on all the Danes who heard him'.[36]

In April 1961 he was presented with the Atoms For Peace Award by James

†The plan, although considered feasible, was later abandoned.

R Killian†, President of the Massachusetts Institute of Technology, on the occasion of the Centenary of the founding of the Institute. This award, carrying with it a cheque for 75 000 dollars, was established by the Ford Motor Company in response to Eisenhower's appeal to the United Nations on 20 July 1955 that 'business and professional men throughout the world ... take an interest and provide an incentive in finding new ways that this science can be used ... for the benefit of mankind and not destruction'. The two former recipients had been Niels Bohr and George von Hevesy. Cockcroft was recognised for 'his early work in the artificial disintegration of atomic nuclei ... his leadership in the establishment of AERE, his active work in the production of radioisotopes and the establishment of an isotope school at Harwell' (though in respect to the latter two items the credit was due mainly to Henry Seligman). There were speeches by Professor Norman Ramsey and Chancellor Beadle, organ recitals by Lady Jeans, and, finally, the presentation of the gold medal, 'a large heavy piece', and a brief reply from Cockcroft in which he acknowledged the advice and encouragement he obtained from

Arthur Compton's Chicago Group, especially the pioneers of reactor development, Fermi, Wigner, Weinberg and Zinn. So with this help and the stimulus of French scientists working with us, the Canadian – British atomic development at Chalk River got off to a flying start, and it was from this base that the British nuclear power programme developed from 1950 onwards. This is the traditional method of development of science and technology, one group building on the work of another so that the great developments of science and technology are due to the combined efforts of the whole scientific world.[37]

After it was all over, George Steiner, then a lecturer in English at Princeton University and shortly to come to Churchill College, remembered seeing the Cockcrofts, whom he had recently met, disappear from view with the gold medal tied up in a pocket handkerchief[38].

†Killian was President Eisenhower's scientific adviser until 1959.

CHAPTER EIGHTEEN

FIRST MASTER OF
CHURCHILL COLLEGE

Cockcroft, it has been seen, was one of those who had long been pressing for some kind of technology university to cope with the greater numbers of scientists and engineers that the country needed. As Director of Harwell, he had established good relations with the universities both in the instituting of Harwell Fellowships and by offering facilities for research. His interest in education was recognised in 1956 when he accepted an invitation[1] from an old Cavendish colleague, Vivian Bowden, to become Vice-President of the Manchester College of Science and Technology, of which the latter was Principal. At that time Bowden was trying to expand the College on the lines of the Massachusetts Institute of Technology and the Continental *Technische Hochschule*.

The MIT had had a famous reputation for many years before the war. In March 1949 Churchill was invited to address a conference there on *The 20th Century, its Promise and its Realisation*:

> I am honoured by your wish that I should take part in the discussions on the MIT; we have suffered in Great Britain by the lack of colleges of university rank in which engineering and the allied subjects are taught. Industrial production depends on technology and it is because the Americans, like the prewar Germans, have realised this and have created institutions for the advanced training of large numbers of high-grade engineers to translate the advances of pure science into industrial techniques that their output per head and consequent standard of life are so high. It is surprising that England, which was the first country to be industrialised, has nothing of comparable status. How right you are, Dr Compton, in this great institution to keep a dean of the humanities in the gaining of which philosophy and history walk hand in hand: human beings and human societies are not structures that are built and machines that are forged, they are plants that grow and must be tended as such.[2]

This set the tone of postwar thinking and several groups moved on different lines. In Cambridge the Shell Company had already endowed a Chair in Chemical Engineering and the IEE a Chair in Electrical Engineering and now, in 1950, senior officers of the Shell Company suggested to a group of leaders of industry that a *postgraduate institution* should be established somewhere in Britain concentrating on advanced technological training, financed by industry and supported by Government. The first idea was that it might be attached to the Cranfield Aeronautical College but objections were raised that this was remote from industrial centres, so Birmingham was suggested, but the idea of a separate postgraduate institution loosely attached to the university did not find favour there.

Lord Cherwell, since his retirement from the Government in 1954, had been concerned in making the UK as conscious, as were the USA and the USSR, of the importance of technology and had campaigned both in the House of Lords and in letters to the Prime Minister about the need to increase the number of scientists and technologists and thereby to make the economy more productive. Whilst in office, Churchill had been too preoccupied to attend to Cherwell's warnings, but after retirement in April 1955 he had been urged by Cherwell and by John Colville his former Principal Private Secretary now a company director, to use the remaining balance of £25 000 of his 80th Birthday Trust to provide 'a nucleus for, and inspiration of, a vast industrial subscription'[3] of around two to three million pounds to be known as the Churchill Technological Trust. In May 1956 Churchill gave his approval but stipulated that a workable scheme should be devised. Colville began to look for support from the leading steel and electrical companies, ICI and Shell whose John Oriel was to play an important part.

The Suez crisis later that year put a brake on the raising of funds for the proposed Trust and Colville suggested that American resources should be tapped. Fortunately, support came from Carl Gilbert, President of the Gillette Company of Boston, a man who had heard Churchill's speech in 1949. Gilbert suggested to Colville that a Churchill college be built 'at, say, Cambridge, fitting into the existing university pattern to hold 600 undergraduates reading science and engineering', also providing fellowships, while the staff would be Anglo – American. During the spring of 1957 Colville asked Sir Alexander Todd, Sir Oliver Franks, Sir Gilbert Fleming and Cockcroft to discuss Gilbert's proposal, reporting to Cherwell that 'some of Cockcroft's ideas strike me as very sensible'. Later that year when Todd and Cockcroft were in the States, they followed up contacts made by Colville with Dean Rusk of the Rockefeller and Henry T Heald of the Ford Foundations and with Henry C Alexander the Chairman of J P Morgan, and met with a favourable response though the Americans were at that time more interested in providing endowments than funds for the actual building of a college.

Meanwhile, Colville had been consulting other industrialists some of whom still favoured a completely separate technological institute, the rest supporting the creation of a new Cambridge college heavily weighted in favour of science and technology both in its teaching and its complement of Fellows and research workers, and having a ratio of postgraduates to undergraduates higher than in the university as a whole. At the same time many scientists felt that an opportunity to found an entirely new British technical university had been missed and that the proposal should have been given wider circulation, but opinions were divided, many welcomed the proposal and were glad that the MIT concept had been aborted, the Colleges of Advanced Technology were being created and they too, would become universities in due course. As for Sir Winston, he was rather disappointed that the college would not resemble the MIT as closely as he would have liked and that it was to be built in Cambridge rather than in Oxford, but by building in Cambridge he conceded that 'after all it will put me alongside the Trinity'.

By the end of 1957 the outlook was sufficiently bright to form a Board of Trustees from industry, science and the academic world. The original Trustees were Lord Tedder, the distinguished wartime air commander now Chancellor of Cambridge University, his Vice-Chancellor and Master of Christ's College Professor B W Downs, Lord Adrian Master of Trinity College and prospective Vice-Chancellor, Sir Alexander Fleck Chairman of ICI, Lord Weeks of Vickers, Lord Chandos Chairman of AEI who was also at that time the President of the Manchester College of Technology, Lord Godber of Shell, Todd and Cockcroft. Later, Lord Knollys of Vickers and English Steel, Noel Annan the Provost of King's College, William Carron the President of the Amalgamated Engineering Union and Colville became Trustees. Sir Winston agreed to be chairman and allowed meetings to be held at his London home. His interventions, though infrequent, could be to the point and he provided further stimulus with a supply of his own brand of 'suitable lubricants for discussion'.[4]

The Trustees formed several committees to advise them on the composition of the College and its educational policy, as well as to prepare Statutes, Ordinances and other matters. From the outset they envisaged that the College should number around 500, of whom one third should be postgraduates and two thirds undergraduates. Seventy per cent should read subjects in natural sciences, engineering or mathematics, and the remainder would study subjects in the humanities, including the social sciences.

The University received the proposal with mixed feelings, some Masters of Colleges and Fellows thought that the University was already big enough. The Master of Jesus, E M W Tillyard, a scholar of Elizabethan literature, led this faction and declared[5] that an expansion of Cambridge was 'an assumption of far greater moment than the foundation of a new college and I believe it to be pernicious'†. Within the University Senate, however, more moderate councils prevailed, and it agreed on 14 May 1958 to recognise the new college when sufficient funds had been raised to guarantee its existence[6]. The Trustees realised that it would be disastrous if an appeal headed by Sir Winston's name were to flop but one million pounds had already been promised so they launched the appeal on the following day. John Oriel and his Company now relieved Sir Alexander Todd of the business of collecting money and by the end of the year they had enough to fulfil the Senate's stipulation; on 24 January 1959 the Senate formally recognised the foundation of Churchill College[7].

The question arose as to who should be the first Master. Todd, who had just been awarded a Nobel Prize for Chemistry and who had done so much in the early stages, appeared to be the obvious candidate and was about to be elected when the Prime Minister, Harold Macmillan intervened to point

---

†Some of the scientists were also unenthusiastic; Lord Adrian for example thought that the proposal should be dropped unless the university was prepared to absorb 700 more students. Only a few years were to elapse before a number of new colleges to accommodate both male and female students were approved without exception.

out that Cockcroft, then 61, was about to retire from the Atomic Energy Authority. Though less concerned in determining the course of civil scientific policy than Todd had been, his international reputation would undoubtedly be an asset to the new college, so dependent on its transatlantic and other overseas connections. On 7 November 1958 Tedder spoke to Cockcroft on the steps of the Athenaeum and told him that he had been chosen to be Master[8].

By an odd chance the Mastership of St John's was vacant again and Cockcroft was on the short list. But as he told his brother Leo,

> I received the offer of the Trustees before I learned I should have had a handsome majority of John's Fellows. So the die is cast! I shall take up my appointment in September '59 but will remain a part-time member of the AEA for two or three years until the College is 'in being'.

There can be little doubt that Cockcroft had more opportunity to impress his personality on a new foundation than he would have had on the long-established traditions of St John's.

On 24 January 1959 the College was formally recognised by the University and two days later the Trustees announced that Cockcroft was to be the first Master. The fact that Churchill had insisted that the appointment of succeeding Masters should be made by the Crown, as at Trinity College, Cambridge and Christ Church, Oxford, aroused much criticism, especially in *The Times*,[9] on the grounds that it might lead to the selection of specialists, or worse, dull unimaginative figures, forgetting that in recent years such diverse and eminent figures as the physicist, Sir J J Thomson and the historian Sir George Trevelyan had been Masters of Trinity. The Trustees further argued that a Crown appointment would considerably widen the choice, as Masters were often elected only from among the Fellows of their own College which at any particular moment might contain no Fellow of great distinction. More perceptive than *The Times* was Cockcroft's one-time lecturer, Ebenezer Cunningham who wrote;

> You will have many problems in creating not only a building but a corporate community and behind these lies the big question of the relation of science and modern society. So many folk are quaking for fear of what lies ahead. We will all pray that the new powers may be well used in the building of a peaceful and healthy world, and so that your students may see science in this setting, free from a superstitious belief that it is an automatic benefit to mankind.[10]

Cockcroft, although continuing to serve as a part-time member of the Authority and often travelling abroad, threw himself into the business of raising funds, especially in the United States where his friendship with influential figures like Dean Rusk and Professor Killian of MIT stood him in good stead —so much so, that Elizabeth jokingly had to warn him not to let the College 'become entirely an American takeover bid!' One of his most spectacular coups was to induce the Ford Foundation to give a million dollars. The negotiations took place during a visit to New York in May 1959 and it is doubtful whether anyone with a lesser reputation than Cockcroft could have achieved it.

Purchase of a site and plans for building had gone ahead. The chosen site was a sloping 40 acre stretch of land, mostly market gardens, at the corner of Storey's Way and the Madingley road, belonging to St John's College. From the high ground the chapel tower of St John's, the brick tower of the University Library and the pinnacles of King's College Chapel may be seen emerging from the trees of the 'Backs'.

A brief for the architect was prepared by the Trustees' Educational Policy Committee under Noel Annan who became chairman of the Building Committee in June 1958, Sir Leslie Martin, Professor of Architecture at Cambridge, being appointed consultant. Later Cockcroft became chairman and once again was able to indulge to the full his delight in architecture. It was his idea that there should be a large lecture hall, rather like the Cockcroft Hall at Harwell, with good acoustics, and which was, in the event, presented by the Wolfson Trust, of which he was a Trustee. As the college was expected to be mainly residential, he favoured the traditional two-room Cambridge sets as opposed to study bedrooms. In the end, both types were included, though two-room sets had later to be abandoned in the interests of economy.

A panel was formed to select the architect by means of a limited two-stage competition under the rules of the Royal Institute of British Architects[11]. On the panel were Cockcroft and Annan, assisted by the well known architects, Sir William Holford, Sir Basil Spence and Sir Leslie Martin. They looked for one who, according to Cockcroft, 'can work in the spirit of this century rather than in the spirit of the past'. The winner was Richard Sheppard, Robson & Partners. One of the deciding factors was the irregular design for the arrangement of the flats for Overseas Fellows. Otherwise the plan followed the traditional pattern of enclosed courts built in brick extending from the focal point which was the dining hall and Common rooms. One unusual feature, surely inspired by Cockcroft, was the buttery, or croft, beneath the dining hall; in most colleges the buttery was merely the store from which provisions could be bought but in Churchill the buttery had a wide dais on which was a long bar and small tables where Fellows and undergraduates could talk and freely mix; below there was a room for billiards and dancing.

Sir Winston, who attended Sir Leslie Martin's presentation of the winning design, had already been assured by Cockcroft that nothing outrageously *avant garde* would be accepted and, after examining the plan, confined himself to a single question: 'What is the distance from the top to the bottom?'†. Martin was momentarily lost for an answer but probably what Sir Winston was considering was the expense likely to be incurred in building nine courts (later reduced to seven) over a wide area, especially in regard to services and administration.

The Trustees wanted Churchill to see the college at least partially completed and great pressure was placed on getting the building under way. A week after Sheppard had been chosen as architect, he and Cockcroft inspected the site and agreed that levelling of the ground should begin immediately. Building was to start in the north-west corner in order to provide a nucleus

---

†He gazed on the drawings sadly, but did not comment; after the meeting he told Cockcroft 'I did not wish to influence the decision'.

of the college including temporary offices, library and dining hall. Permanent buildings would accommodate the first postgraduates and were to be ready by October 1960. Undergraduates were to be admitted in the autumn of the following year whatever stage the building had reached.

The Cockcrofts left Harwell in October 1959 and returned to live at 31 Sedley Taylor Road which served as Master's Lodge until they moved into Churchill towards the end of 1963. Their first official function was to welcome Sir Winston to the site on 17 October 1959, his one and only visit. The occasion was marked by the planting of two trees, an English oak and a black mulberry, Mulberry appropriately enough, being the code name for the artificial harbours built for the Normandy landings, a scheme in which Churchill had taken a close interest. In a brief speech he announced the generous gift from the Ford Foundation and a £50 000 donation from the Transport and General Workers Union in memory of Ernest Bevin and which was to be used for building a library[13]. Then, as R V Jones wrote

> he affirmed his belief in technology, even in striving for the moon: 'Let no one believe that the lunar rockets are merely ingenious bits of prestige. They are the manifestations of a formidable advance in technology. As with many vehicles of pure research, their immediate uses may not be apparent. But I do not doubt that they will ultimately reap a rich harvest for those who have the imagination and power to develop them and to probe ever more deeply into the mysteries of the universe in which we live.[14]

Had not Cockcroft and Walton indeed seen a rich harvest grow from their pure research of 1932, research whose immediate use was not apparent at the time, even to Rutherford! Sir Winston examined specimen panels of brick for the buildings but disliked all of them. Sheppard later proposed a type of brown brick from Stamfordham made by Williamson Cliff.

Cockcroft had now to decide who were the first Fellows to be submitted for election in June 1960. He was, of course, well qualified to pick the leading scientists and engineers and he obtained the assistance of John Morrison to select Fellows of the highest quality representing the humanities. Morrison was a classicist; he became the first Vice-Master and was later elected President of Wolfson College. Fellows on the scientific side included Sir Edward Bullard, Richard Keynes, Kenneth McQuillen, Richard Adrian, Richard Hey and Richard Tizard, the son of one of Cockcroft's oldest friends. Representing the humanities were Frank Hahn, a mathematical economist, (later Professor of Economics at Cambridge University) and C A St J Wilson, an architect and historian. A year later came Stephen Roskill the naval historian and George Steiner, the literary critic, was appointed Director of English Studies. The Bursar, much involved in the early planning and the building, was Major General J R C Hamilton, a retired Royal Engineer who had been Director of Military Operations at the War Office. His Chief Clerk was Harold Pettitt, who had served under Cockcroft when he was a Junior Bursar at St John's.

Several Extraordinary Fellows were appointed including Francis Crick, who with Maurice Wilkins and James Watson (later an Overseas Fellow) had achieved fame by proposing a structure for DNA, thereby establishing the basis of what is now known as molecular genetics, C P Snow the novelist and John Oriel who had raised funds to build the college.

Sir Winston was appointed the first Honorary Fellow and was joined by the sculptor, Henry Moore, who lent two of his works, and by Sir Barnes Wallis the aeronautical engineer, celebrated for designing airships, aeroplanes and wartime devices such as the bouncing bomb.

George Steiner had met Cockcroft while lecturing at Princeton University and had discussed Cockcroft's ideas for giving the arts their proper place in a technological society. Steiner, initially sceptical, had eventually agreed with him, considering that in the case of Churchill College Cockcroft had made it 'a place where the arts were not only welcomed but spoilt'. It is interesting to reflect that Cockcroft's championing of the Arts may have owed something to his daughter Catherine who had read History at Oxford, as we have already noted, and had crossed swords with her father over this—if it is possible to cross swords when one of the adversaries does not wield a sword. She reflected, in a recent letter to the authors,

> It occurred to me in a flash (of inspiration?) that this chap who was just setting up Churchill College on 'C P Snow' principles did not know what was involved in an arts degree. So I wrote (through the night) an essay to end all essays *In defence of a History degree*. He wrote by return of post to say he had for the first time understood what was involved in an Arts degree, that he had always before held them in some contempt, but he could see now that as much disciplined work was required as was of a Science degree. To my shame it was probably the best essay I ever wrote at Oxford, but more to my shame, it was some time before his magnaminity, nay humility, hit me.

So maybe the College owes much to 'Cathie', indeed Cambridge owes, after all, something to Oxford.

Cockcroft was determined to avoid what Steiner described as the 'hierarchical atmosphere of other colleges'[15]. He wanted a place 'where senior and junior, science and the arts, were continually mixing'. The acrimonies and parochial cruelties (marking certain arts faculties) filled him with a sadness when he compared them with the cameraderie he had known in his career as a scientist. One way in which Cockcroft achieved this was in encouraging Fellows and students to take part in the various College activities and to meet in the Buttery and Common rooms so that as he wrote,

> physicists can meet with economists to argue about the physical factors affecting economic growth; we can hear the latest news from Knossos or Pylos, or the 'digs' on the Indian North West Frontier; we can hear about the most recent discoveries of radio sources and quasars or we can discuss architecture and politics. Thus the College provides a general education for students as well as the continual re-education of Fellows.[16]

This belief in informality also led him to make what were innovations at that time in other quarters. For example, Fellows and students were free to bring lady guests to dine or lunch in Hall, unlike other Cambridge colleges.

On 16 December 1960, what Cockcroft described as 'our first grand dinner', to which lady guests from the academic world were invited, was held in the recently completed temporary hall. Elizabeth 'did the flowers and we had our two modern silver pieces out and displayed our Winston Churchill painting (a sea-scape)† and showed the large model of the finished college'.

By this time the first postgraduates had begun to take up residence, coming from universities in America, Britain, Canada, Hong Kong, Holland, Nigeria and elsewhere. The Cockcrofts, who at Harwell and other establishments made a point of getting to know as many of the staff as possible, soon knew their names and entertained them at Sedley Taylor Road. One of them, a New Zealander, remembered being

> shown into the Master's Lodge by Lady Cockcroft dressed-up and feeling rather nervous, not knowing anybody, when a little man with a very pleasant smile came up to me and said very diffidently 'Er—have you had any sherry yet?' And I said 'No thanks, but I would quite like some'. And began to talk to him. And it wasn't until I'd been talking to him for five minutes or more that I realised that I was not talking to the Master's Butler, but to the Master himself. And this to me is one of the things I remember most about the Master. The fact that he was completely unaffected and completely approachable at all times.[17]

Meanwhile, work on the main building, as schemes of this nature almost invariably do, was falling behind schedule. The urgency to complete the college had led to skimpy plans and prolonged negotiations with contractors, increasing cost and delays. On account of this, the design of the central block was revised in the autumn of 1960. Denys Armstrong, the Domestic Bursar, became responsible for supervision of the plans, though Cockcroft continued to supervise and hurry on the work. He was not, wrote a Fellow, 'tolerant of slack or lazy work and he was delighted when his son Christopher, then an undergraduate, took a vacation job with the builders'[18]. On his American visits he made a point of looking at university libraries and halls, jotting down notes for reference, always eager to learn as he had been when planning the new high-voltage laboratory at the Cavendish.

The first undergraduates duly arrived for the Michaelmas term of 1961, but full accommodation was far from being ready. The rate of acceptance was therefore governed by the number of lodgings which could be obtained in Cambridge and the number of Fellows and students which the flats and temporary buildings, in particular, the temporary kitchen, could support. Not until 1967 did it become possible to accommodate the original planned complement of postgraduates. Until then many undergraduates had to bicycle long distances every day, which may have helped to account for the steady progress which the Churchill boats were making in the bumping races on the river.

The only serious acrimony of the kind which Cockcroft deplored arose over the chapel, traditionally a focal point of colleges in the older universities. When the Trustees first considered the brief for the building they decided that nothing more than a meditation room was required. Sir Winston supported them, remarking that there were too many churches and chapels in Cambridge already. The nearest Cockcroft had ever got to expressing publicly his own religious views was in a BBC interview[19] when he placed himself

---

†Sir Winston later gave a still life entitled *The Orchids* to the College.

between the complete agnostic and the complete churchgoer, but he firmly believed that there should be a place in College for worship, just as in the same way he had wanted a chaplain for Harwell. Early in 1961 Canon Noel Duckworth was appointed the first chaplain; he was a celebrated prewar Cambridge cox and had spent much of the war in a Japanese prisoner-of-war camp, afterwards becoming for a while Chaplain of St John's College and then going out to serve in Ghana. While the Churchill College chapel was being built he held services in the Chapel of the Westminster Theological College a few minutes away and the Cockcrofts attended whenever they were able to do so.

Others outside the College likewise believed that the spiritual side should not be neglected. One of the criticisms of the College during the Senate House debate in November 1958 was the failure to provide for a free-standing chapel[20]. Annan, replying for the Trustees, declared that there was no objection to such a building. Subsequently Canon Montefiore, then Chaplain of Caius College (later Bishop of Birmingham), who had been present at the debate, held a collection in his college chapel for a religious building at Churchill. Prompted by Montefiore, the Reverend Timothy (later Lord) Beaumont offered the Trustees up to £30 000 to build a chapel. The Trustees accepted his gift (the actual amount was £26 000) before any appointments to the College were made.

In 1961 Sheppard's revised plans for the building were presented to the Governing Body; they showed a chapel at the entrance to the College, thus according with tradition. Francis Crick immediately resigned, his action receiving much publicity in the national press. The Governing Body rejected the chapel, only a small minority being in favour; Cockcroft remained aloof from discussion and did not vote.

Shortly after, John Killen, one of the Fellows, with the support of the Vice-Master, John Morrison, mooted the idea of a chapel independent of the College. Their proposal was backed by a number of postgraduates. Cockcroft offered his support and became Chairman of the Chapel Society Trust. In this capacity he wrote a decisive memorandum[21] laying down the functions for which a chapel might be used, including services, not necessarily restricted to the Christian religion, meetings of a serious nature, and music and organ recitals. This paper was a major factor in overcoming further opposition. Beaumont, still prepared to be benefactor, however, insisted that the services 'should be in accordance with the usage of the Church of England'.[22]

Three years elapsed before the storm subsided allowing a site to be allocated and a design approved. The chapel was then built by the same contractor who had been responsible for the college, using the same kind of materials but under a separate contract. The undergraduates were by this time represented in the Chapel Society, causing Duckworth to remark to Cockcroft,

> Three years ago such a proposal would have met wholesale and violent opposition. It may indeed be true what Theodore Bercyn said to Henry of Navarre 'Sire, the Church is an anvil that hath worn out many hammers!'[23]

But Duckworth was a popular figure and had exerted himself on behalf of the boat club. A light-hearted proposal by the Junior Common Room was that the chapel should be sited on the river and be over 60 feet long enabling it to accommodate a racing eight. Its actual site, held by the Chapel Trustees at a peppercorn rent, overlooks the playing fields and, ironically, makes it more conspicuous than it would have been if Sheppard's plan had been followed.

Cockcroft was no less diligent on behalf of the College Boat Club than he was over the Chapel. The Club was founded by an enthusiastic group of postgraduates who worked their way up from the bottom to the first division.

> The Master [wrote Canon Duckworth] never missed being present at the races. On one occasion he left a high pressure meeting in London saying that he had important business in Cambridge. Indeed he had, on the tow path, arriving to see all his boats going up.[24]

On account of the increased cost of building the college, General Hamilton proposed that they should amalgamate with the boat clubs of King's and Selwyn; and the Leys School. Cockcroft approved this proposal for economy and in doing so influenced other colleges to adopt similar measures.

His hearing had been failing for some time and he had resisted using a hearing-aid—this may indeed have explained why he so seldom contributed to discussion after dinner at the Royal Society Dining Club and elsewhere. By now, he was wearing an ordinary National Health Service hearing-aid and Canon Duckworth has described the way Cockcroft sometimes handled College Council meetings, 'with a touch of consecrated cunning':

> In the middle of a long, tedious and often contentious wrangling [continued Duckworth] he would switch off his aid, let the noise go on, then switch on and say 'I think we are all agreed'. I had to go and ask for two racing eights. The whole of the Council was against me. At his pre-prompting and at the meeting I made out a case and a request for £600. The wrangling went on. John had switched off. The going-on finally subsided. When he switched on and said 'Do I take we are all agreed?' Silence. 'Thank you Canon. You can go ahead and order!'[25]

Cockcroft had always taken an active part in undergraduate societies and he supported the founding of the Socratic Society by a Canadian postgraduate, Dr Macormack Smyth. It met after evening hall about three times a term to discuss problems of general interest, speakers ranged from Beeching on Government and industry, to Christopher Cornford on the ethics of pop art, to Admiral Sir Caspar John on defence. George Steiner remembered vividly one of the first meetings of the Society which happened to fall on the evening of President Kennedy's assassination[26]. Cockcroft, who invariably attended meetings, had just come back from Washington where he had been attending the centennial of the National Academy of Sciences and everyone expected him to cancel the meeting. But he not only insisted that the speaker, Martin Esslin, an authority on contemporary German drama, should deliver his paper, but conducted the proceedings in such a way that no-one left to watch the latest reports on television, everyone feeling that they had taken part in a memorable and moving occasion.

Probably Cockcroft contributed most to the College by his cultivation of relations with universities in other countries. It was his idea that there should be a number of Overseas Fellowships and he used to invite eminent scholars from abroad to spend six months or a year at the College in this capacity—a practice which is still observed—and led to other Cambridge colleges following his example, though to a lesser extent. In 1960 the Trustees agreed that a Churchill Foundation of the United States should be set up and they appointed Carl Gilbert as chairman, the purpose being to raise funds to support American scholars at Churchill, scholars who were selected by a committee consisting of James Killian, Lee DuBridge and Cockcroft, who regularly attended meetings when visiting the States.

On 5 June 1964 the College, then half completed, was opened by the Duke of Edinburgh; as he walked through the spacious grounds and between the magnificent buildings he quipped 'It looks as though the college has already been opened!'. Referring to the Founder, the Master said

> To those who had the good fortune of living in his time, whether they be plain men whom he led, the scientists who produced during the war miracles of technology, or the great with whom he shared the burden—and there are many

Figure 24   The opening of Churchill College by HRH the Duke of Edinburgh, 5 June 1964.

of those amongst us today—that name has brought inspiration and an echo of his glory. To such as he is, there can be no single sufficient memorial. Yet there is a peculiar appropriateness in our enterprise. The idea of a College as a place of manifold interests mirrors Sir Winston's manysided genius. Here we study the natural sciences and instruments of technology, without which, as Sir Winston foresaw, we cannot sustain the exacting stride of the future.

and he read a message from the Founder

Already the College is training at the highest level the scientists and technologists of which the country and the world stand in such need. I wholeheartedly congratulate those responsible for this achievement and thank them for their dedication of this splendid work as a memorial to my name.

to which the Visitor, His Royal Highness, replied

As Sir Winston himself has written 'it is only by leading mankind in the discovery of the new ways of science and engineering that we shall hold our position and continue to earn our livelihood'. If the discovery of new worlds of science hold the key to our future then what better than a college to turn out more and better scientists and technologists. Churchill College is something quite new. I hope very much that it will have a profoundly stimulating effect upon the whole field of science and technology in this country in the future. Only this influence will perpetuate the true inspiration of Sir Winston Churchill.[27]

Sir Winston was too infirm to be present, but at least he had the satisfaction of knowing that a large part of the College was in being.

On 24 January 1965 Sir Winston Churchill died. That evening Cockcroft assembled College members in Hall and paid a moving tribute to 'our Founder and first Honorary Fellow',[28]

We are met together to do honour to the memory of Sir Winston Churchill.

So long as English is spoken, and history studied, men will marvel at the greatness of Sir Winston. They will think back on him as a titan, and wonder that there should have been such diversity of achievement in one man. Surely they will discern as one of the marks of his greatness that he should have chosen as the first of the memorials to his glory the foundation of this College. Other captains of history have had their palaces, their triumphal arches, their city squares and mausolea. So, no doubt, will Winston Churchill. But this College is the memorial he himself inspired, and in whose beginnings he took pleasure. And he, a man of rhetoric and art, gave his name and active support to a College devoted in large measure to the natural sciences. For it was in the sciences, in technology that his tireless vision had come to see the battleground and promise of the future.

We mourn tonight the passing of our Founder and first Honorary Fellow. It will be difficult to think of a second, of anyone who could justly belong to the same category. But Sir Winston would not wish it so. Though a master historian, his resolve was for the future. It is in the growth, in the achievements of our work here, now and in generations to come, that this resolve shall continue as a living force.

All of us gathered in this Hall tonight are here because Winston Churchill lived, because governments and individuals from many parts of the earth were proud to do him honour. Let us, in whose lives his name will always have a special echo, now pay our tribute of silence.

Later he commented further on the enormous importance of Churchill's great interest in and appreciation of scientific and technological matters, and enumerated his

> personal interventions in the scientific war, including the installation of radar to track low-flying aircraft, the authorisation of the Tizard Mission and the keen interest he took in the battle against the V-weapons, while in the sphere of atomic energy his personal intervention led to the Quebec Agreement which enabled British scientists to make an important contribution to the joint war effort, and also enabled them to develop, through the Canadian – British Chalk River project, an almost complete knowledge of nuclear reactor technology[29].

In May 1966 Peter and Anna Kapitza made their long anticipated visit to the College, staying with the Cockcrofts in the Master's Lodge. Anna Kapitza had declared that they would return to Cambridge when John was appointed Master of a college. Her prophesy had at last come true. It was Kapitza's first visit to England since 1934 and John could not contain his excitement as the date of their arrival drew nearer. For most of May 1966 they stayed at the Master's Lodge and were at once engulfed in a whirl of engagements. A special meeting of the Kapitza Club was held in his honour; he spoke to the Socratic Society, visited some laboratories and addressed the Royal Society

Figure 25   Kapitza and Cockcroft during Kapitza's visit to Churchill College, May 1966. (Courtesy: Churchill College, Cambridge)

in London. He had lost none of his high spirits and irreverence and after returning to Moscow, ended a letter of thanks to Cockcroft: 'Greetings to the Fellows of your College, Vice-Master, Crick, Squire, Richard Adrian, Keynes and of course to the Chaplain and remind him that he must not be frightened to come to the Soviet Union'.[30]

Not long after, Kapitza's old home in Huntingdon Road was transferred to the USSR Academy of Sciences and used to accommodate Russian students working in Cambridge. It was the outcome of discussions with Kapitza on Cockcroft's visit to Moscow in 1965 and it was arranged that when the house was not fully occupied by Russians it would be used by Churchill postgraduates.

As Cockcroft approached his 68th birthday the Governing body had to consider how long he should remain as Master. The Statutes ruled that his term of office could only be extended up to two years after his 70th birthday; the Fellows were quite sure that he was still needed and invited him to serve the full four years[31]. True to character, he combined being Master with a number of other appointments, such as serving as part-time member of the Atomic Energy Authority, sitting on various Government committees, as well as being Chancellor of the Australian National University, all of which took him away from Cambridge and will be described in the last two chapters. It seems to be appropriate here to record the impressions he made on Fellows and undergraduates. In the comparatively short time since its foundation he had become part of the College. As Dr McQuillen recalled, his presence permeated

the whole place, the buildings, the playing fields, the river. He had that same four squareness, solidity as the buildings of the College. He was very much integrated into the place at all levels—the undergraduates, the graduate students, the Fellows... One of my commonest memories of the Master was any time of day from half past eight onwards, sitting at that desk in his study in the Master's Lodge, overlooking, or rather much more overlooked by, a lot of the college—imperturbable, sphinx-like, sitting there writing with a reading lamp at his right hand, quite unmoved, apparently unaware of the procession of people who went past the room all day, gazing in through the window. He had a quality of being able to come into a room full of people without any kind of fuss and yet immediately being felt. He was able to talk to people: he talked to our visitors, our guests, very distinguished people, very shy people, young people, old people —he was able to put them at their ease, talk with them, and equally, he was adept at ending a conversation, when he wanted to move on and talk to someone else, without apparently breaking off suddenly. And yet as a chairman, he seemed singularly ineffectual. We would all talk our heads off, without any very strong lead from the chair, and yet, somehow or other things got done, decisions were taken. He also had a curious lack of assurance on occasion, in little matters. How shall we do this? How shall we do that? Shall we say the Long Grace or the Short Grace at dinner to-night?[32]

It was never easy to fathom what was in his mind, let alone decipher his crabbed handwriting! There were a number of 'Cockcoft watchers' who enjoyed speculating on what lay behind that impenetrable mask. Richard Hey, in particular, remembered how the meaning of occasional, seemingly innocent, remarks would 'explode like a bomb' a day or two later[33]. Richard Tizard, then Senior Tutor, found that Cockcroft responded enigmatically to administrative matters.

> I remember many times going to him about some problem and after I'd had a ten or fifteen minute chat with him I never knew which side of the fence he was going to come down on. He would smile at me in this enigmatic way and I would go out, and it wasn't till I discovered what actually happened later on that I knew whether he was on my side or not. This characteristic sometimes infuriàted me and other Fellows of the College, simply because it was so effective.[34]

Some indication has been given of the way he presided over Council and Governing Body meetings which he conducted in a way similar to those at Harwell and other establishments over which he had presided. As then, he never took the initiative and rarely expressed a view on a matter of substance, nor did he take a vote on a particular issue. Most of the Fellows who knew him well would probably have agreed with General Hamilton that

> his strength and great contribution to the College lay in his whole hearted support to any project or matter with which he agreed and his determination behind the scenes to steer the College in the direction he wanted. He would support all activities in the College, usually by his presence, often unobtrusively. Whilst gaining the affection and loyalty of all members of the College, including staff, he rarely, if ever, gave praise or showed gratitude to an individual. He expected results and obtained them.[35]

He did not always get his way. When there were complaints about the food in Hall, he wrote to Elizabeth from Boston:

> Try lunching in Hall and see whether the food is as awful as the JCR meeting stated. I'll have to have the student meals served to me to check. I was opposed to having different meals (i.e. another menu for High Table) but the younger dons had their way.

He was very popular with the undergraduates and, as John Morrison recalled,

> he was acclaimed with the song *For he's a jolly good fellow* after a graduates' dinner —a distinction not usually accorded to the Master of a College. He was appreciated because he had risen to the top of traditional Cambridge through a grammar school and an engineering firm, and while Master had established strong links with schools in north-west and north-east England.[36]

He just missed the wave of student unrest that germinated on the American campuses in the mid-sixties and spread to Europe in 1968, though he probably would have taken it in his stride. When Joseph Boyce and his wife came to England to visit Churchill in 1964 he showed them round.

> John indicated a lounge and reading room where women were permitted. Emily asked him if they already had women students in the college. John replied 'not yet, but new things like that come to us about five years after you get them!'[37]

On 14 March 1967 Cockcroft could write with restrained pride to Sir Ernest Marsden, the veteran New Zealand physicist and colleague of Rutherford.

The college is making good progress. We expect to have another 160 student rooms by next October. This will complete the third side of the big square. We have also started work on a further block of 70 rooms which will fill the fourth side (thanks to a gift from the Wolfson Trust) and these should be completed by 1968. We should then have accommodation for about 90 per cent of our students, including 20 of the original flats and 40 new flats for married research students. I have a little over two years before I retire so will at any rate see the whole of the building concept of the college realised. We have already reached the maximum number of students and almost a maximum number of Fellows.[38].

CHAPTER NINETEEN

COMMONWEALTH ADVISER

While Churchill College was being built in the early 1960s, Cockcroft gathered his unabated energies for a new phase. This had to do, firstly with education in Australia where he became Chancellor of the Australian National University and, secondly, with his concern for improving the economies and standard of living of developing countries like India, Nigeria and Ghana. At an age when professional men usually ease up on their activities, he thought nothing of flying out to Australia and returning via North America to visit friends and keep in touch with current scientific activities.

His interest in India derived from his friendship with Homi Bhabha, of which the latter took full advantage. It is probable that Cockcroft was deceived by Bhabha's easy western manner and did not appreciate his determination to make India a first-class power, even, probably to the extent of it having a stock of nuclear weapons. A continuous flow of correspondence between the two scientists had gone on while Cockcroft was at Harwell and a member of the AEA. Bhabha wanted to build a low-energy research reactor which could be used for isotope production. There was also the basis for striking a bargain: Britain was interested in acquiring beryllium from India for use as a reactor moderator whilst India needed fuel elements for a DIDO-type reactor. After prolonged negotiations the AEA provided the fuel elements but Britain did not seem to get the beryllium. Indeed, Bhabha made an agreement with the French to extract thorium from the monazite sands of Travancore after failing to get his terms from the British. However Cockcroft helped Bhabha to train some Indian scientists at Harwell, seconded some of his chemical staff to India, and provided unclassified information on nuclear physics[1].

In March 1953 Cockcroft, on his first Indian tour, visited Bhabha at the Tata Institute of Fundamental Research which was almost entirely the outcome of Bhabha's vision. They both had in common a deep interest in architecture and Bhabha had lined the walls of the Bombay Yacht Club—home of the new Institute until the new buildings were ready—with modern paintings of which he was an avid collector. He showed Cockcroft the site of the proposed Atomic Energy Research Establishment at Trombay, overlooking the harbour of Bombay, and for which he was then occupied in preparing plans for trees and gardens.

Cockcroft next went out in January 1961 to attend the opening of the first Canadian – Indian research reactor which was almost a twin of the pioneer NRX reactor built under Cockcroft's direction at Chalk River. Before reaching Bombay he visited scientific establishments in Pakistan, including the new university at Karachi, 'built for some mysterious reason 14 miles out in the Sind Desert'. At Dacca he was at the opening of a scientific congress presided over by an old Johnian Fellow Abdus Salam, Professor of Physics at Imperial College and gave a lecture illustrated by a film to an audience of about 3000 on *Energy for under-developed countries*.

His first stop in India was Calcutta where he inspected a nuclear physics laboratory, it reminded him of 'Cambridge in the 1920s, only more primitive, with wires all over the place and a cyclotron of the Stone Age'. The staff were 'keen but desperately poor. All the science money goes to the Government institutes'. This and other examples were to provide fuel for his pleas for increased technological aid. At the Bose Institute he gave an impromptu three-quarters of an hour talk to a hastily gathered audience—a summary of his Bombay lecture.

In Bombay he stayed at the Bhabha family mansion on the Malabar Hills overlooking the sea. Homi's flat on the top floor gave him ideas for Churchill College: it was a magnificent room with windows all along one side looking out to the harbour and a bedroom off and a dining recess and kitchen to himself, 'I'm sure from seeing this, that our public rooms do not need to be more than 12 feet high—preferably less'. On the lower floors lived Homi's brother and his mother, and Cockcroft had the large guest room on the ground floor to himself with a bearer and cook to minister to him. Most meals, however, he shared with 'Homi or members of his family...the Tatas who run half Indian big business—steel, air lines, hotels, etc.'

At the inauguration of the reactor, which took place in the open, he sat opposite Nehru before an audience of 7000,

> men in white shirts, women in saris making a lovely scene... the speeches were lost in the wind which tore the cotton lining of our canopy to shreds. Nehru went on unperturbed with his speech with great force on the theme of the need for power to take India out of its poverty. 'Power, power, power' were the main words I heard. Most of the rest was lost in the flapping of the canopy and the poor performance of the loud speakers.

Other engagements included a lecture, a radio broadcast and a meeting of the United Nations Scientific Advisory Committee at which F Perrin from France, Rabi and Goldschmidt from the USA and W B Lewis from Chalk River were present, and there were sightseeing tours to antiquities at Aurangabad and the Elephanta caves. From Bombay he flew to Bangalore, visited the Hindustan Aircraft Factory and the Indian Institute for Science, thence on to Mysore, governed by a progressive maharajah, and finally, northwards again to Bihar before returning home from Calcutta.

He had not long been back in Cambridge when he received a letter from Oliphant then in charge of the Research School of Physical Sciences at the

Australian National University informing him that the University Council had unanimously agreed to invite him to become their new Chancellor for a four-year term of office. It would be an honorific post and require an annual visit to Australia for degree giving and other ceremonial occasions.

> If you say 'yes' it will have a very great effect upon the academic outlook and standards of the university, as well as add lustre and distinction to the university itself and to the functions over which you would preside.[2]

The university had been founded at Canberra in 1946 to provide good research facilities for students and good salaries for teachers in an attempt to reverse the flow of talent overseas, especially to the United Kingdom. To this end four research schools comparable to the best to be found overseas were created: physics, social sciences, medicine and Pacific studies. Oliphant, Keith Hancock the historian, Howard Florey the celebrated chemist, and Raymond Firth the social anthropologist had been active in their formation. In 1960 plans for enlarging the university were approved which covered the formation of an Institute of Advanced Studies and a School of General Studies. Cockcroft was no stranger either to Australia or to the University. He had received an honorary degree from it in 1952 and opened a laboratory (named after him) in the Research School of Physical Sciences, and had paid another visit in the course of an extensive tour of Australia in May 1959. In the interval he had been responsible for providing the School with a 30 MeV electron synchrotron from Harwell on 'reversed lend lease', to which was added a Van de Graaff accelerator not long after.

Leonard Huxley was appointed first vice-chancellor. He and his deputy, Professor A D Trendall, agreed that they needed a new Chancellor to replace Lord Bruce, a former Prime Minister of Australia and now advanced in years. Bruce gave way with good grace. Huxley and his colleague concluded that they could have no better person than Cockcroft; Huxley, who had been on the staff of TRE, remembered him from the war years. Cockcroft accepted, later pointing out at his installation, that the limited time required to preside over official functions 'together with a distance of 12 000 miles would ensure that your new Chancellor will not interfere unduly with the affairs of your university'.

He was installed with due ceremony at Canberra on 11 April 1962,

> being fetched by the University Masters and processed in, clad in black gown with a gold hood with page carrying my train! Having arrived safely on the platform the Pro-Chancellor pronounced the Words of Admission, and then there were short speeches by the Governor General [Lord de L'Isle and Dudley], the Prime Minister [Robert Menzies] and then a 20 minute speech by me.

The Cockcrofts (Elizabeth accompanied him on all his Australian tours) stayed in the Chancellor's flat where they 'cooked their own breakfast and either lunched in Hall or get meals sent over'. Cockcroft, recalled Huxley,

> took his duties as Chancellor most seriously. He made it his business to meet as many of the academic staff as time would permit (usually, as Cockcroft noted, when they were foregathered for a tea break) and representatives of students'

organisations. His unassuming manner and natural courtesy was recognised and appreciated by all. Lady Cockcroft also took pains to meet the wives of staff members.

They also visited Perth, where he received an honorary degree and opened a physics laboratory at the university, and Melbourne where he lectured. In the following year Canberra celebrated its Jubilee and Cockcroft was present when the Queen opened the Menzies Library. Of special interest to Cockcroft was the Department of Astronomy's observatory at Mount Stromlo outside Canberra high up in 'a lovely situation with forests all round' and because of its height 'quite cool out of the sun'. A 120 inch reflecting telescope was being built there to increase the number of observations of the stars of the southern hemisphere.

They returned home via New Zealand and stayed with the Governor General, Sir Bernard Fergusson, in Auckland where 'semi-regal pomp with aides, etc was observed'. A more simple, but nonetheless sincere, welcome awaited them at the Marsdens' at Wellington; his connection with Manchester and Rutherford in the 1912–14 period no doubt stimulated many stories that evening. Then they went to look at the geothermal power station at Wairakei; 'it was rather like an inferno with steam coming out from many bore holes 3000 feet deep'.

On the way home Cockcroft discussed with astronomers at the California Institute of Technology a proposal for a jointly-operated Anglo–Australian telescope of extremely large size. The scheme did not meet with immediate approval in Australia but was endorsed when the Government changed there some years later. At Berkeley at the Radiation Laboratory Cockcroft met Edwin McMillan and other Nobel Prize winners. He always enjoyed visiting the Radiation Laboratory where his old friend Ernest Lawrence, who had died in 1958, 'used to reign and build his great machines', and he was interested in the fusion work at the Livermore Laboratory not far away. Dorothea, who had been nursing in Australia for several years, was with her parents and they all returned home just in time for her sister Catherine's wedding to Nicholas Milford, whose elder brother, John, was the young scientist who had impressed Cockcroft not long before in Africa when he read a paper on the distribution of the ozone in the atmosphere.

In 1965 he opened a new observatory for the Australian National University's Department of Astronomy at Siding Spring Mountain, part of a 5000 feet high volcanic range in northern New South Wales and which provided better observation than Mount Stromlo. He was particularly concerned to encourage Anglo–Australian collaboration in the field of astronomy; at his installation as Chancellor of ANU he had spoken of how Australia was now well equipped for radioastronomy and how necessary it was to work with the optical astronomers and he mentioned the work of a joint Anglo–Australian project to measure the diameter of stars. He described this visit in a letter to Eric. There were

lovely views over the surrounding plains devoted to sheep and cattle growing in very large farms up to 1000 acres... The telescopes were of very modern design but medium size†, together with living accommodation for a few permanent staff and observers who travel from Canberra and sleep on the mountain.

While there, he spent some time talking to the local high school at Coonabarabra

> mainly about early days in science. After this we toured the school and I was astonished to find that their Physics equipment was far worse than that at Todmorden Secondary School 50 years ago!

He was now succeeded as Chancellor by Sir Howard Florey, responsible for the wartime developments of penicillin; Cockcroft reminded him that they had both been research students in the late 1920s. 'Florey was engaged with rabbits and I with primitive nuclear accelerators'.[5] Summing up his term of office he was pleased to note that 'the number of undergraduates had grown from 1000 in 1961 to 2400 today with a growth rate of about 35% during the last year', and he spoke of plans for an expansion of undergraduates to 3500 and of postgraduates to over 800 by 1969. The School of Central Studies had grown and more laboratories had been added to the scientific faculties.

Huxley noted

> perhaps the most important service that he rendered the University was in helping to persuade some distinguished scholars in England that the ANU was a worthy institution to join. In particular, he played a vital role in the staffing of our newly created Research School of Chemistry. He helped to convince two very distinguished Australian professors of chemistry in British universities that they should return to Australia to lead the new school in the ANU. This School of Chemistry has achieved enormous success and is one of those of which the University is most proud[6].

He had thoroughly enjoyed his Chancellorship and always welcomed members of the university at Churchill College; a number of them resided there while pursuing their study in Cambridge.

Shortly after returning home from his last tour of duty as Chancellor, Cockcroft met Blackett, who had become Deputy Chairman of the Advisory Council on Technology and Scientific Adviser to the Labour Government's new Ministry of Technology, at Millbank Tower. Copisarow, who was the Ministry's Chief Scientific Officer, had suggested that Cockcroft would be an ideal person to initiate studies of the problems facing the developing countries, problems to which Blackett had given much thought in recent years; he had concluded that the initial requirements for raising the standard of living in developing countries were very expensive while later stages needed more engineers and managers than in the early stages. 'Science', he concluded, 'is no magic wand to convert a poor country into a rich one'.[7] Cockcroft, too, had been concerned about the lack of balance between the poor and wealthy countries and with the other members of UNSAC he had agreed that a United Nations Conference should be convened in 1963 to discuss the best ways of helping developing countries. He was given some insight into the

†In 1971 the Anglo–Australian telescope, one of the largest in the world, was commissioned at the observatory.

practical problems when he went to Africa to attend the opening of the Kariba dam and had been impressed by the efforts being made to stop soil erosion and to improve the production of food.

Blackett wanted Cockcroft to discover how developing countries could best be helped, either through the efforts of government research establishments or through obtaining research and development contracts with industry. He believed that insufficient thought had been given to the kind of material aid appropriate to the economy for which it was intended; for instance, cheaper fertilisers and other chemical plant would be just as effective as the more expensive kinds used in this country. He expected the investigation to take around six months during which Cockcroft would be a consultant[8]. Cockcroft assimilated a quantity of statistical information, not only on sophisticated technology being adapted by some of the developing countries, but also on medium scale technology (along the lines of Blackett's brief) and technological developments suitable for small-scale agricultural holdings and small-scale industries. His report was summarised in a lecture delivered in January 1966 under the auspices of the Overseas Development Institute, an independent body trying to influence the pursuit of wise policies in this comparatively new field[9]. For a man whose interests were in research reactors and high-energy particle accelerators, it is interesting to see him recommending simple one-wheel drive tractors or a multi-purpose vehicle drawn by a pair of oxen, adaptable for use as a plough or a cultivator, or even a groundnut lifting device. He was shocked by the enormous wastage of cereals due to imperfect drying and processing, and the depredations of insects and he drew attention to improved methods of storage of grain, to ways of assessing the effectiveness of fumigation systems and to cheap tropical roofing materials. Afterwards he told Copisarow that he thought economic results would only arise out of a number of initiatives on a wide front in the territories concerned; but that he hoped his small contribution might be catalytic in this respect.

At the same time he was extending his interests in education in the developing countries. In August 1965 he and Sir Joseph Hutchinson represented the Royal Society at a conference organised by the US National Academy of Sciences on Science and Development in Nigeria,[10] the object of which was to see how the Nigerian scientific effort could be improved and to find out the best way countries such as Britain and the United States could help. He stayed in great comfort at the Villa Serbelloni on Lake Como bequeathed by its Italian owner to the Rockefeller Foundation; he had been a guest there two years earlier while working as a member of a Commission chaired by Dr Killian, President of the MIT, on a report for the OECD on 'the next decade of higher education for scientists and engineers in the USA' and he was delighted with the relaxed atmosphere and fine scenery. He remarked that it would make a good retreat where he could settle down and write his memoirs: alas time ran out and those memoirs were never written. As the conference progressed the need to expand the universities and the research institutes in Nigeria quickly became apparent and the Nigerians were encouraged by the promise of practical support. One problem was the lack of teachers for sixth forms to provide suitable candidates for the universities. Unfortunately much of their efforts were frustrated by the lack of a stable political background in which education could flower.

Cockcroft's interest in African countries of the Commonwealth caused him to make two visits to Ghana in the latter part of 1966. On the overthrow of President Nkrumah, one of the problems considered by the new government (the National Liberation Council headed by Lieutenant General Ankrah) was whether or not to continue with the construction of a Russian research reactor and ancillary facilities which Ghana had bought. The NLC made representations to the IAEA on the possibility of inviting Cockcroft to advise on the matter. Professor Joseph Quartey, of the Chemistry Department of the University of Ghana, was at the time an Overseas Fellow at Churchill College. During some discussions which the Ghana authorities asked him to hold with the IAEA he was told that Ghana would be fortunate to have the advice of a person of Cockcroft's eminence and international standing, and that there had, indeed, been an earlier invitation to Cockcroft to advise on certain aspects of the Ghana Academy of Sciences. He at once recommended to the authorities that the possiblity be taken up directly with Cockcroft himself[11].

As Cockcroft was still a serving member of the AEA, sanction had first to be given by the British Government. The Foreign Office was concerned lest Cockcroft's intervention should jeopardise the good relations with Russian scientists which he had done so much to foster, but the Commonwealth Relations Office thought that he should be allowed to go provided his brief was non-political. In the event, he accepted an invitation to assess the technical state of the reactor project; the scientific and personnel requirements, and likely capital and operating costs; the technical problems which would arise if the government decided to abandon the project; and the alternative uses to which the equipment and facilities could be put.

He flew to Ghana on 7 October 1966 as guest of the Government. For the sake of convenience he stayed at the University at Accra where Quartey, then back at the University, looked after his welfare and assisted him in getting the information he wanted[12]. Owing to the previous secrecy of the project, there was considerable difficulty in finding out the costs, and he was only able to submit an interim report before leaving on 15 October, with the final version to be submitted later when the capital and operating costs had been verified. Apart from the technical aspects, in general, he concluded that: in view of the capacity for some 20 years to come of the hydro-electric station (Volta dam) then in existence, a reactor was not likely to be necessary for the purpose of producing power. Account should be taken of the state of the scientific and technological development of Ghana, the scarcity of appropriate scientific manpower, and the financial needs for other fields, such as agriculture and health. However, a final decision on whether the project should be continued or abandoned, after due consideration of all the assembled data, was the sole perogative of the Ghana Government, and discussions should be held with possible users.

Although much had to be done on his short visit, he enjoyed driving through the countryside and admired the women 'wearing beautifully-coloured garments, walking gracefully along the roads carrying baskets of oranges on their heads'. The night before he left, he was entertained by the Vice-Chancellor of the University at a formal dinner 'with African dances and drumming to follow—most impressive!'

As stated earlier, even before the assignment on the nuclear reactor arose, Cockcroft had been invited by the Ghanians to advise on the Academy of Sciences[13]. The invitation had in fact been issued during Nkrumah's own time, through the Royal Society. It had been felt that owing to organisational and other factors such as the limited scientific manpower available, the Academy had not made as great an impact as expected on the health and living conditions of the people. When the assignment on the reactor was discussed, it was decided to cover that and the one on the Academy on two separate visits. So it was that Cockcroft paid a second visit to Ghana, this time with Elizabeth, shortly before Christmas 1966 to chair a committee on the Academy. After a series of meetings and interviews, the committee recommended a reorganisation into two separate bodies—one (the 'Academy') to deal with the learned society aspects, and the other (the 'Council for Scientific and Industrial Research') to deal with the co-ordination and applications of research.

CHAPTER TWENTY

MAN OF PEACE

Cockcroft had good reason to hate war; he had observed it at close quarters in the trenches of the Western Front and although he had fully approved the development of an atomic bomb to forestall the possible use of one by Hitler, six months after the atomic bombs had been dropped on Japan he told his brother Leo,

> I have certainly no wish to spend the rest of my working life perfecting means of blowing the world to pieces. If we can forget about bombs and devote ourselves to peaceful uses it would be an enormous relief.

As has been shown, he had bent his energies to harnessing nuclear power to peaceful applications and to promoting the exchange of the latest information on nuclear research to all concerned. While he was serving as a fulltime member of the AEA he felt under an obligation not to identify himself too closely with the various groups pressing for nuclear disarmament.

He did, however, become one of the Vice-Presidents, along with Blackett, Cherwell, Oliphant, Simon, Skinner, Thomson, G I Taylor and other prominent physicists, of the Atomic Scientists Association formed in 1946. This body aimed to bring before the public the true facts about atomic energy, to help shape policy on such matters, and to promote the international control of atomic energy. In the late 1950s Cockcroft and most members of the Association pressed for a complete cessation of nuclear weapons tests; there was great anxiety concerning the highly radioactive fission products, especially strontium-90, which were brought down by rain from nuclear explosions in the atmosphere, this particular element was known to induce leukaemia, and members pressed the Government to make a statement. In 1957 Cockcroft wrote to Kathleen Lonsdale, the well known crystallographer and another Vice-President, that he thought they 'ought to worry less about tests and much more about disarmament'. She agreed and replied[1] that she considered that 'to abolish tests alone would be to live in a fools' paradise'.†

---

†In a further letter of 27 August 1957 she reiterated the need for disarmament and continued, 'I am not sure that any beginning will be made except by unilateral action and that seems almost impossible in terms of economic necessity.' However, Cockcroft never believed in unilateral action.

Considered views like these were unlikely to find response among the supporters of the Campaign for Nuclear Disarmament which was making itself felt during 1958 and 1959 particularly through the Easter marches from the Atomic Weapons Establishment at Aldermaston to London patronised by ex-Cabinet Ministers and beatniks. His daughter 'Cathie' recalls that, when she was up at Oxford, the subject was discussed with her Father 'and after some distressed walking up and down the sitting room at Harwell at the beginning of the Easter Vac, he finally brought himself to ask me not to (take part) in the March ... he did not know that I had already decided that I could not do that'. Scientists like Cockcroft and Lonsdale were no less determined to do their utmost to limit the possibility of another world war but they believed they could be more effective by providing informed opinion[2].

The need not only for informed scientific debate but for making contact with foreign scientists of similar views had already found expression in the conferences on science and world affairs, more familiarly known as the Pugwash conferences of scientists which were initially prompted by Bertrand Russell, who in December 1954 had drafted a manifesto to which a number of distinguished scientists had appended their signatures, including Einstein shortly before his death, and Max Born and Joliot-Curie. Though not a signatory, Cockcroft publicly supported the manifesto. By 1960 the Pugwash conferences had become an established feature and attracted scientists from both sides of the Iron Curtain, some from the West attending freely without Government backing, those from the East being sent officially.

Since the war official attempts to promote talks on disarmament had been a dismal failure, but in 1958, partly in response to public anxiety about fallout from nuclear tests and partly because the Soviets were afraid of the proliferation of nuclear weapons in countries like China, India and even Germany, it was agreed that a partial nuclear test ban treaty should be negotiated between the Americans, Russians and British. Five years were to elapse before the treaty was signed in Moscow, but a start was made on the scientific level at a Conference of Experts which met in Geneva in July 1958[3]. Cockcroft represented the United Kingdom as an alternate to Penney. Both western and eastern scientists agreed, he wrote later, that 'it was perfectly feasible to detect explosions in the atmosphere and ocean at such distances that no inspection by the other side would be necessary'.[4] The conference concluded that 'a network of 180 seismological stations would be required round the world—about fifty of them in Russia—to be certain of detecting underground explosions of the order of five to ten kilotons'. A major problem, however, was that of distinguishing nuclear explosions from natural phenomena like earthquakes.

The Pugwash meetings from 1960 to 1963 provided a useful unofficial forum for discussing the prolonged negotiations which ultimately led to the test ban treaty, but the erection of the Berlin wall and the resumption of Soviet nuclear tests were hardly an auspicious introduction to the Pugwash conference on disarmament and world security held at Stowe, Vermont in September 1961. It was the first time that Cockcroft had attended. He could not be persuaded to go to the previous conference held in Moscow on the grounds that it was too outnumbered by Russian academicians to have any value. This time the numbers were more in balance and he was in good company with Blackett, Bullard, Penney, Zuckerman† and Rotblat who, as secretary to Pugwash, had been the main driving force in organising the meetings. Among the non-scientists, but specialists in the fields of strategy and politics were Philip Noel-Baker, Wayland Young and Michael Howard, the military historian, later to become Regius Professor of Modern History at Oxford, who was one of a small group which had founded the Institute for Strategic Studies in London, of whose Council Cockcroft was a respected member.

He flew from Italy where he had been attending a meeting of the Killian Commission on American Education and passed the time by composing his report on this subject:

> I hope my journey to Vermont will be worthwhile [he wrote to Elizabeth in Cambridge]. At any rate we might try to get more understanding of the curious present behaviour of the Russians. [The plenary session proved to be] not very edifying since the two opening Russian speeches were mainly political and non-constructive... The first US address was not much better but the second by Harrison Brown [the geochemist] of MIT was at least constructive. Then there was a fierce debate largely devoted to the German question with emotional speeches about the Russian sufferings in the last war. I got very fed up towards the end and said a few words to pull the conference round to its supposed theme... and suggested we got down to details in the following days as to how to go about it.

The conference then broke up into small groups—always more rewarding—to discuss technical details. Cockcroft and Penney, Francis Perrin and Hans Bethe, formed a group with two Soviet Academicians, one of whom, Igor Tamm a theoretical physicist acted as chairman; Cockcroft had known him for thirty years or more. They discussed how to cut off the production of fissile material for military purposes and the elimination of nuclear stock piles. In their joint paper, Cockcroft and Penney pointed out that the important areas for supervision were the chemical plants where plutonium was separated from uranium and the subsequent way in which plutonium was used[6]. In the main, the Russians agreed with these observations.

Michael Howard's impression of Cockcroft at this meeting, and others similar to it, was that he was

> a wise old bird [who] listened carefully, seldom spoke, and when he did speak did so with great authority and dignity. His great talent lay in getting things done[7]. [At Stowe, Howard continued] Cockcroft and Penney were Olympian, making few interjections but those of great weight. But what did emerge, I am afraid, was that the British no longer mattered very much. The Russians and the Americans were talking to one another over the heads of the rest of us, and I think that Cockcroft saw this more clearly than did such disarmament activists as Blackett and Noel-Baker and Rotblat. Still, Cockcroft obviously saw how much good the Pugwash meetings could do in opening up a dialogue with the Russians even if the actual discussions and resolutions were unimportant. His presence, both at Stowe and even more at Cambridge the following year when

---

†It was the first time that Zuckerman, Chief Scientific Adviser to the Government, had talked to Russian government scientists face-to-face.[5]

he gave a reception in his own house, lent a dignity and credibility to the proceedings which were of great value. If he was there, one felt, it must be all right. And I think it was.

By 1962, despite the resumption of atmospheric testing, an 18-nation commission resumed negotiations at Geneva. At the next Pugwash conference held on 25 August in Cambridge, Cockcroft and Bullard in their paper said it would be sufficient to ask to inspect sites in about 10 per cent of suspected tests since a 1 in 10 chance of being discovered would be a sufficient deterrent[8].

According to Cockcroft, however, the Russian delegation was much less relaxed than at Stowe, adhering strictly to the official Soviet line being followed at Geneva, though Professor Tamm tried to break the ice by explaining his proposal for a 'black box'—an unmanned seismic recording system which would obviate the need for on-site inspections of nuclear weapon testing grounds to which the Russians objected[9].

Cockcroft was President of the British Association that year, meeting in Manchester four days after the Pugwash meeting and in his Presidential Address entitled *Investment in Science* delivered in the Free Trade Hall before an audience of 4000 he took advantage of the occasion to condemn both the space race between the Americans and the Russians and the continuing development of thermonuclear weapons. The Press reported him as being the first scientist of renown to speak out openly on these dangers. He warned that while investigations of other planets was exciting, there was no doubt that these ventures were being undertaken

mainly for prestige and as an instrument of power politics, seriously distorting the pattern of scientific development through the diversion of very large numbers of engineers and scientists to these objectives.[10]

On account of the threat of nuclear war, he appealed to scientists and professional men who had special knowledge to make whatever contribution they could

to solve the technical problems of the 'controlled and complete disarmament' which is now the declared objective of the United States, Russia and the British Commonwealth. [He concluded] We must realise, however, that the great difficulties in achieving disarmament are political and not technical. If there was a real will on the part of all major powers to disarm it could be achieved, releasing enormous resources for diversion to urgent needs of our own country and less fortunate countries.

On 6 September he attended a further Pugwash meeting held in London. On this occasion there were only large plenary sessions where political attitudes had to be struck, though again the meeting was redeemed by Tamm and two of his colleagues who joined forces with three American scientists in elaborating the Russian proposal for seismic recording stations in neutral countries. Their proposal was afterwards accepted by the Russians at Geneva as well as a recommendation for retaining a minimum deterrent to the end of the second stage of the disarmament programme.

The next Pugwash conference was held at Dubrovnik towards the end of

September 1963 in a more hopeful atmosphere two months after the signing of the Partial Test Ban Treaty which banned nuclear tests in the atmosphere and in outer space, under water, and also underground if the explosions there would result in an escape of radioactive debris beyond national boundaries. By 22 August over 67 nations had agreed to adhere to the treaty. Cockcroft welcomed the treaty and expressed relief that 'our leaders [including Kennedy and Macmillan]' had not heeded the 'lunatic fringe of science' which was ever on the lookout for 'more exotic types of nuclear weapons'.[11] He went on to discuss how improvements could be made to detect underground tests which were still difficult to distinguish from earthquakes; unmanned seismic stations could be built in regions of high seismic activity, instruments could be buried in holes drilled to about 10 000 feet, and could also be placed on the ocean bed. Attempts to pave the way for a complete ban treaty were made during the following two years. They were supported by Cockcroft who did not believe that general and complete disarmament was yet practicable[12]. While technical advances in seismology now made it possible to detect most nuclear explosions as far distant as 10 000 kilometres from the territory of the country of origin, the fact that the United States was embroiled in the Vietnam war put a blight on political overtures.

In Britain the Labour Party returned to power in October, 1964, after an absence of 13 years, and there was much heady talk about the 'white-hot technological revolution' accompanying plans for revitalising the nation's ailing industrial effort. Harold Wilson, the Prime Minister, decided to appoint a Minister of State with special responsibilities for disarmament and he was advised to invite Cockcroft to take on the job[13]. However, Cockcroft, who had always been a Liberal and had voted for the Liberal candidate at the General Election, felt that it would be inconsistent for him to accept, nor could he neglect his duties as Master of Churchill College. Alun Gwynne-Jones, until then Military Correspondent of *The Times*, was next approached and he accepted the appointment, but not being an MP, he took his seat in the House of Lords as Lord Chalfont.

Less than three months elapsed before Chalfont invited Cockcroft to act as unofficial consultant on the technical aspects of nuclear disarmament[14]. The Geneva talks had again broken down and both British and American governments were anxious to revive them. To this end, Cockcroft was invited to attend a meeting of the Anglo–US committee on disarmament in Washington on 23 June 1965, and Zuckerman, in his capacity as scientific adviser to the Prime Minister on disarmament, and Rabi of the USA also attended. Cockcroft, typically, said nothing during the proceedings, but, no doubt, contributed in his unassuming way to the informal discussions. A 17 nation disarmament conference was reconvened in Geneva that July but the continuing tensions caused by the Vietnam war were not conducive to progress. Cockcroft, like many others, was anxious about the threat to peace of the American military presence in South Vietnam and was a signatory, with eight senior Fellows from Cambridge colleges, of a letter to *The Times*, published on 23 February 1965, urging the Government to take the initiative in bringing about a cease-fire before the conflict degenerated into a threat to world peace[15].

The explosion of the first Chinese atomic bomb in October 1964 made politicians more than ever aware of the dangers of proliferation. In July 1966 Chalfont revived his study group to consider aspects of a comprehensive test ban[16]. Cockcroft and Peierls accepted invitations to be members and Cockcroft visited the Atomic Weapons Establishment at Aldermaston to inform himself about recent experiments by scientists of the Authority which enabled them to distinguish between the earth waves produced by an earthquake and those by a small explosion of around 5 KT†. Cockcroft afterwards wrote to Zuckerman that the new technique gave a 'positive indication that a particular event is an explosion rather than an earthquake'.[17]

Yet in the long run, as Zuckerman rightly pointed out, techniques of identification ultimately depended on decisions by the politicians. It was for governments 'to decide where the balance of advantage lies, whether to live with the risk of the present nuclear balance being upset by the application of the results of some test or tests, or whether to extend the test ban in order to help discourage the proliferation of nuclear weapons'.[18]

The politicians were indeed increasingly being faced with decisions dependent on scientific advice, not only in regard to the proliferation of nuclear weapons, but to vastly expensive projects such as space research, Concorde, the Channel Tunnel, or the construction of a high-energy accelerator for fundamental nuclear research. Cockcroft, it has been seen, had always been anxious to keep the politicians in the picture about Harwell, and had spoken on a number of occasions to the Parliamentary and Scientific Committee[19] (he once appeared in his working tweed suit to address an audience wearing black ties, who had been patiently awaiting him, and left for Harwell immediately afterwards). Unlike his old friends, Blackett, Bowden and Snow, who had accepted the offer of posts in the Labour Government, he decided to join the Liberal Party. He approved of the Liberals for several reasons, firstly, he had been brought up a Liberal in the Manchester tradition, and secondly, because the Liberals not only opposed further nationalisation of industry but also an independent nuclear deterrent.

> I can't imagine why [Cockcroft had written to Oliphant during the 1964 Election] the Conservatives cling to this independent deterrent as a principal prop in their programme.[20]

In May 1965 he was appointed chairman of the Liberal Party Committee on Scientific Policy. The sort of role he envisaged for himself was probably not very different from that of Ernest Chain, who had contributed so much to the development of penicillin, and who was invited by Cockcroft to serve on the committee: Chain agreed to serve on condition that he was not associated politically with the Party, he thought it might provide an excellent platform to put forward proposals for a more vigorous and enlightened scientific policy, he wanted to see 'an active and imaginative research policy run by the minimum of bureaucracy and backed by an organisational efficiency

---

†When the first atomic bomb was exploded its power was described as equivalent to the explosion of 20 000 tons of TNT, and thereafter nuclear explosions have been described as x kilotons of TNT equivalent.

similar to the United States'[21]. Cockcroft, likewise, thought that the Prime Minister should have the benefit of a committee similar to the American President's Scientific Advisory Committee on Science and Technology. In his experience, politicians were 'faced with a decision and had to put up with it'.[22] Topics that appeared on the agenda of Cockcroft's committee included industrial research in government departments, applied research in industry, research associations and universities, and the application of cost benefit analysis to extremely costly projects like Concorde.

In June 1966 Cockcroft was elected Vice-President of the Liberal Party and was entitled to a seat on the Party Council,[23] but he insisted that he would not allow politics to distract him from his other interests which he enumerated as atomic energy, disarmament, science and technology in the developing countries, and international cooperation in science and technology. Nor did he intend to ease up on travel. In March 1967 he and Elizabeth made what proved to be their last visit to the United States. It was a packed tour and proved to be not without its excitements. They flew direct to Dallas where he was to give the keynote address to a convocation at the Engineering School of the Texas A & M University† on the theme *Nuclear Energy: Engineering for the 1970s*. On arrival at the airport they were, he wrote to Eric,

> conducted to a tiny one-engine five-seater plane which just about sat under the Boeing's wings. Our hosts said it was a one hour flip to the University at College Station—a place I'd not been able to find on the map. So after recovering from the surprise we soared aloft and set out south-west. [They ran into headwinds and mist.] After one and three-quarter hours we saw College Station and began to descend rocking furiously until we hit the runway. So we breathed a sigh of relief and were driven off to a nice Motel—Holiday Inn where we stayed in luxury for five nights.

The theme of his address was the fact that in recent years uranium had emerged as a competitive third fuel. Nuclear power, he went on, depended on increasing the amount of fission energy obtainable from reactors, the reactors of the 1970s would extract less than one per cent of the potential energy from each ton of uranium so to improve on that the fast breeder reactor would have to be developed commercially. On Good Friday they went to Houston and the Manned Spacecraft Center—'the whole station must cost hundreds of millions of dollars a year to run—all to land on the moon'. The next day they went round the research laboratories of the Texas Instrument Company which were making transistors and other components for space flights. Then on to the South-west Center for Advanced Studies 'built mainly by private subscription... but now hoping to form up with the University of Texas and get State money' and at a dinner party that evening he spoke about Churchill College.

On Easter Day they flew to Washington where he was to be a member of an international working party of scientists to discuss what the Inter-American Development Bank, founded in 1960 could do to help science and technology in Latin America and to prepare the ground for a Heads-of-State

†Agriculture, Architecture and Medicine.

meeting to be attended by President Johnson;[24] Cockcroft was attending in place of Blackett and represented the Ministry of Overseas Development. Three days later he parted company from Elizabeth, she going to stay with relations while he flew to Los Angeles to be the guest of Dr Ivan Getting who had been the head of the fire-control group in the Radiation Laboratory during the war and was now Managing Director of the Aerospace Corporation responsible for 'systems engineering' for the US Air Force on satellites and ballistic missiles. Not only did he speak to members of the Corporation on science policy but gave a lecture to the Los Angeles Council for World Affairs on technological cooperation in Europe. Then he rejoined Elizabeth in Boston and sorted out some business with Carl Gilbert on the US Churchill Foundation before they returned home.

Though he continued to be enthusiastic about nuclear power, the potential danger to world peace lay heavily on his mind. When he was in Los Angeles he told the World Affairs Council that only the good sophisticated control systems employed in the United States, Great Britain and Russia would prevent the accidental discharge of nuclear missiles. Again, 'as more and more nations acquire nuclear power it would be difficult to keep tight controls over small nations which might use the weapon against each other and set off a chain reaction'.[25]

Another theme of those years was his concern that the rapid developments in technology were overshadowing the work of fundamental scientists. He had recently heard them described as 'absent-minded white-coated egg-heads'[26].

> So it still seems necessary [he told the Patternmakers Company at a Mansion House dinner in the City of London] to remind our politicians that the work of Rutherford led to nuclear power, the work of Fleming, Chain and Florey to the vast antibiotics industry; the work of the chemists to the vast chemical industry; the work of our molecular biologists (in which Cambridge excels) and that of other biologists will undoubtedly lead to equally important practical results in the future. Fundamental science is the goose which lays the golden eggs though they may take 20 to 30 years to hatch!

At the Liberal Arts Conference held at the University of Chicago in February 1966 he was asked to speak on *A Transatlantic View of What (Technological) Knowledge is Worth Having*. He confessed that he was well aware of the danger of assuming that technology would automatically provide all the answers.

> What [he asked] are the social and economic advantages of a supersonic aircraft project costing several billions of dollars as against subsonic flight? What are the relative advantages or disadvantages of different transport systems? Can we reduce the choking-up of our cities with commuters' cars by providing more and better high speed public transport? How can we best rebuild our cities, our road and rail systems to take account of the tremendously rapid increase of the car and truck population which shows little sign of diminishing? What are the economic and social benefits of the space travel programme of the US and USSR? Apart from the technological spin-off, such as microelectronics and microcomputers, what do we gain from explorations in space? There is certainly great scientific interest in determining whether primitive forms of life exist on Mars, but we will find no Martians. So the astronauts will have to travel to other

stellar systems to find evidence of human-like life... How much of your resources are you willing to spend on this?

And he introduced his recent preoccupation with developing countries and 'the need to overcome their very great disabilities and low standards of living'. Drawing on his experience, he illustrated his point by telling them that after independence

Nigeria was left with only one doctor in 30 000 of the population—most of them in cities and only about 500 indigenous scientists and engineers. So it is not surprising that four per cent of the children die before the age of five.

His address was interlaced with comments on the study of the history of civilisations, politics, the influence of literature, the visual arts and music and his belief (practised throughout his life) that learning and knowledge should be a continuous process.

In graduate student years, it is necessary to specialise as I did in Mathematics and Physics. But with increasing age our interests inevitably broaden. Life is all too short to explore all the fascinating avenues which open. [He concluded by quoting A E Housman, also comparing science and the arts] The pleasure of learning and knowing, though not the keenest, is yet the least perishable of pleasures; the least subject to external things and the play of chance and the wear of time. And as a prudent man puts money by to serve as a provision for the material wants of his old age, so too he needs to lay up against the end of his days provision for the intellect.[27]

On 27 May 1967 Cockcroft celebrated his 70th birthday.

I've certainly been lucky [he wrote to Leo] in keeping fit for so long though I notice now that I need occasional naps after lunch and before Hall. I have also noticed some change in my eyes requiring more frequent adjustment of glasses. However, I hope I shall last for a few more years and certainly through my College appointment.

Little did he know that time was running out and that he had only another three months to live.

So the summer passed. There were functions to attend—both festive and grave. There was a dinner of the Cavendish Laboratory specially held in his honour to commemorate his 70th birthday—they are usually held at the end of the Michaelmas term. In a reminiscent mood he told how at the scholarship examination for St John's College he had to do a particular experiment and in traditional Cavendish manner was given a battery which was completely flat!

Appleton was so impressed with this brilliant discovery that I no doubt gained enough marks in the practical to offset my lack of knowledge in the written papers.

He spoke, too, of his appointment to the Jacksonian chair.

History may recall that the contributions of the Cavendish physicists in the war years were not inferior to our contributions made in physics in the prewar years.

Then there was the opening of the new Cripps building at St John's, reminding him of his endearing world as Junior Bursar years ago. The Royal Society Commonwealth Conference on developing countries was held in Oxford where he stayed the night in Merton College 'which was very cold'. As Master of Churchill he attended the memorial service to Lord Tedder who had died on 3 June, having been Chancellor of the University since 1951.

His mind was working hard, especially on how to halt the despoliation of the environment. In July Rabi called on him and told him about a conference the US State Department was planning for 1969, to be followed by another devoted to the problems arising out of nuclear power. Within a few days of Rabi's departure, Cockcroft had written a memorandum which went to U Thant, Secretary General of the United Nations, proposing a list of topics for discussion such as the pollution of rivers and oceans, desalinisation, pollution of the atmosphere by smoke and aircraft, the importance of ensuring global food supplies and fresh water. Earlier that year he had reminded the AEA that he had long suggested to Ralph Bunche of the United Nations the need for another Geneva conference on this subject but Penney told Cockcroft that it was the Government's view that several environmental conferences should take the place of conferences on the peaceful uses of atomic energy because of the 'tremendous commercial pressures engendered by the latter'.[29]

He had visited Harwell on the occasion of its twenty-first anniversary and given a suitable address, referring to its conception at a chance meeting with Chadwick and Oliphant at a Washington hotel in November 1943, when he was on the radar mission and they were about to resume collaboration with the Americans which had been made possible by the Quebec Agreement. After relating the history of the Establishment, illustrated by slides, he concluded:

> Harwell has therefore been a pioneering establishment in many fields and has established a reputation as one of the great International Laboratories of the world. I believe that its great scientific and technological strength and innovating spirit can continue to be used to promote our industrial strength not only in atomic energy but in other industrial fields[30]

a hope that after the initial stimulus had been expended was not fulfilled. It was a kind of 'farewell', for on 6 July he attended his last meeting as Member of the AEA at the Headquarters in Charles II Street. In a letter of thanks for his services the Minister of Technology, Anthony Wedgwood Benn, wrote

> No-one in Britain will ever forget your work as the creator of Harwell where so many of the ideas underlying the present nuclear programme were initiated and developed. Your outstanding work for the Authority will long be remembered, not least by the young scientists to whom you gave so much encouragement and advice.[31]

He would still have plenty to occupy his mind. In recent years he had revived his interest in the family business at Todmorden, and was diligent in attending Board meetings whenever he could.

> *The Observer* reports 30 cotton mills closed down owing to the credit squeeze [he wrote to his elder brother Eric managing the business in November 1966]. Are there any of these in the Todmorden area? [After his 70th birthday he wrote

to Leo] I think we should get some idea of the future organisation of John
Cockcroft & Sons,

suggesting that Eric should retire soon and hand over his responsibilities 'to
the young'.

He was planning further overseas tours. He had agreed to represent the
AEA at the Madame Curie centenary celebrations at Warsaw in October.
Following that, there was to be a visit to Iran, and for 1968 he had accepted
an invitation to return to Australia which he and Elizabeth intended to com-
bine with a visit to Uganda where they would stay with their daughter,
Catherine, and her husband. Abdus Salam, Director of the International
Centre for Theoretical Physics at Trieste, invited him to lecture on *Your Own
Life of Physics* and, as ever, invitations came in from the United States[32].

Politics, too, were claiming more of his time. Timothy Beaumont was then
one of the 'Party Managers' in the Liberal Party and required to propose
names for new appointments. Because of his connection with Churchill College and aware that Cockcroft was a Liberal, indeed he was at that time Vice-
President of the Cambridge City Liberal Association, Beaumont went to
Cambridge on 24 May to persuade him to stand for the Presidency[33].
Cockcroft agreed, making it clear that he would only be able to give limited
time to the Party because of his other commitments and because he was liable
to be abroad a good deal. At that time, Beaumont explained, 'the Presidency
of the Party was not a political appointment (as it is today) and was virtually
never contested. The Executive of the Party nominated an eminent Liberal
who was then elected!' So it happened and Cockcroft agreed to be present at
the Party Conference at Blackpool on 20 September.

It is difficult to visualise him in the hurly burly of the political arena. But
in addition to his Liberal principles, there was his concern about nuclear
disarmament and, as his old friend from the Mond days, W L Webster,
pointed out in a letter from Canada about the importance of helping developing countries: 'Perhaps the British Liberal Party is in as good a position as
any political group to bring debate down to earth'.[34]

On 31 August, after three weeks holiday at Cley, the Cockcrofts sailed from
Harwich (Elizabeth always disliked flying) for Sweden to attend the 17th
Pugwash Conference to be held at Rønneby. The theme was *Scientists and
World Affairs*. Cockcroft spoke of the control of the peaceful uses of atomic
energy and effectively dealt with a German complaint that the powers with
the capability of making nuclear weapons put those nations which were not
able to make bombs at a disadvantage because they could not receive
classified information. Cockcroft pointed out that details of most nuclear
plants were available in the technical press as soon as a nuclear power station
had begun to operate. What, in his opinion, was important was not the
inspection of reactors but the inspection of plutonium separation plants and
the distribution centres of highly-enriched uranium[35]. He felt that he had
made his point and on returning home wrote to Webster: 'The discussions
went quite well and we found ourselves in agreement with the Russians
and US on the non-proliferation treaty; the objections which were raised to
it were mainly by the Germans and Brazilians'.[36]

Until then, Bertrand Russell had been chairman of the Pugwash Continuing Committee but advancing years and other interests had prevented him from devoting much time to its affairs. There was a need for someone more active and who would at the same time command international respect. At the conference Cockcroft was Chairman of the Standing Committee on Future Organisation set up 'to consider and propose modifications in the organisation which would facilitate carrying out activities in the future'.[37] The conference now agreed to create the post of President, not only to preside over conferences but to offer advice to the organisation at other times. Cockcroft was unanimously elected the first President. He immediately announced his intention of endeavouring to raise funds in order to expand the activities of Pugwash.

Apart from this recognition of his unswerving belief in advancing the cause of disarmament, Cockcroft was delighted to meet a number of old friends like the Kapitzas, Perrin, Rabi, Peierls, Abdus Salam and Henry Seligman who was attending as an official observer from the IAEA. The right-hand rule of the road had just been introduced in Sweden and Rabi recalled dining with the Cockcrofts and watching with amusement the uncertain movements of the traffic[38].

On their return journey the Cockcrofts went to Risø to look at the Danish DIDO reactor—a Harwell child—and he discussed its future applications with the staff. Back at Churchill he prepared for his next engagement—the Liberal Party Conference. By a curious chance an unforeseen event engaged him in international relations for the last time. One of the many foreign postgraduates who enjoyed the friendly atmosphere of Churchill College was a young Russian scientist named Vladimir Tkachenko, a protégé of Kapitza's, who was interested in low temperature physics. He had been given leave of absence to continue his studies at Birmingham University and had been invited to spend a month at Churchill where he stayed in the Master's Lodge. Cockcroft liked this tense, rather introverted, but highly intelligent, young man and asked him to come back in the summer. In the meantime he had a letter from Kapitza asking whether it would be possible for Tkachenko's wife to join him in England as he had heard he was feeling lonely[39]. At Rønneby, Kapitza had enquired about Tkachenko and was glad to learn that permission had been granted for his wife to join him.

Just before the weekend of 16 September a young Russian woman arrived at Churchill and was received by Tkachenko who was staying in the college but whether she was his wife or not has never been resolved. Early on the Saturday morning the couple left for London. It appears that Tkachenko went to the Russian Embassy and it was said that he had asked to return home; he was told to come back in an hour's time. As he walked down the Bayswater Road two men in a car abducted him, but a bystander who witnessed the incident fortunately phoned the police. There had recently been several shocking cases of Russians in other countries being forced to return to their homeland. Special Branch officers rescued Tkachenko just before he was bundled into a Moscow-bound plane at London airport[40]. In a flash this created a minor international incident, particularly disturbing for scientists since (and much of this was due to Cockcroft) it would damage the agreement between the Royal

Society and the Russian Academy of Sciences whereby exchanges of scientists between the two countries became possible.

As it happened, it was all due to a misunderstanding[41]. Both British and Russian medical officers agreed that Tkachenko was suffering from a mental breakdown and he was allowed to go home. The British can hardly be blamed for taking immediate steps to stop an abduction; the Russian Ambassador knew perfectly well that his action in abducting anyone is illegal in Britain and he could easily have asked Tkachenko to visit him to discuss the matter, for Tkachenko was not seeking asylum in Britain, he had come to study physical problems. Cockcroft was, of course, inundated with telephone calls from the Police, the Foreign Office and the Press. He felt responsible for the young man who was a student of one of his oldest friends. As it was still the Long Vacation there were only two Fellows in College at the time besides himself—McQuillen, then Vice-Master, and Hey, who was packing his bags for an overseas visit[42]. Hey had already been questioned by a police officer about Tkachenko and recalled speaking to Cockcroft on the phone. From his room across the court he could see the Master seated at his desk by the large window. Cockcroft, in fact, was under the weather, suffering from one of his tiresome colds and had complained of pains in the chest. For this reason he had cancelled a plan to stay with his daughter, Jocelyn, at Sheffield, before going up to Blackpool for the party conference on the coming Wednesday and he had agreed to see a doctor as soon as possible.

Early on the morning of Monday 18 September Elizabeth awoke and realised he was not in bed. She went to the bathroom and found him on the floor. He had died from a heart attack. An autopsy showed that Sir John had had a heart condition earlier in life. He had fulfilled the family motto—*Fortis cadere, cadere non potest* (to die fighting strong and never to yield).

He was buried in St Giles cemetery, not far from the college, alongside his first son Timothy who had died so tragically almost 38 years earlier. All around, emerging from the rough grass, are the head stones marking the resting place of distinguished Cambridge scholars. The inscription on Cockcroft's head stone, mounted above the small curved stone on which the name 'Timothy' is carved, simply gives his principal honours and awards, his appointment as first Master of Churchill College and the dates of his birth and death. It concludes with the following line 'Whose Love was His Strength', composed in a moment of inspiration by his son, Christopher.

At the time of the funeral an important by-election was in full swing in Cambridge. As the cortege made its way to the cemetery a large yellow banner supporting the Liberal Party candidate, David Spreckley, could be seen in the windows of the Master's Lodge. It was Cockcroft's final, quietly defiant, gesture.

A Memorial Service was held in Westminster Abbey on 17 October, in which the psalm 'I will lift up mine eyes unto the hills; from whence cometh my help' reminded us of his love for the Yorkshire moors; the prayers of the Chaplain of Churchill College, the Rev Canon J N Duckworth reminded us of his greatest hope 'Atoms for Peace':

> our thanksgiving to Thee...for our friend and leader John Cockcroft who...
> following the truth where it led him and entering into the secrets of the universe

which Thou hast created... Save us from the perils of our own inventions and
continue to use the power of science not for our destruction... not for death, but
for life

followed by the Oration delivered by John's successor and friend Dr Spence.

We have come this morning to this historic Abbey Church to commemorate the
life of John Cockcroft, scientist, creator and administrator of great projects and
technological statesman whose career was so uniquely characteristic of our time.

There followed a resumé of those wonderful achievements concluding with

Foremost of the New Men, his life was conducted according to Christian principles which have been acclaimed here for centuries; dedication and service, love
of family and home, love for others. He earned the devotion of his colleagues
and the respect and affection of all who knew him; his memory will ever be fresh
in our hearts.

In a way his death helped to heal the wound to Anglo – Soviet scientific relations inflicted by the Tkachenko incident. Kapitza immediately sent a
telegram of condolence to McQuillen who was now acting head of the College
until a new Master was elected.

We had known each other for more than 40 years [continued Kapitza] Sir John
was a physicist of great insight, masterly technological gifts and a brilliant
organiser. With his quiet and charming ways he was a stubborn fighter for
progressive views not only in science but also in international affairs. We know
Sir John as a promoter of peace and international collaboration. It was my
privilege together with Sir John to bring closer the scientists of our two countries. I sincerely hope that this fine tradition will be followed by Churchill
College. Churchill College was the last great achievement to which Sir John
brought so much of his personality, thought and touching love and where he and
Lady Cockcroft with such tact lived up to their high position as first dwellers
in the Master's Lodge of Churchill College.[43]

EPILOGUE

Cockcroft led a full life. Scientist and man of action, he spanned what he liked to call the 'stone age' of nuclear physics and the new world of high-energy particle accelerators financed by governments. He was one of C P Snow's 'new men', familiar with the problems of the academic world, government laboratories, and the 'corridors of power', though he was never tempted by the rewards of the latter. Three strands run through his life, fundamental research, the direction of research establishments, and his enduring belief in the applications of nuclear energy for the good of mankind.

In fundamental research he made no original discovery like his contemporary Chadwick with the neutron. But, as another contemporary, Nevill Mott, said, he could do 'things that the physicists of his day who were trained in the string and sealing wax tradition could not do'. He and Walton, applying the novel quantum theory, solved before anyone else the problem of bombarding the atom with enough energy to change the nucleus. Cockcroft with his knowledge of engineering and mathematics proved that a suitable machine could be built. For that reason, as Ken Bainbridge wrote from America,

> if anyone deserved a Nobel Prize, he did. The Cockcroft–Walton experiments stimulated and induced the tremendous pace of nuclear physics development utilizing machine-produced agents to produce nuclear reactions.

Despite all the attempts to engage him in the formation of science policy, fundamental research remained his dominant interest from the Cavendish cyclotron of the late 1930s, to his insistence, after the war, that fundamental research as well as technological applications should be included in Harwell's programme, and eventually to the frequently delicate negotiations, in which he played a discreet but notable part, leading to the foundation of CERN and the Rutherford Laboratory. His associations with the pioneers of nuclear physics like Rutherford, Bohr, Joliot and Irène Curie, Lawrence and others, ensured that his pronouncements were heard with respect.

He could not remain aloof from events in the world outside the laboratory. Kapitza's detention in Russia left him to run the Mond. A little later, with the onset of war, he became the link between the universities and the defence departments recruiting talent from the former which helped to win the scientific war. It took him away from the 'olive grove of Academe', first into army radar and then to the first atomic energy research establishments at Chalk River and Harwell. The experience he gained in dealing with authority in the early days of the war convinced him that his teams of personally selected young scientists must be given freedom to do the things they wanted to do, just as later he shielded them, as Thonemann said, 'from the political scrimmage which raged unabated at Director level'. It was no accident that Harwell became a nest of talent, producing leaders like Adams, Cottrell, Finniston, Flowers, Pease†, Spence, Seligman, Taylor and others.

His encouragement of the young made possible the revival of physics in postwar Britain. As Adams wrote:

> for me and for many of my generation in England, he was the great patron who provided the conditions in which we grew in stature as scientists and engineers, and to him we owe our development. Without him we would, no doubt, have followed modest careers in government or industrial laboratories, but he pushed us to tackle jobs and projects which we never dreamt we could do or would ever have the opportunity to do and he sent us all over the world.

His portrait looked down on several of them as they worked in their offices in university or research establishments.

In later years, his interest in the young and his concern to remedy the deficiencies in scientific and technological education brought him back to his beloved Cambridge to be Master of the new Churchill College. Its building, like that of Chalk River, Harwell, or the restoration of St John's, was something to which he could not fail to respond, and the College was a place where, as Penney shrewdly observed, 'he did not have to do the things he should have done and did the things he liked doing'. In Canberra the new Australian National University was another place where he relished the not over-onerous duties of Chancellor.

His contribution to the beginnings of nuclear power in Britain is more difficult to assess. Again, as Penney noted, it is easy to start from nothing and design a reactor (and in Cockcroft's day the money was available), it is more difficult to decide on a particular system. Cockcroft worked in a time when reactor physics was limited to a handful of scientists who relied on hand-written notes for lack of text books. His optimism, necessary for research, was tempered with caution more than has been acknowledged. In years to come he may be given credit for his encouragement of thermonuclear research. Since his death the campaigns of the environmentalists and the anti-nuclear lobby, the arguments over the merits of reactor systems, have muddied over the original flow of enthusiasm. But no-one else could have had the assurance to run Harwell as he did. Without him, it would, to quote Thonemann again, 'have been a mundane place instead of a veritable crucible of ideas and development'. In the AEA he was immensely effective at getting things done. His silence and diffidence were totally illusory. His fervent belief in the breaking-down of the barriers of secrecy not only helped to restore Anglo–American scientific relations but, in a global context, was in a large way

---

†R S Pease who became Director of the Culham Laboratory.

responsible for the great international conferences at Geneva in the mid-1950s.

Finally, he must be judged as a man. Oliphant, a friend of 40 years standing, though by no means uncritical of his performance as a scientist, paid this tribute when he unveiled a memorial to Cockcroft in Todmorden town hall.

> His integrity was absolute. He was generous in word and deed, giving full credit to all with whom he worked and always ready to help a colleague in need. At all times he had the courage of his convictions and spoke up for what he believed to be right. His compassion led him to work against war, and for a solution to the problems of poverty and malnutrition in the world. His home life was exemplary—he was lucky in his choice of wife who was his companion in all things—and his love for his children was profound. These are less tangible qualities than his genius as a man of science and his greatness as a leader of men, but they made of John a whole man, in a sense which is rare, and they endeared him to all who knew him well. The only criticisms I ever heard of John were of his inability to compromise with truth in the interests of the establishments he led, or of individuals in them... His capacity for hard and continuous work was phenomenal, his tenacity of purpose enormous, his courage when things went wrong, outstanding. His sense of fair play was not gained on the playing fields of Eton, but was a trait as natural as his ability.
>
> John loved his country with a deep and abiding loyalty. He did not hide his feelings when he believed England to be in the wrong, or when politicians or businessmen failed to do what was necessary to enable her to retain and increase her greatness. But he worked indefatigably, both in public and behind the scenes, to help overcome her deficiencies in education, in industrial development and management, and in defence. In politics he was an old-fashioned liberal, seeking always the middle way of decency and fairness. If he was intolerant in any way it was of the inhumanity, the greed and self-seeking of both the extreme right and the extreme left. He never sought power, but when it came to him, he exercised it with wisdom and restraint. For many men, this would sound like a platitudinous panegyric from the pulpit, but for John Cockcroft it is all hard fact.

No biography of John Cockcroft would be complete without an appreciation of the constant support, encouragement and devotion he received from Elizabeth during their long life together.

In spite of the many problems of bearing and bringing up a family of five children and moving them around in war and peace following in father's footsteps, John's interests were always paramount.

From early married years in Cambridge to life in the Master's Lodge of Churchill College her gentle, kindly manner welcomed colleagues, scientists from near and far, VIPs and their wives to the hospitality of the family home. In the new settlements at Chalk River and in the early days at Harwell she was particularly helpful to the young wives and families. Although Harwell ultimately became a very large establishment Elizabeth continued her unflagging entertainment and many a party, and even Christmas romps, were held in the Cockcroft house for as many as it would hold. But as the numbers grew, the wives of the younger scientists admired her from afar—as one of them said recently : 'He was God and she was Goddess'.

Letters to and from Cockcroft and his family (JDC, EC, CC) belong to the private collection of the Cockcroft family. Papers dealing more strictly with his work, including his Cavendish notebooks and a miscellaneous collection of memoranda, letters, scientific papers, speeches, reviews, etc covering the Cavendish, Army radar, Chalk River, Harwell and Churchill College periods are held in the Churchill College Archive (CKFT). The Archive also has the Cavendish notebooks of Ernest Walton. A number of other sources have been used, including the files of the Cabinet Office (CAB), the Department of Scientific and Industrial Research (DSIR), the Ministry of Supply (AVIA), the War Office (WO), Tube Alloys, Chalk River and Harwell (AB), all of which are to be found in the Public Record Office (PRO) at Kew. The Harwell collection contains personal memoranda and correspondence on a wide range of topics. Also consulted were the Chadwick papers held by the UK Atomic Energy Authority; the Cherwell Papers held by Nuffield College, Oxford; files of the Royal Society; letters exchanged between Ernest Lawrence and Rutherford, Chadwick, Cockcroft and others held by the Bancroft Library, University of California, Berkeley, USA; the Rutherford papers in the Cambridge University Library; the files of the Royal Commission for the 1851 Exhibition; and files relating to the United Nations Scientific Advisory Committee and the International Atomic Energy Agency Scientific Advisory Committee held by the IAEA in Vienna.

Chapter 1—Boyhood in Todmorden
1 Savage E M *The Development of Todmorden from 1700 to 1896*. Todmorden Antiquarian Society. Birch R *A Way of Life Glimpses of Todmorden Past*.
2 Holt W *Looking at Life from Todmorden* Sept 1967.
3 Cockcroft Keith. The following pages are based on an account given to the Todmorden Antiquarian Society in 1976.
4 Holt W *Northern News Reel* 11 Aug 1945.
5 PRO/AB27/3. Quinn A to JDC, 15 July 1952.
6 JDC. 'Rutherford... Life and Work after the year 1919, with Personal Reminiscences of the Cambridge Period' Lecture to the *Physical Society* 1946.

Chapter 2—The Crucible of War
1 Inglefield V E *History of 20th (Light) Division* London 1921.
2 PRO/WO95/2105. War Diary of 92nd Bde, RFA, 1916–18.
3 Cruttwell C R M F *A History of the Great War 1914–18* p 40, Oxford 1964.
4 Inglefield V E *op cit.*
5 PRO/WO95/2105 *op cit*. Entry, 30 Nov 1917.

Chapter 3—Apprentice and Undergraduate
1 Royal Society Memoir. Miles Walker.
2 Dummelow J *Metropolitan – Vickers Electrical Co. Ltd 1899 – 1949.*
3 Royal Society Memoir. Miles Walker.
4 PRO/AB27/57. JDC. Toast of Old Associates, Manchester University Convocation and Manchester University Old Students' Association Dinner, 27 Jan 1957.
5 Royal Commission for 1851 Exhibition Files. Applications for Industrial Bursaries, 3 June 1920.
6 JDC to Royal Commission for 1851 Exhibition, 9 Jul 1921.
7 Fleming A P M to Royal Commission for 1851 Exhibition, 26 May 1921.
8 CKFT2/1. JDC's MSc Thesis, June 1921.
9 *Ibid.* Walker to JDC, 30 Aug 1921.
10 Royal Commission for 1851 Exhibition, JDC to Royal Commission, 24 May 1922.
11 CKFT20/1. JDC's correspondence with E Cunningham.
12 PRO/AB27/3. JDC to Albert Einstein, 26 Feb 1954.
13 JDC 'Rutherford... Life and Work' *op cit.*
14 *Ibid.*
15 Royal Society Biographical Memoir. John Douglas Cockcroft FRS, Vol 14 Nov 1968.

Chapter 4—Cavendish Research Student
1 PRO/DSIR3/21. Rutherford to Sir Frank Heath, 12 Mar 1924.
2 *Ibid.* Rutherford to Heath, 20 June 1924.
3 JDC. 'Rutherford...Life and Work' *op. cit.*
4 Boyce J C 'Some Recollections of J D Cockcroft', Communication to Guy Hartcup, 15 Apr 1979.
5 Boyce J C to Guy Hartcup, May 1980.
6 PRO/DSIR17/50. Rutherford to Secretary Research Board, DSIR, 26 Oct 1927.
7 PRO/DSIR3/22. Rutherford – Kapitza research in intense magnetic fields, March – Aug 1924.
8 PRO/DSIR3/24. Kapitza to Secretary Research Board, DSIR, 18 May 1925.
9 JDC. Review of 'The Collected Papers of Lord Rutherford', Vol III—The Cavendish Laboratory, 1965. *Contemporary Physics* vol 7 No 3 Feb 1966.
10 JDC, Ellis C D and Kershaw H 'A Permanent Magnet for Beta-ray Spectroscopy' *Proc. R. Soc* A **135** 628.
11 Crowther J G *Fifty years with Science* pp 94 – 5 London 1970.
12 CKFT2/2. Minute Book of Kapitza Club, 1925 – 33.
13 Royal Society Memoir. *op cit.*
14 CKFT2/2. JDC's *PhD Thesis* 'The condensation and reflection of molecules from surfaces' 1928.
15 Boyce J C to Guy Hartcup, 15 Apr 1979.
16 Rutherford Papers ADD7653 K7 Kapitza to Rutherford 11 Oct 1925.
17 *Ibid.* Kapitza to Rutherford 27 Apr 1927.
18 CKFT20/40. Rutherford to Kapitza 7 May 1927.
19 Milner C J Letter to *New Scientist* 2 Feb 1978.

Chapter 5—Artificial Disintegration of the Elements
1 Rutherford Sir E 'Scientific aspects of intense magnetic fields and high voltages' *Nature* Vol 120 3 Dec 1927.
2 Martin Sir L to Guy Hartcup 5 Dec 1980
3 McMillan E M 'Early History of Particle Accelerators' from *Nuclear Physics in Retrospect* ed R H Steuwer, University of Minnesota 1979. Appendix Walton to McMillan 11 April 1977.

4   *Ibid*. App. Walton to McMillan 11 April 1977.
5   CKFT20/80. JDC's Memorandum to Rutherford *The Probability of Artificial Disintegration by Protons* Dec 1928.
6   Allibone T E extract from unpublished autobiography.
7   Royal Commission for 1851 Exhibition. File on Ernest Walton.
8   CKFT20/80. JDC's note *The Development of high voltage experiments in Cambridge*.
9   Milner C J to Guy Hartcup 29 Oct 1979.
10 Walton Ernest to Guy Hartcup 29 Feb 1980
11 Clarke J to Guy Hartcup 17 Oct 1979
12 Rutherford Papers. ADD 7653/PA 138. Opening of High-Tension Laboratory, Metro–Vick 28 Feb 1930.
13 JDC and Walton. *Proc. R. Soc.* A **29** p44 1930.
14 McMillan E M *op cit*. Walton to McMillan 14 May 1977.
15 CKFT11/1 JDC's letters home from USSR Aug 1931.
16 Crowther J G *op cit*.
17 CKFT11/1. *op cit*.
18 Bowden Lord to Guy Hartcup 4 Oct 1979.
19 Clarke J to Guy Hartcup 7 Oct 1979.
20 JDC. 'Some Personal Recollections of Low Energy Physics' Rice University, USA, Feb 1963; 'Physics in the Thirties' *Aus. Inst. of Phys.* Vol 1 No 7 Oct 1964.
21 CKFT20/80. JDC to Karl Darrow 1937.
22 CKFT1/4. Walton to JDC 9 Dec 1937.
23 *Ibid*.
24 Oliphant Sir M *Rutherford. Recollections of the Cambridge Days* Netherlands, Elsevier 1972 chapter 6.
25 PRO/AB27/4. JDC to J A Gray (Ontario) 17 Feb 1959.
26 JDC and Walton. Letter to *Nature* **129** p649 30 Apr 1932.
27 Rutherford Lord 'The Transmutation of the Atom' *Listener* 18 Oct 1933.
28 Pocock R BBC portrait of Sir John Cockcroft 19 Sept 1968.
29 CKFT20/1. JDC to Crowther 3 May 1932.
30 MacCarthy D Review in *New Statesman* 'Wings over Europe' 7 May 1932.
31 CKFT27/1. G von Hevesy to JDC 9 May 1932.
32 Lawrence E O Papers. Bancroft Library, Berkeley University, USA 72/116/C, Carton 4, Folder 5 EOL to JDC 20 Aug 1932.
33 CC. Gamow G to JDC 7 Sept 1932.
34 CKFT20/10. JDC to Gamow 29 Sept 1932.
35 CC. Wertenstein L to JDC 3 May 1932.
36 CC. Physics Research Institute of Moscow to JDC 16 May 1932.
37 Weisskopf V 'Physics in the XXth Century' *Riv. Nuovo Cimento* **1** Numero Speciale 1969.

Chapter 6—The New Physics

1   Allibone T E Papers. Rutherford to Allibone May 1932.
2   Royal Society Memoir *op cit*.
3   CKFT20/4. Boyce to JDC 8 Jan 1933; CKFT20/80, JDC to A M Tyndale 1933— reasons for visit to USA.
4   Lawrence Papers *op cit*. Carton 4, Folder 5, EOL to JDC 2 June 1933.
5   Rutherford Papers. ADD7653 C57. JDC to Walton and P I Dee June 1933.
6   JDC. *Some Personal Recollections of Low Energy Nuclear Physics. op cit*. 1963.
7   *Ibid*.
8   *Ibid*.
9   Rutherford Papers *op cit*. JDC to Rutherford 22 July 1933.
10 *Ibid*. JDC to Rutherford 22 July 1933

11 CKFT11/3 JDC to his mother 16 June 1933.
12 Childs H 1968 *An American Genius. E.O. Lawrence* (New York: E P Dutton) chapter 8
13 Lawrence Papers *op cit*. JDC to EOL 28 Feb 1934.
14 *Ibid*. EOL to JDC 14 Mar 1934.
15 CKFT20/80. JDC to Merle Tuve 30 Apr 1934.
16 Lawrence Papers *op cit*. Rutherford to EOL 13 March 1934.
17 Rutherford Papers *op cit*. EOL to Rutherford 1934.
18 JDC. Rutherford Memorial Lecture *Proc. R. Soc.* **217** pp1–8 1953.
19 CKFT20/81. Boyce to JDC 11 Mar 1934.
20 CKFT8/8. Tuve and Hafstad *Phys. Rev.* 1 June 1934.
21 CKFT20/81. Hafstad to JDC 7 Sept 1934.
22 BBC Portrait of Sir John Cockcroft *op cit*. T E Allibone.
23 CKFT20/90. JDC to K T Bainbridge 14 Dec 1934.
24 Rutherford Papers. ADD7653/01. Oliphant to Rutherford 25 Aug 1935.
25 Peierls Sir R 'The growth of physics in Cockcroft's time' *Atom* **161** p54 Mar 1970.
26 CKFT4/5. JDC's speech at Cavendish Dinner Dec 1937
27 Lawrence Papers *op cit*. Carton 15. Folder 34, EOL to Rutherford 21 Mar 1936.
28 JDC. *Some Personal Recollections of Low Energy Nuclear Physics. op cit.*
29 Boyce J C *Some Recollections of J D Cockcroft. op cit.*
30 CKFT20/81. Bainbridge to JDC 12 Dec 1937.
31 CKFT20/81 JDC to Bainbridge 14 Dec 1934.

Chapter 7—The Mond and Fellow of St John's: War Clouds

1 PRO/DSIR17/52. Kapitza to Rutherford 4 Mar 1929; CKFT20/40. Kapitza to Rutherford 16 Apr 1930.
2 Clarke J to Guy Hartcup 17 Oct 1979.
3 CKFT20/43. Kapitza to Eric Gill and Niels Bohr 1932–34.
4 CKFT27/1. H C Hughes to JDC 3 May 1932.
5 *The Times* Statement by USSR Embassy 24 April 1935.
6 *The Times* Statement by Rutherford 24 April 1935.
7 PRO/DSIR11/53. Royal Society Mond Managing Committee Meeting 11 Oct 1935.
8 CKFT20/15. JDC's correspondence with Kapitza.
9 CKFT11/4. JDC's letters to his mother from USSR Sept 1936.
10 CKFT20/16. Kapitza to Nevill Mott July 1964.
11 CKFT20/31. E C Stoner to JDC 29 June 1935.
12 CKFT20/81. Bainbridge to JDC 24 Nov 1936.
13 Crook A C 1978 *Penrose to Cripps. passim* (Cambridge: Cambridge University Press)
14 Crook *op cit*.
15 CKFT20/15. Anna Kapitza to JDC 30 Mar 1939.
16 CC. Rutherford to JDC 27 Sept 1937.
17 CKFT11/3. JDC to his mother 21 Oct 1937.
18 CKFT20/81. JDC to Bainbridge 27 Dec 1937.
19 Crook *op cit*.
20 CKFT20/52. Ernest Lawrence to JDC 5 Oct 1938.
21 *Ibid*. JDC to Lawrence 24 Oct 1938.
22 CKFT20/52. JDC to Cooksey 21 Aug 1939.
23 Massey Sir H 'Atomic Energy and the Development of Large Teams and Organisations' *Proc. R. Soc.* A **342** p491 1975.
24 CKFT 20/15. Anna Kapitza to JDC 30 Mar 1939.
25 CKFT4/38. JDC's speech at Cavendish Dinner in honour of his 70th birthday 27 May 1967.

Chapter 8—A Roving Commission

1 PRP/AVIA12/189. JDC *General Account of Army Radar*, written for the Ministry of Supply July 1945 *passim*.
2 PRO/AVIA7/3269. ADEE to War Office 23 Oct 1939.
3 JDC 'Account of Army Radar' *Deep River Review* Oct 1946 (excerpt from reference 1 above).
4 CKFT20/14 JDC's correspondence with Joliot 1939–40.
5 Oliphant Sir M to Guy Hartcup 2 June 1980.
6 Lawrence Papers *op cit.* Carton 14, Folder 6, EOL to Oliphant 22 May 1940.
7 PRO/AIR2/71/93. Joubert to Gough 6 Jul 1940.
8 JDC Review of 'The Prof in Two Worlds' by Lord Birkenhead *Sunday Times* Nov 1961.
9 PRO/AVIA10/1. British Technical Mission to N America 1940.
10 Wilson Carroll L to Guy Hartcup 1 Sept 1980.
11 PRO/AVIA12/189. JDC *General Account of Army Radar. op cit.*
12 PRO/AVIA22/2286. JDC to Gough 30 Sept 1940.
13 Mackenzie C J to Guy Hartcup 20 June 1980.
14 PRO/AVIA10/2. JDC's report on visit to A L Loomis's Laboratory 3 Nov 1940.

Chapter 9—A Period of Frustration

1 CKFT27/6. Burton's congratulatory letter to JDC 10 June 1944.
2 CKFT20/81. JDC to Bainbridge 2 Jan 1941.
3 PRO/AVIA22/2308. J A Ratcliffe's history of beginnings of Army Operational Research Group.
4 CKFT25/15. Pile to JDC Jan 1948.
5 CKFT4/10. JDC *Science and the War Effort* lecture to Min of Supply Feb 1943.
6 PRO/AVIA7/3541. Dunworth's report on visit to N America Sept–Oct 1942.
7 Cherwell Papers G.327. papers on GL III.
8 PRO/AVIA22/1384. Meeting at British Thomson Houston 30 Sept 1943.
9 Cherwell Papers *op cit.*
10 PRO/AVIA22/1383. JDC to Paris 15 Sept 1943.
11 PRO/AVIA22/1388. JDC to Paris 12 Nov 1943.
12 PRO/AVIA12/179. JDC's *General Account of Army Radar. op cit.*
13 PRO/AVIA22/1388. JDC to Paris 26 Nov 1943.
14 PRO/CAB122/364. Deputy Chief of Imperial General Staff to Lt. Gen. G N Macready, British Army Staff 7 Jan 1944.
15 PRO/WO32/10911. Report on Flying Bomb Attacks 18 Jul 1944.
16 PRO/AVIA22/846. Special Fuse Production *passim*.
17 PRO/AVIA22/850. Paris to Director General Research and Development Ministry of Supply 7 Apr 1942.
18 CKFT3/13. JDC's Address to British Thomson Houston Summer School 1948.
19 PRO/AVIA22/82. Major Gen. Evetts to Paris 1 Jul 1943.
20 PRO/AVIA7/3536. JDC's Report on Radar Mission 28 Dec 1943.
21 PRO/CAB122/364. Lt. Gen. Macready to Admiral Sir Percy Noble British Admiralty Delegation, 16 Jan 1944.
22 PRO/AB27/2. JDC's mixed correspondence 1946–50.
23 PRO/AVIA12/189. JDC's *General Account of Army Radar. op cit.*
24 CKFT25/12. A V Hill to JDC 30 Oct 1942.
25 *Ibid.*
26 CKFT25/12. JDC's ADRDE correspondence.
27 CKFT20/4. Black to JDC 21 Feb 1945.
28 PRO/AVIA21/189. JDC's *General Account of Army Radar. op cit.*
29 CKFT20/84. JDC to Scientific Press Dept USSR Embassy 12 Oct 1941.

30 CKFT25/12. Kapitza to JDC 9 Feb 1943.
31 PRO/AVIA7/2796. JDC to Webster 12 Aug 1941.
32 *Ibid.* JDC to Webster letters May 1942.
33 PRO/AVIA10/65. Minutes of Anglo–US meetings in Washington 22 Nov–11 Dec 1943.
34 PRO/AVIA7/2253 and PRO/AVIA7/3536. JDC's report to Duncan Sandys 8 Dec 1943.
35 PRO/AB1/113. Perrin M W to Chadwick 24 Feb 1944.
36 CKFT27/6. Bedford L H to JDC 12 June 1944.
37 PRO/AB6/674. JDC's views on being ADSR in Ministry of Supply to Sir A Rowlands 28 Mar 1949.
38 Zuckerman Solly 1978 *From Apes to Warlords* (London: Hamish Hamilton) p362.
39 CKFT4/10. Gough to JDC 21 Jan 1943.
40 CKFT20/9. Ratcliffe to JDC 1945.
41 CKFT20/30. Schonland to JDC Sept 1944.

Chapter 10—Beginnings of Atomic Energy in England and Canada

1 CKFT25/17. JDC to Tizard 31 May 1939.
2 CKFT10/1. Meitner to Sir O W Richardson 15 May 1940.
3 CKFT4/33A. JDC to Royal Scottish Museum and Glasgow Institute of Physics and Physics Society 17–18 Mar 1966.
4 Kemmer N to Guy Hartcup Oct 1980.
5 CKFT25/27. Chadwick to JDC 19 June 1960.
6 PRO/AB1/210. JDC on post-MAUD Committee period.
7 Laurence G C 'Early Years of Nuclear Energy Research in Canada', Personal account, not dated.
8 *Ibid.*
9 Chadwick Papers. Folder 7 1939–43. JDC to Chadwick 24 Oct 1943.
10 PRO/AB1/129. Anglo–US relations 1943–44. Halban to Chadwick 9 Feb 1944.
11 PRO/AB1/278. JDC to Appleton 8 May 1944; JDC. 'The Early Days of the Canadian and British Atomic Energy Projects' IAEA Special No 2 Dec 1962.
12 Seligman H to Guy Hartcup 17 May 1979.
13 PRO/AB1/113. JDC's request for Dee 13 May 1944.
14 Kemmer N to Guy Hartcup 3 Oct 1980.
15 CKFT6/7. JDC's review of *Niels Bohr: The Man and the Scientist* by Ruth Moore *Sunday Telegraph* Sept 1967.
16 Butler G C to Guy Hartcup 22 May 1980.
17 PRO/AB1/278. JDC to Appleton 10 Oct 1944.
18 Goldschmidt B to Guy Hartcup 29 May 1979.
19 Steiner G to Guy Hartcup 10 Jan 1980; Hyde M *The Atom Bomb Spies* (London: Hamish Hamilton) 1980.
20 CKFT3/33A. JDC to Royal Scottish Museum *op cit.*
21 Kemmer N to Guy Hartcup Oct 1980; PRO/AB16/52. Atomic Scientists Association 16 Mar 1948.
22 Milford C to T E Allibone Mar 1983.

Chapter 11—'England has need of you'

1 CKFT25/8. JDC's draft autobiography 1967.
2 CKFT25/7. Tube Alloys Consultative Council Meeting 6 April 1945.
3 Gowing M and Arnold L 1974 *Independence and Deterrence* (London: Macmillan) Vol 1 pp38–9.
4 CKFT25/27. Oliphant to JDC 14 Sept 1945.
5 CKFT25/8. JDC's autobiography *op cit.*

6   CKFT25/20. Memo from Dunworth *et al* to Chadwick 30 Aug 1945.
7   CKFT25/20. Memo from British scientists in Canada to JDC 27 Dec 1945.
8   CKFT20/7. Dee to JDC 26 Jul 1945.
9   PRO/AB27/3. Exchange of letters between JDC and Anderson 17 Sept-31 Oct 1945.
10 CKFT25/8. JDC's autobiography *op cit.*
11 PRO/AB27/1. JDC to Franks 23 Nov 1945.
12 JDC 'Expectations from Science' *New Scientist* 4 Nov 1965.
13 How Sir F to Guy Hartcup 27 Aug and 30 Sept 1980.
14 Penney Lord to Guy Hartcup 14 Oct 1980; PRO/AB27/8. JDC to Plowden 3 Aug 1956.
15 CKFT25/8. JDC's autobiography *op cit.*
16 Gowing M *Independence and Deterrence. op cit.* (London: Macmillan) Vol 1 p42.
17 How Sir F to Guy Hartcup 30 Sept 1980.
18 CKFT25/8. JDC's autobiography *op cit.*
19 PRO/PREM8/367. MacDonald to Halifax 27 Mar 1946.
20 Willson D to Guy Hartcup Aug 1982.
21 Amphlett C B to Guy Hartcup 21 Oct 1980.
22 CKFT4/13. JDC's speech on receiving Freedom of Todmorden Oct 1946.
23 PRO/AB27/2. JDC to MacKenzie 29 Oct 1946.
24 Penney Lord 'Sir John Cockcroft' *Nature* Vol 216 11 Nov 1967.
25 JDC (ed) 1965 *The Organisation of Research Establishments* Introduction (Cambridge: Cambridge University Press)
26 Allen J F to Guy Hartcup 22 Dec 1980.
27 Amphlett C B to Guy Hartcup 21 Oct 1980.
28 How Sir F to Guy Hartcup *op cit.*
29 Cottrell Sir A to Guy Hartcup 21 Oct 1980.
30 CKFT20/82. Spence to JDC 14 Jan 1953.
31 McMillan E M to Guy Hartcup.
32 Royal Society Memoir of Robert Spence.
33 Seligman H to Guy Hartcup.
34 CKFT25/27. JDC to Ministry of Works men Jan 1947.
35 CKFT25/8. JDC's autobiography *op cit.*
36 Lawrence Papers Carton 2, Folder 8, Pickavance to EOL 4 Oct 1947.
37 CKFT25/8. JDC's autobiography *op cit.*
38 Willson D to Guy Hartcup Aug 1982.
39 PRO/AB27/8. Glyn to JDC undated.

Chapter 12—Successes and Disappointments

1   PRO/AB16/389. British Atomic Energy Programme.
2   *Picture Post* 7 Dec 1946.
3   JDC 'Early Experiments: Atomic Energy: a symposium by experts' *The Listener* 13 Mar 1947.
4   PRO/AB16/419. Chatham House Atomic Energy Study Group 1946–7.
5   Cherwell Papers K79, JDC to Cherwell 6 Jan 1948.
6   PRO/AB27/1. JDC to Rowlands 25 Feb 1949; PRO/AB6/144. JDC to Tizard 1949.
7   CKFT3/14. JDC General lecture on atomic energy, University of Witwatersrand, Johannesburg 23 Aug 1949.
8   Richards D 1977 *Portal of Hungerford* (London: Heinemann) pp349–70.
9   PRO/AB27/8. Oliphant to JDC 6 Feb 1950.
10 PRO/AB27/8. Dee to JDC 15 Mar 1950.
11 PRO/AB27/8. Wilson to JDC 3 Mar 1950.

12 JDC *The development and future of atomic energy* Romanes Lecture Oxford 2 June 1950.
13 JDC. *Pure Science* a lecture delivered in Oxford 9 Aug 1951, published in *Atomic Scientists News* Nov 1951.
14 PRO/AB6/77. JDC. *Organisation of atomic energy work in Britain* 18 May 1951.
15 Gowing *Independence and Deterrence. op cit.* Vol 2 chapter 22 p401 (London: Macmillan).
16 PRO/AB27/2. JDC to W Davies 7 Aug 1947.
17 Lawrence Papers. Carton 4, Folder 6, EOL to JDC 31 Jul 1951.
18 PRO/AB27/3. Willson to JDC 4 Apr 1951.
19 Willson D to Guy Hartcup Aug 1982.
20 CKFT27/9. Nobel Prize citation Nov 1951.
21 CKFT3/2. JDC's Nobel Prize lecture.
22 Statutes of St John's College Cambridge.
23 PRO/AB27/7. Morgan to JDC 9 Apr 1952.

Chapter 13—Policy-making in Whitehall

1 Tizard Sir H to Select Committee on Estimates 1946.
2 Tizard Papers (HTT467). JDC to Tizard 18 Dec 1949.
3 *Ibid.* Tizard to JDC 18 Jan 1950.
4 *Ibid.* JDC to Tizard 26 May 1951.
5 PRO/AB16/1789. JDC to Portal 9 May 1951.
6 PRO/AB27/8. Ministry of Defence to JDC 31 July 1951.
7 PRO/AB27/8. JDC to Macfarlane (Ministry of Supply) 12 Nov 1951.
8 PRO/AB16/178. Similar letter from JDC to Morgan 20 Mar 1952.
9 Chapman Pincher to Guy Hartcup 17 Sept 1981.
10 Cockburn Sir R *Science, Defence and Society* Truman Wood Lecture to Royal Society of Arts 15 Mar 1967.
11 PRO/AB27/8. Oliphant to JDC 16 Jan 1950.
12 CKFT14/1. Transcript of ad-lib disc. *This Technological Age* 10 Nov 1952.
13 Willson D to Guy Hartcup Aug 1982.
14 Cockburn Sir R BBC 'Portrait of Sir John Cockcroft' *op cit.*
15 Cook Sir W to Guy Hartcup 28 Oct 1979.
16 JDC. Review of Ronald Clark's 'Tizard' *Cambridge Review* 1965.
17 CKFT4/30. JDC *Scientists and Government* Leeds University 8 Feb 1963.
18 Todd Lord to Guy Hartcup 18 Nov 1980.
19 PRO/AB27/11. JDC to Todd 6 May 1952.
20 CKFT4/30. JDC *Scientists and Government. op cit.*
21 Royal Society Memoir *op cit.*
22 CKFT3/13. JDC to British Thomson Houston Summer School *The Need for Technical and Scientific Staff* 1948.
23 PRO/AB27/11. Royal Society Discussion on *Technology in Universities* 29 Jan 1952.
24 *Ibid.*
25 Mitchell J S to Guy Hartcup 29 Apr 1980.
26 CKFT4/30. JDC *Scientists and Government. op cit.*
27 Zuckerman Lord *Scientific Advice during and since World War II. Proc. R. Soc.* A 342–456 1975.
28 CKFT17/5. Royal Society Evidence of Fellows to Trend Committee Oct 1962.
29 CKFT17/9. Sir Winston Churchill to JDC 12 Nov 1961.
30 *Ibid.* JDC to Sir Winston Churchill 16 Nov 1961
31 CKFT17/1. JDC Evidence given to Committee on Higher Education (Robbins) Oct–Nov 1961.

Chapter 14—'Putting Nuclear Power on the map'

1 CKFT25/8. JDC's autobiography *op cit.*
2 *Ibid.*
3 *Ibid.*
4 *Ibid.*
5 PRO/AB6/339. JDC Memorandum 3 Sept 1948.
6 PRO/AB6/513. JDC to Woodward 10 Nov 1948.
7 PRO/AB6/513. JDC to M W Perrin 16 Oct 1948.
8 PRO/AB6/339. JDC *UK nuclear power reactor programme* 22 Nov 1949.
9 CKFT25/8. JDC's autobiography *op cit.*
10 *Ibid.*
11 *Ibid.*
12 Willson D to Guy Hartcup Aug 1982.
13 Gowing *Independence and Deterrence. op cit* Vol 2 p288 (London: Macmillan).
14 *Ibid.*
15 CKFT25/8. JDC's autobiography *op cit.*
16 *Proc IEE* **100** Pt I No 123 May 1953.
17 CKFT25/8. JDC's autobiography *op cit.*
18 Gowing M *Independence and Deterrence* Vol 2 p292 (London: Macmillan).
19 Willson D to Guy Hartcup Aug 1982.
20 CKFT25/8. JDC's autobiography *op cit.*
21 PRO/AB27/13. Comments on *The future development of the UK nuclear power programme* by Hinton and given to the Institution of Civil Engineers Aug 1958.
22 CKFT25/8. JDC's autobiography *op cit.*
23 *Ibid.*
24 PRO/AB27/24. JDC to Appleton 11 Apr 1956.
25 Mott Sir N Appreciation of Sir John Cockcroft *Varsity* 14 Oct 1967.
26 CKFT20/86. JDC to Ed *Technology of Youth* Moscow 22 Feb 1967.

Chapter 15—Member of the Atomic Energy Authority

1 CKFT20/31. Skinner to JDC 4 Mar 1951.
2 PRO/AB6/77. JDC's memo *Organisation of atomic energy work in Britain* May 1951.
3 Chapman Pincher 'Why Britain has no atom' *Daily Express* 7 July 1951.
4 JDC to Parliamentary Select Committee on Estimates 19 Feb 1947.
5 Willson D to Guy Hartcup Aug 1982.
6 JDC to Parliamentary Select Committee on Estimates 7 May 1952.
7 Birkenhead Lord 1961 *The Prof in Two Worlds* (London: Collins) p31.
8 CKFT20/28. Lady Rutherford to JDC 1 Jul 1953.
9 CKFT27/10. M W Perrin to JDC 1 June 1953.
10 Hinton Sir C *Atomic Energy Developments in Great Britain* lecture given to American Atomic Energy Forum, New York 31 Oct 1953.
11 Plowden Lord to Guy Hartcup 18 May 1980.
12 Penney Lord to Guy Hartcup 14 Oct 1980.
13 PRO/AB16/1789. JDC to Morgan 23 Nov 1951.
14 Willson D to Guy Hartcup Aug 1982.
15 CKFT20/27. Plowden to JDC 23 Dec 1954.
16 Cmd 9389. *A Programme of Nuclear Power* Feb 1955.
17 CKFT20/25. Oliphant Sir M to JDC 4 Sept 1956.
18 Oliphant Sir M to Guy Hartcup 2 June 1980.
19 Plowden Lord to Guy Hartcup 18 May 1980.
20 AERE11/Staff/13. JDC's memo to Heads of Divisions.
21 CKFT25/8. JDC's autobiography *op cit.*

22 Spence R. Twenty-one years at Harwell *Nature* **314** 22 Apr 1967.
23 AERE11/Staff/13 *op cit.*
24 CKFT4/36. JDC's address to Weymouth School 29 Oct 1965.
25 Willson D to Guy Hartcup Aug 1982.
26 CKFT18/24. Golovin Igor 1976 *Life of I V Kurchatov* (Leipzig: Urania Verlag).
27 AERE11/OC/2 JDC's record of discussion with Kurchatov 25 Apr 1956; CKFT18/23A. JDC's papers on controlled thermonuclear research.
28 Thonemann P to Guy Hartcup 4 Dec 1980; R M Heckstall-Smith 'The ZETA Episode—A study of the interface relations between science and society', an unpublished BSc thesis (Social Sciences) submitted to South Bank Polytechnic 1975.
29 JDC. 'The next stages with ZETA' *New Scientist* 30 Jan 1958.
30 *Ibid.*
31 AERE11/OC/2. DM253. JDC to EOL 4 Nov 1955.
32 Runcorn S K (ed) 1963 *Physics in the 1960s* JDC. *Controlled Thermonuclear Research* (Edinburgh: Oliver and Boyd).
33 Cherwell Papers. D250. JDC to Cherwell *Review of High Energy Project* 20 Jan 1955. CKFT25/24. JDC *Notes The origins and early history of NIRNS.*
34 Science Research Council. *Nimrod. The 7GeV proton synchrotron* p14, 1979.
35 *Ibid.* p19.
36 *Ibid.* p33.
37 PRO/AB27/56. JDC. *Biological implications of atomic energy* address to Postgraduates Medical Federation, London University 11 Oct 1956.
38 Lawrence Papers. Carton 37. JDC to EOL 2 Nov 1957.
39 AB6/76. Liaison with Risley. JDC to Hinton 5 April 1949.
40 Lawrence Papers Carton 37 *op cit.*
41 Arnold L *The Accident at Windscale in October 1957.* Lecture at Leeds University Workshop 12 June 1979.
42 *Ibid.*
43 PRO/AB27/4. A B Jones Speech at Cockcroft presentation 3 Feb 1957.
44 CKFT17/4. J V Dunworth AERE Organisation, paper given to conference on training of scientists for industry 1957.
45 JDC. Prize-giving speech, Gresham's School summer 1958, reported in *The Gresham.*
46 PRO/AB27/8. JDC *Human Relations in Research Establishments* 30 Jan 1951.
47 CKFT20/79. Bragg to JDC 14 Feb 1951.
48 JDC (ed) *The Organisation of Research Establishments. op cit.* F A Vick on AERE Harwell.
49 *The Observer* Profile of Sir John Cockcroft 9 Dec 1951.
50 CKFT27/9 Sir R Glyn to JDC 15 Nov 1951.
51 CKFT27/13. Lord Glyn to JDC 30 Jan 1959.
52 Betjeman J and Piper J 1949 *Berkshire Architectural Guide* (London: Murray) p128.
53 CKFT27/11. Betjeman to JDC 1 Jan 1957.
54 CKFT11/17. File on JDC's visits to N America 1946–55.
55 CKFT13/18. JDC's speech to Prior Court School 24 June 1950.
56 Bretscher H to Guy Hartcup 25 Apr 1980.

Chapter 16—Scientist/Diplomat

1 Rowlands Sir A to Parliamentary Select Committee on Estimates 19 Feb 1947.
2 *Robert Oppenheimer, Letters and Recollections* ed by Alice Kimball Smith and Charles Weiner. Speech to the Association of Los Alamos Scientists 2 Nov 1945.
3 CKFT25/8. JDC's autobiography *op cit.*
4 Lawrence Papers Carton 4, Folder 5, EOL to JDC 10 June 1946.

5 *Ibid.* EOL's secretary to JDC 17 Aug 1946.
6 *Ibid.* JDC to EOL 25 Aug 1946.
7 *Ibid.* EOL to JDC 30 Aug 1946.
8 PRO/AB16/388. Co-ordination of Anglo–US effort. JDC's report of discussion with Carroll Wilson, 10 May 1947.
9 CKFT25/8. JDC's autobiography *op cit.*
10 Gowing M *Independence and Deterrence* Vol 1 *op cit.* (London: Macmillan) Chap 8.
11 Lilienthal David E *Journals* 1964 Vol II *The Atomic Energy Years* 1945–50 (New York: Harper and Row) p385.
12 CKFT25/8. JDC's autobiography *op cit.*
13 Lawrence Papers Carton 4, Folder 6. Brode to EOL 3 June 1949.
14 CKFT3/80. JDC *The process of technological innovation* lecture given to the Engineering Institutions, Southern Branch 25 Feb 1965.
15 Dirac P A M 'Is there an Aether?' *Nature*, Vol 168 24 Nov 1951.
16 Gowing M *Independence and Deterrence* Vol 1 *op cit.* (London: Macmillan) pp415–6.
17 PRO/AB27/3. Makins to JDC 10 Jan 1953.
18 Royal Society Memoir *op cit.*
19 PRO/AB16/388, *op cit.* D E H Peirson to Longair (British Embassy Washington) 12 Feb 1948.
20 JDC 1964 Review of 'Nuclear Secrecy and Foreign Policy' by Harold L Nieburg Washington in *Disarmament and Arms Control* Vol 2 No 4 (London: Pergamon) pp454–6.
21 Wilson Carroll to Guy Hartcup 1 Sept 1980.
22 Sherfield Lord to Guy Hartcup 2 Nov 1982.

Chapter 17—International Scientist

1 Goldschmidt B 'The Origins of the International Atomic Energy Agency' *IAEA Bull.* 20th anniversary, Vol 19, No 14 Aug 1977
2 PRO/AB27/46 European Atomic Energy Society papers 15 June 1954.
3 AERE/11/EAES/6. Goldschmidt to JDC 19 Dec 1956.
4 Bernstein J 1978. *Experiencing Science* chapter 2 Rabi I 'The Modern Age' (New York: E P Dutton) p120.
5 AERE/11/Conf/78. International Conference on peaceful uses of atomic energy 1955. Rabi's meeting with British nuclear physicists in Cambridge 24 Aug 1954.
6 *Ibid.*
7 CKFT4/30. JDC *The United Nations and Atomic Energy* Hammerskjöld Memorial Lecture 26 Nov 1963.
8 CKFT4/22. JDC Address at opening of Calder College of Further Education 17 September 1955.
9 CKFT27/11. Richard Foot to JDC 1 Jan 1957.
10 CKFT4/30 JDC *The United Nations and Atomic Energy. op cit.*
11 *Daily Worker* 'Profile of Sir John Cockcroft' 13 Aug 1955.
12 JDC *Peaceful Uses of Atomic Energy*—2nd Geneva Conference 12 Sept 1958.
13 IAEA Scientific Advisory Committee File 24 Feb 1958–10 Aug 1960. Plowden to Cole, 20 Oct 1958.
14 IAEA/SC/110-1 SAC. JDC to Cole 27 Mar 1961.
15 *Ibid.* Seligman to JDC 4 Apr 1961.
16 JDC. *The impact of atomic energy on society* 10th regular session of the General Conference Vienna 23 Sept 1966.
17 CKFT17/14. JDC to Rabi 23 June 1967.
18 PRO/AB27/35. Thonemann to JDC 6 Oct 1958.
19 Popović Mary S to Guy Hartcup 21 June 1979.
20 CKFT4/30. JDC *Scientists and Government. op cit.*

21 CKFT17/4. NATO Study Group Rome 14 Sept 1959.
22 Chadwick Papers Box 1/2. JDC to Auger 24 Oct 1951.
23 Royal Society File. British Committee for cooperation with UNESCO in natural sciences 16 Nov 1951.
24 Chadwick papers *op cit*. Box 26/1, R A Butler to Sir David Brunt, Secretary of Royal Society 25 Nov 1952.
25 Fry D W to Guy Hartcup 5 Dec 1980.
26 Chadwick Papers *op cit*. JDC's report on CERN meeting at Brussels 27 Jan 1953.
27 AERE11/CERN3B. CERN Science Policy Committee. Bakker to JDC 10 Feb 1959.
28 Adams Sir J to Guy Hartcup; Kowarski L *An account of the origin and beginning of CERN* CERN 61-10 10 April 1961.
29 CKFT18/20. Willems *et al* to JDC 1 Jul 1963.
30 Adams Sir J to Guy Hartcup *op cit*.
31 CKFT23/9. Sir Michael Adeane to JDC Dec 1957.
32 PRO/AB6/398. Relations with India. JDC to Bhabha 8 Jan 1957.
33 CKFT27/12. Trevelyan to JDC 4 Jan 1957.
34 *Ibid*. Tizard to JDC 1 Jan 1957.
35 CKFT27/11. Mrs E Atherton to JDC 1 Jan 1957.
36 PRO/AB27/27. JDC's visit to Copenhagen to receive Niels Bohr Gold Medal 4–8 Oct 1958.
37 CKFT22/47. JDC receives Atoms for Peace Award April 1961.
38 Steiner G to Guy Hartcup 10 Jan 1980.

Chapter 18—First Master of Churchill College

1   CKFT13/1. Bowden to JDC 9 Jul 1956.
2   Churchill Winston S Address to MIT 31 Mar 1949.
3   Cherwell Papers E97. Colville to Sir Winston Churchill and Lord Cherwell Apr 1956–Apr 1957.
4   CKFT12/78. Churchill College historical file.
5   Tillyard E M W as reported in *The Observer* 8 June 1958.
6   Cambridge University Reporter. Council of the Senate's notice 14 May 1958.
7   *Ibid*. 22 Jan 1959.
8   CKFT12/78. Churchill College history file *op cit*.
9   *The Times* 27 Jan 1959.
10 CKFT27/13. Cunningham to JDC 22 Jan 1959.
11 CKFT12/27. Churchill College architects' competition.
12 Hamilton Maj. Gen. J R C *Personal Narrative of Building of Churchill College*, unpublished.
13 CKFT12/78. Churchill College History file *op cit*. Sir W Churchill's speech 17 Oct 1959.
14 Jones R V Royal Society Memoir of Sir Winston Churchill.
15 Steiner G 'Sir John Cockcroft' *Varsity*. *op cit*. 14 Oct 1967.
16 JDC 1964 'Churchill College—A Modern University College', *Science* **146** No 3643 pp502–4.
17 Joyce D BBC 'Portrait of Sir John Cockcroft' *op cit*.
18 Duckworth Canon N to Guy Hartcup 21 May 1980.
19 CKFT4/32. JDC in BBC radio interview—'Let's find out' 6 June 1966.
20 Cambridge University Reporter *op cit*. 18 Nov 1958.
21 CKFT12/48. JDC Draft instruction to architect on use of a chapel (undated).
22 *Ibid*. Beaumont to JDC 4 Jan 1962.
23 *Ibid*. Duckworth Canon N to JDC 23 Feb 1965.
24 Duckworth Canon N to Guy Hartcup 21 May 1980.

25 Duckworth Canon N to Guy Hartcup 24 Apr 1980.
26 Steiner G to Guy Hartcup 10 Jan 1980.
27 HRH The Duke of Edinburgh's and JDC's speeches at opening of Churchill College 5 June 1964.
28 CKFT12/78. Churchill College history file *op cit.*
29 JDC 'Sir Winston Churchill' *Nature* 30 Jan 1965.
30 CKFT20/17. Kapitza to JDC 6 Aug 1966.
31 CKFT20/86. Morrison to JDC 28 Apr 1965.
32 McQuillen K BBC 'Portrait of Sir John Cockcroft' *op cit.*
33 Hey R Conversations with Guy Hartcup 1979–80.
34 Tizard R BBC 'Portrait of Sir John Cockcroft' *op cit.*
35 Hamilton Maj. Gen. J R C to Guy Hartcup 22 June 1980.
36 Morrison J BBC 'Portrait of Sir John Cockcroft' *op cit.*
37 Boyce J C 'Some Recollections of J D Cockcroft', communication to Guy Hartcup *op cit.*
38 CKFT14/3. JDC to Marsden 14 Mar 1967.

Chapter 19—Commonwealth Adviser

1 PRO/AB6/398. Relations with India. JDC and Bhabha correspondence Nov 1947–Jan 1957.
2 CKFT14/2. Oliphant to JDC 22 Mar 1961.
3 JDC. Address at his Installation as Chancellor at Australian National University 11 Apr 1962.
4 Huxley Sir L to Guy Hartcup 11 Feb 1980.
5 CKFT14/4. JDC at Presentation of Degrees at Australian National University 11 Apr 1962.
6 Huxley Sir L to Guy Hartcup *op cit.*
7 Blackett Lord *Science and technology in an unequal world* (First Nehru Memorial Lecture) 13 Nov 1967. A Copisarow to Guy Hartcup 14 Sept 1981.
8 CKFT20/55. Blackett to JDC 30 Mar 1965.
9 JDC *Technology for developing countries* Overseas Development Institute 26 Jan 1966.
10 CKFT16/1. Nigeria Conference Aug 1965.
11 Quartey J A K to Guy Hartcup 19 Jan 1981.
12 CKFT15/1. JDC's visit to Ghana 15 Oct and 9 Dec 1966; CKFT15/2. Correspondence on Ghana reactor.
13 CKFT15/9. Ghana Academy of Sciences—background papers; CKFT15/15. Ghana Academy of Sciences—Report of Committee of Experts Dec 1966.

Chapter 20—Man of Peace

1 PRO/AB27/6. Atomic Scientists Association—policy and correspondence. JDC to Lonsdale 13 June 1957.
2 Milford C to T E Allibone Mar 1983.
3 Jacobson H K and Stein E *Diplomatists, Scientists and Politicians* (Ann Arbor, Michigan: University of Michigan Press) 1966. An American view of negotiations leading to the partial test ban treaty.
4 CKFT4/31. JDC *Scientists and World Affairs.* National Liberal Club 29 Jan 1966.
5 Zuckerman Lord to Guy Hartcup 26 Mar 1981.
6 JDC and Sir W Penney *Problems of the cessation of fissile material for military purposes and the elimination of weapons and stockpiles.* Proc 8th Int Conf on Science and World Affairs Vermont Sept 1961.
7 Howard M to Guy Hartcup 27 Oct 1979.

8   CKFT18/17. Sir E Bullard and JDC. *Problems of reduction and elimination under international control of weapons of mass destruction and their means of delivery* 9th Pugwash Conf on Science and World Affairs, Cambridge, England Aug 1962.
9   CKFT4/31. JDC *Scientists and World Affairs. op cit.*
10 JDC Presidential Address to Brit Association *Nature* 1 Sept 1962.
11 CKFT18/2. JDC *The Nuclear Test Ban* 11th Pugwash Conf Dubrovnik Sept 1963.
12 CKFT4/29. JDC *Problems of Disarmament* California Institute of Technology 1 May 1962.
13 Zuckerman Lord to Guy Hartcup 26 Mar 1981.
14 CKFT18/1. Chalfont to JDC 29 Dec 1964.
15 *The Times* 'Seeking settlement in Vietnam' R F Kahn J D Boyd J D Cockcroft *et al* 23 Feb 1965.
16 CKFT18/1. Chalfont to JDC 6 Jul 1966.
17 *Ibid.* JDC to Zuckerman 28 Nov 1966.
18 Zuckerman Sir S *Technological Aspects of Proliferation* Institute of Strategic Studies, Adelphi Paper No 29 Oct 1966.
19 Powell C and Butler A 1980 *The Parliamentary and Scientific Committee. The First Forty Years* (London: Honor Croome Press) see JDC's 4 speeches 1951–58.
20 CKFT20/86. JDC to Oliphant 16 Oct 1964.
21 CKFT28/5. Liberal Party Research and Development Committee. Chain's letter 19 Mar 1965.
22 CKFT28/1. Liberal Party general correspondence JDC to Stuart Blume University of Sussex, 1966.
23 CKFT28/1. Election to Vice President Liberal Party 27 June 1966.
24 CKFT20/53. Inter-American Development Bank 1967.
25 CKFT11/20. JDC Address to Los Angeles World Affairs Council 30 March 1967.
26 CKFT11/21. JDC *The Technology Gap* Speech to Pattenmakers Company dinner Mansion House Feb 1967.
27 CKFT6/6. JDC *A transatlantic view of what knowledge is worth having* University of Chicago Liberal Arts Conference Feb 1966.
28 CKFT17/13. JDC to Rabi 27 Jul 1967. List of topics sent to U Thant.
29 CKFT17/14. Penney to JDC 9 May 1967.
30 CKFT3/32. JDC's address at Harwell's 21st Anniversary Jan 1967.
31 CKFT25/22. Anthony Wedgwood Benn to JDC 3 Aug 1967.
32 CKFT11/24. Abdus Salam to JDC 21 Mar 1967.
33 CKFT28/4. Beaumont to JDC 11 May 1967; Lord Beaumont to Guy Hartcup 3 Sept 1981.
34 CKFT20/86. Webster to JDC 31 Aug 1967.
35 JDC. *The control of the peaceful uses of atomic energy* 17th Pugwash Conf. Rønneby, Sweden Sept 1967.
36 CKFT20/86. JDC to Webster 13 Sept 1967.
37 17th Pugwash Conf Proceedings. Election of Officers and Continuing Committee.
38 Rabi I to Guy Hartcup 30 June 1980.
39 CKFT12/55. JDC-Kapitza correspondence. Apr 1967.
40 *The Times* 18 Sept 1967.
41 *Nature* 'Russian Salad' Vol 215, 23 Sept 1967.
42 McQuillen and Hey to Guy Hartcup Aug 1980.
43 Kapitza P *Nature* Vol 215 30 Sept 1967.

SELECT BIBLIOGRAPHY

The following books contain references, either to Cockcroft, or provide useful background reading for his numerous and varied activities.

Allibone T E 1972 *Rutherford, the father of nuclear energy* (Manchester: Manchester University Press)
—— 1984 *Metropolitan – Vickers Electrical Company and the Cavendish Laboratory* in *Cambridge Physics in the Thirties* ed J H Hendry (Bristol: Adam Hilger)
Andrade E N da C 1964 *Rutherford and the Nature of the Atom* (London: Heinemann Educational)
Baxter J P 3rd 1968 *Scientists against Time* (Cambridge: MIT Press)
Birkenhead Lord 1961 *The Prof in Two Worlds* (London: Collins)
Childs H 1968 *An American Genius—Ernest Orlando Lawrence* (New York: E P Dutton)
Clark R 1965 *Tizard* (London: Methuen)
—— 1965 *Sir John Cockcroft* (London: Phoenix)
Cockburn S and Ellyard D 1981 *Oliphant. The Life and Times of Sir Mark Oliphant* (Australia: Axiom Books)
Cockcroft J 1965 *The Organisation of Research Establishments* (Cambridge: Cambridge University Press)
Crowther J G 1970 *Fifty years with Science* (London; Barrie and Jenkins)
—— 1974 *History of the Cavendish Laboratory* (London: Macmillan)
Eve A S 1939 *Rutherford* (Cambridge: Cambridge University Press)
Frisch O 1979 *What Little I Remember* (Cambridge: Cambridge University Press)
Goldschmidt B 1967 *Les Rivalités Atomiques, 1939–1966* (Paris: Fayard)
Gowing M 1964 *Britain and Atomic Energy, 1939–1945* (London: Macmillan)
Gowing M and Arnold L 1974 *Independence and Deterrence, Britain and Atomic Energy 1945–1952* Vol 1 *Policy Making* (London: Macmillan)
—— 1974 *Independence and Deterrence, Britain and Atomic Energy 1945–1952* Vol 2 *Policy Execution* (London: Macmillan)
Hewlett R G and Anderson O E 1969 *History of the US Atomic Energy Commission* Vol 1 *The New World 1939–1946* (Pennsylvania State University Press)
Hewlett R G and Duncan F 1969 *History of the US Atomic Energy Commission* Vol II *Atomic Shield 1947–1952* (Pennsylvania State University Press)
Jacobson H K and Stern E 1966 *Diplomatists, Scientists and Politicians. The United States and the Nuclear Test Ban Negotiations* (Ann Arbor, Michigan: University of Michigan Press)
Kapitza P 1964 *Collected Papers* ed D Ter Haar Vol I 1916–34 (Oxford: Pergamon)

Lilienthal D E 1964 *Journals. The Atomic Energy Years, 1945–1950* Vol II (New York: Harper and Row)

Longstaff M 1980 *Unlocking the Atom. A Hundred Years of Nuclear Energy* (London: Muller)

Moore R 1967 *Niels Bohr: the Man and the Scientist* (London: Hodder and Stoughton)

Oliphant M 1972 *Rutherford. Recollections of the Cambridge Days* (Amsterdam: Elsevier)

Richards D 1977 *Portal of Hungerford* (London: Heinemann)

Rotblat J 1972 *Scientists and the Quest for Peace* (Cambridge, Mass: MIT Press)

Rozenthal S (ed)1967 *Niels Bohr* (Amsterdam: North-Holland)

Smith A K and Weiner C (ed) 1980 *Robert Oppenheimer, Letters and Recollections* (Cambridge, Mass: Harvard University Press)

Snow C P 1981 *The Physicists* (London: Macmillan)

Streuwer R H (ed) 1979 *Nuclear Physics in Retrospect* (Minneapolis, Mn : University of Minnesota)

Weart S R 1979 *Scientists in Power* (Cambridge, Mass: Harvard University Press)

Zuckerman S 1978 *From Apes to Warlords 1904–1946* (London: Hamish Hamilton)

SIR JOHN COCKCROFT'S SCIENTIFIC PUBLICATIONS AND PRINCIPAL LECTURES

1925 (With R T Coe, J A Lyacke and Miles Walker) An electric harmonic analyser *J.IEE* **63** 69

The temperature disribution in a transformer or other laminated core of rectangular cross-section in which heat is generated at a uniform rate. *Proc. Camb. Phil. Soc.* vol XXII pt 5

1928 The effect of curved boundaries on the distribution of electrical stress round conductors *J.IEE* **66** 385.

Skin effect in rectangular conductors at high frequencies *Proc. R. Soc.* A **122** 533

The design of coils for the production of strong magnetic fields *Phil. Trans.* A **227** 317

On phenomena occuring in the condensation of molecular streams on surfaces *Proc. R. Soc.* A **119** 293

PhD Thesis *The Condensation and reflection of molecules from surfaces*.

1930 (With E T S Walton) Experiments with high velocity positive ions *Proc. R. Soc.* A **129** 447

1932 (With E T S Walton) Experiments with high velocity positive ions (I) Further developments in the method of obtaining high velocity positive ions *Proc. R. Soc.* A **136** 619

(With E T S Walton) Experiments with high velocity positive ions (II) The disintegration of elements by high velocity protons *Proc. R. Soc.* A **137** 229

(With C D Ellis and H Kershaw) A permanent magnet for beta-ray spectroscopy. *Proc. R. Soc.* A **135** 628

1933 (With E T S Walton) Disintegration of light elements by fast neutrons *Nature* **131** 703

A magnet for alpha-ray spectroscopy *J. Sci. Instrum.* **10** 71

1934 (With E T S Walton) Experiments with high velocity positive ions (III) The disintegration of lithium, boron, and carbon by heavy hydrogen ions. *Proc. R. Soc.* A **144** 703

1935 (With C W Gilbert and E T S Walton) Experiments with high velocity ions (IV) The production of induced radioactivity by high velocity protons and diplons. *Proc. R. Soc.* A **148** 225

1936 (With W B Lewis) Experiments with high velocity positive ions (V) Further experiments on the disintegration of boron. *Proc R. Soc.* A **154** 246.

27th Kelvin Lecture. *The transmutation of matter by high energy particles and radiation.* 17th Mackenzie Davidson Memorial Lecture. *High velocity positive ions. Their application to the transformation of atomic nuclei and the production of artificial radioactivity. Brit J. of Radiol.* Vol X (New Series) No III March 1937

1937 Cornell University Lectures. (1) *Transmutation of elements* (2) *Liquefaction of hydrogen and helium.*
High speed positive rays of hydrogen and deuterium and artificial radioactivity. *Current Science* Special No on 'Canal Rays' Sept 1937.
The transmutation of elements. Réunion Internationalle de Physic-Chemie-Biologie. Congrès du Palais de la Découverte, Paris Oct 1937

1939 Royal Institution Lecture *New phenomena in liquid helium.*

1945 Rutherford. Life and work after the year 1919, with personal reminiscences of Cambridge period. *The Physical Society.*

1950 Romanes Lecture, University of Oxford. *The development and future of nuclear energy.*

1951 Nobel Prize Lecture. *Experiments on the interaction of high speed nucleons with atomic nuclei.*

1952 The Rutherford Memorial Lecture delivered at Canterbury University College, Christchurch, New Zealand.

1954 Sidgwick Memorial Lecture. *Nuclear Physics since Rutherford.*

1955 James Forrest Lecture. *The development of nuclear power.*

1956 Lecture to Nobel Laureates, Lindau. *Scientific and technical problems in the development of nuclear power.*

1958 James Forrest Lecture. *The further development of the United Kingdom nuclear power programme.*

1959 100th Anniversary of the Academic Convocation of Cooper Union for the Advancement of Science and Art. *Science and Society.*

1960 Weizmann Institute of Science. *The impact of the physical sciences on the world today.*

1961 Robert Grosseteste Memorial Lecture, Lincoln. *The development of science and technology in the future.*

1962 British Association, Presidential Address. *Investment in Science.*

1966 International Atomic Energy Agency. *The impact of atomic energy on society.*

Index

References to notes are indicated by a suffix italic *n* to the page number.
References to quotes are indicated by italicised page numbers.